D1593467

# HENRY BRADSHAW SOCIETY

ffounded in the year of Our Lord 1890
for the editing of Rare Liturgical Texts

VOLUME CXV

*ISSUED TO MEMBERS FOR THE YEAR 2003*
AND
PUBLISHED FOR THE SOCIETY
BY
THE BOYDELL PRESS

# FOUR IRISH MARTYROLOGIES

## DRUMMOND, TURIN, CASHEL, YORK

*Edited by*
Pádraig Ó Riain

LONDON
2002

First published for the Henry Bradshaw Society 2002
by The Boydell Press
an imprint of Boydell & Brewer Ltd
PO Box 9, Woodbridge, Suffolk IP12 3DF, UK
and of Boydell & Brewer Inc.
PO Box 41026, Rochester, NY 14604–4126, USA
website: www.boydell.co.uk

ISBN 1 870252 19 5

ISSN 0144–0241

A catalogue record for this book is available
from the British Library

Library of Congress Cataloging-in-Publication Data
applied for

This publication is printed on acid-free paper

Printed in Great Britain by
St Edmundsbury Press Ltd, Bury St Edmunds, Suffolk

# TABLE OF CONTENTS

To the Memory of
William O'Sullivan
(1921–2000)

# PUBLICATION SECRETARY'S PREFACE

Because of the vagaries of preservation, proportionately fewer liturgical manuscripts, especially missals and breviaries, survive from medieval Ireland than from England and continental countries; but among those manuscripts which do survive from Ireland, a striking number is made up of martyrologies in various forms – whether native vernacular *féliri* ('metrical calendars'), or liturgical calendars annotated to a greater or lesser extent, or historical martyrologies proper, based on the model of Ado or Usuard. The compilation of martyrologies, particularly those commemorating native Irish saints, was clearly an enterprise which excited and inspired medieval Irish ecclesiastics, and the surviving Irish martyrologies are a source of outstanding importance for the study of the early Irish church. Since the inception of the Henry Bradshaw Society, the publication of Irish martyrologies has been one of the Society's principal concerns. Among its early publications the Society can number the fundamental editions of various Irish martyrologies: Whitley Stokes's editions of the martyrologies of Gorman (vol. IX) and Óengus (vol. XXIX), and Lawlor's edition of the martyrology compiled by the late eleventh-century Welsh scholar Rhigyfarch ap Sulien, which has its roots in Irish tradition (vols XLVII–XLVIII), and Best and Lawlor's edition of the martyrology of Tallaght (vol. LXVIII). The present edition of *Four Irish Martyrologies* by Professor Pádraig Ó Riain, one of the world's foremost authorities on Hiberno-Latin hagiography, continues and develops the Society's interest in Irish martyrologies, and brings into print the few remaining texts, all of them descendants in some way of the 'Martyrology of Óengus', which preserve Irish martyrological tradition. The texts edited here include the 'Martyrology of Drummond', composed at Armagh in the second half of the twelfth century, probably for use at Glendalough; the 'Martyrology of Turin', now preserved in the Biblioteca Nazionale in Turin but originally compiled in the late twelfth century in the area around Tara; the 'Martyrology of Cashel', composed in the vicinity of Lismore, the original text of which does not survive intact but has been brilliantly reconstructed by Professor Ó Riain from notes made (in

Latin) by John Colgan in the seventeenth century; and a Hiberno-Latin redaction of the 'Metrical Calendar of York', preserved in the aforementioned Turin manuscript and containing many distinctive Irish interpolations. All the martyrological texts edited here are provided with comprehensive annotation, which will in itself be an indispensable tool for all future work on the saints of the early Irish church, and Ireland's relationship with European martyrological tradition. It is a pleasure to be able to issue this volume to members of the Henry Bradshaw Society for the year 2003.

Michael Lapidge,
for the Publications Committee
June 2002

# PREFACE

Athough begun in the mid-1980s, my work on the edition of these texts has had since to give way on numerous occasions to more pressing commitments. In the meantime, the original plan to edit the two recently discovered martyrologies in the National Library, Turin – which I term the Martyrology of Turin (MTur) and the Irish Martyrology of York (IMY) – has expanded to include two other texts, the Drummond Martyrology (MDr), of which a new edition was long overdue, and the Martyrology of Cashel (MC), which has never before been edited. Influencing the decision to add the two latter texts was the fact that they share with MTur a derivation from the Martyrology of Óengus (MO) in its annotated form. Moreover, these three, and perhaps also IMY, appear to have responded to the same perceived need for new texts of this kind in the period that followed the holding of the synod of Clane in 1162 and the beginning of the English Conquest of Ireland in 1169. Also noteworthy is the fact that MDr, MTur and IMY have been preserved in their original manuscripts, a rare occurrence in the history of the transmission of the Irish record of the saints. And finally, all four texts edited here have another, less fortunate, characteristic in common; each is lacunose. MDr lacks parts of September and October, MTur and IMY lack November and December and MC, although reasonably well preserved for the months of January to March, is poorly represented for the period April to December.

A curious feature of the transmission of the Irish record of the saints is its periodic character and nowhere is this more obvious than in the martyrological record. An initial phase of composition in the early ninth century was followed by over three hundred years of apparent inactivity until, in the later twelfth century, several new martyrologies, including, very probably, all the texts edited here, were compiled. Another lull in activity followed until the late fourteenth century when multiple copies began to be made of the version of MO annotated in the late twelfth century. Significantly, since it may indicate that they were already then out of reach, none of the texts in this volume was copied or brought up to date during this period of intense rewriting of earlier materials. The final phase of martyrological activity was in the early seventeenth century when, in the wake of Reformation and Counter-Reformation, the record of the saints was used extensively to inform the religious debates of the period. In any case, through the publication of an up-to-date edition of the four texts in this volume, a substantial and representative part of the later medieval Irish martyrological record has been made easily accessible.

In the course of my preparations for the edition I have received assistance from several colleagues and friends, to whom I am greatly indebted. I am particularly indebted to the late William O'Sullivan, who showed a tremendous interest in the work in all its stages, providing extensive guidance on many of its aspects, but especially on the problems associated with the manuscript hands. He also enlisted the aid of such experts in English palaeography as Ian Doyle, A. Piper, and Michael Ruddick, whose opinions have proved very helpful. My colleagues Kevin Murray and Diarmuid Ó Murchadha carefully read and commented on large parts of the work, and Donna Thornton was very helpful in relation to the edition of the Irish Martyrology of York. Dagmar Ó Riain-Raedel provided considerable back-up support over the whole period, and made available her expert knowledge of the continental martyrologies containing Irish material. Helen Davis of Boole Library, University College, Cork, was most obliging in searching out and making available printed and manuscript sources, and Elmarie Uí Cheallacháin produced the initial electronic versions of most of the texts. Help with various enquiries came from Patrizia di Bernardo Stempel, Robert Godding, Daniel McCarthy, Dáibhí Ó Cróinín, and Olivier Szerwiniack.

I am indebted to the Biblioteca Nazionale, Turin, and to the Pierpont Morgan Library, New York, for permission to publish manuscript material in their care. The consultation of the manuscript sources has been greatly facilitated by grants from both the Academic Travel Grant Scheme and Arts Faculty Research Fund at University College, Cork, and from the Humboldt Stiftung, Bonn. I am also grateful to the Faculty of Arts, University College, Cork, and the Publications Committee of the National University of Ireland for generous grants towards publication costs. Finally, I should like to thank Professor Michael Lapidge for his assistance and encouragement.

# ABBREVIATIONS

(For editions, see Bibliography. For manuscripts, see General Index.)

| | |
|---|---|
| A | *Acta Sanctorum Hiberniae*, ed. J. Colgan |
| *AASS* | *Acta Sanctorum*, eds J. Bolland et al. |
| ab. | abbas |
| AClon | Annals of Clonmacnoise, ed. D. Murphy |
| AFM | Annals of the Four Masters, ed. J. O'Donovan |
| AH | Armagh |
| AI | Annals of Inisfallen, ed. S. Mac Airt |
| ALC | Annals of Loch Cé, ed. W. M. Hennessy |
| *Altempsianus* | version of MU used by Sollerius (Du Sollier) |
| AM | Antrim |
| anch. | anchorita/anchorite |
| *Antverp. Maj.* | version of MU used by Sollerius (Du Sollier) |
| Apr. | April(is) |
| AU | Annals of Ulster, eds S. Mac Airt, G. Mac Niocaill |
| Aug. | August(us) |
| b. | barony |
| B | Brussels MS 5100–4 |
| Bede, *De temporum* | *De temporum ratione*, ed. C. W. Jones |
| *Bruxellensis* | Brussels version of MU used by Sollerius (Du Sollier) |
| cc. | columns |
| C | NLI MS G 10 |
| CE | Clare |
| *Centulensis* | version of MU used by Sollerius (Du Sollier) |
| CGSH | *Corpus Genealogiarum Sanctorum Hiberniae*, ed. P. Ó Riain |
| ch. | church |
| CK | Cork |
| CN | Cavan |
| CW | Carlow |
| Co./co. | county |

| | |
|---|---|
| DB | Dublin |
| Dec. | December |
| diac. | diaconus |
| disc. | discipulus |
| DL | Donegal |
| DN | Down |
| DY | Derry |
| E. | East |
| ep. | episcopus |
| F | Franciscan Library MS A 7 |
| Feb. | Februarius |
| FH | Fermanagh |
| *Gen. Reg. SS.* | *Genealogiae Regum et Sanctorum Hiberniae*, ed. P. Walsh |
| *Grevenus* | version of MU used by Sollerius (Du Sollier) |
| GY | Galway |
| *Hagenoyensis* | version of MU used by Sollerius (Du Sollier) |
| IMY | The Irish version of the Martyrology of York |
| Jan. | Ianuarius |
| July | Iulius |
| June | Iunius |
| KE | Kildare |
| KF | Franciscan Library, Killiney |
| KK | Kilkenny |
| KY | Kerry |
| L | Laud Misc. 610 MS |
| L. | Lower |
| Lb | Leabhar Breac MS |
| LD | Longford |
| LH | Louth |
| LK | Limerick |
| LL | Book of Leinster MS |
| LM | Leitrim |
| LS | Laois |
| LU | Leabhar na hUidhre MS |
| *Lubeco-Col.* | versions of MU used by Sollerius (Du Sollier) |
| Mai. | Maius |
| Mar. | Martius |
| m./mm. | martyr/martyres |
| MA | The Martyrology of Ado, ed. J. Dubois |

| | |
|---|---|
| *Matric. Carthus. Ultraj.* | version of MU used by Sollerius (Du Sollier) |
| MC | The Martyrology of Cashel |
| MCamb | Martyrologium Cambrense, ed. H. J. Lawlor |
| MCh | The Martyrology of Christ Church, eds Crosthwaite, Todd |
| MDr | The Martyrology of Drummond |
| MG | The Martyrology of Gorman, ed. W. Stokes |
| MH | The *Martyrologium Hieronymianum*, eds H. Delehaye, H. Quentin |
| MH | Meath |
| Migne, *Ephem.* | *Computus vulgaris qui dicitur ephemeris*, ed. J.-P. Migne |
| MN | Monaghan |
| MO | The Martyrology of Óengus, ed. W. Stokes |
| MO | Mayo |
| *Molanus* | version of MU used by Sollerius (Du Sollier) |
| mon. | monachus |
| MR | *Martyrologium Romanum*, eds H. Delehaye et al. |
| MS | manuscript |
| MT | The Martyrology of Tallaght, eds R. I. Best, H. J. Lawlor |
| MTur | The Martyrology of Turin |
| MU | The Martyrology of Usuard, ed. J. Dubois |
| MY | The Martyrology of York |
| N. | North |
| nat. | *natale* |
| NLI | National Library of Ireland |
| Nov. | November |
| Oct. | October |
| OY | Offaly |
| P | RIA MS 23 P 3 |
| p. | parish |
| PL | *Patrologia Latina*, ed. J.-P. Migne |
| pr. | presbyter |
| r. | river |
| R1 | Rawlinson B 505 MS |
| R2 | Rawlinson B 512 MS |
| RIA | Royal Irish Academy |
| RN | Roscommon |
| *Rosweyd.* | version of MU used by Sollerius (Du Sollier) |

| | |
|---|---|
| S. | South |
| sacerd. | sacerdos |
| SCO | Scotland |
| Sep. | September |
| SO | Sligo |
| st/St | saint |
| T | *Trias Thaumaturga*, ed. J. Colgan |
| TE | Tyrone |
| tl. | townland |
| TY | Tipperary |
| U. | Upper |
| v./vv. | virgo/virgines |
| *Vita Columbae* | ed. A. O. and M. O. Anderson |
| *Wallis* | Translation of Bede, *De temporum ratione* by F. Wallis |
| W. | West |
| WD | Waterford |
| WH | Westmeath |
| WW | Wicklow |
| WX | Wexford |

CHAPTER ONE

# THE MARTYROLOGY OF DRUMMOND: INTRODUCTION

## 1 *Manuscript and Previous Editions*

As a rule, the earliest manuscript copies of Irish martyrologies are several centuries later than the date of composition of their texts. For example, the earliest manuscript containing the Martyrology of Óengus, which was composed about the year 830, dates to about 1400, and the Martyrology of Gorman, which may be dated to about 1170, survives in a unique copy made by Mícheál Ó Cléirigh in 1630.[1] It is noteworthy, therefore, that the Martyrology of Drummond, henceforth MDr, has been preserved in what would appear to be its original manuscript,[2] commonly known as the Drummond Missal, which is now kept in the Pierpont Morgan Library, New York, where it is numbered MS 627. The manuscript, which has been described most thoroughly by H. Oskamp,[3] is made up of 109 folios in the hands of two main scribes, with additions in at least one other hand.[4] The martyrology is on folios 1 to 18, with one leaf, containing the text from the 22 September to the 10 October, now lost between folios 13 and 14. The manuscript takes its name from a long sojourn in Drummond Castle, Perthshire, Scotland, where it was kept from at least as early as the eighteenth century until its purchase by the Pierpont Morgan Library in 1916.

In addition to the martyrology, the manuscript contains a missal, and both missal and martyrology were last published by G. H. Forbes in

---

[1] Stokes, *Félire hÚi Gormáin*.

[2] For a variant view, see Schneiders, 'The Drummond Martyrology', at pp. 137–8.

[3] Oskamp, 'The Irish Quatrains'. Since then, Gibbs Casey, 'Through a Glass Darkly', pp. 206–7, has also published a description of the manuscript. For an earlier, less detailed, account, see Henry, Marsh-Micheli, 'A Century of Irish Illumination', pp. 122–3.

[4] Gibbs Casey, 'Through a Glass Darkly', p. 207, identifies seven hands.

1882.[5] Since then, only M. Schneiders has examined the text of the martyrology, in an article published in 1990.[6] His examination includes very useful tables, showing the source, where known, of each entry, together with a list of the entries shared by MDr with the closely-related Martyrology of Christ Church, henceforth MCh. The missal has yet to be studied in detail. However, its neumes have been recently examined by S. Gibbs Casey, with some valuable results concerning, among other matters, the date of the manuscript.[7]

## 2 Provenance of the Manuscript: Glendalough?

There is no evidence to show when or how the manuscript came into the possession of the Drummond family. F. N. Robinson stated that the Drummonds were already the owners in the fourteenth century, but presented no evidence to support this view.[8] Unfortunately, therefore, there is no clue in the recent history of the manuscript as to where it may have been compiled originally, or kept in the period before it reached Drummond Castle in Scotland. The previous editor of martyrology and missal, G. H. Forbes, had little to say on the subject of the manuscript's provenance, beyond noting the particular attention paid in it to St Cóemgen (Kevin) of Glendalough.[9] A poem of two verses in Irish on f. 108, one attributed to Cóemgen, the other to Ciarán of Saigir (Seirkieran), commemorates a welcome given by the former to the latter.[10] As F. Henry and G. L. Marsh-Micheli were the first to note, these verses probably relate to the presence at Glendalough of a church called after St Ciarán.[11] Also, the manuscript contains a *Commemoratio de Sancto Martino et Patricio et Nicholao et Coemgino* at ff. 104–6, which again underlines the importance of St Cóemgen to the scribe of

---

[5] Forbes, *The Ancient Irish Missal*. A previous edition of the martyrology was published by (A. P.) Forbes (*Kalendars of the Scottish Saints*, pp. 1–32), who had rediscovered the manuscript in the Drummond Library in 1861. Some marginal notes have been edited by Robinson, 'The Irish Marginalia in the Drummond Missal'.

[6] Schneiders, 'The Drummond Martyrology'.

[7] Gibbs Casey, 'Through a Glass Darkly'.

[8] Robinson, 'The Irish Marginalia in the Drummond Missal', p. 195. The view is restated by Gibbs Casey, 'Through a Glass Darkly', p. 205, citing an 'internal file' which appears to have been prepared by Robinson.

[9] Forbes, *The Ancient Irish Missal*, p. 88.

[10] For the text, see Oskamp, 'The Irish Quatrains', p. 90.

[11] Henry, Marsh-Micheli, 'A Century of Irish Illumination (1070–1170)', p. 123.

these folios. This obvious concern of the scribe has led to the assumption that the Drummond manuscript was produced at Cóemgen's main church of Glendalough. First proposed by Henry and Marsh-Micheli, this position has since also been adopted by both Oskamp and, more recently, Gibbs Casey.[12]

In the face of previous agreement on a Glendalough provenance, it may seem unwise to question it. However, it is worth noting that almost all its supports are located in the final section of the manuscript (ff. 91–108), where, as Oskamp has explained,[13] all the leaves, except one bifolio at 99–100, are singletons, as against the remainder of the manuscript which consists of gatherings. Accordingly, Oskamp, although pointing out that liturgists would need to examine the texts of the final section,[14] allowed for the possibility that several leaves, including those supporting a Glendalough provenance, might have been added to the main gatherings, perhaps when it became clear that the manuscript was destined for that monastery.

It is indeed striking that where Glendalough bias might be expected in the early part of the manuscript, and especially in the text of the martyrology, it is conspicuously absent. Thus, although Cóemgen's feast is noted at 3 June, no special attention is paid to it. The entry, which reads *Eodem quoque die, apud Hiberniam, sancti Coemgeni confessoris natale*, shows none of the elaboration, however formulaic, present in other entries. For example, the entry for Áed of Clonmore in Co. Carlow, who is commemorated at 11 Apr., refers to the saint's lineage and habits with the words *Item, apud Hiberniam, Aed sanctus vir nobilis genere, sed nobilior moribus, clarus Christi confessor ad astra perrexit*. Similarly, the comments on Ruadán of Lorrha in north Tipperary at 15 Apr., which read *In Hibernia insola, sanctus prespeter et confessor Ruadan, mirandae sanctitatis et miraculorum vir, hoc die conscendit ad Christum*, draw attention to his miraculous power. In fact,

---

[12] Ibid. Cf. Henry, *Irish Art in the Romanesque Period*, p. 51; Oskamp, 'The Irish Quatrains', p. 82. Gibbs Casey, 'Through a Glass Darkly', p. 208, proposes a correlation between some masses in the missal, especially two on the Trinity, and the physical layout of Glendalough. She also draws attention to the occurrence of an iris leaf motif on f. 31v, which is otherwise attested only in British Library MS Egerton 3323, a manuscript of Glendalough provenance.

[13] Oskamp, 'The Irish Quatrains', p. 84.

[14] Ibid. Despite Oskamp's suggestion that the texts were perhaps 'alternatives for or additions to the main missal', in fact they relate to other missals in much the same way as the texts in the main section of the manuscript.

there are over 40 elaborate entries of this kind, none of them pointing directly to Glendalough as a likely provenance for the martyrology.[15]

## 3 *Provenance of the Manuscript: Armagh (1)*

The internal evidence of provenance points rather to a church with a particular interest in St Patrick, most likely Armagh. The entry for the saint's day at 17 Mar., which reads *Apud Hiberniam Occiani insolam, natale sancti Patricii arch[i]episcopi Scottorum*, ultimately derives from the Martyrology of Ado (MA), whose Irish adaptation was the source used by MDr for the vast majority of its non-Irish saints.[16] However, the reference to Patrick's status as 'archbishop of the Irish' is an addition to the Irish version of MA. Moreover, this description is repeated at 24 Mar. in MDr, where, uniquely in an Irish martyrology, the octave of Patrick's feast is also noted. The intervening period between feast and octave contains a similar reference to the Armagh saint at 19 Mar., where Auxillus is described as 'a disciple and brother and fellow bishop of St Patrick, bishop and apostle of the Irish'.[17]

The prominence given to certain non-Irish saints might also be best explained by reference to Armagh. It is already stated in the seventh-century *Liber Angeli* that Armagh showed special reverence to 'the principal martyrs Peter and Paul, Stephen, and Laurence'.[18] This reverence, which served as a support for the church's claim to primacy,

---

[15] The elaborate entries, involving use or retention of superlative forms, more extended, or unique, descriptions, that I have noted are: 4 Jan. (Ciar), 10 Jan. (Diarmait), 13 Jan. (Sulpicius), 15 Jan. (Benedictus), 16 Jan. (Furseus), 24 Jan. (Manchanus), 1 Feb. (Brigida), 9 Feb. (Mochuaróc), 24 Feb. (Cuimmíne Iensis), 1 Mar. (David), 5 Mar. (Ciarán, Carthach), 17 Mar. (Patricius), 19 Mar. (Auxaile), 21 Mar. (Benedictus), 24 Mar. (Domangart, Octavae Patricii), 28 Mar. (Maria Magdalena), 1 Apr. (Ambrosius), 11 Apr. (Áed), 15 Apr. (Ruadán), 18 Apr. (Laisrén), 24 Apr. (Ananias, Azarias, Misael), 14 May (Carthachus), 24 May (Augustinus), 9 June (Columba, Baíthíne), 17 June (Moling), 18 June (Báetán, Furudrán), 7 July (Máel Ruain), 11 July (Translatio Benedicti), 26 July (Transformatio Domini), 3 Aug. (Inventio corporis Stephani), 11 Aug. (Airerán), 29 Aug. (Iohannes Baptista), 4 Sep. (Ultanus), 9 Sep. (Ciaranus), 10 Sep. (Finnianus), 12 Oct. (Mobí), 21 Oct. (Munnu), 25 Oct. (Gormanus), 11 Nov. (Martinus), 7 Dec. (Buite), 12 Dec. (Finnianus), 18 Dec. (Flannán), 26 Dec. (Stephanus), 29 Dec. (Airerán).

[16] Below § 11.

[17] This is also found in a note to MT (Best, Lawlor, *The Martyrology of Tallaght*, p. 100). Other possible evidence of a Patrician character to the entries selected for inclusion in MDr is the allocation of 14 Apr. to St Tassach, who is reputed to have rendered the last rites to Patrick.

[18] Bieler, *The Patrician Texts in the Book of Armagh*, pp. 122.28, 186.33.

almost certainly continued into the twelfth century. The new church consecrated at Armagh in 1126 was, for instance, named after Peter and Paul.[19] It is possible, therefore, that the exceptional importance attached to these saints in the martyrology is also due to an Armagh involvement in its production. The numerous entries relating to Peter and Paul, either together or separately, at 18 Jan. (Peter), 25 Jan. (conversion of Paul), 25 Feb. (discovery of Paul's head), 28 June (vigil of Peter and Paul), 29 June (feast of Peter and Paul), 30 June (feast of Paul), 2 July (Processus, Martinianus, and Peter and Paul), 23 July (Apollinaris and Peter), 26 July (Peter as witness), 1 Aug. (Peter in Rome), 4 Aug. (Aristarchus, disciple of Paul), 18 Oct. (Luke, disciple of Paul), 17 Dec. (Ignatius and Peter), are, by the standard of the text, quite elaborate. This applies also to the entries on Stephen at 3 Aug. (discovery of his body) and 26 Dec. (martyrdom), and, although the remarks about him are quite brief, Laurence of Rome is one of two saints only to have vigil (9 Aug.), feast (10 Aug.) and octave (17 Aug.) noted.[20]

The missal reflects a similar concern with Peter and Paul, for example at 51b–52a, where a mass in honour of the apostles names Peter, Paul, and Andrew in each of its three texts.[21] Similarly, at 64a, the same three names are intercalated into a prayer and, at 59a, the name of Peter is substituted for those of other saints with the comment *Petro patrono nostro intercedente*. As Forbes pointed out,[22] this substitution surely shows that the church for which the missal was written was under the special patronage of the senior apostle.

The apostle Andrew is the other saint beside Laurence to have vigil (29 Nov.), feast (30 Nov.) and octave (7 Dec.) recorded in the martyrology. The prominence given to Andrew might indicate a concern, natural in Armagh, with the centres of the neighbouring island of Britain already enjoying or then seeking primacy. Scotland's first archbishop was not finally appointed until the late fifteenth century. However, in 1164 the Pope rejected the metropolitan church of York's claims to authority over the Scottish Church and a year later, in 1165, lent his authority to the consecration of a bishop of St Andrews by other Scottish bishops.[23] The southern English metropolitan church of Canter-

---

[19] AU 1126.
[20] This prominence might also be explained by reference to Glendalough, whose abbot Lorcán (Laurence) may have had a role in the preparation of MDr.
[21] Forbes, *The Ancient Irish Missal*, p. 31.
[22] Ibid., p. 37.
[23] Webster, *Medieval Scotland: the Making of an Identity*, p. 67.

bury received due recognition at 24 May, where the author of MDr, who normally abbreviated, uncharacteristically retained almost the whole of the commentary on St Augustine present in his source.[24] Finally, by describing David of Wales as 'archbishop of the island of Britain' at 1 Mar., the author showed his awareness of what has been described by W. Davies as the obsession with its status prevailing at St David's ever since Rhigyfarch wrote his Life of its saint about 1095.[25] A campaign conducted by Bishop Bernard during the first half of the twelfth century included a letter from the Chapter of St David's to Pope Honorius, written between 1124 and 1130, claiming metropolitan status.[26]

## 4  *Provenance of the Manuscript: Armagh (2)*

There are many other aspects of the text that would make sense of an Armagh role in its production. For instance, its evident interest in St Martin, a saint greatly favoured at Armagh, is shown by the extensive notice he received on 11 Nov., where details over and above those listed in MA are provided, and again, at 13 Jan., where the comments on Sulpicius Severus include a reference to his having written the Life of St Martin, a version of which was kept at Armagh.[27] This interest was maintained in the missal which, at the canon of the mass (39a), added Martin to the list of saints commemorated *in sollempnibus diebus*, followed by five others, including Gregory, whose work was likewise well known in Armagh,[28] and Patrick, the only Irish saint in the list.[29]

The use of the Martyrology of Ado (MA) as the main source of non-Irish saints, which is dealt with below in greater detail (§§ 10–11), likewise points to a provenance in the primatial church. Examination of the Commentary on the Martyrology of Óengus (MO), which appears to have been prepared at Armagh, shows that it also made extensive use of

---

[24] The 24 May, rather than 26 May, was chosen because of the influence of MO.

[25] Davies, *Wales in the Early Middle Ages*, p. 160. For an edition of the 'original' Life, see James, *Rhigyfarch's Life of St David*. Cf. Wade-Evans, *Vitae Sanctorum Britanniae et Genealogiae*, pp. 150–70.

[26] See Cross and Livingstone, *The Oxford Dictionary of the Christian Church*, p. 1441.

[27] For the copy of the Life kept at Armagh, see Kenney, *The Sources*, p. 668. A connexion with St Martin may also explain the inclusion of Severinus of Cologne at 23 Oct.

[28] Extracts from the pope's *Moralia* are preserved in the Book of Armagh.

[29] Forbes, *The Ancient Irish Missal*, p. 20 (= 39a). Also added are Augustinus, Hieronymus, and Benedictus.

a copy of MA as a source of information on non-Irish saints.[30] We may be reasonably sure, therefore, that what was possibly the only Irish copy of this martyrology was kept at Armagh.

The emphasis on the church of Iona, which is the only 'Irish' church (always placed *apud Hiberniam*) named in the text, is perhaps also to be explained most satisfactorily in terms of Armagh.[31] Clearly, the author was determined to have Iona seen as an Irish church, a concern which seems also to have informed the activities of the Columban churches in Ireland throughout the twelfth century. As I argue elsewhere,[32] the Preface added to the metrical text by the Commentator of MO can best be understood if it was composed in the time of Gilla Meic Liac (d. 1174), archbishop of Armagh, and, for sixteen years previous to his succession to Patrick, abbot of Derry.[33] Since the abbacy of Derry was at this time effectively the headship of the confederation of churches historically associated with Iona, should MDr have been compiled at Armagh during Gilla Meic Liac's long tenure, 1148–74, it would very naturally have evinced a particular interest in the 'Irishness' of the Scottish church.[34]

The interest in nuns and female saints apparent in the text of the missal, where, despite their absence from the usual form of the prayers, *sanctimoniales* are singled out for mention three times,[35] might also be most easily explained in terms of Armagh. Attached to the abbey of St Peter and Paul's at Armagh was a convent of nuns, named, curiously enough, after St Brigit. It could well be, therefore, that it was this circumstance, rather than any possible connexion with Kildare, that led to the addition of Brigit's name, together with that of Eugenia, to an invocation in the canon of the mass.[36]

---

[30] Ó Riain, 'Die Bibliothek des Verfassers', at pp. 89–91. See also below §§ 10–11.

[31] There are four references to Iona, at 24 Feb., 2 Mar., 22 Mar., 25 May. Moreover, the inclusion of some saints (Oisíne, 1 Jan.), and the importance attached to them (Buite, 7 Dec.), may have been due to their association with the Columban *familia*. Columba is also named, with Patrick and Cóemgen, in a collect towards the end of the missal (104b).

[32] Ó Riain, 'The Martyrology of Óengus'.

[33] AU 1174.

[34] For a discussion of the position of Derry in the twelfth century, see Herbert, *Iona, Kells, and Derry*, pp. 109–23.

[35] Forbes, *The Ancient Irish Missal*, 3 (21a–22a).

[36] Ibid., p. 21 (= 41a); Gwynn, Hadcock, *Medieval Religious Houses*, pp. 312–13. It should also be noted that Find Ua Gormáin, possibly a member of a family which, as I point out below (§ 6), may have been involved in the writing of MDr, had been bishop of Kildare until his death in 1160. Previously, Find had been abbot of the Cistercian/Benedictine abbey of Newry which might explain the interest shown in Benedict, who is mentioned four times (15 Jan., 21 Mar., 11 July, 15 Nov.), and added, with others, to a list of saints in the canon of the mass.

## 5 *Provenance of the Manuscript: Armagh (3)*

An Armagh provenance would also accord well with the known connexions between the metropolitan church and Glendalough. In the course of the twelfth-century reform, both churches had become centres of the Augustinian canons regular. Armagh adopted the rule during the tenure as archbishop of Máel Máedóc (Malachy), who died in 1148, and Glendalough followed suit during the abbacy of Lorcán (Laurence) Ua Tuathail (1153–62), who appears also to have been instrumental in the foundation of houses of canons elsewhere in Leinster.[37] Involvement of the canons in the production of missal and martyrology is indicated by a number of factors. *Augustinus*, for example, is among the names added to the text of the canon of the mass (39a). Similarly, although no attempt is made to elaborate on the entry for Augustine himself at 28 Aug., the cults most favoured by the Irish canons, which included those of Mary, Peter and Paul, John the Evangelist and John the Baptist, are very prominent in the text.[38] As we have already seen, Peter and Paul, who were patrons of the Augustinian house established at Armagh in 1126, with mention on sixteen days, were plainly of more than usual interest to the martyrologist.[39] The extent of his interest in Mary and the two Johns may be measured both by the number of their feasts and also by other references. Mary's days include the feasts of the Annunciation (25 Mar.), Purification (2 Feb.), 'ad Martyres' (13 May), Vigil of Assumption (14 Aug.), Assumption (15 Aug., cf. 18 Jan.), and Birth (8 Sep.), to which may be added her position as sister of Mary, mother of Philip and James (1 May). Between them, John the Apostle and John the Baptist figure in no fewer than nine feasts.[40]

A large number of native saints given prominence in the text were likewise associated with churches which had become centres of the Augustinian canons in the course of the twelfth century. Of twenty-three elaborate entries, at least nine concern saints directly associated with foundations of the canons.[41] These are Diarmait of Inis Clothrann

---

[37] Gwynn, Hadcock, *Medieval Religious Houses*, pp. 175 (Ferns), 184 (Leighlin).

[38] Ibid., pp. 156–98.

[39] 18 Jan., 25 Jan., 22 Feb., 25 Feb., 25 Apr., 26 Apr., 31 May, 28 June, 29 June, 30 June, 2 July, 23 July, 26 July, 4 Aug., 18 Oct., 17 Dec.

[40] John the Apostle (26 Jan., 28 Mar., 6 May, 26 July, 27 Dec.); John the Baptist (23 June, 24 June, 29 Aug., 5 Nov.).

[41] Omitted from consideration are the Patrician and related entries included above (§ 3).

(10 Jan.), Ciarán of Saigir (5 Mar.), Ruadán of Lothra (15 Apr.), Laisrén of Leithglenn (18 Apr.), Airerán of Clonard (11 Aug., 29 Dec.), Ciarán of Clonmacnoise (9 Sep.), Finnian of Movilla (10 Sep.), and Finnian of Clonard (12 Dec.). Moreover, some other saints who received high praise, such as Manchán of Liath Mancháin near Clonmacnoise (24 Jan.), were connected with churches likely to have been dependencies of Augustinian priories.

As a consequence of the leading role played by the canons in the reform of the Irish Church, the Augustinian priory at Armagh would doubtless have maintained regular contact with the house of canons founded, it seems, by Lorcán Ua Tuathail at Glendalough in the 1150s.[42] According to the Annals of Ulster, Gilla Meic Liac, archbishop of Armagh, officiated at Lorcán's consecration as archbishop of Dublin in 1162, having previously presided over a synod of the clergy of Ireland at Clane, which was attended by 26 bishops and numerous abbots. The stated purpose of this synod, the last before the arrival of the Anglo-Normans in 1169, was 'to enjoin rule and good conduct'.[43] This provided a very likely background for the production of liturgical texts of the kind represented by the Drummond missal and martyrology.[44] Moreover, the overseeing role assumed by Armagh in this enterprise may be inferred from the further decree of the synod of Clane that 'no one should be lector in a church in Ireland, except an alumnus of Armagh'.

Therefore, although there can be no absolute certainty about it, there is a good deal of circumstantial evidence to indicate that the Drummond manuscript originated in Armagh, whence it made its way, probably almost immediately, to Glendalough. If, as must seem very likely in the light of the decrees promulgated at Clane, some form of Armagh imprimatur applied to texts servicing the need for 'rule and good conduct', then one can easily envisage a situation in which a new liturgical manuscript requested by Glendalough was brought there in more or less complete form from Armagh.

[42] Gwynn, Hadcock, *Medieval Religious Houses*, pp. 176–7.
[43] The text of AU 1162 reads: *ic erail riagla ocus sobesa*, 'enjoining rule and good conduct'.
[44] See also Ó Riain, 'The Martyrologies of Flann Ua Gormáin'.

## 6 *Date of the Manuscript*

Unfortunately, neither missal nor martyrology was provided with a date of composition. Also, the critical apparatus added to the martyrology in the form of dominical letters and lunar observations has not yielded any dating evidence.[45] Against this, however, much of the textual argument put forward here in favour of an Armagh provenance depends on a date for the manuscript in the latter half of the twelfth century. The enjoinment of 'rule and good order' proclaimed at the synod of Clane in 1162 would have provided an ideal point of departure for the preparations that led to the production of the martyrology in the first place.[46] Similarly, the description of Patrick as *archiepiscopus Scottorum* at 17 Mar. is very much in keeping with the reaffirmation by the clergy of Ireland at Clane of 'the orders of archbishop of Ireland' for the saint's successor at Armagh. On the other hand, a date this late for the Drummond manuscript would be at variance with some previous opinion on the subject, based on palaeographical and art-historical criteria. Thus the art-historians, Henry and Marsh-Micheli, proposed a late eleventh or early twelfth-century date for the manuscript,[47] and, although this has since been rejected by Oskamp, who instead opted for a date shortly before 1172,[48] his evidence for the much later date, since also espoused by Schneiders,[49] has not been

---

[45] Forbes (*The Ancient Irish Missal*, pp. v–vi) drew attention to a 'very curious feature' of the system of dominical letters, whereby the interrupted series of letters, brought about by omission of a letter at 24 Jan., was resumed at 25 May. D. Mc Carthy, Trinity College, Dublin, who examined the evidence at my request, concluded that 'no reliable inference can be drawn from this data' (personal communication, dated 22 Sep. 1999).

[46] What may also reflect this concern is both the interest shown in Ambrosian chant (1 Apr.) and the use of neumes in the body of the missal.

[47] Henry, Marsh-Micheli, 'A Century of Irish Illumination', pp. 111, 122–3, where a late eleventh-century date is preferred. Cf. Henry, *Irish Art in the Romanesque Period*, p. 51, where the early twelfth century is specified. Best and Lawlor, the editors of the Martyrology of Tallaght (MT) (pp. xxi–xxii), adopted the eleventh-century date, as did Hennig ('A Feast of All the Saints of Europe', p. 53; idem, 'Grundzüge der martyrologischen Tradition Irlands', p. 95), and Grosjean ('S. Patrice d'Irlande', p. 156), both of whom may simply have been following suit.

[48] Oskamp, 'The Irish Quatrains', p. 82.

[49] Schneiders, 'The Drummond Martyrology', pp. 105–6. On the other hand, Schneiders (ibid., p. 137) would place the Drummond martyrology probably in the period before 1100, and certainly before 1148, when Malachy of Armagh, whose feast is not recorded in the text, died. However, although this feast, as well as those of many other recently deceased, is commemorated in MG, with the solitary exception of Tigernach of Boirche (d. 1061), no such feasts are noted in MDr. Moreover, the use made of the Commentary on MO (see § 8),

published.[50] Gibbs Casey has also opted for a date in the second half of the twelfth century, mainly on the grounds that there is a reference in a prayer on f.108v to tithing, which was first introduced into Ireland at the Synod of Kells-Mellifont in 1152.[51]

Another complication is the fact that, whereas Oskamp would place the user of what is regarded as the latest hand in the manuscript – the 'non-Irish' hand on folios 107–8 – in the fourteenth century, more recent expert palaeographical opinion would assign it to no later than the mid-twelfth.[52] More precisely, I. Doyle and A. Piper would place the Drummond 'non-Irish' hand in the period before 1150, whereas M. Gullick, although in general agreement with the other two scholars, would be prepared to place the hand, which he describes as 'conservative/rustic', at the latest in the second third of the twelfth century.[53] Therefore, on palaeographical criteria, the 'non-Irish' hand of the Drummond manuscript cannot be assigned to much later than 1150.

The gap between the dating implications of the palaeographical evidence and the conclusion to be drawn from textual emphases in both martyrology and missal, which, as I show below (§§ 8–9), is supported by an examination of the sources used in the martyrology, may not be unbridgeable. The person responsible for the non-Irish hand could have learned to write it many years before he paraded his skill on the last few folios of the Drummond manuscript. As I show elsewhere, Flann Ua Gormáin, 'arch-lector' of the school at Armagh until his death in 1174, and probable brother of Máel Muire Ua Gormáin, author of the Martyrology of Gorman (MG), is very likely to have been involved in the production of the Commentary on the Martyrology of Óengus.[54] In that case, since there is strong textual evidence to show that both martyrology and missal of the Drummond manuscript were also compiled at Armagh, and since, according to his obituary notice,[55] Flann had spent twenty-one

---

which I have dated to the early 1170s (Ó Riain, 'Die Bibliothek des Verfassers'), renders such an early date impossible.

[50] Probably the earliest attempt to date the manuscript was by J. W. Legg who, in *Missale ad usum Ecclesie* (p. 1409), published in 1891, placed it in the thirteenth century.

[51] Gibbs Casey, 'Through a Glass Darkly', p. 208. She also suggests that the maledictory marginalia in Irish may have been directed at Diarmait mac Murchada who was apparently to blame for the burning of Glendalough in its entirety in 1163.

[52] E. A. Lowe, as reported by Oskamp, 'The Irish Quatrains', p. 87, was of the opinion that the same scribe wrote this hand as wrote the Irish salutation on f. 108.

[53] The opinions of these scholars were furnished at the request of the late W. O'Sullivan.

[54] Ó Riain, 'The Martyrologies of Flann Ua Gormáin'.

[55] AU 1174.

years among the Franks and Saxons prior to his return to Armagh in 1154, it is not beyond the bounds of possibility that the hand is his. Flann would have learned to use a non-Irish hand precisely in the period that expert opinion would assign to the hand of folios 107–8.[56]

Whatever the final explanation of the presence in the Drummond manuscript of a pre-1150 non-Irish hand, there is, as I now propose to show, quite compelling internal evidence to indicate that the martyrology cannot have been written ahead of the Commentary on MO, which I have dated elsewhere to about 1170.[57]

## 7 *The Sources of the Martyrology of Drummond (MDr)*

In common with the martyrologies that preceded it, MDr recorded the feasts of both Irish and non-Irish saints. A breakdown of its entries, carried out comprehensively by Schneiders, shows that more entries relate to non-Irish than to Irish saints.[58] Moreover, as in other martyrologies of this kind, precedence is normally, but not invariably, given to non-Irish saints.[59] Since A. P. Forbes's edition of the martyrology in 1872, it has been recognised that it depended on the Martyrology of Óengus (MO) for the majority of its Irish saints.[60] On the other hand,

---

[56] Possibly relevant to the argument at this point is the fact that in both MG and MDr mention is made at 25 Oct. of an otherwise unrecorded Gormán, of Cell Gormáin, now Kilgorman in County Wexford. In MG, the description *aiste*, 'of the metres', is attached to the saint, whereas, in MDr, the saint is said to have been a *peregrinus*, 'pilgrim'. Could there be a play on the names and histories of the authors of the texts here? The description in the metrical MG would certainly set its known author, Máel Muire, as would that in MDr, if the much-travelled Flann were to have been its author.

[57] Ó Riain, 'Die Bibliothek des Verfassers', pp. 101–2.

[58] Schneiders, 'The Drummond Martyrology', pp. 117–18, counts 777 entries in toto, which breaks down into 468 non-Irish and 309 Irish saints. Since there is a lacuna from 22 Sep. to 10 Oct., no symbolic importance can be attached to the number 777.

[59] On many days an Irish saint is listed without any companion, as at 17 Mar., where we find only Patrick, 'archbishop of the Irish'. The majority of the exclusively Irish days are in the months of February to May, with 31 examples, the other months having only four examples between them (ibid., pp. 116–17; Irish saints are indicated in Schneiders's table of entries by the use of the capital letters, B, C, and F).

[60] Forbes, *The Ancient Irish Missal*, p. xi, states that he was made aware of this dependence by W. Reeves, but in this he had been anticipated by his brother, A. P. Forbes (*Kalendars of the Scottish Saints*, pp. xvii–xviii). Very occasionally, pace Schneiders, who states that he did not know the text (p. 120n), he may also have drawn on MG, a copy of which appears to have reached Armagh very soon after the composition of the text. Thus, among the Irish saints not drawn from MO or its Commentary are three, Guaire and Díraid (27 July) and Cruimther Fráech (20 Dec.), who are otherwise in MG, but not in MT.

although some non-Irish saints likewise were drawn from MO, the majority of these derive from a copy of the Martyrology of Ado (MA), which, as G. H. Forbes was the first to note, is closely related to the text of the Martyrology of Christ Church (MCh).[61] It is proposed to re-examine each of these interrelationships here, beginning with that between MDr and MO.

## 8 The Martyrology of Drummond (MDr) and the Martyrology of Óengus (MO)

According to the table provided by Schneiders, the author of MDr drew a total of well over 300 saints, Irish and external, from the metrical text of MO.[62] The majority of these entries were taken directly from the metrical text, including at least one ghost saint, Molotha, at 2 Sep., whose name is based on a misreading of the verbal form *molthae*, 'praise thou'.[63] However, as was first suggested by R. I. Best and H. J. Lawlor, saints were drawn not only from the metrical text of MO but also from its Commentary.[64] These included several ghost saints, one of the more striking examples of which, already singled out by Best and Lawlor, was *Femmi* (21 Jan.), who is otherwise attested only in the Commentary on MO. The Commentator had misconstrued a line of Óengus's quatrain for the day, which reads *Fuinche, feidm as uaisliu*, 'Fuinche, effort that is highest', taking *feidm* 'effort' (written *feim*, for example, in the R1 version of MO) to be the personal name Feimme, otherwise borne by the sister of Daig son of Cairell of Iniskeen.[65]

---

[61] Ibid.

[62] The figure quoted by Schneiders ('The Drummond Martyrology', p. 118) is 319, but this does not take account of the 43 or so saints drawn from the Commentary, many of whom are listed by Schneiders under entries from an unknown source. That MDr was using a copy of the first, or Armagh, line of transmission of the Commentary can be seen, for example, in its preference for *Ruphi* (27 Aug.) and *Agappa* (30 Aug.) against *Ruphin* and *Agatha* of the manuscripts of the second line of transmission. For a discussion of the lines of transmission, see Ó Riain, 'The Martyrology of Óengus'.

[63] All manuscripts of MO agree with MDr in reading *Molotha* (*Molatha*). However, Stokes was no doubt correct to restore the form *molthae*, which is required by sense and metre. No trace of a saint named Molatha is found in MH at 2 Sep.

[64] Best, Lawlor, *The Martyrology of Tallaght*, p. xxii, where mention is made of 'a few names incorporated from the scholia' of MO. Cf. Schneiders, 'The Drummond Martyrology', p. 114.

[65] Forbes, *The Ancient Irish Missal*, p. <3>, had already drawn attention to the confusion with *feidm*, which he also took to be a name.

In fact, entries relating to over 40 saints, mostly real, sometimes imaginary, were taken from an annotated version of MO.[66] Thus, at 31 Jan., reference is made to a phantom saint named Bríg who is likewise elsewhere first recorded in the Commentary on MO. Again, a line in Óengus's quatrain for the day – *co mbríg romóir*, 'with great vigour' – had first been wrongly taken by the Commentator to refer to a saint named Bríg who was then duly adopted by MDr.[67] Equally clear proof of dependence is provided by the inclusion at 8 Mar. of St Áed who figures nowhere else among the saints of the day. The person intended seems to be Beoaid of Ardcarne, whom the metrical text of MO records as *epscop Beoaed bágach*, 'Bishop Beoaid the warlike', with alliteration between the name and the following adjective. In this case, the Commentator took the bishop's name to derive from *áed beo*, 'living Áed/fire', which in turn provided MDr with the basis of its entry.[68]

Schneiders argued that MDr must have been using a less than fully annotated MO, because, although it took 'nearly all the Irish saints' of the metrical text, it failed to include all those listed in the Commentary.[69] In fact, since many additions and omissions were made to the Commentary by individual copyists, we cannot know what was

---

[66] The 42 feasts are: 13 Jan. (Sulpicius), 15 Jan. (Maurus), 19 Jan. (Marius), 20 Jan. (Féichín), 21 Jan. (Feimme), 24 Jan. (Manchanus), 31 Jan. (Bríg), 8 Feb. (Onchú), 1 Mar. (David), 8 Mar. (Conna, Áed), 10 Mar. (Constantinus), 11 Mar. (Óengus), 15 Mar. (Lucas), 24 Mar. (Domangart), 25 Mar. (Annuntiatio, Passio Domini), 26 Mar. (Mochellóc), 1 Apr. (Ambrosius), 20 Apr. (Omnes sancti Europae), 24 Apr. (Ananias etc.), 13 May (Tigernach), 16 May (Finguine), 5 June (Aglahes/Agatha), 7 June (Mocholmóc), 12 June (Mothairén/Mothoria), 17 June (Colmanus filius Luachan), 21 June (Diarmait), 15 July (Divisio apostolorum), 26 July (Transformatio Domini), 24 Aug. (Patricius), 5 Sep. (Bricín), 10 Sep. (Finnianus), 12 Oct. (Mobí), 21 Oct. (Munnu), 26 Nov. (Siricius), 27 Nov. (Secundinus), 28 Nov. (Tres filii Bochrai), 4 Dec. (Fer Dá Leithe), 8 Dec. (Ichtbrichtán), 9 Dec. (Feidelm, Mugain), 11 Dec. (Eiltíne), 26 Dec. (Iarlaithe), 28 Dec. (Innocenti). Schneiders ('The Drummond Martyrology', pp. 120–2) could find only 16 entries on Irish saints drawn from the Commentary; in fact, as the list above shows, there were 28.
[67] Cf. Ó Riain, 'Some Bogus Irish Saints', p. 3.
[68] The gloss is in both lines of transmission of MO. In my index to Ó Riain, *Corpus Genealogiarum Sanctorum Hiberniae*, pp. 226, 271, the name is written as if the ending included the diphthong *áe*. I would now incline towards regarding the ending as an example of the *-(a)id* found in such names as *Amalgaid, Cúscraid*.
[69] Schneiders, 'The Drummond Martyrology', p. 114. On the grounds that MDr contains Irish saints not found in MO, Schneiders suggests that the version being used cannot have been the immediate or remote exemplar of any of the surviving versions. However, as he goes on to point out, the possibility that the author of MDr was drawing on 'additional Irish sources' for these cannot be ruled out. In fact, the number of entries on Irish saints that cannot be traced elsewhere, either at all or on the particular day, is tiny. Two cases in point are Máel Doid at 24 Mar., who is normally remembered on the 13 May, and Mothuu at 1 Aug., who is nowhere else recorded.

originally the sum total of its entries. A basic late twelfth-century version is indeed reflected in all surviving manuscripts, but not fully represented by any. However, we can be certain that MDr was using a version drawn up no earlier than the late twelfth century, because, as I shall now show, many of the entries borrowed from the Commentary had in fact previously been taken by the Commentator from the Martyrology of Gorman (MG), which dates at the latest to about 1170.

## 9 The Martyrologies of Drummond (MDr), Óengus (MO) and Gorman (MG)

Although an objection might be raised at this point that the Commentator of MO could just as well have been drawing on MDr, there are several grounds for rejecting this line of argument. In the first place, since mistakes of the kind *Femmi* for *feidm* or *Bríg* for *bríg* derive directly from attempts to interpret the metrical text of MO – the task set for himself by the Commentator – borrowing by him of misinterpretations perpetrated by others is rendered less likely. Besides, in the case of the mistaken entry at 21 Jan., there is possible evidence of a particular interest on the part of the Commentator in the substitute saint Feimme whose name is again intercalated at 17 Sep., this time in the guise of sister of Daig of Iniskeen, at the expense of Euphemia of Calcedonia.[70]

The most compelling reason for insisting that MDr was the borrower and the Commentary the source, and not vice versa, is the fact that of the entries in question, at least eleven can be shown to derive ultimately from MG, which, as I showed elsewhere, was used extensively by the Commentator.[71] A case in point is the entry for 26 Nov. which records the *natale* in Ireland of Banbán and 'Sericius'. The latter name, more correctly Siricius, is plainly not Irish. Nor was the saint, who is none other than the late fourth-century Pope of that name. His spurious Irish

---

[70] In this case, however, the mis-identification, which may have been influenced by the fact that Feimme is also separately recorded in MG on that day, is now confined to the *y* line of transmission, as represented by manuscripts F and Lb.

[71] Ó Riain, 'Die Bibliothek des Verfassers', pp. 89–91. The eleven entries are 8 Feb. (Onchú), 7 June (Mocholmóc), 17 June (Colmanus), 21 June (Diarmait), 5 Sep. (Bricín), 21 Oct. (Munnu), 26 Nov. (Siricius), 28 Nov. (Filii Bochrai), 4 Dec. (Fer Dá Leithe), 9 Dec. (Feidelm, Mugain), 11 Dec. (Eiltíne). In all cases, MDr agrees both with the Commentary and with MG against the metrical text of MO in the detail of the entry, be this the form of name used (8 Feb., 7 June, 5 Sep., 21 Oct., 4 Dec., 9 Dec., 11 Dec.), the inclusion of the saint (17 June, 21 June), or the number or attribute(s) of the saint(s) (26 Nov., 28 Nov.).

connexions are, however, otherwise documented in the Commentary, which reads *ó Maig Bolcc hi Feraib Cúl Breg*, 'from Mag Bolg in Fir Chúl of Brega'.[72] On verbal evidence, the Commentator's inspiration for this entry clearly came from MG, where the gloss on *epscop Siric* reads *Maighe Bolcc i Feraibh Cúl i mBreghaibh*.[73] Similarly, at 5 Sep., MDr records a St Bricín who is absent under this guise from the metrical text of MO but present both in the Commentary, which reads *Bricin Tuama Drecon isin Breifne*, 'Bricín of Tuaim Drecoin (now Tomregan on the Cavan-Fermanagh border) in Bréifne', and in MG where Bricín is stated, in very similar terms, to have been attached to *Tuaim Drecain i mBrefne Chonnacht*.[74] A third case, involving a saint completely absent from the metrical text of MO but present in the Commentary, occurs at 17 June, where MDr records the feast of Colmán mac Luacháin. This saint is described in the Commentary, again in verbal agreement with MG, as being from *Laind mic Luachain i Midhe*, 'Lann Meic Luacháin (now Lynn) in Mide'. There can be no doubt but that in these three representative examples the Commentary, having drawn on MG, itself became the source of MDr. By extension, on the assumption that this course of derivation applies to all 11 entries shared by both Commentary and MDr with MG, we may infer that MDr cannot have been compiled before about 1170.[75]

## 10  *The Martyrology of Drummond (MDr) and the Martyrology of Ado (MA)*

The martyrology composed by Ado, bishop of Vienne in France, between 853 and 860 quickly became one of the most popular texts of its kind. Within the decade after its composition it had already formed the basis of the Martyrology of Usuard (MU), compiled about 865, and, together with MU, it served as one of the principal liturgical sources of information on the feastdays of the saints in the centuries that

---

[72] The place in question is now the parish of Moybolgue, otherwise Bailieborough, on the Meath-Cavan border.
[73] The entry is at 25 Nov.
[74] A reference to Connacht is also added to the version in the Commentary on MO in manuscripts R1, F, and Lb.
[75] For the most recent discussion of the date of MG, see Ó Riain, 'The Martyrologies of Gorman'.

followed.[76] Curiously, however, the earliest evidence of the presence of a copy of either text in an Irish church dates to about 1168–70, when a copy of MU served as the main source of the non-Irish saints listed by Máel Muire Ua Gormáin in the metrical martyrology he composed at the priory of Cnoc Muire (Knock Abbey), near the diocesan church of Louth. Soon after this a copy of MA was used extensively at Armagh in the course of the compilation of the Commentary on the Martyrology of Óengus (MO).[77]

As already stated, the use made of MA as the main source of entries on non-Irish saints points to Armagh as the place of origin of MDr.[78] Moreover, as in the case of the Commentary on MO, if we except a small number of entries, the material taken from MA is habitually abbreviated in MDr. As it happens, the first two entries, which read *Octavas Dominicae natiuitatis in hoc die celebratur* and *Hoc quoque die, circumcissio Domini nostri Iesu Christi secundum legem Moysi*, are more expansive than the corresponding entries of MA.[79] From there on, however, although usually consistent with the introductory words of the source entry, the text tends very quickly to taper off. The entry on Pope Telesphoros at 5 Jan., where only the first clause of the source text is retained, aptly illustrates the normal procedure:

MA *Romae natale sancti Telesphori, qui septimus post Petrum apostolum pontifex ordinatus, sedit annos undecim, menses tres, dies viginti unum, illustreque martyrium duxit.*
MDr *Romae natale sancti Thelespori papae et martyris.*

Examination of all the entries shows that the source was very much a 'mixed' text, now agreeing with the first family of MA manuscripts, here designated MA (1), then following the reading of the second family or MA (2). Predominantly, however, the agreement is with MA (1) against MA (2).[80]

---

[76] For MA and MU, see Dubois, *Le Martyrologe d'Adon*, idem, *Le Martyrologe d'Usuard*. For a close analysis of the relationship between MA and MDr, see Schneiders, 'The Drummond Martyrology'.

[77] Ó Riain, 'Die Bibliothek des Verfassers', pp. 93–6.

[78] MDr may have drawn also on a version of MH, possibly MT. Examples are the use of the words or phrases *presbyter* (13 Sep.) and *et alii/aliorum* (8 May, 19 Oct.).

[79] The first entry simply reads *Octavae Domini* in MA, and the second, which is found only in the second family of MA manuscripts, reads *Circumcisio Domini nostri Iesu Christi secundum carnem*. For a brief account of the textual history of MA, see Dubois, *Le Martyrologe d'Adon*, pp. xx–xxviii.

[80] Where the families of MA disagree in the month of January, eleven readings (2.1, 4.1, 9.1, 10.1, 14.1, 16.1, 18.2, 22.1, 24.1, 25.2, 26.1) follow MA (1), four (1.2, 4.1, 6.1, 28.1)

MDr's appearance of regularly adapting its source may only partially reflect the habit of its author. As Forbes was first to point out, there is abundant evidence to show that the source had already been adapted, among other ways, to local usage.[81] This becomes clear from a comparison with the Martyrology of Christ Church, Dublin (MCh), which survives in the thirteenth-century section of a manuscript in Trinity College, Dublin.[82] The dependence of both texts on the same version of MA shows itself in the presence in each of many shared adaptations. Thus, although MCh retains the full text of MA's entry on Pope Telesphorus, and as a rule is much less abbreviated than MDr, the two versions regularly agree to differ with MA in the spellings of saints' names, in the inclusion of additional saints, in the omission of saints, in the wording of entries, in the selection of saints' days, and in the precedence given to certain saints.[83]

This is not to suggest that the examples of disagreement with Ado's text are all attributable to an Irish adaptor. On the contrary, comparison with the Martyrology of Usuard (MU) and its *auctaria*, as cited by Du Sollier, shows that many of the changes had been made long before the text reached Ireland.[84] In fact, the Irish version of MA sometimes agrees with MU against MA proper in both wording and spelling,[85] and, although this may involve only minor variations, the extent of the agreement, especially with some *auctaria*, clearly shows that the source text had at some stage been collated with a version of MU. In addition, several *auctaria*, and especially the *Bruxellensis* version, agree with the Irish MA against MA proper on a regular basis with regard to spelling,

---

MA (2). Much the same pattern obtains throughout. Cf. Schneiders, 'The Drummond Martyrology', pp. 110–11.

[81] Forbes, *The Ancient Irish Missal*, p. vi.

[82] The manuscript is numbered 576. For the text, see Crosthwaite and Todd, *The Book of Obits and Martyrology*. For the date of the manuscript, see Colker, *Trinity College Dublin: Descriptive Catalogue*, pp. 1038–40; Hawkes, 'The Liturgy in Dublin', pp. 57–8, followed Todd in wrongly assigning the manuscript to the fourteenth century.

[83] Spelling: 16 Apr. (*Calixti/Callisti, Carici/Caristi*), 5 June (*Brancii/Bonifacii*). Addition: 19 June (Celsus), 22 Oct. (Severus, Leogathus). Omission: 20 June (Novatus). Wording: 18 Jan. (transposition of *sedit Romae*), 20 Jan. (addition of a reference to Milan). Selection of days: 18 July (Iusta, Rufina), 19 July (Ioseph). Precedence: 17 Oct. (Florentius), 3 Nov. (Germanus).

[84] Sollerius (Du Sollier), *Martyrologium Usuardi Monachi*.

[85] Wording: 10 Jan. (*primi/-*), 22 May (*supplicio coronata/suppliciis passa*), 16 June (a whole clause). Spelling: 5 Mar. (*Foccae/Phocae*), 25 Apr. (*Letania/Litaniae*). There are also quite a number of examples of what seems to have been direct use of MU; see notes at 27 Jan., 16 Feb., 6 Mar., 12 Mar., 18 Mar., 19 Apr., 31 May, 6 June, 27 July, 29 July, 1 Aug., 15 Aug., and 5 Sep.

additions of words or names, changes of days and precedence of saints.[86]

Of all the *auctaria* used by Du Sollier, the *Bruxellensis* version, from a 14/15th-century manuscript belonging to a house of canons in Brussels,[87] is closest to the text of the Irish MA. For example, only these place the feast 'in Italy' of the 'Irish' Columbanus on the 13 Nov., eight days ahead of the regular feast on the 21 Nov., a misplacement, if such it is, scarcely attested elsewhere.[88] Similarly, at 15 Dec., they stand quite alone in rendering corruptly the name *Valerianus* as *Aurilianus*.[89] This kind of agreement is most likely due to the two texts having belonged to the same line of transmission which, given the association of *Bruxellensis* with canons, may have represented a standard version of the Augustinian canons regular.[90]

There is some evidence to suggest that sources other than MU or one of its *auctaria* may also have been quarried for materials during transmission. For example, in the month of November alone, the inclusion of the names Caesarius (1 Nov.), Domninus (4 Nov.), Leontius and Faustius (22 Nov.) can best be explained by reference to the Hieronymian Martyrology.

## 11 *The Irish Martyrology of Ado*

The nonetheless ultimately Irish character of the version of MA underlying MDr and MCh finds its clearest expression in the entries on the native saints which the two derivative texts hold in common.[91] Included

---

[86] Spelling: *Calixti* (16 Apr.). Addition: Celsus (19 June), *et martyris* (16 Jan.), *de Mediolano* (20 Jan.). Selection of days: see 18–19 July (Iusta, Rufina, and Ioseph, as in *Bruxellensis*). Precedence: 16 June (Ciricus, as in *Bruxellensis*), 21 July (Praxedes, as in *Bruxellensis*).
[87] *AASS* Iunii vi, p. LX. Unfortunately, *Bruxellensis* does not appear to have survived. Forbes, *The Ancient Irish Missal*, p. x, states that MDr agrees most closely with *Grevenus*, but this is not the case.
[88] For another mention of the feast, in some Premonstratensian copies of MU, see Overgaauw, *Martyrologes manuscrits*, p. 1056. The Premonstratensian canons also followed the rule of St Augustine.
[89] Similarly, at 27 Nov., only these two versions list the feast of Amator, which is placed in other martyrologies on the previous day.
[90] This is not to say that agreement between the Irish MA and *Bruxellensis* is completely regular. For instance, at 12 Jan. only the Irish MA adds *sancti*. Similarly, at 16 Jan. only *Bruxellensis* lists Maurus, who in all others is at 15 Jan.
[91] For a discussion of these, see now Schneiders, 'The Drummond Martyrology', pp. 127–32.

in the list of shared saints in this category are some who were already in Ado's text, but even here the two texts clearly derive from an intermediate common source. Thus, at 1 Feb., MDr and MCh agree almost word for word in reading *Item apud Hiberniam, dormitatio beatissimae uirginis Brigidae ueneranter hodie commemoratur*, whereas MA reads *Item apud Scotiam, sanctae Brigidae virginis, cuius vita miraculis claruit*.[92] Similarly, at 17 Mar., the words *Apud Hiberniam, Occiani insolam, natale sancti Patricii archepiscopi Scottorum*, common to MDr and MCh, may be compared to the version of MA which reads *In Scotia, natale sancti Patricii episcopi et confessoris*.[93] According to Schneiders, who provides a useful list of the entries concerned,[94] MDr drew a total of 122 entries, non-Irish and Irish, from its source copy of MA. In fact, this figure is approximate only, for Schneiders derived several entries from MO which might just as easily have come from MA. However, it gives an idea of how extensively this source, which may have contained as many as fifty native saints, was used by MDr.[95]

Perhaps the most important aspect of the presence of native saints in the source text is the evidence of provenance they provide,[96] which, as might be expected, points to the involvement of Augustinian canons. Almost a third of the saints, including Áed (Ferns), Brendan (Clonfert), Cainnech (Dungiven, Monaincha),[97] Cóemgen (Glendalough), Columba

---

[92] Both MCh and MA add further, but distinct, comments.

[93] As at 1 Feb., MCh and MA add further, but quite distinct, comments.

[94] Schneiders, 'The Drummond Martyrology', pp. 142–5.

[95] Schneiders, ibid., pp. 142–5, counts 24. However, over twenty saints, including Patricius and Brigida, may be added to his list. For the full list see the next note.

[96] Very often, the author of MDr renders the names in an Irish form. This was doubtless because of his simultaneous consultation of MO, otherwise seen, for example, in his conflation of MA and MO at 21 Apr., where not only Máel Rubae but also his mother (*cum sancta matre* MDr, *cona máthair* MO) is listed. The full list of native saints in the Irish MA is as follows: 9 Jan. (Fáelán), 16 Jan. (Furseus), 31 Jan. (Áed), 1 Feb. (Brigida), 6 Feb. (Mel), 11 Feb. (Etchén), 15/16 Feb. (Berach/Berchán), 17 Feb. (Fintan), 19 Feb. (Baíthín), 21 Feb. (Fintan), 28 Feb. (Sillán), 15 Mar. (Filii Nessan), 17 Mar. (Patricius), 19 Mar. (Auxaile, Laichtín), 21 Apr. (Máel Rubae), 30 Apr. (Ronanus), 7 May (Ciaróc, Brecán), 9 May (Sanctanus), 10 May (Comgallus), 16 May (Braendinus), 22 May (Baíthíne), 3 June (Coemginus), 9 June (Columba, Baíthíne), 11 June (Mac Táil), 13 June (Mac Nisse), 18 June (Báetán, Furudrán), 7 July (Máel Ruain), 10 Aug. (Blaan), 19 Aug. (Mochtae), 23 Aug. (Eogan), 31 Aug. (Áedán), 2/3 Sep. (Lon/Lomanus, Colmán, Mac Nisse), 4 Sep. (Ultanus), 6 Sep. (Mac Cuilinn), 11 Oct. (Cainnech), 31 Oct. (Faelanus), 9 Nov. (Sinche), 17 Nov. (Dúilech), 25 Nov. (Finnchú), 27 Nov. (Secundinus), 12 Dec. (Finnianus), 18 Dec. (Maigniu). The Welsh David was also added at 1 Mar. For Schneiders's list, see 'The Drummond Martyrology', pp. 128–30.

[97] The house of regular canons in Kilkenny appears to have been founded shortly after 1200.

(Derry),[98] Comgall (Bangor), Finnian (Clonard), Fintan (Clonfert), Mac Nisse (Clonmacnoise), Máel Rubae (Bangor, Apurcrossan), Mochta (Louth), Patrick (Armagh etc), and Sillán (Bangor), are directly associated with churches at or near which houses of canons are known to have been founded by the third quarter of the twelfth century,[99] and several others, such as Ciar of Kilkeary near Toomyvara and Fursa of Killursy near Annaghdown, whose brother Fáelán is also mentioned, are associated with churches close to, and probably controlled by, houses of canons. This may also apply to some Dublin saints (Dúilech of Clogher, Mac Cuilinn of Lusk, Máel Ruain of Tallaght, Maigniu of Kilmainham, and Meic Nessáin of Ireland's Eye), whose churches were possibly attached either to the priory of the Holy Trinity or to that on St Patrick's Island (later Holmpatrick). On that evidence, it would seem that the choice of native saints added to the Irish MA is most likely to have been made by an Augustinian canon.

Where is this Irish version likely to have been prepared? Although by no means plentiful, the evidence again points to Armagh which, as is clear from the Commentary on MO, possessed a copy of MA,[100] fuller, it seems, than that used by the authors of MDr and MCh. At 16 Feb., for instance, in their comments on St Iuliana, MO and MA refer to the province of Nicomedia, a detail absent from MDr and MCh. Similarly, at 23 Nov., where the subject is Pope Clement, MO and MA contain a reference to the city of Cersona, omitted from MDr and MCh. The least that can be said, therefore, is that the apparently fuller copy held by Armagh could well have served as the immediate source of the Irish MA consulted by MDr and MCh. Moreover, the great interest in St Patrick shown by the Irish MA, which used the title *archiepiscopus Scottorum* at 17 Mar., and which probably contained the lengthy commentary on him now preserved only in MCh, as well as the extensive note on his follower Secundinus at 27 Nov., points to the Augustinian house of Sts Peter and Paul at Armagh as a very likely place of origin.

Use of the title *archiepiscopus Scottorum* possibly also dates the Irish adaptation of MA to the period after the synod of Clane in 1162, when, as we have already seen (§ 5), the clergy of Ireland, having enjoined

---

[98] Columba is placed *apud Hiberniam*. For evidence of the presence of Augustinian canons in Derry by as early as about 1170, see the entry on Columba in MG at 9 June, which describes him as 'abbot of the Black Monks' of that church.

[99] Gwynn, Hadcock, *Medieval Religious Houses*, pp. 153–6.

[100] Ó Riain, 'Die Bibliothek des Verfassers', pp. 93–6.

'rule and good conduct', reaffirmed the orders of 'archbishop of Ireland' to the successor of Patrick.

## 12 *The Martyrology of Christ Church (MCh) vis-à-vis the Martyrology of Drummond (MDr)*

Since it more properly belongs in the textual tradition of the Martyrology of Ado (MA), I do not propose to examine the Martyrology of the Holy Trinity or Christ Church (MCh) here.[101] However, the fact that it shares with MDr a common source, which it very probably reflects quite closely, merits some discussion. In fact, given the probable involvement of Augustinian canons in the preparation of both texts, their possession of a common source can be easily explained. Christ Church, where MCh was compiled, and Glendalough, where MDr was kept, shared an affiliation to the canons regular, forged, it would appear, by Lorcán Ua Tuathail, who was abbot of Glendalough from about 1153, until his appointment as archbishop of Dublin in 1162.[102] The Glendalough priory of St Saviour's is thought to have been founded by Ua Tuathail some time after his assumption of the abbacy, and the introduction of the regular canons to Christ Church is usually put after Ua Tuathail's arrival there in 1162.[103] There is no evidence to show that Ua Tuathail himself was involved in the transactions that brought the texts to Dublin and Glendalough. However, it is very likely that requests to the authorities at Armagh for new, up-to-date martyrologies and missals, which led to the production of MDr and MCh, came from the two Augustinian priories associated with him.[104]

## 13 *Authorial Habits*

Although well able to formulate his own version of the required Latin words or phrases,[105] on occasion the author of MDr was prone to lapse

---

[101] For discussions of the martyrology, see Hennig, 'The Sources', pp. 416–24; Schneiders, 'The Drummond Martyrology', pp. 109–11.

[102] For the dates, see Gwynn, Hadcock, *Medieval Religious Houses*, pp. 80–1, 170.

[103] Ibid., p. 177.

[104] In view of its many Irish saints, the source copy of MA shared by Christ Church and Glendalough must already have been used by an Irish religious community.

[105] 13 Jan. (a–a), 24 Apr. (b–b), 27 Apr. (b–b), 23 May (b–b), and 24 May (d–d).

into grammatical error, sometimes through habit,[106] at other times through apparent carelessness, as when he substituted genitive for nominative, singular for plural, plural for singular, and feminine for masculine declension.[107] Slight misspellings of names also occur occasionally, as in the case of *Ampliani* for *Amphiani* at 5 Apr., *Alax-* for *Alex-* at 24/25 Apr., and *Marcelli* for *Marcellini* at 26 Apr. He was also a reasonably good Irish scholar who, where appropriate,[108] supplied genitive forms of personal names. However, he twice allowed himself to be misled into believing that Cuanna was a female, at 4 Feb. and 10 Apr., presumably because of the ending in -*a*.

Misreadings of the source are rare enough, but incorrect conflations of two separate entries have been noted at 4 Jan., 3 Feb., 14 July and 24 July. Finally, the indiscriminate use of *Britannia* for *Alba/Scotia* (8 Jan., 17 Apr., 21 Apr., 25 June, 10 Aug.), Wales (1 Mar.), and the rest of the island (20 Mar., 24 May, 22 June, 24 Aug., 31 Aug., 17 Sep.) is worthy of note.[109]

## 14  *Summary of Conclusions*

The foregoing discussion indicates that previous opinion on the Martyrology of Drummond may require modification in two important respects. First, its manuscript would appear to have been written not at Glendalough but at Armagh. Secondly, its date would seem to lie, with that of other similar texts, such as the Martyrology of Gorman and the Commentary on the Martyrology of Óengus, in the period about 1170. The evidence for an Armagh provenance for the manuscript derives mainly from emphases present in the texts of both martyrology and missal, whereas all the support for Glendalough is found on single and perhaps added folios at the end of the manuscript. An Armagh provenance would also accord very well with what is otherwise known of martyrological production about this time, on the eve of the English conquest of Ireland. However, this event may not have been the only influence on the sudden surge in martyrological activity. The initial

---

[106] As when he wrote *in Hiberniam* (31 Jan., 8 Apr., 13 May) for *in Hibernia*, probably under the influence of the frequently used formula *apud Hiberniam*.
[107] For one example of each, see 21 Mar. (c), 23 Mar., 22 Mar., 15 May (b). For his use of Irish and Latin, see also Schneiders, 'The Drummond Martyrology', pp. 132–4.
[108] For example, 2–3 Sep., 12–14 Sep., 17 Sep.
[109] Cf. Schneiders, 'The Drummond Martyrology', pp. 108–9.

impetus appears to have come from the synod held at Clane in 1162, which enjoined 'rule and good conduct' on the Irish clergy.[110] Finally, there is palaeographical evidence to suggest that Flann Ua Gormáin, a member of the same hereditary learned ecclesiastical family as Máel Muire, author of the Martyrology of Gorman, was involved in the production of the Martyrology of Drummond. The hand he would undoubtedly have learned to use during his twenty years outside Ireland may be the non-Irish hand now visible on folios 107–8 of the manuscript.

## 15  *Editorial Method*

Punctuation, use of capitals, and division of the entries according to number are editorial. Otherwise the text is presented in accordance with the manuscript, with silent expansion of all abbreviations, except where it seemed wiser to draw attention to the manuscript reading. The ligature -*æ* is always written out -*ae*. Parentheses are used in the *apparatus criticus*, either singly to indicate that one source disagrees slightly with the other, or in pairs to set off the bracketed letters or words peculiar to the bracketed source.

The text has been established from a microfilm copy of the original manuscript, collated with the standard editions of the main sources used by the author and the texts most closely related to these.[111] From the variants cited, the source used will normally be apparent. Parallel text from MO is, where necessary, translated. Where native saints drawn from the Irish version of MA are concerned, both the reading of MO and the corresponding reading of MCh are normally given, the latter in a note to the entry.

---

[110] The synod is mentioned in a single sentence only in Gwynn, *The Twelfth-Century Reform*, p. 62.

[111] For the Martyrology of Ado, see Dubois, *Le Martyrologe d'Adon*; for the Martyrology of Christ Church, which has also been consulted in manuscript, see Crosthwaite, Todd, *The Book of Obits and Martyrology*; for the Martyrology of Óengus, see Stokes, *Félire Oengusso Céli Dé*, and for the Martyrology of Usuard and its auctaria, see Dubois, *Le Martyrologe d'Usuard*, and Sollerius, *Martyrologium Usuardi Monachi*.

# CHAPTER TWO

# THE MARTYROLOGY OF DRUMMOND: TEXT

## JANUARY

Ianuarius habet dies triginta et unum iuxta solem, et triginta dies iuxta lunam

### [1 January] KAL. EN.

1  <sup>a</sup>Octavas Dominicae natiuitatis in hoc die celebratur.<sup>a</sup>
2  <sup>b</sup>Hoc quoque die, circumcissio Domini nostri Iesu Christi secundum legem Moysi<sup>b</sup>.
3  Et in Hibernia, sancti confessoris Osini.
4  Et aliorum plurimorum sanctorum martyrum confessorum atque uirguinum.

<sup>a–a</sup>Octaue Domini MCh, MA. <sup>b–b</sup>*om.* MCh.

**1. Octavae Nativitatis Dominicae.** Here the wording varies from that of MCh and MA (1), agreeing instead in its essentials with that of the *Bruxellensis* version of MU, which reads: *octava dies Dominicae nativitatis.*
**2. Circumcisio.** This is not in MA (1), whereas MA (2), which was influenced by MU, the first historical martyrology to notice the feast, reads *carnem* for *legem Moysi*, a reading peculiar to MDr. MO also refers to the circumcision on this day.
**3. Osíne.** This is not in MO, but MT names the saint's church as Cluain Mór – now Clonmore tl./ p., Ferrard b., Co. Louth – whose foundation was attributed to Colum Cille (Herbert, *Iona, Kells and Derry*, p. 233, § 41). The connexion with Colum Cille may explain the inclusion of the saint (Introduction, § 4).
**4. Et alii.** This addition is also the final entry at 1 Jan. and 31 Dec. of the *Martyrologium Romanum*, where it reads: *et alibi aliorum plurimorum sanctorum martyrum et confessorum, atque sanctarum virginum*, followed by the response *Deo gratias*.

## [2 January] IIII NON. EN.

1 Natale sancti<sup>a</sup> Macarii abbatis.
2 <sup>b</sup>Manchini quoque et Scothini<sup>b</sup> confessorum in Hibernia insola commemoratur.

<sup>a</sup>beati MA. <sup>b–b</sup>Mainchine . . . Scothíne MO.

**1. Macarius.** The text, which reflects the Irish MA, corresponds to MA (1), subject to the use of *sancti* for *beati*, which is more in keeping with MU.

## [3 January] III NON. EN.

1 Romae, natale sancti Anterois<sup>a</sup> pape et martyris <sup>b</sup>natale celebratur.<sup>b</sup>
2 <sup>c</sup>Fintani quoque et Finnlog<sup>c</sup> in Hibernia celebratur.

<sup>a</sup>Anteros MCh, MA. <sup>b–b</sup>*om.* MCh, MA, *which add more detail.* <sup>c–c</sup>Fintan . . . Findlug MO.

**1. Anteros.** The author seems to have treated the name as an Irish first declension noun, with palatal genitive. He also duplicated *natale*.

## [4 January] II NON. EN.

1 Natale sancti Titi <sup>a</sup>episcopi et<sup>a</sup> apostolorum discipuli apud Affricam <sup>a</sup>in hac die celebratur.<sup>a</sup>

<sup>a–a</sup>*om.* MCh, MA.

**1. Titus.** The entry agrees with MA (1), subject to the description of Titus as bishop, which derives from the more extensive commentary on the saint, as in MA (2) and MU. *Apud Affricam* corresponds to the first two words of the following entry in MCh and MA, where it more properly belongs.

## [5 January] NON. EN.

1 Romae, natale sancti Thelespori <sup>a</sup>papae et martyris.<sup>a</sup>
2 Item apud Hiberniam, sanctissima uirgo Ciar<sup>b</sup> ad Christum conscendit.

<sup>a–a</sup>*om.* MCh, MA, *which add more detail.* <sup>b</sup>Ciar MO.

**1. Telesphorus.** The final words agree with the so-called *Parvum Romanum* – identified by Quentin (*Les martyrologes historiques*) as a forgery compiled by Ado himself – and with the *Centulensis* version of MU, which also use the words *papae et martyris*.
**2. Ciar.** The use of the superlative, as in *sanctissima*, was usually reserved for saints of special interest to the author, who seems to have been an Augustinian

canon (Introduction, § 5). Ciar was patron of Cell Chéire, now Kilkeary tl./ p., Upper Ormond b., Co. Tipperary. Although the affiliations of this church are unknown, it lay near Toomyvara, a dependency of the Augustinian priory at Monaincha. Ciar also figures in the Life of Brendan of Clonfert, the site of an Augustinian priory from about the middle of the twelfth century.

## [6 January] UIII IDUS

1  Epifania Domini [a]nostri Iesu Christi [b]in hoc die celebratur.[ab]
2  Et[c] sanctae Macrae uirginis [d]et martyris natale celebratur.[d]

[a–a]*om.* MCh, MA (1). [b–b]*om.* MA (2). [c]eodem die (passio) MCh, (MA). [d–d]*om.* MCh, MA, *which add more detail.*

**1. Epiphania Domini.** The words *nostri Iesu Christi* accompany the notice of this feast in MA (2), as well as in some versions of MU, including *Antverp. Maj.* and *Bruxellensis.*
**2. Macra.** The words *et martyris* also follow *uirginis* in the *Matric. Carthus. Ultraj.* version of MU.

## [7 January] UII IDUS

1  [ab]Ieiunium Christi[b] cum diabolo temptaretur.[a]

[a–a]*om.* MCh, MA. [b–b]tossach corgais Issu, 'the beginning of Jesus's Lent' MO.

**1. Ieiunium Christi.** The entry is from MO, which was also the source here of both MG (*tossech coir a corghais*) and MTur (*initium ieiunii*). Although omitted from the surviving copy of MT, the entry may have been in the original version because it is also in MCamb, which reads *initium ieiunii Christi*. As Forbes pointed out, this feast falls forty days before 15 Feb. when Christ's victory over the devil is commemorated. See also the note to MTur at 7 Jan.

## [8 January] UI IDUS

1  Herapolim[a] Campaniae, natale[b] sancti [c]confessoris Seuerini[c] fratris beatissimi Uictorini clarissimi uiri in[d] miraculis [e]celebratur hodie.[e]
2  Item apud Hiberniam, [f]Ercnat sancta uirgo et Nectan in Britania[f] eodem die migrauerunt ad Christum.

[a](Apud) Neapolim MCh, (MA). [b]*om.* MCh, MA. [c–c]*reversed* MA. [d]*om.* MA. [e–e]*om.* MCh, MA. [f–f]Ercnat úag . . . Nechtan de Albae, 'E. the virgin, N. of Alba' MO.

**1. Severinus.** *Her-* is probably a misreading of *Ne-* of the source. Several versions of MU, including *Antverp. Maj.* and *Centulensis,* also omit *apud.* Since it is already in MA, the superlative *beatissimi* does not reflect a particular interest in the saint.

27

**2. Ercnat, Nechtan in Britannia.** The use of *Britannia* for *Alba* of MO also occurs at 21 Apr., and 25 June. Moreover, churches in Scotland are assigned to *Britannia* at 17 Apr. and 10 Aug. See also Schneiders, 'The Drummond Martyrology', pp. 108–9.

## [9 January] U IDUS

1 Apud[a] Antiochiam,[b] sancti Iuliani martyris et Bassilissae coniugis eius [c]natalicia celebrantur.[c]
2 Uitalis[d] quoque sanctus hoc die.
3 Et apud Hiberniam, Faelan[e] ad Christum migrauerunt.

[a]Eodem die apud MCh, MA. [b]*add* natale MA. [c–c]*different wording* MCh, MA. [d]Uitalis MO. [e]Fáelán MO.

**1. Iulianus.** Although second in MCh and MA (1), which give precedence to the virgin Marciana, Iulianus and his wife are likewise first in MU.
**2. Vitalis.** Although also in MA (2), MDr took this saint from MO.
**3. Fáelán.** This entry was in the Irish MA, with MCh reading, more or less as here, *Et apud Hiberniam, Felan ad Cristum migrauit.* It is also in the *Grevenus* version of MU, which reads: *Felani abbatis et confessoris.* The saint is associated with the church of Cluain Móescna, later Kylmisken, Lynn p., Fartullagh b., Co. Westmeath. The verb also governs *Uitalis*, whence its plural form.

## [10 January] IU IDUS

1 Apud Tebaidem, natale sancti Pauli primi[a] heremitae [b]hodie celebratur.[b]
2 Et apud Hiberniam, beatissimus Diarmait[c] et confessor Christi ad Dominum perrexit.

[a]*om.* MA. [b–b]*om.* MCh and MA, *which add more detail.* [c]Diarmait MO.

**1. Paulus.** Except for the addition of *primi*, which is regular in the manuscripts of MU, the wording agrees with MA (1).
**2. Diarmait.** Diarmait was associated with the island of Inis Clothrann (Inchcleraun), Cashel p., Rathcline b., Co. Longford, which became the site of an Augustinian priory about the middle of the twelfth century. This may explain why he is described as *beatissimus* (Introduction, § 5).

## [11 January] III IDUS

1 [a]Reuersio pueri Christi de Aegypto in hac die commemoratur.[a]

[a–a]a hEgipt . . . tánic macc már Maire, 'out of Egypt came Mary's great son' MO.

**1. Reversio pueri Christi.** Although the feast is also in MT, which reads *educt(io) Christi ex Egipto*, MDr appears to be based here on MO. The more usual day was 7 Jan., as in both MCh and (MA), which read *Relatio pueri (Iesu) ex Egipto.*

## [12 January] II IDUS

1 Apud Achaiam, natale sancti[a] Saturi martyris ciuis Arabiae [b]hodie celebratur.[b]
2 Et apud Hiberniam, sanctus confessor Ladcend[c] ad astra conscendit.

[a]*om.* MA. [b–b]*om.* MCh, MA, *which add more detail.* [c]Laidcenn MO.

**1. Saturus.** The *Centulensis* version of MU also prefaces *Saturi* with *sancti.*

## [13 January] IDUS EN

1 Romae, uia Lauicana, [a]quadraginta milites sub Galliano imperatore martyrio coronati sunt.[a]
2 [b]Sanctus quoque Sulpicius[c] confessor, qui uitam sancti Martini Toronensis episcopi eloquentissimo sermone dictauit, hodie migrauit ad Christum.[b]

[a–a]corone militum quadraginta sub Gallieno imperatore MCh, MA. [b–b]*om.* MCh, MA. [b]Sulpic MO.

**1. Quadraginta milites.** The phrasing, which is not paralleled elsewhere, is probably due to the author.
**2. Sulpicius.** Although the saint's more usual day was 17 Jan., MT, which spells the name *Supplicius*, and MO place him here. The description of the saint may be compared to the Commentary on MO, which reads .i. *qui libros Martini fecit.* The unusually elaborate character of the entry may be due to Armagh interest in the saint's Life of Martin (Introduction, § 4).

## [14 January] XUIIII KAL. FEB.

1 Apud Nolam, Campaniae urbem,[a] beati Felicis prespeteri [b]natale celebratur.[b]
2 Eodem die, [c]Glucerus diaconus martyrii[c] tormentis beatam uitam finiuit.

[a]*om.* MCh, MA, *add* natale MA. [b–b]*om.* MCh, MA, *which add more detail.* [c–c]Pais Gluceri deochain, 'The passion of G. the deacon' MO.

**1. Felix.** The wording of the entry agrees with MA (1) against MA (2), which has *sancti* for *beati.*

THE MARTYROLOGY OF DRUMMOND

## [15 January] XUIII KAL. FEB.

1 Ambacuc[a] et Michiae profetarum, [b]hodie natale commemoratur.[b]
2 [c]Eodem die quoque,[d] natale sancti Mauri abbatis, discipuli beati[e] Benedicti[f] [g]et eximi patris monachorum Europae, celebratur.[cg]
3 In hac quoque die, sancta uirgo Ita[h] apud Hiberniam migrauit ad Christum.

[a]Abacuc MCh, MA. [b-b]om. MCh, MA, *which add more detail.* [c-c]In territorio Andegavorum, depositio beati Mauri monachi MA. [d]om. MCh. [e]sancti MCh. [f]add abbatis MCh. [g-g]om. MCh. [h]Íte MO.

**1. A(m)bacuc.** The spelling with *-mb-* is also in MT and MTur.
**2. Maurus.** Whereas MA took this saint to be the abbot of Glanfeuil, its Irish version followed the majority of the *auctaria* of MU and the Hieronymian tradition by taking the saint to be a disciple of St Benedict. The Commentary on MO likewise describes Maurus as *monachus et discipulus Benedicti abbatis*, and also contains (21 Mar., 11 July) a reference to Benedict's status as *pater monachorum Europae*. For a similar description of the saint, see Ó Riain, *Corpus*, § 712.34. See also Hennig, 'The Sources', p. 419.

## [16 January] XUII KAL. FEB.

1 Romae, uia Salaria in cymitherio Priscillae, natale sancti Marcelli papae [a]et martyris.[ab]
2 [cd]Et apud Hiberniam,[d] natale sancti Fursei[e] Scotigenae[f] confessoris atque abbatis celebratur.[cf]

[a-a]om. MA. [b]more detail MCh, MA. [c-c]different wording MA (2). [d-d]eodem die MCh. [e]written Fur sei MDr. [f]om. MCh.

**1. Marcellus.** The wording agrees with MA (1) against MA (2), which omits from *Romae* to *Priscillae*. The *Bruxellensis* version of MU likewise adds *et martyris*.
**2. Furseus.** MA (2) and MU also list Fursa, and some *auctaria* describe him as both abbot and confessor. However, no other source places him *apud Hiberniam* or uses *Scotigena* of him.

## [17 January] e* XUI KAL. FEB.

1 In Aegypto, apud Thebaidem, hodie[a] beati Antonii monachi [b]natale celebratur.[b]

[a]om. MCh, MA. [b-b]om.MCh, MA, *which add more detail.*

*At this point the letters of the week begin to be prefixed to the Roman notation. However, they do not correspond to the usual system which would have *c* at the 17 Jan. The consequent irregularity continues throughout.

30

## [18 January] f XU KAL. FEB.

1 Cathedra sancti Petri apostoli, qua primum [a]Romae sedit.[a]
2 Eodem quoque[b] die, natale sanctae Priscae uirginis et martyris.
3 [c]Annuntiatio quoque assumptionis beatissimae Dei genetricis Mariae semper uirginis fidelibus Romanis.[c]

[a–a]*reversed* MA. [b]*om.* MCh, MA. [c–c]*om.* MCh, MA.

**1. Cathedra Petri.** Several *auctaria* of MU agree with the Irish MA in the order of the words *primum Romae sedit.*
**2. Prisca.** The wording here agrees with MA (1) against MA (2), which reads *et passio sanctae Priscae virginis.*
**3. Annuntiatio assumptionis.** This entry is from MO, which reads: *Mórad i rRóim . . . bás mórmáthar Issu*, 'the magnifying . . . in Rome . . . [of] the death of the great mother of Jesus'. The Hieronymian tradition (as in MT) specifies the arrival in Rome of the news.

## [19 January] g XIIII KAL. FEB.

1 In Smirna, natale[a] sancti Germanici martyris [b]celebratur hoc die.[b]
2 Item[c] eodem die, Romae,[d] sanctorum martyrum Marii et Marthae [e]uxoris suae[e] cum filiis duobus[f], Audifax et Ambacuc,[g] [b]qui simul martyrio coronati sunt.[b]

[a]*om.* MA. [b–b]*om.* MCh, MA, *which add more detail.* [c]*om.* MA. [d]*add* natalis MA. [e–e]*om.* MCh, MA. [f]suis MCh, MA. [g]Abacuc MCh, MA.

**2. Marius, Martha.** This feast is placed here in the Irish version of MA rather than on the following day (MA 1, 2), probably because of the influence of MO. The addition of the detail *uxoris suae* reflects the similar wording of the Commentary on MO. See also the note to MTur at 19 Jan.

## [20 January] a XIII KAL. FEB.

1 Romae, Fabiani episcopi [a]natale celebratur.[a]
2 Et[b] eodem die, natale sancti Sebastiani martyris[c] Medolanensis.[d]
3 Et apud Hiberniam, natale sanctorum confessorum, [e]Molaca, Oenu, Fechin,[e] celebratur.

[a–a]*om.*MCh, MA, *which add more detail.* [b]*om.* MCh, MA. [c]*om.* MCh. [d]*om.* MA, de Mediolano MCh. [e–e]Molaca, Moecu . . . ocus Óenu MO.

**2. Sebastianus.** The reference to *Medolanensis* (sic.)/*de Mediolano* is otherwise found in Florus (Dubois, *Le Martyrologe d'Adon*, p. 66), in the *Bruxellensis* version of MU, and in the Commentary on MO.
**3. Molaca etc.** The name *Moecu* is explained in the Commentary on MO as a derivative of *Féichín*, whence the preference here for the non-hypocoristic form.

## [21 January] b XII KAL.

1 Romae, natale sanctae Agnetis[a] martyris[b] [c]hodie celebratur.[c]
2 Et apud Hiberniam, quoque natale sanctarum uirginum, [d]Fanche et Femmi,[d] celebratur.

[a]*add* uirginis et MA. [b]*om.* MCh. [c-c]*om.* MCh, MA, *which add more detail.* [d-d]Fuinche, feidm, 'F., effort' MO.

**1. Agnes.** See also 28 Jan. below and the note to MTur at 21 Jan.
**2. Feimme.** Although read by G. H. Forbes as *Feinmi,* and by A. P. Forbes as *Femini,* the spelling of the manuscript is quite clearly *Femmi,* which is taken from the Commentary on MO. Forbes's suggestion that the name was based on a misreading of the word *feidm,* 'effort', which follows *Fuinche,* has been generally accepted (Introduction, § 8). However, it should be pointed out that the transformation had already taken place in the Commentary.

## [22 January] c XI KAL. FEB.

1 In Hispania,[a] natale[b] sancti Uincentii[c] diaconi [d]et martyris[d] celebratur.[e]
2 Apud Hiberniam, quoque sanctae uirgines id est [f]filiae Comgaill et sanctus confessor Colman[f] hodie ad Christum migrauerunt.

[a]Hispaniis MCh, MA. [b]*om.* MCh. [c]Uicentii MCh. [d-d]*om.* MCh. [e]*om.* MCh, MA, *which add more detail.* [f-f]Estecht ingen Comgaill, Colmán, 'Death of the daughters of C., C.' MO.

**1. Vincentius.** The text corresponds to MA (1), with MA (2) following MU by adding *civitate Valencia* to *Hispaniis.*

## [23 January] d X KAL. FE.

1 Romae, natale sanctae Emerentianae uirginis et martyris Christi.[a]
[a]*after* uirginis MCh, MA, *which add further detail.*

## [24 January] IX KAL. FE.

1 Apud Effessum, natale sancti Timothei apostoli.
2 Et[a] apud Antiochiam, sancti Babilli[b] episcopi [c]cum tribus discipulis suis.[c]
3 In Hibernia, natale sancti Manchani *Conchenn* (?) uiri sapientissimi.

[a]*om.* MCh, MA. [b]Babylac MA. [c-c]*om.* MCh, MA, *which add more detail.*

**1. Timotheus.** The entry corresponds to MA (1), with MA (2) agreeing with some *auctaria* of MU by describing Timothy as *discipulus beati Pauli.*

**2. Babillus.** Like MTur (*Babilli*) below, the Irish MA follows the Tallaght tradition – MT (*Babili*), MO (*Babill*) – in its declension of the name of the saint, more properly *Babylas/Babylae*. It also follows the Commentary on MO in referring to the saint's three 'disciples', more correctly 'little ones' (*parvuli*, MT, MDr, *deidbléin*, metrical text of MO).
**3. Manchanus.** This is from the Commentary on MO. G. H. Forbes claimed to have 'no idea' as to the force of the word after *Manchani*, which he transcribed conjecturally as the meaningless *concumes*. (His brother, A. P. Forbes, had simply omitted the word.) In fact, the word seems to consist of a reversed *c*, which is the normal abbreviation for *con*, followed by *c* with a line over it, followed by what looks like *es*, but might also be read as *h* with a dot after it. For the connexion between the saint and *coinchinn*, 'dog-heads', see the Commentary on this day, and Plummer, *Irish Litanies*, p. 64.

## [25 January] e* UIII KAL.

1  Conuersio sancti Pauli ᵃad fidem.ᵃ
2  Eodem die quoque,ᵇ natale° sancti Annaniae apud Damascum celebratur.ᵈ

ᵃ⁻ᵃ*om* MCh, MA. ᵇ*om.* MCh, MA. °*om.* MCh. ᵈ*om.* MCh, MA, *which add more detail.*

*Since the letter was omitted on the previous day, this should be *f*. Forbes, *The Ancient Irish Missal*, pp. v–vi, takes the omission to have been deliberate.

**1. Paulus.** I have otherwise found the words *ad fidem* only in MTur and in the, unpublished, thirteenth-century Waterford calendar in Corpus Christi, Cambridge, MS 405.
**2. Ananias.** Of the two recensions of MA, this entry is in the first only.

## [26 January] f UII KAL.

1  Natale sancti Policarpiᵃ ᵇdiscipuli Iohannis apostoli.ᵇ

ᵃ*add* martiris MCh, *add* episcopi MA. ᵇ⁻ᵇqui beati Johannis apostoli discipuli MCh, MA.

**1. Polycarpus.** MA (1) and MU preface *natale* with the name of Polycarpus's place, *apud Smyrnam*, which is omitted in MA (2).

## [27 January] g UI KAL. FEB.

1  Constantinapolim,ᵃ natale sancti Iohannisᵇ °hoc die celebratur,° qui Crisostomus appelatur.
2  Et apud Hiberniam, sancta uirgo Murgeiltᵈ hodie celebratur.

ᵃConstantinopolitani (*after* Johannis) MCh, MA. ᵇ*add* episcopi MCh, MA. °⁻°*om.* MCh, MA. ᵈMuirgein MO.

**1. Iohannes.** The placing of *Constantinapolim* first corresponds to some *auctaria* of MU, including *Antverp. Maj.* and *Centulensis.*

**2. Muirgeilt.** The saint celebrated on this day in MO and MT was Muirgein, abbot of Glenn Uisen, and none of the surviving manuscript witnesses has the form *Murgeilt.* However, the Commentary on MO, which proposed an alternative identification with a daughter of Echu mac Maireda, drew here on the 'Death-tale of Echu', the only copy of which, in LU 39a–41b, contains the statement: *iss é ainm dorat di Muirgein .i. gein in mara, nó Muirgeilt .i. geilt in mara,* 'the name he gave her was Muirgein, that is birth of the sea, or Muirgeilt, that is mad one of the sea'.

## [28 January] a U KAL.

1  Natale sanctae Agnae[a] secundo [b]a nativitate.[b]

[a]Agnetis MCh (*with* tis *above line in different ink*), MA. [b–b]*om.* MA.

**1. Agnes.** This second feast of Agnes (cf. 21 Jan.), which fell on 27 Jan. in the Hieronymian tradition (cf. MTur below), commemorates her birthday. (However, the unpublished Waterford calendar in Corpus Christi, Cambridge, MS 405, describes it as the octave of her main feast.) The form *Agnae* agrees with MA (2). The addition *a nativitate* is already in Bede's martyrology. The *Bruxellensis* version of MU reads: *de nativitate secundo.*

## [29 January] b IU KAL.

1  [a]Natale sanctorum episcoporum [b]Hipoliti, Pauli, Gillae, Constantini[b] commemoratur.[a]

[a–a]*om.* MCh, MA. [b–b]epscoip . . . Hipolitus, Paulus, Gillas, Constantinus MO.

**1. Hippolytus etc.** The order of the saints is the same as in MO. *Gillas* is for *Gildas*, author of *De Excidio Britanniae*, who is placed by MT, the source of MO, among the Irish saints. Constantinus and Gildas are again brought together in the *Grevenus* version of MU.

## [30 January] c III KAL. FEB.

1  Hierusolimis,[a] Mathiae[b] episcopi.[c]
2  Et apud Hiberniam, sanctus Enan[d] confessor migrauit ad Christum.

[a]Jerosolimis MCh. [b]*preceded by* beatissimi MA. [c]*add more detail* MCh, MA. [d]Enán MO.

**1. Matthias.** This is the second entry in MCh and MA. The first concerns Hippolytus whom MDr, drawing on MO, had entered on the previous day.

TEXT

## [31 January] d II KAL. FEB.

1  In Hiberniam, natale sancti [a]Aedae episcopi et sancti Maelanfaid[a] commemoratur.
2  Sancta quoque uirgo Brig[b] etiam in Hiberniam hodie migrasse fertur ad Christum.

[a-a]Aed . . . Maelanfaid MO. [b]co mbríg romóir, 'with very great vigour' MO.

**1. Áed, Máel Anfaid.** Bishop Áed was added to the Irish version of MA, with MCh reading: *Eodem die; sancti Edani episcopi*. To be noted is the fact that the (*Lubeco-Col.*) and *Grevenus* versions of MU also contain this saint, with the words (*ipso die, sancti*) *Edani episcopi et confessoris*. However, the spelling of his name here, as well as that of his companion, *Maelanfaid*, is based on MO. Despite using *in* for the more usual *apud*, the author retained the accusative *Hiberniam*.

**2. Bríg.** Neither MT nor MG enter Bríg on this day, the implication being that the Commentator of MO, followed by MDr and, much more recently, by the editor of MO, erroneously took the phrase *co mbríg romóir*, 'with very great vigour', to contain the name of a saint (cf. Introduction, § 8).

## [1 February] e KAL. FEB.

1  Apud[a] Antiochiam, [b]passio sancti[b] Ignatii episcopi.[c]
2  Item apud Hiberniam, dormitatio[d] beatissimae[e] uirginis Brigidae ueneranter hodie[f] commemoratur[g].

[a]*preceded by* Eodem die MA. [b-b]beati MA (1), sancti MA (2). [c]*add* et martyris MA. [d]dormitio MCh. [e]beate MCh. [f]hoc die MCh. [g]*add more detail* MCh.

**1. Ignatius.** If we except the use of *sanctus* for *beatus*, the wording here is in general agreement with MA (1). Although third in both recensions of MA, it is also first in MU.

**2. Brigida.** Although already in the original MA, which refers to Brigit's altar-beam miracle, the notice of the saint here is based on the reworded version of the Irish MA, which shares with MT the use of the word *dormitatio*, 'falling asleep'. MCh adds a eulogy of Brigit which probably also formed part of the Irish MA.

## [2 February] f IIII N. FE.

1  [a]Purificatio sanctae Mariae [b]semper uirginis.[ab]
2  Et apud Hiberniam, sancta uirgo Findech[c] hoc die in Christo quieuit.

[a-a]*om.* MA. [b-b]*om.* MCh. [c]la Findig MO.

**1. Purificatio Mariae.** The Irish MA joins with the Commentary, which reads *purgatio Sanctae Mariae apud Romanos* (Stokes, 'On the Calendar of Oengus', p. xlv), some *codices pleniores* of MH, and several *auctaria* of MU, including *Bruxellensis*, in emphasising the Marian aspect of this feast, traditionally regarded as a feast of the Lord (cf. Auf der Maur, 'Feste und Gedenktage', p. 203).

[3 February] g III N. FE.

1  <sup>ab</sup>Apud Uiennam<sup>b</sup>, natale<sup>c</sup> Blassi <sup>d</sup>martyris sancti.<sup>d</sup>
2  <sup>e</sup>Et eodem die apud Castrinam urbem, natale Ualdburgae sanctae uirginis.<sup>ae</sup>

<sup>a–a</sup>*om.* MA. <sup>b–b</sup>*om.* MCh. <sup>c</sup>*add* Sancti MCh. <sup>d–d</sup>episcopi et martiris MCh. <sup>e–e</sup>Ipso die, sancte Wereburge (*with second* e *above line in different ink*) uirginis MCh.

**1. Blasius.** The first recension of MA lists this saint under 15 Mar., where the second recension spells the name as *Blavius*. However, most *auctaria* of MU place him on 3 Feb. *Apud Uiennam* is mistakenly taken from the entry on St Eventius, which followed in the source.
**2. Ualdburga.** In the spelling of her name, Werburga of Chester (*Castrina urbs*) is confused here with Walburga, abbess of Heidenheim, whose feast fell on 1 May, as below. Some *auctaria* of MU also assign Werburga to this day.

[4 February] a II N. FEB.

1  Et apud Hiberniam, sancta uirgo Cuanna<sup>a</sup> ad Christum migrauit.

<sup>a</sup>Cuannae MO.

**1. Cuanna.** There is nothing in MO to suggest that the saint was a female. See also the second entry at 10 Apr.

[5 February] b N. FEB.

1  <sup>a</sup>Apud Siciliam, ciuitatem<sup>a</sup> Catanensium, pasio sanctae Agathae uirginis sub <sup>b</sup>Decio imperatore.<sup>b</sup>

<sup>a–a</sup>in Sicilia civitate MA. <sup>b–b</sup>*reversed* MA, *add more detail* MCh, MA.

**1. Agatha.** The wording of the Irish MA, as reflected here by MDr and MCh, corresponds closely to the *Centulensis* version of MU, which reads: *Apud Siciliam, civitate Catenensi, passio sanctae Agathae virginis, sub Decio imperatore.*

## [6 February] c UIII ID.

1 <sup>a</sup>Natale sanctae Luciae<sup>b</sup> uirginis.<sup>a</sup>
2 Et apud Hiberniam, <sup>c</sup>Mel sanctus episcopus<sup>c</sup> et confessor eodem die perrexit ad Christum.

<sup>a–a</sup>*om.* MCh, MA. <sup>b</sup>Lucia MO. <sup>c–c</sup>epscop Mel MO.

**1. Lucia.** The Commentary on MO, which concludes that Lucy of Syracuse (13 Dec.) is intended, quotes an extensive passage about her.
**2. Mel.** Bishop Mel, patron of the diocesan church of Ardagh, was in the Irish MA, with MCh reading: *Ipso die, episcopus Mel.*

## [7 February] d UII ID.

1 Apud Hiberniam, sancti confessores <sup>a</sup>Mellan et Lomman<sup>a</sup> ad Christum migrauerunt.

<sup>a–a</sup>Mellán . . . Lommán. MO.

## [8 February] e UI ID.

1 In Hibernia insola, natale sanctorum confessorum <sup>a</sup>Onchu et Fiachra<sup>a</sup> ad Christum perrexerunt.

<sup>a–a</sup>Haue . . . ind éicis . . . Fiachrae, 'The descendant of the poet, F.' MO.

**1. Onchú.** The name *Onchú* was taken from the Commentary on MO, where it glosses *Haue ind éicis* of the metrical text.

## [9 February] f U ID.

1 <sup>a</sup>Apud Alaxandriam,<sup>a</sup> sanctae Appolloniae uirginis <sup>b</sup>et martyris.<sup>b</sup>
2 Item apud Hiberniam, <sup>c</sup>Mochuaroc, uir sanctus et sapientissimus,<sup>c</sup> ad Christum perrexit.

<sup>a–a</sup>Alexandriae MA. <sup>b–b</sup>*more detail* MCh, MA. <sup>c–c</sup>Mochuaróc ind ecnai, 'M. of the wisdom' MO.

**1. Appolonia.** The wording of the reference to Alexandria in the Irish MA agrees with MU.
**2. Mochuaróc.** The more elaborate character of this entry, shown by the use of the superlative *sapientissimus*, probably indicates an interest in Mochuaróc's church, which was in the Decies district (cf. Introduction, § 5).

## [10 February] g IIII ID.

1  Romae,ᵃ uia Lauicana, nataleᵇ ᶜdecem militum.ᶜ
2  ᵈEodem die,ᵈ sancte Scolasticae uirginis ᵉnatale celebratur.ᵉ
3  Et apud Hiberniam, sanctus confessor Cronanᶠ ad Christum migrauit.

ᵃ*preceded by* Item MCh, MA. ᵇ*om.* MCh, MA. ᶜ⁻ᶜ*reversed* MCh. ᵈ⁻ᵈApud castrum Cassinum MA. ᵉ⁻ᵉ*om.* MCh, MA. ᶠCrónán MO.

**1. Decem milites.** This entry is in third place in MCh and MA.
**2. Scholastica.** This saint is only in the second recension of MA.

## [11 February] a III ID.

1  Apud Hiberniam, sanctus ᵃepiscopus Etchen et confessor, et sancta uirgo Gopnatᵃ hoc die ad Christum perrexerunt.

ᵃ⁻ᵃMo Gopnat . . . epscop Etchen MO.

**1. Etchén, Gobnat.** Etchén of Clonfad, Killucan p., Farbill b., Co. Westmeath, was in the Irish MA, with MCh reading: *Eodem die episcopi Etchani*. He is also in the *Grevenus* version of MU, which reads: *In Hibernia, Eciani episcopi et confessoris*. MDr drew both Gobnat and the Irish form of Etchén's name from MO.

## [12 February] b II ID.

1  In Hispania,ᵃ ciuitate Barcinone, natale sancte Eulaliae uirginis et martyris.ᵇ
2  Sanctus quoque ᶜSimplex episcopus et Damianus cum multitudine martyrumᶜ hoc die coronati sunt.

ᵃHispaniis MCh, MA. ᵇ*add more detail* MCh, MA. ᶜ⁻ᶜepscop Simplex . . . Damán . . . co maccraid, 'Bishop S., D. with many youths' MO.

**2. Simplex, Damianus.** Although MDr clearly draws this entry from MO, MA also refers to *passio sancti Damiani militis*.

## [13 February] c IDUS FEB.

1  Natale sanctiᵃ Agabi profete in Nouo Testamento.ᵇ
2  Item apud Hiberniam, sanctus Modomnocᶜ confessor eodem die migrauit ad Christum.

ᵃ*om.* MCh. ᵇ*add* apud Antiochiam MCh, MA, *add more detail* MA. ᶜModomnóc MO.

## [14 February] d XUI KAL. MAR.

1  Romae, natale sancti<sup>a</sup> Ualentini prespeteri.<sup>ab</sup>
2  <sup>c</sup>Marcellus quoque cum sanctorum martyrum multitudine hoc die migrauit ad Christum.<sup>c</sup>

<sup>a</sup>*added later above line* MCh. <sup>b</sup>*add more detail* MCh, MA. <sup>c–c</sup>*om.* MCh, MA, Marcellus . . . ochtmoga caín cinged, 'M., 80 fair champions' MO.

## [15 February] e XU KAL.

1  <sup>a</sup>Uictoria Christi de diabulo post ternas temptationes ab eodem Christo superatas celebratur.<sup>a</sup>
2  Eodem die, apud Hiberniam, sancti confessoris Beraig.<sup>b</sup>

<sup>a–a</sup>*om.* MCh, MA, buaid Maicc Dé dia námait, 'the Son of God's triumph over his enemy' MO. <sup>b</sup>Beraig MO.

**1. Victoria Christi.** The reference to the three temptations, which accords with the Gospel account, is absent from MO.
**2. Berach.** Although the Irish spelling of the saint's name is from MO, the entry as such is probably from the Irish MA, with MCh – which reads *Eodem die, sancti confessoris Berchani* – mistakenly placing the saint, who was patron of Termonbarry p., Ballintober N. b., Co. Roscommon, on the following day. The *Grevenus* version of MU also places him on this day, with the words: *In Hibernia, Beracii episcopi et confessoris.*

## [16 February] f XIIII KAL.

1  Cumis<sup>a</sup> sanctae Iulianae uirginis <sup>b</sup>et martyris.<sup>b</sup>

<sup>a</sup>*preceded by* Et (in) MCh, (MA), *add* natale MA. <sup>b–b</sup>*more detail* MCh, MA.

**1. Iuliana.** Although also placed first in the *Bruxellensis* version of MU, this entry is in second place in MCh and MA. As pointed out in the note for the previous day, MCh mistakenly placed Berchanus (recte Berachus) here.

## [17 February] g XIII KAL.

1  Apud Hiberniam, sanctorum confessorum <sup>a</sup>Cormac et Fintan<sup>a</sup> ad Christum perrexerunt.

<sup>a–a</sup>Chormaicc . . . la . . . Fintain MO.

**1. Fintan.** Although the Irish form of his name is from MO, Fintan of Clonenagh (tl./p., Maryborough W. b., Co. Offaly) was in the Irish MA, with MCh reading: *Eodem die, sancti confessoris Fintani.* Fintan had already entered the external martyrological record in the ninth-century Martyrology of Usuard, which reads: *In Scothia sancti Fintani presbiteri et confessoris magnae virtutis viri.* From Usuard, the name passed to the second recension of MA. The *Grevenus* version of MU wrote the name as *Fymianus* and described the saint as a bishop.

## [18 February] a XII KAL.

1  In[a] Hierusolimis, beati Semeonis[b] martyris.[c]
2  Et apud Hiberniam, sancti confessores [d]Molipa et Colman[d] hoc die ad Christum perrexerunt.

[a]*om.* MCh, MA. [b]*add* episcopi et MCh, MA. [c]*add more detail* MCh, MA. [d–d]Colmán, Moliba MO.

**2. Colmán.** This saint, who is usually assigned to Moray in Scotland, did not find his way into the Irish MA. However, with other Irish saints, he is in the *Grevenus* version of MU, which reads: ... *In Hibernia, Culani episcopi et confessoris. Item Berethoi ... Item Colomanni episcopi et confessoris.*

## [19 February] b XI KAL.

1  Apud Hiberniam, sanctus confessor Baithin[a] perrexit ad Christum.

[a]Baethíne MO.

**1. Baíthín.** Patron of Tibohine, now tl./p., Frenchpark b., Co. Roscommon, Baíthín was in the Irish MA, with MCh reading: *Eodem die sancti confessoris Baithini.*

## [20 February] c X KAL.

1  Apud Tyrum, quae est urbs maxima Fenicis,[a] beatorum martyrum [b]natale celebratur[b], quorum numerum [c]Dei sola[c] scientia collegit.[d]
2  [e]Gaius quoque uenerabilis episcopus hoc die cum sua turba e martyrio coronatus est.[e]

[a]Phoenicis MA. [b–b]*om.* MCh, MA. [c–c]solius Dei MA. [d]colligit MCh, MA, *which add more detail.* [e–e]Gaius int epscop ... imma slecht trichae trénfher, 'G. the bishop round whom were slain 30 champions' MO.

**1. Beati Martyres.** Several versions of MU agree with the reading *sola* for *solius.*

## [21 February] d IX KAL.

1  Apud Hiberniam, sancti Fintain[a] hoc die natale celebratur.

[a]Fintain MO.

**1. Fintan.** Although Fintan, alias Fintan Corach, was included in the Irish MA –
with MCh reading *Eodem die sancti confessoris Fintani* – the Irish spelling of
the saint's name came from MO. His inclusion in the Irish MA may have been
due to his attachment to the diocesan centre of Clonfert, the site of an Augustinian priory, probably since before the middle of the twelfth century.

## [22 February] e UIII KAL.

1  Apud Antiochiam, cathedra sancti Petri.

## [23 February] f UII KAL.

1  Apud Smirnam,[a] natale[b] sancti[c] Seremi[d] monachi.[e]
2  [f]A quibusdam quoque Mathias apostolus gloriosum martyrium pro
Christo consummasse fertur.[f]

[a]Smirmum MCh, Syrmium MA. [b]*om.* MA. [c]beati MA. [d]Sereni MCh, MA. [e]*more detail*
MCh, MA. [f–f]Mathias int apstal ar Chríst céssais riaga, 'M. the apostle suffered tortures
for Christ' MO.

**1. Serenus.** The name of the saint's place is also spelt with medial *-rn-* in some
*auctaria* of MU, including *Bruxellensis*.
**2. Matthias.** MDr followed MO here, in the process duplicating Matthias's
feast, which is also on the following day. The *Grevenus* version of MU added an
Irish saint named *Tyminus, episcopus et confessor*, whom Grosjean, 'Édition du
Catalogus', § 666, has taken to be *Finianus*.

## [24 February] g UI KAL. MAR.

1  Natale sancti Mathiae apostoli.
2  Et apud Hiberniam, [a]Cummain Iensis monasterii clarus abbas[a] ad
Christum perrexit.

[a–a]abb hÍae . . . Cummíne MO.

**1. Matthias.** See the note on the second entry of the previous day.
**2. Cuimmíne.** For a possible explanation of the naming of the saint's church of
Iona, see Introduction, § 4.

## [25 February] a U KAL. MAR.

1  [a]Natale sancti Teolis.
2  Et sancti Pauli apostoli capitis inuentio commemoratur.[a]

[a-a]Fofrith cenn Póil apstail . . . hí féil . . . Teolis, 'The head of the apostle P. was found on the feast of T.' MO.

**1. Teolis.** The more correct form of this saint's name, which is from MO, is possibly Theonas/Theon, whose feast fell, according to MH, on 26 Feb. Cf. Ó Riain, 'Some Bogus Irish Saints', p. 7.

**2. Inventio capitis Pauli.** The *Aquicinctinus* version of MU likewise records this feast, with the words: *Inventio capitis sancti Pauli apostoli*. For a note on the MO version of the entry, see Hennig, 'Studies in the Latin texts', 74, § 27.

## [26 February] b IU KAL. MAR.

1  In ciuitate Pergen[a] Pampilie,[b] natale sancti[c] Nestoris episcopi.[d]

[a]Perge MA. [b]Pamphili(a)e MCh, (MA). [c]beati MA. [d]*add more detail* MCh, MA.

**1. Nestor.** Among the entries added to the *Grevenus* MU on this day is *In Hibernia, Oghani episcopi*. Cf. Grosjean, 'Édition du Catalogus', § 570.

## [27 February] c III KAL. MAR.

1  Natale sancti confessoris Comgan[a] in Hibernia insola ad Christum migrauit.

[a]Chomgain MO.

## [28 February] d II KAL. MAR.

1  In territorio Lugdunensi,[a] natale[b] Romani abbatis.[c]
2  Et apud Hiberniam, abbas sanctus Sillan[d] ad Christum perrexit.

[a]*add* locis Uirensibus MCh, (MA). [b]beati MA. [c]*add more detail* MCh, MA. [d]Sillain MO.

**2. Sillán.** This saint, who was abbot of Bangor, the seat of an Augustinian priory founded by Malachy, was in the Irish version of MA. The entry in MCh reads: *Eodem die; confessoris Sillani*.

## [1 March] e KAL. MARTII

1  [a]Sanctus Dauid archepiscopus Brittaniae insolae perrexit ad Christum.[a]
2  Et apud Hiberniam, sancti episcopi et confessores [b]Senan et Moynenn[b] ad astra perrexerunt.

[a-a]Dauid Cille Muni MO, *om.* MA. [b-b]Senán, Moinenn MO.

**1. David.** Although MDr and MCh, which reads *eodem die, sancti Dauid*, differ in their wording, it is probably save to assume that David was in the Irish MA. Several versions of MU, including *Grevenus*, which adds comments on the saint's relationship with Patrick, refer to David on this day. As for his description as archbishop, which is shared by the Commentary on MO and the *Grevenus* MU, see Davies, *Wales in the Early Middle Ages*, p. 161, where attention is drawn to the 'serious claims for metropolitan status' made by St David's in the twelfth century (cf. Introduction, § 3) .

**2. Moinenn.** The *Grevenus* MU places a saint *Monanus levita et confessor* in *Scotia* on this day, but our saint is more likely to be represented, albeit corruptly, in the same source for the following day, which reads: *In Hibernia, Tedgnae et Monendabis* [=*Monend ab[bat]is* ?] *abbatum.* Cf. Grosjean, 'Édition du Catalogus', § 510.

[2 March] f UI N. MAR.

1 Apud Hiberniam, sanctus abbas ᵃFergna monasterii Hiensisᵃ ad Christum perrexit.

ᵃ⁻ᵃFergnai Iae MO.

**1. Fergna.** For a possible explanation of the specification of the saint's church here, very unusual in MDr, see Introduction, § 4.

[3 March] g U N. MAR.

1 In Hibernia insola natale sanctorum confessorum ᵃMoacro et Celeᵃ natalicia celebrantur.

ᵃ⁻ᵃCéle Críst . . . Momacru MO.

**1. Céile, Momacru.** For the use of *Céile* for *Céile Críst*, literally 'Christ's client', see also MG at 3 Mar. Most of the manuscript witnesses to MO agree with MDr in not having medial *m* in their versions of the name *Moacru*.

[4 March] a IIII N. MAR.

1 Natale sancti Lucii papae et martyris.ᵃ
2 Romae,ᵇ uia Appiae, nataleᶜ sanctorum martyrum noncentorum.ᵈ

ᵃ*add more detail* MCh, MA. ᵇ*preceded by* Item MCh, MA. ᶜ*om.* MCh, MA. ᵈnongentorum MCh, MA.

**1, 2.** The *Grevenus* MU reads here: *In Hibernia, sancti Mogruddonis episcopi et confessoris.* Cf. Grosjean, 'Édition du Catalogus', § 501.

43

## [5 March] b III N. MAR.

1 Apud Antiochiam, passio sancti Foccae[a] martyris.[b]
2 Et apud Hiberniam, sancti confessores [c]Ciaran et Cartach[bc] ad Christum cui devote seruierint migrauerunt.

[a]Phocae MA. [b]*more detail* MCh, MA. [c-c]Carthach . . . Ciarán MO.

**1. Phocas.** All versions of MU agree with the Irish MA in spelling the saint's name with initial *F-*.
**2. Ciarán, Carthach.** The more elaborate than usual wording may be due to the author's apparent interest in the affairs of the Augustinian canons (Introduction, § 5); Saigir Chiaráin – now Seirkieran p., Ballybritt b., Co. Offaly – the church of these saints, appears to have become an Augustinian priory before the arrival of the Normans in 1169 (Gwynn, Hadcock, *Medieval Religious Houses*, p. 195). Several versions of MU, including *Lubeco-Col.* and *Grevenus*, likewise record Ciarán, the latter reading: *In Hibernia, Kerani episcopi et confessoris.*

## [6 March] c II N. MAR.

1 Nicomediae,[a] natale sancti Uictoris et Uictorini martyrum.[b]

[a]In Nicomedia (*with a above line*) MCh. [b]*om.* MCh, MA, *which add more detail.*

**1. Victor, Victorinus.** Some *auctaria* of MU also attach *martyrum* to the names of the two saints.

## [7 March] d NON. MAR.

1 In Mauritania, ciuitate Tiburtinorum,[a] passio sanctarum martyrum[b] Perpetuae et Felicitatis.[c]

[a]Tuburbitanorum MA. [b]*after* Felicitatis MA.

**1. Perpetua, Felicitas.** The spelling *Tiburtinorum* is also reflected in some *auctaria* of MU, including *Centulensis* which reads: *civitate Tyburtina.*

## [8 March] e UIII ID. MAR.

1 Apud Hiberniam, sancti confessores, [a]Senan, Aed et Conna,[a] in hoc die ad Christum perrexerunt.

[a-a]Senan . . . Conandil . . . epscop Beoáed MO.

**1. Áed, Conna.** Either the metrical text of MO was read as *Co(n)na dil . . . epscop beo Aed*, 'dear Conna . . . lively bishop Áed', or, more likely, the forms of the names were taken from the Commentary which identifies Conandil as

TEXT

Conna and Beoáed as Áed *beo*, 'lively, live'. Some *auctaria* of MU record Irish saints here, including *Grevenus* which reads: *Cenani* (recte *Senani*), *Conalli, Crouani*. The *Altempsianus* MU refers to Senán only, spelling his name *Seinavi*.

## [9 March] f UII ID. MAR.

1 [a]Pasio quadraginta militum ut quidam ferunt quibus in tenebroso loco positis sol ob signum supernae claritatis et consolationis emicuit.[a]

[a-a]Bás cethorchat míled . . . dia tuargaib fri hilchu grian i lluc dub dorchu, 'The death of forty soldiers . . . to whom the sun arose with paeans in a black, dark place' MO.

**1. Quadraginta milites.** Although most *auctaria* of MU also refer to the feast of the forty soldiers on this day, rather than on the 11 Mar., where it is placed by MA, MDr appears to have reproduced here in translation, as on the following day, most of the quatrain of MO.

## [10 March] g UI ID. MAR.

1 Natale sanctorum martyrum, Alexandri et Gaii[a] de Umenia.[b]
2 [c]Hoc quoque die, ut fertur, Constantinus imperator, sub quo sancta crux Christi Helena beata matre eius procurante inuenta est in Hierusalem, e corpore migrauit ad Christum.[c]

[a]Ga MCh, Caii MA. [b]Eumenia MCh, MA, *which add more detail*. [c-c]*om*. MCh, MA, Dorograd co haingliu Constantin . . . lass fríth . . . crann croiche in Choimmded, 'Constantine, by whom was found the tree of the Lord's cross, has been summoned to the angels' MO.

**1. Caius.** The spelling of the name with initial *G-* is common in MU and its *auctaria*. The MU in use in Ireland, as represented by MG, also spelt the name *Gaius*.
**2. Constantinus.** For the second day in succession, most of the metrical text of MO is reproduced in translation, with the addition of some details (Helena, Hierusalem) from the Commentary.

## [11 March] a U ID. MAR.

1 Apud Sephastem[a] Armeniae urbem,[b] natale[c] quadraginta militum tempore Lucinii[d] regis.[e]
2 Item apud Hiberniam, sancti confessores [f]Libren, Senan, Constantin, et Oengus[f] ad Christum migrauerunt.

[a]Sebastem MCh, (MA). [b]minoris MCh, MA. [c]*om*. MCh. [d]Licinii MA. [e]*add more detail* MCh, MA. [f-f]Librén, Senan . . . Constantin MO.

45

**1. Quadraginta milites.** This entry is only in the first recension of MA. See also above at 9 Mar.
**2. Librén . . . Óengus.** The name of Óengus, author of MO, was added to some versions of the metrical text. Moreover, the Commentary, as in most versions, also refers to him. The *Lubeco-Col.* and *Grevenus* versions of MU read here: *In Scotia, sancti Constantini regis et martyris.*

## [12 March] b IIII ID. MAR.

1 Rome, [a]natale beati[a] Grigorii,[b] papae,[c] doctoris et apostoli Anglorum.[d]

[a-a]beatorum pontificum MCh, MA. [b]Gregorii MCh, MA. [c]om. MCh, MA. [d]*add more detail* MCh, MA.

**1. Gregorius.** The plural *beatorum pontificum* in MCh and MA takes account of Pope Innocent who follows Gregory in these sources. Several versions of MU join MDr in using a singular form.

## [13 March] c III ID.

1 Apud Hiberniam, natale sanctorum confessorum [a]Mochoemoc et Cuangus[a] in hoc die celebratur.

[a-a]Mochóemóc . . . Cuangus MO.

**1. Mochóemóc.** The *Grevenus* MU reads here: *In Hibernia, Mochomogi confessoris*, adding also *Geraldi abbatis* and *Kevocae (Kennocae) virginis.*

## [14 March] II.ID. MAR.

1 Romae, [a]natale[b] sanctorum[a] martyrum quadraginta et[c] octo.[d]

[a-a]*om.* MCh. [b]*passio* MA. [c]*om.* MCh. [d]*septem* MA, *add more detail* MCh, MA.

## [15 March] ID. MAR.

1 Lucas[a] sanctus euangeliza a quibusdam in hoc die ad Christum migrasse fertur.
2 Item apud Hiberniam, sancti [b]fili Nessan[b] ad Christum eodem die perrexerunt.

[a]Lucas MO. [b-b]maicc Nessáin, 'the sons of N.' MO.

**1. Lucas.** In the Commentary on MO, Lucas is glossed *euangelista.*
**2. Filii Nessáin.** Although the form of the saints' name is from MO, the entry was in the Irish MA, with MCh reading: *Eodem die, sanctorum filiorum Nessani.*

## [16 March] XUII KAL. AP.

1  Romae, natale sancti Ciriaci martyris.[a]
2  Et apud Hiberniam, sancti confessores [b]Abban et leprosus Finan[b] ad
   astra hoc die perrexerunt.

[a]*om.* MCh, MA, *which add more detail.* [b-b]Abbán . . . Fínán . . . Lobur, 'A., F. the leper'
MO.

**2. Abbán, Fínán.** These two saints are also in the *Grevenus* MU, which reads:
*In Scotia, . . . Albani episcopi et confessoris . . . In Hibernia, Finiani abbatis et
confessoris.*

## [17 March] XUI KAL. AP.

1  Apud Hiberniam, Occiani insolam, natale sancti Patricii archepiscopi
   Scottorum.[a]

[a]*add more detail* MCh.

**1. Patricius.** This entry is also in MA which reads: *In Scotia natale sancti
Patricii episcopi et confessoris . . .* The redactor of the Irish MA rewrote the
entry so as to reflect recent developments in the Irish Church, such as the emergence in the twelfth century of metropolitan bishops (Introduction, §§ 3, 11).
MCh adds a very long eulogy on the saint which may have also formed part of
the Irish MA.

## [18 March] XU KAL.

1  Natale sancti[a] Alaxandri[b] episcopi [c]et martyris.[c]

[a]*om.* MCh. [b]Alexandri MCh, MA. [c-c]*om.* MCh, MA, *which add more detail.*

**1. Alexander.** The formulation *et martyris* is also attached to this saint in
several *auctaria* of MU.

## [19 March] XIU KAL.

1  Apud Hiberniam, sancti confessores Lachtin[a] et Auxaile, discipulus,
   et frater, et coepiscopus sancti Patricii episcopi, Scottorum apostoli,
   eodem die ad Christum perrexerunt.

[a]Molachtóc MO.

**1. Auxillus (Auxaile), Laichtín.** The entry on Auxillus derives from the Irish
MA, with MCh reading: *eodem die Auxilli et Lactani.* However, the text peculiar
to MDr, from *discipulus* to *episcopi*, is closely related to a gloss added to MT at

19 Mar., which reads: *Auxilinus episcopus et coepiscopus et frater sancti Patricii episcopi* . . . Laichtín also figures in the (*Grevenus*) and *Lubeco-Col.* versions of MU which read: (*In Hibernia*), *sancti Lactini* (*episcopi et*) *confessoris.*

## [20 March] XIII KAL. APRILIS.

1  In Britania,[a] natale[b] sancti Guberti.[c]
2  [d]Item sanctus Policronus episcopus cum sancta martyrum turma eodem die perrexit ad astra.[d]

[a]Britanni(i)s MCh, (MA). [b]*om.* MCh, MA. [c]Cuthberti MCh, MA, *which add more detail.* [d-d]Policroni . . . co mórshluag, 'P., with a huge host' MO.

**1. Cuthbertus.** The spelling of the saint's name recalls that of Bede, which reads: *Gut(h)bertus.*

## [21 March] d XII KAL.

1  Apud Casinum castrum, natale[a] sancti Benedicti eximi[b] abbatis, cuius uitam uirtutibus et miraculis gloriosam in Dialagorum libris beatus papae[c] [d]Grigorius scripsit.[de]
2  Item apud Hiberniam, sanctus confessor Enna[f] hoc die migrauit ad Christum.

[a]*om.* MCh. [b]*om.* MCh, MA. [c]papa MCh, MA. [d-d]*reversed* MCh, MA. [e]scribit MCh. [f]Endae MO.

**1. Benedictus.** The retention here of the whole entry of the source may be explained by the importance of Benedict, *summus abbas monachorum Europae* (Commentary on MO at 21 Mar.). For Benedict, see also 15 Jan., 11 July, 15 Nov.
**2. Énna.** This saint is also in the *Grevenus* MU, which reads: *In Hibernia, Endei abbatis.*

## [22 March] e XI KAL.

1  Apud Hiberniam, sanctus confessor [a]Falbe, abbas Hiensis[a] monasterii, ad astra perrexerunt hoc die.

[a-a]Failbe . . . Iae MO.

**1. Fáilbe.** For comments on the specification of the saint's church, unusual in MDr, see Introduction, § 4. The author's use of plural verb with singular subject may be noted. For the reverse procedure, see the entry for the following day.

## [23 March] f X KAL.

1 Apud Hiberniam, sanctus confessor <sup>a</sup>Momedoc, et filia sancta uirgo
Feradig<sup>a</sup> hoc die ad Christum migrauit.

<sup>a–a</sup>Ingen . . . Feradaig . . . Momaedóc, 'Daughter of F., M.' MO.

**1. Momedóc, Filia Feradaig.** As on the previous day, the verb does not agree
with its subject.

## [24 March] g IX KAL. AP.

1 Romae,<sup>a</sup> sancti Pigmeni<sup>b</sup> prespeteri <sup>c</sup>natale celebratur.<sup>c</sup>
2 Item apud Hiberniam, sancta uirgo <sup>d</sup>Scire et sancti confessores
Mochta<sup>d</sup> et <sup>e</sup>Cammin eodem die comitati sancti ad Christum.
3 Hoc quoque die, sanctus confessor et prespeter Domangart, nobili
atauorum germine regum, natus est.
4 Item eodem die,<sup>f</sup> octabas sancti Patricii archepiscopi.
5 Item <sup>g</sup>eodem die,<sup>g</sup> natale sanctorum confessorum Esco[p] Mac
Cairthinn et Mael Doid.<sup>e</sup>

<sup>a</sup>*add* natale MA. <sup>b</sup>Pingmeni MCh. <sup>c–c</sup>*om.* MCh, MA *which add more detail.* <sup>d–d</sup>Scíre . . .
Mochtae MO. <sup>e–e</sup>*om.* MO. <sup>f</sup>*A space is left between this and the following word in the
manuscript.* <sup>g–g</sup>*Between* eodem *and* die, *a superfluous* confessor *has been added.*

**2. Caimín.** Patron of Inis Celtra, Holy Island – now tl./p., Leitrim b., Co.
Galway – on Lough Derg of the river Shannon, Caimín is variously assigned
either to this day, as in MG, MTur, MD, or to the following day, as in MT and
the Commentary on MO. The *Grevenus* MU reads: *Kanini confessoris.*
**3. Domangart.** The Commentary on MO, as in MSS R1 and Lb, also refers on
this day to Domangart who was patron of the church of Ráth Murbuilg, now
Maghera p., Upper Iveagh b., Co. Down, substituting him for St Mochta of
Louth. The elaborate character of the entry, which includes a reference to the
saint's noble ancestors, is one of the pointers to Ua Gormáin involvement in the
production of MDr. This family had Down connexions, which may explain the
emphasis on the saint's ancestry (Introduction, § 6).
**4. Octavae Patricii.** This entry, unique in the Irish martyrological record, is a
strong indication of an Armagh provenance for MDr (Introduction, § 3).
**5. Mac Caírthinn, Máel Doid.** Mac Caírthinn's name, accompanied by the title
of bishop, is also recorded in the Commentary on MO for this and the previous
day (not 18 Mar., as Stokes wrongly assumed). Máel Doid, presumably the saint
of Muckno, now a p., Cremorne b., Co. Monaghan, is usually commemorated on
13 May.

## [25 March] a UIII KAL. AP.

1 Apud ciuitatem Galilaeae Nazareth, annuntiatio Dominica <sup>a</sup>per angelum Gabrielem ad Mariam uirginem, quando dixit ei angelus: Ecce concipies et paries filium et uocabis nomen eius Iesum.

2 <sup>b</sup>Eodem quoque die, Dominus noster Iesus Christus sub Tiberio Cesare, et Pontio Pilato preside, Anna et Caipha sacerdotibus, pro salute mundi crucifixus est.<sup>ab</sup>

<sup>a–a</sup>*om.* MCh, MA. <sup>b–b</sup>crochad . . . Issu Críst, 'Crucifixion of J. C.' MO.

**1. Annuntiatio Dominica.** The added material, ultimately derivative of MA (2), may be compared to the Commentary on MO, which reads: . . . *per Gabrielem arcangelum ad Mariam uirginem, quando dixit ei angelus, ecce concipies et paries filium, et uocabitur nomen eius Iesus.*
**2. Crucifixio.** Compare the Commentary on MO, which reads: . . . *et eodem die pasus est sub Pontio Pilato.*

## [26 March] b UII KAL. AP.

1 Apud Hiberniam, sancti confessores <sup>a</sup>Mochelloc et Sinchell<sup>a</sup> in hoc die ad Christum perrexerunt.

<sup>a–a</sup>I lLetha . . . Mochellóc . . . féil in tSinchill, 'M. in Letha, feast of S.' MO.

**1. Mochellóc.** The Commentary on MO offers various opinions as to the significance of the placename it attaches to Mochellóc – Letha being usually representative either of Brittany (Letavia) or the Roman region (Latium) – including a location for it *apud Hiberniam.* Mochellóc is also commemorated in the *Lubeco-Col.* and *Grevenus* versions of MU, which read: *sancti Mohallock episcopi et confessoris.* In *Grevenus*, he is also remembered under the guise of *In Hibernia, Mottelogi abbatis et confessoris.*

## [27 March] c UI KAL.

1 <sup>a</sup>Christi gloriosissima resurrectio.<sup>a</sup>

<sup>a–a</sup>asréracht, scél ndermar, Issu, 'J. arose, a glorious tale' MO.

**1. Resurrectio Christi.** Although MDr drew the feast from MO, it is also in most *auctaria* of MU. See also MTur on this day.

## [28 March] d U KAL.

1 Natale sanctae <sup>a</sup>Mariae Magdalena,<sup>a</sup> quae et Maria soror Marthae et Lazari erat, ut Iohannes euangeliza testatur.

<sup>a–a</sup>Maria . . . Magdalena MO.

**1. Maria Magdalena.** For a discussion of the implications of the placing here of Mary's feast, which more regularly fell in the West on 22 July, as again in MDr, see Ó Riain, 'Anglo-Saxon Ireland', p. 19. The comment on Mary's relationship to Martha is based on John 12: 3.

## [29 March] e IIII KAL.

1 Apud Hiberniam, sanctae uirgines <sup>a</sup>filiae Baite<sup>a</sup> ad Christum perrexerunt.

<sup>a–a</sup>líth ingen mBaiti, 'feast of the daughters of B.' MO.

## [30 March] f III KAL.

1 In Hibernia, sancti confessores<sup>a</sup> Mochua, Colman, ac Tola<sup>a</sup> ad Christum perrexerunt.

<sup>a–a</sup>Mochuae . . . Colmán . . . Tolai MO.

## [31 March] g II KAL.

1 Romae,<sup>a</sup> sanctae Balbinae uirginis<sup>b</sup> filiae Cyrini<sup>c</sup> martyris <sup>d</sup>natale celebratur.<sup>d</sup>

2 <sup>e</sup>Eodem quoque die, Annisius martyr cum turba magna martyrum ad Christum migrauit.<sup>e</sup>

<sup>a</sup>add natale MA. <sup>b</sup>om. MA. <sup>c</sup>Quirini MCh, MA. <sup>d–d</sup>om. MCh, MA, which add more detail. <sup>e–e</sup>Croch . . . Anissi co cléir, 'The cross of A., with a band' MO.

**1. Balbina.** The auctaria of MU also add virginis to Balbinae.

## [1 April] a KAL. APRILIS

1 Romae, beatae<sup>a</sup> Teothosiae,<sup>b</sup> sororis illustris<sup>c</sup> martyris Hermetis, <sup>d</sup>natale celebratur.<sup>d</sup>

2 <sup>e</sup>Eodem quoque die, ut a quibusdam fertur, sanctus Ambrosius confessor et Medolanensis episcopus, magnae sanctitatis et eloquentiae atque doctrinae illustris uir, conscendisse ad Christum, cuius pulcerrimos et utilissimos ymnos Romana aeclessia frequentat.<sup>e</sup>

<sup>a</sup>beatissim(a)e MCh, (MA). <sup>b</sup>Theodosie MCh, Theodorae MA. <sup>c</sup>illustrissimi MCh, MA. <sup>d–d</sup>om. MCh, MA, which add more detail. <sup>e–e</sup>om. MCh, MA, Ambrois co méit glaine, 'A. with great purity' MO.

**1. Theodosia.** The form of the name, more correctly Theodora, as in MA, is due to confusion with Theodosia of Cappadocia, whose feast fell on the following day.

**2. Ambrosius.** Although almost invariably placed here in Irish martyrologies, Ambrosius's regular feast fell on 4 Apr. The Ambrosian chant, probably intended here by the reference to the 'most beautiful and useful hymns' sung in the Roman church, survives only in manuscripts of the twelfth century or later. Therefore, when this note was written, its popularity may have been quite recent. Otherwise only the Commentary on MO adverts to Ambrose's hymns with the words: [Ambrosius] *qui fecit imnos et episcopus Mediolani ciuitatis in Italia.*

## [2 April] b IIII N. AP.

1 Natale sancti Nicetii, Lugdunensis episcopi, cuius[a] uita miraculis claruit.[b]

[a]*add* et MA. [b]*add more detail* MCh, MA.

## [3 April] III N.

1 Tesalonicae,[a] natale sanctarum uirginum Agappae[b] et Chioniae sub Diocletiano persecutore.[c]

[a]Thessalonica MA. [b]Agapes MCh, (MA). [c]*om.* MCh, MA, *which add more detail.*

**1. Agape, Chionia.** This entry is confined to MA (1).

## [4 April] d II N.

1 Apud Hiberniam, sanctus confessor et episcopus Tigernach[a] migrauit ad Christum.

[a]Tigernach MO.

**1. Tigernach.** This saint is also in the *Grevenus* MU, which reads: *In Hibernia, Beghani abbatis . . . In Scotia, Tigernagi episcopi et confessoris, secundum alios die sequenti.* The reference to the following day is borne out by such other *auctaria* as *Bruxellensis* and *Molanus* which place him there. However, in the Irish martyrologies, it is 'Beghanus', more correctly Becán, who is assigned to the following day.

## [5 April] e N. AP.

1 Apud Cessariam Liciae, natale[a] sancti Ampliani[b] celebratur.[c]
2 Et apud Hiberniam, sanctus confessor Becan[d] ad Christum hoc die migrauit.

[a]*om.* MCh. [b]Amphiliani MCh, Amphiani MA. [c]*om.* MCh, MA. [d]Beccáin MO.

**1. Amphianus.** Against his usual habit, the author has here selected the final entry of his source, as reflected by MCh and MA.
**2. Becán.** See note to the previous day.

### [6 April] f UIII ID.

1  Xixti[a] papae et martyris [b]natale celebratur.[b]
2  [c]Sanctus quoque Herenius cum magna turba martyrum hoc die migrauit ad Christum.[c]

[a]*preceded by* Romae, sancti MA. [b–b]*om.* MCh, MA, *which add more detail.* [c–c]Herenius in t-epscop ata móra míli, 'Bishop H., whose thousands are many' MO.

**1. Xystus.** The text agrees with MA (1) against MA (2).
**2. Hereneus.** Although drawn here from MO, this saint is also in some *auctaria* of MU.

### [7 April] g UII ID.

1  Apud Hiberniam, sanctus confessor Finan[a] ad Christum migrauit.
[a]Fínan MO.

### [8 April] a UI ID.

1  In Hiberniam, sanctus confessor Cennfaelad[a] ad Christum migrauit.
[a]Cennfaelad MO.

### [9 April] b U ID.

1  Apud Sirmium,[a] natale septem uirginum quae [b]simul martyryo coronatae sunt.[b]
2  Eodem quoque, sanctus Quadratus[c] obiit.

[a]Syrinium MCh. [b–b]in unum meruerunt coronari, quinto idus Aprilis MCh, MA. [c]Chadráti MO.

**2. Quadratus.** Some manuscript witnesses to MO, i.e. R[1], Lb, also spell the name with initial *Qu-*.

### [10 April] c IIII ID. AP.

1  Natale[a] Ezechelis profetae.
2  Et apud Hiberniam, sancta uirgo Cuanda[b] ad Christum perrexit.
[a]*om.* MCh, MA. [b]Cuannae MO.

**2. Cuanda.** As at 4 Feb. above, probably because of the feminine Latin ending in *-a*, *Cuanda* is taken to be a female.

### [11 April] d III ID.

1 Apud Cretam, urbem Cortinae, beati Pilippi episcopi, qui uita et doctrina claruit temporibus Antonini Ueri, Lucii Aurelii et[a] Commodii imperatorum.
2 Item apud Hiberniam, Aed[b] sanctus uir nobilis genere, sed nobilior moribus, clarus Christi confessor ad astra perrexit.

[a]*before* Lucii MCh, MA. [b]Maedóc MO.

**1. Philippus.** Unusually, the whole of the entry of the source is retained here.
**2. Áed.** This saint was associated with Clonmore tl./p., Rathvilly b., Co. Carlow. The switch from *Máedóc* of the metrical source text to *Áed* is not in the Commentary on MO, the usual influence in cases of this kind.

### [12 April] e II ID.

1 Romae, uia Aurelia miliario tertio,[a] natale sancti Iulii episcopi et confessoris.[b]

[a]*add* in coemeterio Calepodii MA. [b]*add more detail* MCh, MA.

**1. Iulius.** The entry reflects the first line of transmission of MA.

### [13 April] f ID. Ap.

1 Apud Hispaniam, natale sancti[a] Herminigildi.[b]
2 [c]Eodem quoque die, Paulus sanctus diaconus cum turba magna martyrum ad astra conscendit.[c]

[a]*om.* MCh. [b]Hermigildi MCh, *add more detail* MCh, MA. [c–c]cona phrímshluag . . . Pól deochoin, 'P. the deacon with his main host' MO.

**1. Hermenegildus.** Although first in some *auctaria* of MU, MCh and MA place this entry third. A possible reason for the saint's inclusion is the fact, mentioned in MA (1), that Pope Gregory, who was popular at Armagh, had written about him. Gregory devoted a chapter of his *Dialogi* (iii, 31) to the saint.
**2. Paulus.** As so often (cf. 20 Feb., 31 Mar., 6 Apr., 17 Apr.), a formula involving *turba* is used here to translate MO's reference to the saint's many companions.

## [14 April] g XVIII KAL. MAI.

1 Apud Hiberniam, sanctus ªepiscopus et confessor Tassachª hoc die ad Christum migrauit.

ª⁻ªin rígepscop Tassach, 'the royal bishop T.' MO.

## [15 April] a XVII KAL. MAI.

1 In Hibernia insola, sanctus prespeter et confessor Ruadanª mirandae sanctitatis et miraculorum uir hoc die conscendit ad Christum.

ªRódán MO.

**1. Ruadán.** This saint probably receives greater than usual attention, including a reference to his miracles, because of the presence at his church in Lothra (Lorrha) of an Augustinian priory founded about the middle of the twelfth century (Introduction, § 5). An entry in the *Grevenus* MU for this day, which reads *In Hibernia, Candani episcopi*, has been taken to refer, albeit corruptly, to Ruadán (Grosjean, 'Édition du Catalogus', § 101).

## [16 April] XVI KAL.

1 Apud Corinthum, ªnatale sanctorumª Calixtiᵇ et Cariciᶜ cum aliis septem omnium in mare mersorum.
2 ᵈEodem quoque die, sancta Carisa et beatus Felix diaconus ad astra migrauerunt.ᵈ

ª⁻ªom. MCh, MA. ᵇCallisti MA. ᶜCaristi MA. ᵈ⁻ᵈLa Carissim . . . in deochain Felic, 'With C. the deacon F.' MO.

**1. Callistus, Carisius.** Of the two recensions of MA, only MA (1) treats this as the first entry. However, it is also first in MU. Several *auctaria* of MU agree with the Irish MA in spelling the name *Calixti*.
**2. Carisa.** This saint is a doublet of Carisius above, based on a corruption in the Irish transmission of MH, as represented by MO.

## [17 April] c XV KAL.

1 Apud Brittaniam, sanctus ªDonnan cum socia turba suaª hoc die martyrio coronatus est.

ª⁻ªcona chléir . . . Donnán, 'D. with his troop' MO.

**1. Donnán.** MDr appears sometimes to use the word *Britannia* in the narrower sense of Scotland, reflecting *Alba* of the Commentary on MO in this instance. Cf. 8 Jan., 21 Apr., 25 June, 10 Aug.

## [18 April] d XIV KAL. MAI.

1 Apud Hiberniam, sanctus episcopus et confessor Lasren[a] gloriose ad Christum conscendit.

[a]Laisrén MO.

**1. Laisrén.** This saint was patron of the diocesan centre of Leighlin, Co. Carlow, the site of an Augustinian priory, which may explain the use of *gloriose* here. The addition of *episcopus*, absent from MO, probably reflects Leighlin's status as an episcopal seat. Two *auctaria* of MU, *Lubeco-Col.* and *Grevenus*, also remember Laisrén on this day, with the words: *Laceriani episcopi et confessoris.* For good measure, *Grevenus* adds: *In Hibernia, Lasriani abbatis et confessoris.*

## [19 April] e XIII KAL.

1 Apud Corinthum, natale[a] [b]Timonis beati,[b] de illis septem diaconibus primis.

[a]*om.* MCh, MA. [b-b]*reversed* MCh, sancti Timonis MA.

**1. Timo.** The text agrees with MA (1) against MA (2). Although last in MA, and penultimate in MCh, the saint is first in MU.

## [20 April] f XII KAL.

1 [a]Romae, celebris sollempnitas omnium sanctorum totius Europae commemoratur.[a]

[a-a]féil i rRuaim . . . nóeb nEorapa uile, 'the feast in Rome of the saints of the whole of Europe' MO.

**1. Omnes Sancti.** For a discussion of this feast, see Hennig, 'A Feast of All the Saints of Europe'. The text reflects the gist of an entry already in MT. However, this latter, which is also reflected by the Commentary on MO, as in the manuscripts Lb, P and R1, specifies the saints of Britain and Ireland, together with St Martin.

## [21 April] g XI KAL.

1 Romae, sancti Sotheris papae [a]natale celebratur.[a]
2 [b]Et in Brittania, sanctus confessor Maelrubae cum sancta matre hoc die ad Christum perrexit.[b]

[a-a]*om.* MCh, MA *which add more detail.* [b-b]I nAlbain . . . cona máthair . . . Maelrubai, 'M. in Scotland with his mother' MO.

**1. Soter.** This is one of the entries confined to MA (1).

**2. Máel Rubae.** Although the detail concerning the saint's mother is added from MO, the entry formed part of the Irish MA, with MCh reading: *Et in Britannia; sancti confessoris Maelrubai.* Note the use of *Britannia* for the Irish *Alba,* as at 8 Jan., 17 Apr., 25 June., 10 Aug.

## [22 April] a X KAL. MAI.

1  Uienna,[a] sancti Iuliani [b]episcopi et[b] confessoris celebratur.[c]
2  [d]Hoc quoque die, quidam putant quod beatus apostolus Pilippus uitam martyrio consummauit.[d]

[a]Viennae MA. [b-b]*om.* MA. [c]*om.* MCh, MA. [d-d]*om.* MCh, MA, Pilip apstal MO.

**1. Iulianus.** This is the final entry in MCh and MA. Moreover, it is confined to MA (1). Two *auctaria* of MU, *Lubeco-Col.* and *Grevenus,* agree with the Irish MA in describing the saint as a bishop.

## [23 April] b IX KAL.

1  In Persidia,[a] ciuitate Diospoli, passio sancti Georgii martyris.[b]
2  Et apud Hiberniam, sanctus [c]episcopus et confessor Ibar[c] hoc die ad Christum migrauit.

[a]Perside MCh, MA. [b-b]*add more detail* MCh, MA. [c-c]epscoip Ibair MO.

## [24 April] c UIII KAL.

1  Lugduno Galliae, natale[a] sancti Alaxandri [b]martirys. Et aliorum numero triginta quatuor martyrum qui cum eo passi sunt.[b]
2  [c]Hoc quoque die, tres uiri, Annanias Azarias et Misael, de camino ardentissimi rogi euassise referentur.[c]

[a]*om.* MCh. [b-b]*different wording and more detail* MCh, MA. [c-c]*om.* MCh, MA, Búaid na trí macc n-ennac hi surn, 'The triumph of the three innocent children in the furnace' MO.

**2. Ananias etc.** The names of the three, absent from the metrical text of MO, probably came from the Commentary (*Annamsas, Acarias, Misael*). For the actual wording of the entry, compare MH, which reads: . . . *de camino ignis ardentis sunt liberati.* Several *auctaria* of MU likewise note this feast.

## [25 April] d UII KAL.

1  Apud Alaxandriam, natale[a] sancti Marci euangelizae.[b]
2  Romae, Letania[c] maior, ad[d] sanctum Petrum celebratur.[e]
3  Et apud Hiberniam, sanctus [f]episcopus et confessor Maccaille[f] hoc die ad Christum perrexit.

<sup>a</sup>*om.* MCh. <sup>b</sup>*add more detail* MCh, MA. <sup>c</sup>*Litaniae* MA. <sup>d</sup> *after* ad *MDr first wrote and then expuncutated* x. <sup>e</sup>*om.* MA, *more detail* MCh. <sup>f–f</sup>epscop . . . Mac Caille MO.

**1. Marcus.** The text of the entry agrees with MA (1) against MA (2).
**2. Litania maior.** MU and its *auctaria* agree with the Irish MA in spelling the word *Letania.* The *litaniae maiores,* 'great litanies', were celebrated in Rome on Mark's day.

[26 April] e UI KAL.

1 Romae, natale sancti Ancleti<sup>a</sup> papae, qui quartus<sup>b</sup> post beatum Petrum, cum rexisset aecclesiam annis nouem<sup>c</sup> persecutione Domitiani martyrio coronatus est.
2 <sup>d</sup>Eodem quoque<sup>d</sup> die, natale<sup>e</sup> <sup>f</sup>Marcelli<sup>g</sup> sancti<sup>f</sup> papae <sup>h</sup>et martyris.<sup>h</sup>

<sup>a</sup>Cleti MCh. <sup>b</sup>secundus MCh, MA. <sup>c</sup>duodecim MA. <sup>d–d</sup>ipso MCh, MA. <sup>e</sup>*om.* MCh, MA. <sup>f–f</sup>*reversed* MCh, MA. <sup>g</sup>Marcellini MCh, MA. <sup>h–h</sup>*om.* MCh, MA, *which add more detail.*

**1. Anacletus.** Several *auctaria* of MU, together with MA (2), agree with MCh's spelling of the name as *Cletus.* At least one of the *auctaria, Hagenoyensis,* agrees with the Irish MA in allotting a reign of nine years to Anacletus.

[27 April] f U KAL. MAI.

1 Romae, sancti Anastassi pape <sup>a</sup>natale celebratur,<sup>a</sup> qui <sup>b</sup>tribus annis ac diebus decem Romanam rexit cathedram.<sup>b</sup>

<sup>a–a</sup>*om.* MCh, MA. <sup>b–b</sup>sedit annos tres, dies decem MCh, MA.

[28 April] g IIII KAL.

1 <sup>a</sup>Natale sancti Cristifori cum plurimorum martyrum turba hoc die celebratur.
2 Et apud Hiberniam, natale sancti confessoris Cronani.<sup>a</sup>

<sup>a–a</sup>*om.* MCh, MA, Cristofer la Cronan . . . luid mór míled martrai, 'C. with C., many soldiers went to martyrdom' MO.

**1. Christophorus.** Although in both MT (whence its admission to MO and, *via* MO, to MDr) and Bede's martyrology on this day, this feast is otherwise commemorated on the 25 July, where it is repeated in MDr. Its place in MT and Bede suggests that it was added to the Northumbrian *vorlage* of these two texts (Ó Riain, 'Anglo-Saxon Ireland').

TEXT

## [29 April] a III KAL.

1 Apud Hiberniam, natale sanctorum confessorum <sup>a</sup>Coningin et Fiachnae.<sup>a</sup>
2 Item natale <sup>b</sup>sancti Germani prespeteri<sup>b</sup> cum sanctorum turba martyrum.

<sup>a–a</sup>Coningen . . . la Fiachnae MO. <sup>b–b</sup>Germain chruimthir MO.

**1. Coiningen.** There is a dot in the manuscript over the second *n* of *Coningin*.
**2. Germanus.** This saint, who was attached to a church in Alexandria, is also in several *auctaria* of MU. MDr's *prespiterus* reflects *cruimthir* of MO, which, despite the *diaconus* of MT, in turn translates *presbiterus* of MH. Despite the reference to *turba martyrum* here, MO does not allude to any others.

## [30 April] b II KAL.

1 Romae,<sup>a</sup> passio sancti Cirini<sup>b</sup> martyris.
2 Hoc quoque die, apud Hiberniam, natale sancti confessoris Ronani<sup>c</sup> celebratur.

<sup>a</sup>*add* uia Appia MCh. <sup>b</sup>Quirini MCh. <sup>c</sup>Rónán MO.

**1. Quirinus.** In MA this feast is at 30 Mar. Its inclusion here in both MDr and MCh, where it is the penultimate entry, may be due to the influence of MO. However, several *auctaria* of MU likewise commemorate Quirinus on this day, some referring to his *elevatio* or *translatio*. Similarly, although the spelling *Cirini* probably reflects *Ciríni* of MO, at least one version of MU, viz. the English *Altempsianus*, reads *Cyrini*.
**2. Ronanus.** This also derives from the Irish version of MA, with MCh reading: *eodem die, sancti confessoris Ronani.*

## [1 May] c KAL. MAI.

1 Natale<sup>a</sup> Heremiae profetae.
2 Et<sup>b</sup> sanctorum<sup>c</sup> apostolorum Pilippi et Iacobi filii Mariae, sororis<sup>d</sup> matris Domini, unde et<sup>e</sup> frater<sup>e</sup> Domini dicebatur.<sup>f</sup>
3 <sup>g</sup>Item,<sup>h</sup> in Germania,<sup>i</sup> natale sanctae Ualdburgis<sup>j</sup> uirginis.<sup>gk</sup>
4 Item, apud Hiberniam, natale sancti confessoris Mochoemi.<sup>l</sup>

<sup>a</sup>*om.* MCh, MA. <sup>b</sup>*add* natalis MCh, MA. <sup>c</sup>*om.* MA. <sup>d</sup>que fuit soror MCh, MA. <sup>e</sup>fratres MCh, MA. <sup>f</sup>dicebantur MCh, MA. <sup>g–g</sup>*om.* MA. <sup>h</sup>*om.* MCh. <sup>i</sup>*add* pago Sualauelda MCh. <sup>j</sup>Uualdburgis MCh. <sup>k</sup>*add more detail* MCh. <sup>l</sup>Nethchoimi MO.

**1, 2. Hieremias, Philippus et Iacobus.** The text of both entries agrees with MA (1) against MA (2).

**3. Ualdburgis.** MDr had already used this form of name at 3 Feb. for Werburga of Chester. The *Bruxellensis* MU agrees with MCh in adding *pagus Sualanelda* (recte *Sualavelda/Sualafelda*) to *Germania*.
**4. Mochóeme.** Several manuscripts of MO agree with MDr's spelling of this saint's name.

## [2 May] d UI N. MAI.

1 Apud Hiberniam, natale sancti confessoris Nechtain[a] hoc die celebratur.

[a]Nechtain MO.

## [3 May] e U N. MAI.

1 Hierusolimis, inuentio Sanctae Crucis ab Helena sancta[a] regina, sub Constantino imperatore.[b]
2 Et apud Hiberniam, natale sancti confessoris Conlaid[c] hoc die celebratur.

[a]*om.* MCh, MA. [b]principe MCh, MA, *which add more detail.* [c]Conláid MO.

**1. Sancta Crux.** Although usually mindful of papal entries in his source, MDr here disregards the entry on Pope Alexander I, which follows in MCh, MA.

## [4 May] f IIII N.

1 Apud Hiberniam, natale sanctorum confessorum Mochua[a] et Sillani[b] diaconi.

[a]Mochuae . . . i féil Siluain dechain, 'M. on the feast of S. the deacon' MO.

**1. Silvanus.** All but one of the manuscript witnesses of MO spell the name of this saint, who was bishop of Gaza in Palestine, in Irish style as *Sillain*. This misled MDr into placing him *apud Hiberniam* (Cf. Ó Riain, 'Some Bogus Irish Saints', p. 7).

## [5 May] g III N.

1 Apud Alaxandriam,[a] natale[b] sancti Eutimi[c] diaconi in carcere morientis.[d]

[a]Alexandriam MCh, MA. [b]*om.* MCh, MA. [c]Entimii C, Euthymi MA. [d]quiescentis MCh, MA.

## [6 May] II N. MAI.

1  Natale sancti Iohannis apostoli ante portam Latinam.[a]
2  Item, beati Lucii Cyrinensis episcopi.[b]

[a]*add* Rome *and more detail* MCh, MA. [b]*om.* MCh, MA, *which add more detail.*

**2. Lucius.** In both MCh and MA this is the third and last entry. The entry in between, omitted by MDr, relates to Evodius, bishop of Antioch.

## [7 May] N. MAI.

1  Apud Hiberniam, natale sanctorum confessorum [a]Ciaroc et Brecain[a] hoc die celebratur.

[a–a]Mochuaróc la Breccán MO.

**1. Ciaróc, Brecán.** These saints were in the Irish version of MA. The entry in MCh reads: *eodem die, sanctorum confessorum Ciaroc et Bretani.* The R1 version of MO agrees with MDr in spelling the name as *(Mo)Chiaróc.*

## [8 May] c UIII ID.

1  Mediolano,[a] natale[b] sancti Uictoris martyris.[c]
2  [d]Et sancti Maximi[e] martyris.
3  Et aliorum.[d]

[a]Mediolana MCh, Mediolani MA. [b]*om.* MCh, MA. [c]*add more detail* MCh, MA. [d–d]*om.* MCh, MA. [e]Maxim MO.

**2. Maximus.** This saint is taken from MO, where he is combined with Uictor.
**3. Et alii.** The final entry in MT for this, as for many other days, begins with the words *et aliorum*, which may explain the use of these words by MDr.

## [9 May] d UII ID.

1  In Persidia,[a] natale[b] sanctorum martyrum tricentorum[c] decem.
2  [d]Et apud Hiberniam, natale sancti episcopi et confessoris Sanctani.[d]

[a]Perside MCh, MA. [b]*om.* MCh, MA. [c]trecentorum MCh, MA. [d–d]epscop Sanctain MO.

**2. Sanctanus.** This is from the Irish version of MA, with MCh reading: *Eodem die; sancti episcopi Sanctani.*

## [10 May] e UI ID.

1 <sup>a</sup>Natale sanctorum martyrum Romae,<sup>a</sup> Gordiani,<sup>b</sup> Epimachi <sup>c</sup>et Ianuarii.<sup>c</sup>

2 Et apud Hiberniam, natale sancti abbatis Comgalli.<sup>d</sup>

<sup>a–a</sup>*more detail* MCh, MA. <sup>b</sup>*add* et MCh, MA. <sup>c–c</sup>atque Ianuarij MCh, *more detail* MA. <sup>d</sup>Comgall MO.

**1. Gordianus etc.** This is the second entry in MCh and MA, where that on Job, who is relegated to the following day in MDr, precedes it.

**2. Comgallus.** This is from the Irish MA, with MCh reading: *natalis sancti Comgalli abbatis et confessoris.* The *Grevenus* MU also recalls Comgall with the words: *In Hibernia, Congalli abbatis.*

## [11 May] f U ID.

1 Romae,<sup>a</sup> natale sancti Antimi.

2 <sup>b</sup>Eodem quoque die, natale sancti Iob amici Dei.<sup>b</sup>

3 Item, in Hibernia, natale sanctorum confessorum <sup>c</sup>Cormaic et Critoc.<sup>c</sup>

<sup>a</sup>*add* uia Salaria, mil(l)iario uicesimo secundo MCh, (MA). <sup>b–b</sup>buaid nIóib . . . do ríg nél ba fordarc, 'the triumph of Job; to the king of clouds he was manifest' MO. <sup>c–c</sup>Mochritóc . . . ocus cruimther Cormacc, 'M. and Presbyter C.' MO.

**1. Anthimus.** The wording agrees with MA (1) against MA (2).

**2. Iob.** Job is commemorated in MCh and MA on the previous day. The source here is, however, MO, with *amicus Dei* paraphrasing *do ríg nél ba fordarc*, 'to the king of clouds he was manifest'.

## [12 May] g IIII ID. MAI.

1 Romae,<sup>a</sup> natale sanctorum Nerei et Acheillei<sup>b</sup> fratrum, qui<sup>c</sup> ob <sup>d</sup>Christi confessionem<sup>d</sup> capite cessi sunt.

2 Et apud Hiberniam, <sup>e</sup>sancti confessoris Erci<sup>e</sup> natale celebratur.

<sup>a</sup>*add* in cimiterio Pretextati MCh, (MA). <sup>b</sup>Achillei MCh, MA. <sup>c</sup>*add more detail* MCh, MA. <sup>d–d</sup>*reversed* MCh, *om.* MA. <sup>e–e</sup>la hErc nóebdai, 'with saintly E.' MO.

## [13 May] a III ID.

1 Natale sancte Mariae ad Martyres.<sup>a</sup>

2 Et in Hiberniam, natale sancti Tigernaig anchoritae et confessoris.

<sup>a</sup>*add more detail* MCh, MA.

**1. Maria ad Martyres.** The Irish MA follows MA (1) here, *natale* being omitted from MA (2).

**2. Tigernach.** A reference to Tigernach Bairche (d. 1061), absent from the metrical text of MO, is contained in the Lb version of its Commentary. Tigernach, whose obit describes him as 'chief confessor' of Ireland was abbot of Movilla, now a tl. in Newtownards p., Ards Lower b., Co. Down, the site of a house of Augustinian canons. For other examples of the ungrammatical *in Hiberniam*, see 31 Jan., 8 Apr. above. The *Grevenus* MU places Carthach here, with the words: *In Hibernia, Karthagii episcopi.*

## [14 May] b II ID.

1 Natale[a] sancti Paucomi[b] monachi.[c]
2 Item ipso die, in Hibernia, natale sancti episcopi et confessoris Carthachi,[d] cuius uita uirtutibus plena refulsit.

[a](Natalis) patris nostri (MCh), MA. [b]Pachumi MCh, Pachomii MA. [c]*om.* MCh, MA, *which add more detail.* [d]Charthaig MO.

**1. Pachomius.** Only in MA (1) is this the first entry.
**2. Carthach.** MO does not describe Carthach as a bishop. However, by the twelfth century, his church of Lismore, Co. Waterford, had become a diocesan centre. For the *Grevenus* MU record of this saint, see the previous day.

## [15 May] c ID. MAI.

1 Lamasco,[a] passio sanctorum Petri et Andriae, Pauliae[b] et Dionisiae.
2 Et apud Hiberniam, natale sancti confessoris Dublitrech.[c]

[a](Apud) Lamosacum MCh, (MA). [b]Pauli MCh, MA. [c]Duiblitir MO.

**1. Petrus etc.** This is the final entry in MCh, MA. The incorrect genitive form *Pauliae* was probably influenced by the surrounding *Andriae* and *Dionisiae*.
**2. Dubliter.** The genitive form *Dublitrech* is found in the L, Lb and F manuscripts of MO.

## [16 May] d XUII KAL. IUNII

1 Apud Hiberniam, natale sancti abbatis et confessoris Braendini.[a]
2 In Hibernia quoque, natale sanctorum confessorum [b]Carnich et Finnguni.[b]

[a]Brénainn MO. [b]Carnig . . . hAui Suanaig, 'C., the descendant of S.' MO.

**1. Br(a)endinus.** This is from the Irish MA, with MCh reading: *In Hybernia insula, natalis sancti Brendani abbatis et confessoris.* The *Grevenus* MU joins the *Bruxellensis* version in referring to Brendan, elaborately, with the words: *In Hibernia, sancti Brandani abbatis, qui abstinentia virtute magnus, trium fere millium monachorum e extitit pater.*

**2. Cairnech, Finguine.** Here MDr is following the Commentary, whose R1 version, which is often closest to the original, has *Finnguni* for the more correct *Fidmuine* (descendant of Suanach). The *Altempsianus* MU also records the feast of Cairnech, albeit in his Cornish version, with the words: *In Cornubia, sancti Karnoci episcopi.*

### [17 May] e XUI KAL.

1  In Tuscia, natale<sup>a</sup> sancti Torpetis martyris sub Nerone principe passi.<sup>b</sup>

<sup>a</sup>*om.* MCh. <sup>b</sup>*om.* MCh, MA, *which add more detail.*

**1. Torpes.** MCh, MA (1) (but not MA (2)), and MU place this entry first.

### [18 May] f XU KAL. IUNII

1  Apud Hiberniam, natale sanctorum confessorum <sup>a</sup>Brain, Medoc, Domnoc.<sup>a</sup>

<sup>a–a</sup>Momáedóc . . . Modomnóc . . . Brain MO.

### [19 May] g XIIII KAL. IUNII

1  Romae, natale<sup>a</sup> sanctae Potentianae<sup>b</sup> uirginis.<sup>c</sup>
2  <sup>d</sup>Item, Urbani martyris cum suis sanctis tam plurimis.<sup>d</sup>

<sup>a</sup>*om.* MCh. <sup>b</sup>Pudentianae vel Potentianae MA. <sup>c</sup>*add more detail* MCh, MA. <sup>d–d</sup>cliara Urbáin, 'the troops of U.' MO.

**2. Urbanus.** Compare the entry on the following day. The *Grevenus* MU also places Pope Urban (25 May) on this day.

### [20 May] a XIII KAL.

1  Romae,<sup>a</sup> natale sanctae Basillae<sup>b</sup> uirginis et martyris Christi.<sup>c</sup>
2  Item, Urbani papae et martyris et Marcellosi.<sup>d</sup>

<sup>a</sup>*add* uia Salaria MCh, MA. <sup>b</sup>Basillis MCh. <sup>c</sup>*add more detail* MCh, MA. <sup>d</sup>Marcelosi MO.

**2. Urbanus.** The description of Urban I agrees with the entry in MA (2) at 25 May, the Pope's usual day. The entry of the same name, in reference to an apparently different saint, on the previous day may have influenced the author of MDr.

### [21 May] b XII KAL.

1  Apud Hiberniam, natale sanctorum confessorum <sup>a</sup>Colmani et Barrinni.<sup>a</sup>

<sup>a–a</sup>Colmán . . . Barrfhind. MO.

[22 May] c XI KAL. IUNII

1 Apud<sup>a</sup> Corsicam, natale<sup>b</sup> sanctae Iuliae uirginis,<sup>c</sup> quae crucis <sup>d</sup>supplicio coronata<sup>d</sup> est.

2 Apud Hiberniam, natale sanctorum confessorum <sup>e</sup>Ronani et Baithini.<sup>e</sup>

<sup>a</sup>*preceded by* Eodem die MCh, MA. <sup>b</sup>*om.* MA. <sup>c</sup>*om.* MCh, MA. <sup>d–d</sup>suppliciis passa MA. <sup>e–e</sup>Rónáin . . . Báithéne MO.

**1. Iulia.** This is preceded in MCh and MA by an entry on an African saint. The wording of the Irish MA agrees with MU against MA.
**2 Baíthíne.** The description of this saint is from the Irish MA, with MCh reading: *Hybernia, sancti Boetheni abbatis et confessoris.*

[23 May] d X KAL. IUNII

1 Apud Ligoneas,<sup>a</sup> passio sancti Desiderii episcopi, <sup>b</sup>qui a rege Uandalorum crucis tormento passus est.<sup>b</sup>

<sup>a</sup>e *above* a *in MS of* MDr, Lingones MCh, MA. <sup>b–b</sup>*more detail* MCh, MA.

[24 May] e IX KAL.

1 In Brittania,<sup>a</sup> natale<sup>b</sup> sancti Augustini episcopi<sup>c</sup> <sup>d</sup>primi Anglorum, quem Grigorius beatus papa ad Anglos missit in fide Christi catacizandos.<sup>d</sup>

2 Item, apud Hiberniam, sanctorum confessorum <sup>e</sup>Athbi et Colmani.<sup>e</sup>

<sup>a</sup>Britannis MCh, MA. <sup>b</sup>*om.* MCh, MA. <sup>c</sup>*add* et confessoris MCh, MA. <sup>d–d</sup>*different wording* MCh, MA. <sup>e–e</sup>Colmán . . . Aidbe MO.

**1. Augustinus.** The feast is placed here rather than two days later (26 May), where MCh and MA list it, because of its presence in MO.

[25 May] f UIII KAL. IUNII g*

. 1 Romae, Eleutheri papae, qui <sup>a</sup>duodecim annis Romanam rexit aecclesiam.<sup>a</sup>

2 Et apud Hiberniam, sancti confessoris et prespeteri <sup>b</sup>Dunchada abbatis Iensis<sup>b</sup> natale.

<sup>a–a</sup>sedit annos duodecim (quindecim) MCh, (MA). <sup>b–b</sup>Dunchad hIae MO.

*The attachment of two dominical letters to this day was seen by Forbes, *The Ancient Irish Missal*, p. v, as compensation for the omission of a letter at 24 Jan.

**1. Eleutherus.** This is the final entry in MA (1), the penultimate in MCh. The confusion as to the length of the pope's reign, more correctly fifteen years, was probably due to the use of the Roman notation, *xu* being misread as *xii*. **2 Dúnchad.** For a possible explanation of the naming of Iona, alone of the 'Irish' churches, see Introduction, § 4. *Dunchada* is genitive of *Dúnchad*.

[26 May] a UII KAL.

1 ᵃDepositio sanctiᵇ uenerabilis Bedae prespeteri.ᵃᶜ
2 Et apud Hiberniam, natale sanctorum confessorum ᵈColmani et Beccani.ᵈ

ᵃ⁻ᵃ*om.* MA. ᵇ*om.* MCh. ᶜ*add more detail* MCh. ᵈ⁻ᵈCholmáin . . . Beccán MO.

**1. Baeda.** This is the final entry in MCh. Several *auctaria* of MU also place Bede here, as well as on the following day.

[27 May] b UI KAL.

1 Natale sancti ᵃAculei prespeteri cum ingenti martyrum multitudine.ᵃ

ᵃ⁻ᵃAculius cruimther cona chléir as nóebu, 'Presbyter A. with his most holy troop' MO.

**1. Acculus.** This saint, otherwise named *Aquilinus*, is also here in the *Grevenus* and *Lubeco-Col.* versions of MU.

[28 May] c U KAL. IUNII

1 Natale sancti Iohannis papae ᵃet confessoris.ᵃ

ᵃ⁻ᵃ*om.* MA, *which adds more detail.*

[29 May] d IIII KAL.

1 Romae,ᵃ nataleᵇ sancti Restituti.
2 Etᶜ septem germanorum.
3 Et apud Hiberniam, sanctae uirginis Cummaneᵈ natale celebratur.

ᵃ*add* uia Aurelia MCh, MA. ᵇ*om.* MCh, MA. ᶜuia Tyburtina MCh, MA. ᵈCummain MO.

**1, 2. Restitutus, septem germani.** Although written here as one entry, these were separate martyrdoms.
**3. Cummain.** The author frequently supplies a genitive form of the Irish name, as here in *Cummane* from *Cummain*.

## [30 May] e III KAL.

1 Romae,[a] natale sancti Felicis papae [b]et martyris.[b]

[a]*add* uia Appia (Aurelia), in cimiterio MCh, (MA). [b-b]*om.* MCh, MA, *which add more detail.*

## [31 May] f II KAL.

1 Romae, natale[a] sanctae Petronillae uirginis filiae[b] beati[c] Petri apostoli.[d]
2 Et[e] sancti Crescentiani.

[a]*om.* MCh, MA. [b]H(a)ec fuit filia MCh, (MA). [c]beatissimi MCh, MA. [d]*add more detail* MCh, MA. [e]Turribus Sardini(a)e, natale MCh, (MA).

**1. Petronilla.** Several versions of MU agree with MDr, against MCh and MA, in the use of the wording *filiae beati Petri apostoli.*
**2. Crescentianus.** Another entry separates Crescentianus from Petronilla in MCh and MA.

## [1 June] g KAL. IUNII

1 Apud Cessariam Palestinae, natale sancti Pampilii[a] prespeteri.[b]
2 Hoc quoque die, Teclam[c] uirginem martyrio esse coronatam quidam referunt.

[a]Pamphili(i) MCh, MA. [b]*add more detail* MCh, MA. [c]Teclae MO.

**1. Pamphilius.** This is preceded in MCh and MA by an entry on Nicomedes whose main feast fell on 15 Sep., where it is recorded in MDr.
**2. Thecla.** The formula *quidam referunt*, or words to that effect, frequently marks the use of MO as a source. For a listing of examples, see Schneiders, 'The Drummond Martyrology', pp. 123–4. Alone of the *auctaria* of MU, *Grevenus* also places Thecla here.

## [2 June] a IIII N. IUNII

1 Romae, Marcellini prespeteri et Petri exorcizae sub Diocletiano [a]imperatore coronatorum.[a]

[a-a]*om.* MCh, MA, *which add more detail.*

**1. Marcellinus, Petrus.** This is one of the longest entries in MA, of whose two recensions only the second attaches the word *imperator* to Diocletianus.

## [3 June] b III N.

1  Et<sup>a</sup> in Campania, beati Herasini<sup>b</sup> episcopi et martyris.<sup>c</sup>
2  Eodem quoque die, apud Hiberniam, sancti Coemgini<sup>d</sup> confessoris natale.

<sup>a</sup>item MCh, *om.* MA. <sup>b</sup>Erasmi MA. <sup>c</sup>*add more detail* MCh, MA. <sup>d</sup>Cóemgen MO.

**1. Erasmus.** This is the (second) last entry in (MCh) and MA. However, it is the first in MU. The mis-spelling of the saint's name in the Irish MA was due to confusion of the minims, *mi* being read as *ini*.
**2. Coemginus.** The lack of elaboration in this entry argues against the Glenda-lough provenance previously suggested for MDr (Introduction, § 2). The entry was also in the Irish MA, with MCh reading *In Hybernia, natalis sancti Coemgini abbatis et confessoris.* The *Grevenus* MU twice lists the saint, with the words: *In Hibernia, Kelvini abbatis*, and *Coemgini confessoris.*

## [4 June] c II N.

1  Natale sancti <sup>a</sup>Apollinaris martyris cum ingenti martyrum multitudine.<sup>a</sup>

<sup>a–a</sup>Apollinaris . . . cona chléir, 'A. with his troop' MO.

**1. Apollinaris.** Apollonius of Egypt may be intended here. See MTur at 4 June.

## [5 June] d NON.

1  Natale<sup>a</sup> sanctae Agathae<sup>b</sup> gloriosae feminae multisque uirtutibus clarae.
2  Brancii<sup>c</sup> quoque<sup>d</sup> episcopi et martyris et aliorum servorum Dei.

<sup>a</sup>Item MCh. <sup>b</sup>Aglahe(s) MCh, (MA). <sup>c</sup>Bonifacii MA. <sup>d</sup>*om.* MCh.

**1. Aglahes; 2. Bonifacius.** The reading *Agatha* for *Aglahes* was probably influ-enced by the Commentary on MO, which refers to *Agatha cum aliis uirginibus.* The spelling *Brancius* for *Bonifacius* was already in the Irish MA. For both entries MA provides much more detail and a largely divergent text.

## [6 June] e UIII IDUS IUNII f

1  Natale<sup>a</sup> sancti Pilippi diaconi qui fuit unus de septem primis.<sup>b</sup>
2  Et apud Hiberniam, natale sancti confessoris Maelaithchen.<sup>c</sup>

<sup>a</sup>*om.* MCh, MA. <sup>b</sup>*om.* MCh, MA. <sup>c</sup>Maelaithgin MO.

**1. Philippus.** Phillip was among the first deacons, whence the addition of *primis* here, as in several *auctaria* of MU.
**2. Máel Aithgin.** Some manuscripts of MO (R1, F) also spell the name with *-ch-*.

## [7 June] g UII IDUS

1  Apud<sup>a</sup> Constantinapolim,<sup>b</sup> natale sancti Pauli eiusdem urbis<sup>c</sup> episcopi.<sup>d</sup>
2  Et apud Hiberniam, natale sancti confessoris Mocholmoc.<sup>e</sup>

<sup>a</sup>*om.* MCh, MA. <sup>b</sup>Constantinopoli MA. <sup>c</sup>civitatis MA. <sup>d</sup>*add more detail* MCh, MA. <sup>e</sup>Choluimb MO.

**1. Paulus.** Several *auctaria* of MU agree with the Irish MA in writing *Constantinopolim.*
**2. Mocholmóc.** Several manuscripts of the Commentary on MO render the saint's name as *Mocholmóc.* However, the retention of the prefix *mo-* is against the usual practice of MDr. Both the *Grevenus* and *Molanus* versions of MU likewise commemorate this saint, who was patron of the diocese of Dromore, with the words: *In Hibernia, Colmanni episcopi et confessoris.*

## [8 June] a UI IDUS

1  In Gallia,<sup>a</sup> natale sancti Medardi episcopi et confessoris.
2  Et<sup>b</sup> sancti Carilifi<sup>c</sup> confessoris.
3  Et apud Hiberniam, natale sanctorum confessorum <sup>d</sup>Medrain et Murchon.<sup>d</sup>

<sup>a</sup>Galliis Suessionis ciuitate(m) (MCh), MA. <sup>b</sup>Item eodem die MCh, MA. <sup>c</sup>Carilefi MCh, (MA). <sup>d–d</sup>Medráin . . . Murchon MO.

**1. Medardus.** The wording agrees with MA (1).

## [9 June] b U IDUS IUNII

1  In Gallia,<sup>a</sup> passio sancti Uincentii leuitae et martyris.
2  <sup>b</sup>Item eodem die, apud Hiberniam,<sup>b</sup> natale sanctorum confessorum<sup>c</sup> Columbae abbatis<sup>d</sup> et Baithini sucessoris eius.<sup>e</sup>

<sup>a</sup>Gallis, ciuitate Aginno, loco Pontiano, MCh, (MA). <sup>b–b</sup>in Hibernia MCh. <sup>c</sup>abbatum MCh. <sup>d</sup>*om.* MCh. <sup>e</sup>*add much more detail* MCh.

**1. Vincentius.** This is the second of two entries in MA. The words *leuitae et* are *in rasura* in MCh.
**2. Columba, Baíthíne.** The presence of this entry in the Irish version of MA, together with its length as represented by MCh, point to a greater than average interest on the part of the author in Columban affairs (see also Introduction, § 4). Columba also found admission to MA itself, albeit only in its second recension, with the words *In Scotia, sancti Columbae presbyteri et confessoris,* and to MU, with the additional words *magnae et mirandae virtutis viri.*

## [10 June] c IIII IDUS

1  <sup>a</sup>In Colonia, passio sancti Mauri<sup>b</sup> abbatis et martyris.<sup>a</sup>

<sup>a–a</sup>*om.* MA. <sup>b</sup>Maurini MCh.

**1. Maurinus.** This saint, whose relics were first discovered in the church of St Pantaleon in Cologne in 966, is also commemorated in the *Martyrologium Romanum*, as well as in most *auctaria* of MU.

## [11 June] d III IDUS

1  Natale sancti Barnabbae apostoli.<sup>a</sup>
2  Et apud Hiberniam, natale beati episcopi et confessoris Meic Thail.<sup>b</sup>

<sup>a</sup>*add more detail* MCh, MA. <sup>b</sup>Maicc Tháil MO.

**2. Mac Táil.** This saint is from the Irish MA, with MCh reading *Eodem die, sancti Mectail.*

## [12 June] e II IDUS

1  Medulani,<sup>a</sup> natale sanctorum martyrum<sup>b</sup> Nazarii et Celsii,<sup>c</sup> <sup>d</sup>sub Nerone coronati sunt.<sup>d</sup>
2  Et apud Hiberniam, natale sanctorum confessorum <sup>e</sup>Coeman et Mothoriae.<sup>e</sup>

<sup>a</sup>Mediolani MCh, MA. <sup>b</sup>*om.* MCh. <sup>c</sup>*add* pueri MCh, MA. <sup>d–d</sup>*much more detail* MCh, MA. <sup>e–e</sup>Chóemain . . . Torannán MO.

**1. Nazarius, Celsus.** These saints are also commemorated on 27 July (28 July in MA). Moreover, Celsus is also included in the list below for 19 June. The wording of the entry agrees with MA (1).
**2. Mothorias (Mothairén/Torannán).** Several manuscripts of the Commentary on MO, which locate the saint, among other places, in Scotland, give a variant form *Mothoria/Mothairea* of his name. In his Scottish guise, he found his way into the *Grevenus* MU, which reads: *In Scotia, Termani archiepiscopi et confessoris.*

## [13 June] f IDUS

1  Romae, natale sanctae Feliculae uirginis et martyris.<sup>a</sup>
2  Item, apud Hiberniam, natale sancti confessoris <sup>b</sup>Meic Nissi.<sup>b</sup>

<sup>a</sup>*add more detail* MCh, MA. <sup>b–b</sup>Macc Nissi MO.

**2. Mac Nisse.** This is from the Irish MA, with MCh reading: *Eodem die, sancti confessoris Me[c]nisi.*

## [14 June] g XUIII KAL. IULII

1  Helesei[a] profetae qui apud Samariam[b] Palestinae requiescit.[c]
2  Et apud Hiberniam, sanctus confessor Nem[d] eodem die migrauit ad Christum.

[a]Helisei MCh, MA. [b]Samaria MCh. [c]om. MCh, MA, *which add more detail.* [d]Nem MO.

## [15 June] a XUII KAL.

1  Apud Siciliam,[a] natale[b] sanctorum martyrum Uiti, Modesti et Crescentiae.[c]

[a]Sciciliam MCh. [b]om. MCh, MA (2). [c]*add more detail* MCh, MA.

## [16 June] b XUI KAL.

1  Apud Antiochiam quoque,[a] natale sanctorum martyrum Ciricii et Iulitae matris eius [b]qui post dira tormenta martyrii sui cursum obtruncatione capitis compleuerunt.[bc]

[a]*om.* MCh, MA. [b–b]*different wording* MA. [c]impleuerunt MCh, *add more detail* MCh, MA.

**1. Cyricus etc.** Forbes took the use of *quoque* to indicate that the source text did not have this as its first entry. However, although not so in MU, except in its *Bruxellensis* version, it is also first in MCh and MA. The wording of the Irish MA agrees with MU against MA.

## [17 June] c XU KAL.

1  Apud Hiberniam, natale sancti confessoris Moling[a] pleni profetiae spiritu ceterisque uirtutibus prediti.
2  Item, [b]Colmani filii Luachan[b] uiri Dei et relegiosi.

[a]Moling MO, *dot over* n *of* Moling MDr. [b–b]*om.* MO.

**1. Moling.** MDr shows an awareness here of Moling's reputation for prescience. The saint's main church, at St Mullins, tl./p./b., Co. Carlow, was close to Inistioge, where, possibly already at this stage, there was a house of Augustinian canons. Moling is also remembered here in the *Grevenus* MU, albeit in woefully corrupt form, with the words: *In Hibernia, Enolich confessoris*
**2. Colmanus filius Luachan.** This entry was taken from the Commentary on MO which in turn took it from MG. It is probably this Colmanus, rather than his namesake from Druim Lias, who was intended by the *Grevenus* MU, which reads on the following day: *In Hibernia, Colmanni abbatis.*

## [18 June] d XIIII KAL.

1  Romae,[a] natale sanctorum martyrum Marci et Marcilliani,[b] Tranquillini et Martiae.[c]

2  Item, apud Hiberniam, natale sanctorum confessorum [d]Baithain et Furudran,[d] mirandae sanctitatis uirorum.

[a]*add* uia Ardiatina MCh, (MA). [b]*add* pr(a)eclarissimi generis MCh, (MA). [c]Marci(a)e MCh, (MA), *add more detail* MCh, MA. [d–d]Baithín . . . Furudrán MO.

**1. Marcus et al.** Despite MDr, Tranquillinus and Marcia were not themselves martyrs but parents of Marcus and Marcellianus. Otherwise, the wording agrees with MA (1) against MA (2).

**2. Báetán, Furudrán.** This is from the Irish MA, with MCh reading: *Eodem die sanctorum confessorum Baithini et Furudrani.* The two saints, who, judging by the additional words of praise, appear to have been of more than usual interest to the author, were associated with the church of Dunleer, now tl./p., Ferrard b., Co. Louth.

## [19 June] e XIII KAL.

1  Mediolani, natale sanctorum martyrum[a] Gerbassi[b] et Protassi [c]et Celsi pueri.[c]

[a]*after* pueri (Protasii) MCh, (MA). [b]Geruasii MCh, MA. [c–c]*om.* MA.

**1. Celsus.** This would appear to represent the octave of Celsus who was previously commemorated at 12 June above, and again at 27 July. Although omitted in MA and MU, the *Bruxellensis* version of MU also refers to Celsus on this day. The spelling of *Gerbassi* was influenced by MO, which in some manuscripts (R[1], L) reads *Gerba(i)ssi.*

## [20 June] f XII KAL. IULII

1  [a]Romae, natale sancti Siluerii papae qui anno uno Romanam cathedram rexit.[a]

2  Et apud Hiberniam, Faelani.[b]

[a–a](Sancti) Silvestri (Silverii) pape qui sedit Rome (-) anno uno MCh, (MA), *add more detail* MCh, MA. [b]Fáelán MO.

**1. Silverius.** The confusion in MCh of the name *Silvester*, which had been adopted by four popes, with *Silverius*, which had been the name of one only, was a natural one. The entry is in MA (1) only, where it is preceded by that of St Novatus.

**2. Fáelán.** The Commentary on MO places Fáelán in *Alba*, which MDr elsewhere (8 Jan., 17 Apr., 21 Apr., 25 June, 10 Aug.) translates as *Britannia.*

## [21 June] g XI KAL.

1  Apud Siciliam,[a] natale sanctorum martyrum Rufini et Martiae.[b]
2  Et apud Hiberniam, natale sanctorum confessorum ac prespeterorum Cormaic[c] ac Diarmata.

[a]*add* ciuitatem Siracusis MCh, (MA). [b]Marcie MCh, (MA). [c]Cormacc MO.

**2. Cormac, Diarmait.** The addition of Diarmait, who is not in MO, is based on a mistaken entry in the Commentary on Óengus, which identified *áinle*, 'champion', of the metrical text with Diarmait of Dísert Diarmata (Castledermot, Co. Kildare).

## [22 June] a X KAL.

1  In Brittania,[a] natale[b] sancti Albani martyris.[c]
2  Item, in ciuitate Nola Campaniae, natale sancti Paulini episcopi et confessoris.[c]
3 Item, apud Hiberniam, natale sancti confessoris Cronain.[d]

[a]Britannis MCh. [b]*om.* MCh. [c]*add more detail* MCh, MA. [d]Cronán MO.

**1, 2. Albanus, Paulinus.** The wording of both entries agrees with MA (1) against MA (2).

## [23 June] b IX KAL.

1  Uigilia sancti Iohannis Baptistae.
2  Et apud Hiberniam, natale sancti confessoris Mochoe.[a]

[a]Mochoe MO.

## [24 June] c UIII KAL.

1  Natiuitas beati Iohannis Baptizae precursoris Domini, filii[a] Zachariae et Elizabeth.[b]

[a]*after* Elizabeth MCh, MA. [b]*add more detail* MCh, MA.

**1. Iohannes Baptista.** The wording of the entry agrees with MA (2) against MA (1).

## [25 June] d UII KAL.

1  [a]In Britania, sancti confessoris Moluoc.[a]
2  Item, in Hibernia, natale sanctorum confessorum [b]Sincheill et Telle.[b]

[a]m'Luóc . . . de Albae, 'M. of Alba' MO. [b-b]Sinchill . . . Telli MO.

**1. Moluóc.** The use of *Britannia* for *Alba*, as at 8 Jan., 17 Apr., 21 Apr., 20 Jun., 10 Aug., may be noted. This saint, who was attached to the church of Lismore in Scotland, was in the Irish MA, with MCh reading: *In Scocia, Sancti Lugudi abbatis et confessoris.* He is also remembered in the (*Lubeco-Col.*) and *Grevenus* versions of MU, which read: (*sancti*) *Moloci episcopi et confessoris.*

### [26 June] e UI KAL.

1  Romae, Iohannis et Pauli fratrum ᵃqui sub impio Iuliano martyrio coronati sunt.ᵃ

ᵃ⁻ᵃ*much more detail* MCh, MA.

**1. Iohannes, Paulus.** The wording of the entry agrees with MA (2) against MA (1).

### [27 June] f U KAL.

1  ᵃIn Hispania, ciuitate Cordubae,ᵃ natale sanctiᵇ Stoliiᶜ et aliorum decem et septem.ᵈ

ᵃ⁻ᵃEodem die, Cordube in Hispaniis MCh, (MA). ᵇsanctorum MCh, MA. ᶜZoili MCh, MA. ᵈocto MCh, novem MA.

**1. Zoilus.** This is the last of three entries in MCh and MA. The spelling of the saint's name derives from the tendency in MDr to render *z* as *st*.

### [28 June] g IIII KAL.

1  Uigiliaᵃ apostolorum Petri et Pauli.
2  Ipso die, nataleᵇ sancti Leonis papae ᶜet confessoris.ᶜ
3  Et in Hibernia, natale sancti confessoris Crummain.ᵈ

ᵃ*add* sanctorum MCh. ᵇ*om.* MCh. ᶜ⁻ᶜ*om.* MA. ᵈCrummíne MO.

**2. Leo.** Several *auctaria* of MU agree with the Irish MA in adding *et confessoris* to the description of the saint. MCh and the second line of transmission of MA add further detail.

### [29 June] a III KAL.

1  Romae, natale sanctorumᵃ apostolorum Petri et Pauli, qui sub scelestissimoᵇ Nerone ᶜpasi sunt,ᶜ Basco et Tusco consulibus.ᵈ

ᵃbeatorum MCh, MA. ᵇ*om.* MCh, MA. ᶜ⁻ᶜ*before* sub MCh, MA. ᵈ*add more detail* MA.

**1. Petrus, Paulus.** The text of the entry agrees with MA (2) against MA (1).

## [30 June] b II KAL.

1 Celebratio[a] iterum sancti Pauli apostoli.
2 [b]Stoli quoque et Timothei.[b]

[a]*preceded by* natale et MA. [b]Sauli is Tiamdai MO.

**1. Paulus.** The text of the entry agrees with MA (1) against MA (2).
**2. Zoilus, Timotheus.** Zoilus is the saint already commemorated above at 27 June. Here the entry is taken from MO, several of whose manuscripts show initial *st* in the spelling of the name.

## [1 July] c KAL. IULII

1 In Monte Hor depossitio Aaron sacerdotis primi.
2 Item,[a] eodem die sanctae Monegundis uirginis.

[a]*om.* MA.

**2. Monegundis.** The text of the entry agrees with MA (1) against MA (2).

## [2 July] d UI N.

1 Romae, in cymitherio Damasi, natale sanctorum Processi et Martiniani, qui a beatis apostolis Petro et Paulo [a]instructi et baptizati[a] sunt.[b]

[a–a]baptizati et instructi MCh, MA. [b]*add more detail* MCh, MA.

**1. Processus, Martinianus.** Probably because of the connexion with Peter and Paul (Introduction, § 3), and against its usual practice, MDr retains here a good deal of the detail of its source, including the name of the cemetery.

## [3 July] e U N.

1 Apud Edissam[a] Mesopotamiae urbem,[b] translatio corporis sancti Tomae apostoli.

[a]Edessam MCh, MA. [b]*om.* MCh, MA.

**1. Thomas.** The text agrees with MA (1) against MA (2).

## [4 July] f IIII N.

1 Ossee et Aggei.[a]
2 Item,[b] Toronis,[c] translatio sancti Martini episcopi et confessoris, et ordinatio [d]eius in episcopatum,[d] et dedicatio basilicae ipsius.

3  Et apud Hiberniam, natale sancti confessoris Finnbairr.[e]

[a]*add* prophetarum MCh, MA. [b]*om.* MCh, MA. [c]Turonis MCh, MA. [d-d]episcopatus ejus MCh, MA. [e]Findbarr MO.

## [5 July] g III N.

1  Apud Siriam,[a] sancti Domicii martyris.[b]
2  Eodem die sanctus [c]Agath*us* martyr cum turba martyrum[c] migrauit ad Christum.

[a]*add* natalis MA. [b]*add more detail* MCh, MA. [c-c]don martir Agatho cona chléir, 'to the martyr A. with his troop' MO.

**2. Agatho.** There would appear to be no authority for the spelling *Agathus* either in the manuscripts of MO or in the Hieronymian tradition.

## [6 July] a II N. IULII

1  Iesaie[a] et Iohel profetarum.
2  Et octauae[b] apostolorum.
3  Et apud Hiberniam, natale sanctae uirginis Moninne.[c]

[a]Isaye MCh, Natale Isaiae MA. [b]Octavas MA. [c]Moninne MO.

**1, 2. Isaias, octavae apostolorum.** The text of both entries agrees with MA (1) against MA (2).
**3. Moninne.** This saint also found her way, albeit corruptly, into the *Grevenus* MU, which reads: *In Hibernia, Nonninae virginis.*

## [7 July] b N. IULII

1  Apud Hiberniam, natale sancti episcopi et confessoris Maelruain,[a] cuius uita uirtutibus et miraculis plena refulsit.

[a]Maelruain MO.

**1. Máel Ruain.** The elaborate nature of the comments on this saint, who founded the church of Tallaght, may be noted. The entry was in the Irish MA, with MCh reading: *Et in Hibernia, sancti Maelruein* (with second *e* changed to *a* in different ink) *confessoris.*

## [8 July] c UIII IDUS

1  Romae,[a] natale[b] sancti Zenonis et aliorum decem milium ducentorum et trium.

2 Et apud Hiberniam, natale sanctorum confessorum ᶜBrocain et
Diarmata.ᶜ

ᵃ*add* ad guttam iugiter manentem MCh, (MA). ᵇ*om.* MCh, MA. ᶜ⁻ᶜBroccán . . . la Diarmait
MO.

**1. Zeno.** This is the first entry in MA for the following day, but the *Bruxellensis*
MU agrees with the Irish MA in placing it here. MCh follows MA (2) and MU
by adding here an entry on St Kilian, which reads: *natalis sancti Kiliani martiris
cum sociis suis Othmanno et Thothimanno.* The reference to Kilian's companions is absent from MA (2) but present in the majority of the *auctaria* of MU.

[9 July] d UII IDUS

1 In ciuitate Tiriae,ᵃ nataleᵇ Anatholiae uirginisᶜ et Audacis, ᵈqui sub
Decio imperatore martyrio coronati sunt.ᵈ
2 Et apud Hiberniam, natale sanctorum confessorum ᵉGarban et
Onchon.ᵉ

ᵃCyrie MCh, Tyrae MA. ᵇ*om.* MCh, *add* sanctorum MCh, MA. ᶜ*om.* MA. ᵈ⁻ᵈ*much more
detail* MA. ᵉ⁻ᵉOnchon . . . Garbán MO.

**2. Garbán.** This saint may also be intended by the entry in the *Grevenus* MU,
which reads: *In Hibernia, Germani confessoris.* Cf. Grosjean, 'Édition du
Catalogus', § 345.

[10 July] e UI IDUS

1 Romae, septem fratrum, filiorum sanctae Felicitatis, id est Ianuarii,
Felicis, Pilippi, Siluani, Alaxandri, Uitalis, Martialis,ᵃ ᵇqui sub
Antonino principe passi.ᵇ
2 Et in Hibernia, sancti confessoris Cuain.ᶜ

ᵃMarcialis MCh. ᵇ⁻ᵇ*more detail* MCh, MA. ᶜCuan MO.

[11 July] f U IDUS

1 Translatio sancti Benedicti abbatis, ᵃquando corpus eius post monasterium illius a gentibus destructum ad Galliam, id est ad monasterium
Floriac*um*, translatum est et sepultum est honorifice in eo.ᵃ
2 Et in Hibernia, natale sancti confessoris ᵇMeic Conloce.ᵇ

ᵃ⁻ᵃ*Different wording and more detail* MCh, MA. ᵇ⁻ᵇmacc . . . Conlogae MO.

**1. Benedictus.** *Floriacum*, for the more correct adjectival form *Floriacense*, was
probably due to the occurrence of the nominal form only in the source (MA,
MCH).

## [12 July] g IIII IDUS

1  Apud Aquiliam,<sup>a</sup> natale sancti Hermogorae<sup>b</sup> episcopi.
2  Item, <sup>c</sup>Nazarii et Felicis cum aliis sanctis tam plurimis.<sup>c</sup>

<sup>a</sup>Aquileiam MCh, MA. <sup>b</sup>*add* primi eiusdem ciuitatis episcopi MCh, MA. <sup>c–c</sup>Nazair . . .
Felix . . . cona shluag mór, 'N., F. with his great host' MO.

**1. Hermagoras.** The text agrees with MA (1) against MA (2).
**2. Nabor, Felix.** MDr took over from MO, which in turn had drawn on MT, the
erroneous *Nazarius* (for *Nabor/Navor*). Although apparently absent from the
Irish MA, the two saints are commemorated on this day in most of the *auctaria*
of MU. See also MTur at 12 July.

## [13 July] a III IDUS

1  Estrae<sup>a</sup> et Iohel profetarum.
2  <sup>b</sup>Eodem die quoque,<sup>b</sup> pasio<sup>c</sup> Margaritae uirginis.<sup>d</sup>
3  Item, <sup>e</sup>sancti Euangelii<sup>e</sup> uiri Dei.
4  Et in Hibernia, sancti confessoris Moshiloc.<sup>f</sup>

<sup>a</sup>Esdr(a)e MCh, (MA). <sup>b–b</sup>In Antiochia MA. <sup>c</sup>*add* sanctae MA. <sup>d</sup>*add more detail* MA.
<sup>e–e</sup>Euangeli nóebdai MO. <sup>f</sup>Iam' Silóc, 'with M.' MO.

**2. Margarita.** Although also in MA (2) and most of the *auctaria* of MU on this
day, MCh (and MG) commemorate Margaret on the 20 July, her regular day in
the West.

## [14 July] b II IDUS

1  Apud Pontum, natale sancti Foccae<sup>a</sup> episcopi <sup>b</sup>et martyris.<sup>b</sup>
2  Item, <sup>c</sup>Iacobi episcopi cum decem paruulis.<sup>c</sup>

<sup>a</sup>Phocae MCh, MA. <sup>b–b</sup>*om.* MCh, MA , *which add more detail.* <sup>c–c</sup>in t-epscop Iacob . . . co
ndechenbur noíden, 'Bishop Jacob, with ten infants' MO.

**2. Iacobus.** The bishop, who is the same saint as on the following day, was
taken from MO, which mistakenly placed the feast here. The ten infants, who
are likewise more correctly commemorated on the following day, had no
connexion with Bishop Jacob.

## [15 July] c IDUS IULII

1  Nisibi, natale sancti Iacobi episcopi <sup>a</sup>et confessoris.<sup>a</sup>
2  Eodem die, diuisio apostolorum <sup>b</sup>ad predicandum.<sup>b</sup>

<sup>a–a</sup>*om.* MA, *which adds more detail.* <sup>b–b</sup>In dá apstal déac . . . fos-dáil . . . Íssu, 'The twelve
apostles, Jesus divided them' MO.

**1. Iacobus.** See note to the previous day.
**2. Divisio Apostolorum.** This feast, which is supposed to be of Irish origin (Hennig, 'Zu Anfang und Ende', p. 309), is also in MCh, which reads: *Eodem die, diuisio apostolorum*. Since the text of the entry in some *auctaria* of MU includes MDr's additional words, *ad predicandum*, it seems likely that these came from the external source of the Irish MA. However, the Commentary on MO, which also claims that Adamnán instituted the feast, contains a similar entry. Cf. Hennig, 'The Notes', p. 146.

[16 July] d XUII KAL. AUGUSTI

1  In Hostia,[a] sancti Hilarini martyris.[b]
2  Item eodem die, [c]sancti Mammetis cum felice turba martyrum tolerante.[c]

[a]Ostia MA. [b]*om.* MCh, MA, *which add more detail.* [c-c]co sluag suabais in maccáin Mammetis, 'with the host of the youth M.' MO.

**2. Mammes.** The *Lubeco-Col.* and *Grevenus* versions of MU likewise record the feast of Mammes on this day.

[17 July] e XUI KAL.

1  In Kartagine, natale[a] sanctorum martyrum Scillitanorum, id est Sperati, Narthali, Cithini, Beaturii,[b] Felicis, Aquilini, Laetacii, Ianuariae, Generosae,[c] Bessiae, Donatae, et Secundae, sub Taurino[d] prefecto.[e]

[a]*om.* MCh. [b]Beturii MA. [c]Gerose MCh. [d]Satur(n)ino MCh, (MA). [e]*add more detail* MCh, MA.

**1. Speratus etc.** In the spelling of such names as *Cithini* and *Bessiae*, MDr agrees with MA (1).

[18 July] f XU KAL.

1  Apud[a] Hispaniam, natale sanctarum martyrum[b] Iustae et Rufinae.[c]
2  Item eodem die, [d]sanctae Cristinae cum septem fratribus.[d]

[a]*preceded by* Eodem die, Hispali MCh, MA. [b]*om.* MA. [c]*add more detail* MA. [d-d]co mmórfhessiur bráthre in Christina noebdae, 'with the seven brothers of holy C.' MO.

**1. Iusta, Rufina.** This corresponds to the second entry in MCh. MA has the entry (and the preceding one of MCh) on the following day, but the *Bruxellensis* MU agrees with the Irish MA in placing it here.
**2. Christina.** This is probably the same saint as at 24 July.

## [19 July] g XIIII KAL.

1 Natale sancti<sup>a</sup> Ioseph, qui cognominatus est Iustus. Quique cum beato Mathia ut <sup>b</sup>numerus duodecimus<sup>b</sup> impleretur<sup>c</sup> <sup>d</sup>statutus est sorte.<sup>d</sup>
2 Item eodem die, <sup>e</sup>sancti Sisinni cum turba sancta martyrum patiente.<sup>e</sup>

<sup>a</sup>beati MCh, MA. <sup>b</sup>numerum duodecimum MCh, (MA). <sup>c</sup>impleret MCh, MA. <sup>d–d</sup>ab apostolis statuitur MCh, MA, *add more detail* MCh, MA. <sup>e–e</sup>Sisenni . . . co mmórbuidin brestai, 'S., with a great, spirited band' MO.

**1. Ioseph.** MDr's *statutus est sorte* is an attempt to summarise the remainder of the entry in MCh and MA. Again MA has this entry on the following day. Of the *auctaria* of MU, only *Bruxellensis* agrees with the Irish MA.

## [20 July] a XIII KAL.

1 Apud Damascum, natale sanctorum martyrum<sup>a</sup> <sup>b</sup>Maximini, Iuliani, Macrobi, Cassi, Paulae, Sabinae,<sup>bc</sup> Romulae,<sup>d</sup> cum aliis decem.

<sup>a</sup>*om.* MCh, MA. <sup>b–b</sup>*differently arranged* MCh, MA. <sup>c</sup>Sabini MCh, MA. <sup>d</sup>*om.* MCh, MA, Romula MO.

**1. Maximinus etc.** MDr followed MO in its spelling of *Sabinae* (*Sabina* MO) and in its inclusion of the unrelated saint *Romula*, whose feast more properly belongs on the 23 July.

## [21 July] b XII KAL.

1 Romae, natale<sup>a</sup> sanctae Praxedis uirginis.<sup>b</sup>
2 Item eodem die, sancti <sup>c</sup>Heliae martyris.<sup>c</sup>

<sup>a</sup>*om.* MCh. <sup>b</sup>*add more detail* MCh, MA. <sup>c–c</sup>Heli martir MO.

**1. Praxedes.** This is preceded in MA by an entry on Daniel the prophet. However, the *Bruxellensis* version of MU also begins with this saint.
**2. Helia.** Despite Stokes, who took the form in MO to represent *Helius*, the correct name is *Helia*. The *Grevenus* MU also places this feast here.

## [22 July] c XI KAL.

1 Natale sanctae Mariae Magdalenae.
2 Et depositio<sup>a</sup> sancti Mandregisili<sup>b</sup> <sup>c</sup>abbatis et<sup>c</sup> confessoris.<sup>d</sup>
3 Et apud Hiberniam, natale sancti confessoris Mobiu.<sup>e</sup>

<sup>a</sup>ipso die MCh, *preceded by* Monasterio Fontinella MA. <sup>b</sup>Uuandregisili MCh, (MA). <sup>c–c</sup>*om.* MA. <sup>d</sup>*more detail* MA. <sup>e</sup>Mobiu MO.

**2. Wandregesilius.** Of the two recensions of MA, this entry is in MA (2) only. However, it is also in MU.

# TEXT

## [23 July] d X KAL.

1 Apud Rauennam, natale sancti Apollinaris episcopi [a]et martyris, quem Petrus apostolus ordinauit Rauennae.[a]

[a-a]*much more detail* MCh, MA.

## [24 July] e IX KAL.

1 Romae,[a] natale sancti Uincentii martyris.
2 [b]Cum duodecim sanctis militibus martyrium patientibus.[b]
3 [c]Et in Italia,[c] sanctae Cristinae uirginis et martyris.[d]
4 Et apud Hiberniam, sancti confessoris Declain.[e]

[a]*add* uia Tyburtina, mil(l)iario decimo (nono) MCh, (MA). [b-b]dá noí míled mathe, 'eighteen good soldiers' MO. [c-c]Eodem die apud Italiam in Tyro que est circa lacum Uulsinum natalis MCh, (MA). [d]*om.* MA, *which adds more detail.* [e]Declan MO.

**1. Vincentius.** Second in MA (1), this entry is absent from MA (2).
**2. Sancti milites.** This is taken from the text of MO for the previous day, which also lists Vincentius. MDr mistakenly assumed that the twelve (eighteen according to MO) soldiers were with the saint.
**3. Christina.** The wording agrees with MA (1), which places the entry first. However, the word *martyris*, absent from MA, is also found in some *auctaria* of MU. See note to 18 July.

## [25 July] f UIII KAL. AUG.

1 Natale sancti[a] Iacobi Zebedei apostoli.
2 Et[b] in Licia,[c] natale[d] sancti Cristoferi qui uirgis ferris[e] attritus, et flammis[f] estuantis incendii Christi uirtute salua*tus*, ad postremum[g] sagittarum ictibus perfosus,[h] [i]gladio decollatus est.[i]
3 Et[d] in Hispania,[j] sancti Cucustatis[k] martyris.[l]
4 Et apud Hiberniam, natale sanctorum confessorum [m]Mocholmoc, Moshiloc et Nesain.[m]

[a]beati MA. [b]Eodem (die) MCh, (MA). [c]*add* ciuitate Samo(n) (MCh), MA. [d]*om.* MA. [e]ferreis MCh, MA. [f]a flammis MCh, MA. [g]ultimum MCh, MA. [h]confossus MCh, MA. [i-i]*more detail* MCh, MA. [j]Hispannie MCh, Hispaniis MA, *add* ciuitate Barcinona MCh, MA. [k]Cucufatis MCh, MA. [l] *more detail* MCh, MA. [m-m]Mocholmóc, Moshilóc ... Nessán MO.

**1. Iacobus.** The text agrees with MA (1) against MA (2).
**2. Christopherus.** This very long entry by the standards of MDr may have been due to the increased interest in the saint in the twelfth century; cf. Farmer, *Dictionary*, p. 78. Christopher's feast is also recorded above at 28 Apr.
**3. Cucufas.** The wording agrees with MA (1) against MA (2).

## [26 July] g UII KAL.

1  Romae,[a] sancti Iacinthi[b] martyris.[c]
2  Et in eodem die, [d]in monte Tabor transformatio Domini Salvatoris nostri coram quinque testibus, Moysi, Heliae, Petro, Iohanne et Iacobo.[d]

[a]*add* in Portu (natale) MCh (MA). [b]Hyacinthi MA. [c]*om.* MA, *add more detail* MCh, MA. [d–d]tarmchruthud . . . Íssu i Sléib Thabóir, 'the transfiguration of Jesus on Mount T.' MO.

**2. Transformatio Domini.** This is taken from the Commentary on MO, which reads: *Transformatio Christi in monte Tabor coram .u. testibus, Moysi scilicet et Heliae, Petro et Iohanni et Iacobo.* Although some *auctaria* of MU, including *Grevenus*, assign this feast to the following day, the *Bruxellensis* version places it here.

## [27 July] a UI KAL.

1  [a]In Effesso,[a] [b]natale sanctorum[b] [c]septem dormientium.[c]
2  Item, sanctorum martyrum Nazarii et Celsi.
3  Et apud Hiberniam, sanctorum confessorum Guari et Dírad.

[a–a](Et) apud Ephesum (MCh), MA. [b–b]*om.* MCh. [c–c]*greater detail and different wording* MA.

**1. Septem Dormientes.** This is the final entry in MCh, and the second in MA, which names four of the saints without describing them as *dormientes*. However, this term is almost universal in the *auctaria* of MU.
**2. Nazarius, Celsus.** These Milan saints, who are not in MCh and MA, have already been entered at 12 June Their presence here may be due to the fact that, together with MH, several *auctaria* of MU record their feasts at 28 July.
**3. Guaire, Díraid.** This is apparently one of the few entries on Irish saints drawn neither from MO nor from its Commentary. The two saints are also listed in MG, as *Diraid* gl. *epscop Ferna*, 'bishop of Ferns', and *Guarian*, who, according to the corpus of saints' genealogies (Ó Riain, *Corpus*, § 722.89), was attached to the church of Etardruim (now Edermine tl./p., Ballaghkeen S. b., Co. Wexford).

## [28 July] U KAL.

1  Necomediae,[a] pasio sancti Pantaleonis martyris.[b]
2  Eodem quoque[c] die,[d] [e]sancti Teophili[e] et Perigrini confessoris.[f]

[a]Nichomedie MCh, (MA). [b]*om* MCh, MA, *which add more detail.* [c]*add* Lugduni MCh, MA. [d]*om.* MCh, MA. [e–e]*om.* MCh, MA, Teophil MO. [f]presbyteri MA, *preceded by* presbiteri et MCh, *add more detail* MA.

82

**2. Teophilus, Peregrinus.** Here MDr conflates his sources, drawing Teophilus from MO and Peregrinus from MA (1). Interestingly, although the Celtic saint Samson is in MCh on this day, and was thus probably in the Irish MA, MDr does not list him.

### [29 July] IIII KAL.

1 Romae,[a] natale[b] beati Felicis pontificis [c]et martyris.[c]
2 Et[d] sancti Luppi episcopi[e] et confessoris.[f]
3 Et[g] sanctorum martyrum Simplicii, Faustini, et Beatricis, [h]sub Diocletiano passorum.[h]

[a]*add* Uia Aurelia MCh, MA. [b]*om.* MCh, MA. [c-c]*om.* MCh, MA, *which add more detail.* [d]Trecas, depositio MCh, eodem die, depositio MA. [e]*add* de Trecas MA. [f]*om.* MA, *which adds more detail.* [g](Item) eodem die (natale) MCh, (MA). [h-h]*much more detail in* MCh, MA.

**1. Felix.** Although omitted from MCh and MA, the words *et martyris* are found in several *auctaria* of MU.
**2. Lupus.** In MCh and MA, this and the following entry are placed in reverse order. In the *auctaria* of MU, the formulation *et confessoris,* absent here from MA, is regular.

### [30 July] d III KAL.

1 Romae, natale[a] sanctorum martyrum[b] Abdon et Sennis,[c] [d]sub Decio imperatore.[d]

[a]*om.* MCh. [b]*om.* MCh, MA. [c]*add* subregulorum MCh, MA. [d-d]*more detail* MCh, MA.

### [31 July] e II KAL. AUG.

1 Cesariae, pasio sancti Fabii martyris.[a]
2 Et in Hibernia, sancti [b]Colmain confessoris et episcopi.[b]

[a]*add more detail* MCh, MA. [b-b] epscop . . . Colmán MO.

**1. Fabius.** The wording of the entry, which is placed second in MA (2), agrees with MA (1). MCh adds here a list of the relics kept at Christ Church.

### [1 August] f KAL. AUGUSTI

1 Romae, [a]sancti Petri[a] uincula.
2 [b]Apud Antiochiam,[b] natale sanctorum Machabeorum.
3 [c]Et in Italia,[c] Eusebii episcopi et confessoris.[d]

4 ᵉEt octoginta milium martyrum.ᵉ
5 Et in Hibernia, sanctorum confessorum Rioc et Mothuu.
6 Et aliorum plurimorum.

ᵃ⁻ᵃad sanctum Petrum ad MCh, MA. ᵇ⁻ᵇAntiochi(a)e MCh, (MA). ᶜ⁻ᶜApud Italiam, ciuitatem Uercellus sancti MCh, (MA). ᵈ*more detail* MA. ᵉ⁻ᵉochtmogae mór míle, 'eighty great thousands' MO.

**1. Ad sanctum Petrum.** Several *auctaria* of MU agree with the reading *sancti Petri (ad) vincula.*
**2. Machabei.** Between this and the previous entry, MCh inserted two others, corresponding to entries 8 and 9 in MA (1). Several *auctaria* of MU agree with MDr in placing this entry second and in reading *Apud Antiochiam.*
**4. Octoginta milia martyrum.** Although also in MO, I have been unable to trace this entry elsewhere in the martyrological record.
**5. Rióc, Mothuu.** MDr drew here on a source other than MO. Rióc is assigned to this day in MT and MG, but Mothuu would seem to be otherwise unrecorded. G. H. Forbes suggested that he might represent Nathí, but this would be an uncharacteristic corruption. His brother, A. P. Forbes, had rendered it [Molua].
**6. Alii plurimi.** This was probably added by the author of MDr.

[2 August] g IIII N. AUG.

1 Romae,ᵃ natale sancti Stefani papae et martyris.ᵇ
2 ᶜEt in Bithinia,ᶜ natale sanctae Teothotae cum tribus filiis suis, ᵈqui sub Diocletiano imperatore ignibus combustiᵈ ᵉmartyrii palmam sumpserunt.ᵉ

ᵃ*add* in cimiterio Calixti MCh, (MA). ᵇ*add more detail* MCh, MA. ᶜ⁻ᶜIn prouincia (*in right margin*) Bythinia, urbe Nicea (MCh), MA. ᵈ⁻ᵈ(ignibus combustorum) tempore Diocleciani MCh, (MA). ᵉ⁻ᵉ*more detail* MCh, MA.

[3 August] a III N. AUG.

1 Hierusolimis, inuentio corporis beatissimi Stefani protomartyris et sanctorum Gamalielis, Nicodimi et Abibon,ᵃ sicut reuelatum est a Domino beato prespetero Luciano.ᵇ
2 Item sancti ᶜIohannis Metrapolis.ᶜ

ᵃAbilon (*with* o *corrected from* d) MCh. ᵇ*add more detail* MCh, MA. ᶜ⁻ᶜMetropoil ind Eoin, 'John's metropolis' MO.

**1. Stephanus.** The unusually detailed nature of this entry may be due to a particular interest on the part of an Armagh author in the protomartyr (Introduction, § 3).
**2. Ioannes.** See MTur at 3 Aug.

84

TEXT

[4 August] b II N. AUG.

1  Natale sancti[a] Aristarchi, discipuli beati[b] Pauli apostoli.
2  Et apud Hiberniam, natale sancti confessoris Molua.[c]

[a]beati MCh, MA. [b]sancti MCh, MA. [c]Molua MO.

**1. Aristarchus.** MDr agrees here with MA (1) against MA (2).

[5 August] c N. AUG.

1  Natale[a] sancti [b]episcopi Casiani.[b]
2  Et [c]Herenti martyris.
3  Et sancti Asualti regis Anglorum[c].

[a]Augustidum, natalis MCh, (MA). [b–b]*reversed* MCh, MA. [c–c]Herenti . . . la hOsualt nóeb
. . . ardrí Saxan, 'H., with holy Oswald, high king of the Saxons' MO.

**1. Cassianus.** This is the second entry in MCh, MA.
**3. Osualdus.** Already in MA proper, the entry on Oswald was retained in the
Irish MA, with MCh reading: *sancti Oswaldi regis et martyris*. However, MDr
appears to have based his entry either on MO or on an *auctuarium* of MU, of
which several read: *Oswaldi regis Anglorum*.

[6 August] d UIII IDUS

1  Romae,[a] natale sancti Xisti episcopi et martyris,[b] et[c] sanctorum
   diaconorum[d] Felicissimi et Agapiti sub Decio imperatore.[e]
2  Et in Hibernia, natale sancti episcopi et confessoris Mochua.[f]

[a]*add* uia Appia, in cimiterio Calixti MCh, (MA). [b]confessoris MCh. [c]*add* (in) cimiterio
Pretextati MCh, (MA). [d]*after* Agapiti MCh, MA, *add* eiusdem MA. [e]*add more detail*
MCh, MA. [f]lam' Chua, 'with M.' MO.

**1. Xystus.** The text agrees with MA (1) against MA (2).
**2. Mochua.** The use of *episcopi*, which is absent from MO, deserves notice. The
saint was attached to Clondalkin, near Dublin, a church with no apparent episcopal ambitions.

[7 August] e UII IDUS

1  Apud Tusciam,[a] natale sancti Donati episcopi et martyris.[b]

[a]*add* ciuitatem Arecium MCh, civitate Aretio MA. [b]*add more detail* MA.

## [8 August] UI IDUS AUG.

1 Romae,[a] natale sancti Ciriaci martyris, [b]cum aliis numero uiginti et uno, qui omnes sub[c] Maximiano imperatore[d] gladio decollati[e] sunt.[b]

2 Et in Hibernia, natale sanctorum confessorum [f]Beoain et Colmani episcopi.[f]

[a]*add* uia Ost(i)ensi, mil(l)iario septimo MCh, (MA). [b-b]*different wording and more detail* MA. [c]iubente MCh. [d]Augusto, *add* pro confessione nominis Christi MCh. [e]iugulati MCh. [f-f]Beoain . . . Colmán epscop MO.

**1. Cyriacus.** The text of the entry agrees with MA (1) against MA (2).

## [9 August] g U IDUS

1 Uigilia sancti Laurentii.

2 Et[a] eodem die, Romae, sancti Romani militis [b]et decollati.[b]

3 Et apud Hiberniam, natale sancti [c]Nathi prespeteri[c] et confessoris.

[a]*om.* MCh, MA. [b-b]*more detail* MCh, MA. [c-c]Nathí . . . cruimther, 'N. the presbyter' MO.

## [10 August] a IIII IDUS

1 Natale[a] sancti Laurentii archidiaconi et martyris sub Decio imperatore.[b]

2 Et in Britannia, sancti confessoris Blaain.[c]

[a]*preceded by* Romae MA. [b]*om.* MCh, MA, *which add more detail.* [c]Bláan MO.

**1. Laurentius.** The text of the entry agrees with MA (1) against MA (2).

**2. Blaan.** Although this was in the Irish MA, with MCh reading: *Et in Scotia, sancti Blani abbatis*, MDr took the form of the saint's name from MO. The entry is also in the *Lubeco-Col.* and *Grevenus* versions of MU, which read: *In Scotia, sancti Blani episcopi et confessoris.*

## [11 August] b III IDUS

1 Romae,[a] natale sancti Tiburtii martyrys.[b]

2 Et in Hibernia, uiri sancti et confessoris [c]Airerain et sapientissimi.[c]

[a]*add* inter duos Lauros MCh, (MA). [b]*add (much) more detail* MCh, (MA). [c-c]Airerán n-ecnai, 'A. of the wisdom' MO.

**2. Airerán.** Various churches are attached to this saint in the Commentary on MO, including Clonard, the site of a house of Augustinian canons. This connexion may explain the use of the superlative *sapientissimi* (cf. Introduction, § 5).

## [12 August] c II IDUS

1 Romae, natale sanctorum Cristanti[a] et Dariae.
2 Et in Hibernia, natale sanctorum confessorum [b]Lasriani et Segini.[b]

[a]Crissanti MCh. [b–b]Lassréin . . . Segéni MO.

**1. Chrysanthus, Daria.** This entry is under 1 Dec. in MA, and is otherwise in MCh at 30 Nov. However, it is listed here in MH, as well as in the *Bruxellensis* version of MU.

## [13 August] d IDUS AUG.

1 Romae, natale[a] sancti Hipoliti martyris, sub Decio imperatore.[b]
2 Et apud Hiberniam, sancti confessoris Momedoc[c] natale celebratur.

[a]om. MCh, MA. [b]add more detail MCh, MA. [c]Momáedóc MO.

**1. Hippolytus.** The text agrees with MA (1).
**2. Momáedóc.** Some manuscripts of MO also write the name as *Momedoc*.

## [14 August] e XUIIII KAL. SEPTIMBRIS

1 Uigilia Assumptionis sanctae Mariae.
2 Eodem diae, natale [a]sanctorum confessorum et[b] prespeterorum Eusebii et[c] Grigorii.[a]
3 Natale sancti quoque Furtunati.[d]
4 Et apud Hiberniam, natale sancti confessoris Fachtnae.[e]

[a–a]different wording and much more detail MA. [b]ac MCh. [c]atque MCh. [d]Fortunati MO. [e]Fachtnai MO.

**3. Fortunatus.** Most manuscript witnesses to MO agree with MDr in spelling the name as *Furtunati*.
**4. Fachtna.** This saint, who was attached to the cathedral church of Rosscarbery, is also remembered in the *Grevenus* MU, which reads: *In Hibernia, Fachua episcopi.*

## [15 August] f XUIII KAL.

1 Assumptio[a] sanctae [b]Dei genetricis[b] Mariae [c]ad angelos.[c]
2 Et eodem die, apud Hiberniam, natale sancti confessoris Fir Da Crích.[d]

[a]om. MCh, MA. [b–b]om. MA. [c–c]dormicio MCh, (MA). [d]Fer Dá Chrích MO.

**1. Assumptio.** Some *auctaria* of MU agree with MDr in using the term *assumptio*.

## [16 August] g XUII KAL.

1  Romae, sanctae Serenae, uxoris quondam Diocletiani Augusti.
2  <sup>a</sup>Et<sup>b</sup> Metis, natale sancti Arnulfi episcopi et confessoris.<sup>a</sup>
3  Et sancti Adrionis<sup>c</sup> martyris.

<sup>a–a</sup>*om.* MA. <sup>b</sup>eodem die MCh. <sup>c</sup>Adrionis MO.

**1. Serena.** This is the second entry in MCh and MA.
**2. Arnulfus.** This entry is in MA at 18 July but, following Wandelbert, also here in MU.
**3. Ario.** MDr and MO share the corrupt form *Adrio(nis)* for *Ario(nis)*.

## [17 August] a XUI KAL.

1  Apud<sup>a</sup> Cessaream Capadociae, natale sancti Mammetis martyris.<sup>b</sup>
2  <sup>c</sup>Eodem quoque<sup>d</sup> die, octauae sancti Laurentii martyris.<sup>c</sup>

<sup>a</sup>*preceded by* Et MCh. <sup>b</sup>*add more detail* MCh, MA. <sup>c–c</sup>*om.* MA. <sup>d</sup>*om.* MCh.

**1. Mammes.** This is the second entry in MCh and MA.
**2. Laurentius.** The entry is absent from MA, but present in MU, which, according to its editor, J. Dubois, was the first historical martyrology to include the octave, in much the same wording as here.

## [18 August] b XU KAL.

1  Apud Prenestinam,<sup>a</sup> natale sancti Agapiti martyris sub Auriliano imperatore.<sup>b</sup>
2  Eodem quoque die, apud Hiberniam, natale sanctorum confessorum <sup>c</sup>Dega et Ernine.<sup>c</sup>

<sup>a</sup>*add* ciuitatem, mil(l)iario ab urbe tricesimo tertio MCh, (MA). <sup>b</sup>*add more detail* MCh, MA. <sup>c–c</sup>Mernóc . . . Daig MO.

**2. Erníne.** The form *Erníne* for *Mernóc* of the metrical text of MO is also in the Lb version of the Commentary.

## [19 August] c XIIII KAL.

1  <sup>a</sup>Natale sanctorum martyrum Magni et Andree,<sup>a</sup> cum sociis suis duobus milibus <sup>b</sup>quincentis nonagenti<sup>b</sup> et septem.
2  Et apud Hiberniam, natale sanctorum confessorum <sup>c</sup>Mochtai et Enain.<sup>c</sup>

<sup>a–a</sup>natalis sancti Magni seu sancti Andree martirum MCh, (MA). <sup>b–b</sup>quingentis nonaginta MCh, MA. <sup>c–c</sup>Mochtae . . . Enán MO.

**1. Magnus seu Andreas.** By reading *martyrum*, and taking Andreas as distinct from Magnus, the Irish MA followed MA (2).
**2. Mochtae.** This saint was in the Irish MA, with MCh reading: *et in Hybernia sancti* (added above line) *Mocthei confessoris.*

## [20 August] d XIII KAL.

1  Sancti<sup>a</sup> Samuelis profetae.<sup>b</sup>
2  Et<sup>c</sup> eodem die, natale<sup>c</sup> Forfirii,<sup>d</sup> hominis Dei.<sup>b</sup>
3  Et sanctorum martyrum <sup>e</sup>Diascori et Pampilii.<sup>e</sup>

<sup>a</sup>Natale MA. <sup>b</sup>*add more detail* MCh, MA. <sup>c</sup>*om.* MCh, MA. <sup>d</sup>(beati) Porphirii MCh, (MA). <sup>e–e</sup>Dioscorus . . . Pampil MO.

**1. Samuel.** Of the recensions of MA, this is in MA (1) only.
**3. Dioscorus.** Several manuscripts of MO also spell the name as *Diascorus.*

## [21 August] e XII KAL.

1  In<sup>a</sup> ciuitate Salona, natale sancti Anastassii martyris.<sup>b</sup>
2  Item, sancti Uincentii<sup>c</sup> martyris.
3  Et apud Hiberniam, sancti <sup>d</sup>episcopi et confessoris Senaich.<sup>d</sup>

<sup>a</sup>Et in MCh, MA. <sup>b</sup>*add more detail* MCh, MA. <sup>c</sup>Uincenti MO. <sup>d–d</sup>epscop Senach MO.

**1. Anastasius.** Although third in MCh and MA, this entry is also first in some *auctaria* of MU.

## [22 August] f XI KAL.

1  Romae,<sup>a</sup> natale sancti Timothei martyris.<sup>b</sup>
2  Et <sup>c</sup>Iuliani cum sociis suis.<sup>c</sup>

<sup>a</sup>*add* uia Ostiensi, in cimiterio eiusdem MCh, (MA). <sup>b</sup>*much more detail* MCh, MA. <sup>c–c</sup>maccraid . . . Emiliani, 'the youths of E.' MO.

**1. Timotheus.** This follows the wording of MA (2).
**2. Iulianus recte Emilianus.** None of the manuscripts of MO reads *Iuliani*. However, a saint of this name was commemorated on the previous day in MT, albeit without reference to companions. It may be that MDr simply misread a form like *Emulani* of the L manuscript of MO; cf. Schneiders, 'The Drummond Martyrology', p. 125n.

## [23 August] g X KAL.

1 <sup>a</sup>Apud Romam urbem,<sup>a</sup> natale<sup>b</sup> Hipoliti, Ciriaci,<sup>c</sup> et Archilai.
2 Et apud Hiberniam, natale sancti confessoris et episcopi Eogain.<sup>d</sup>

<sup>a–a</sup>in portu urbis Rom(a)e MCh, (MA). <sup>b</sup>*add* sancti MCh, MA. <sup>c</sup>Quiriaci MCh, MA. <sup>d</sup>Eogain MO.

**1. Hippolytus etc.** This is the penultimate entry in MCh and MA. The spelling *Ciriaci* agrees with that of MO.
**2. Eogan.** The church of this saint, Ardstraw, became a diocesan centre in the twelfth century, whence the description here of Eogan as a bishop, a detail absent from the early ninth-century MO. The entry was in the Irish MA, with MCh reading, corruptly: *Eodem die, sancti confessoris et episcopi Cogani.*

## [24 August] a IX KAL.

1 In India, natale<sup>a</sup> sancti<sup>b</sup> Bartholomei apostoli.
2 Et in Brittania, natale sancti Patricii<sup>c</sup> episcopi et confessoris.

<sup>a</sup>*om.* MCh. <sup>b</sup>beati MA. <sup>c</sup>SenPhátric, 'the senior P.' MO.

**1. Bartholomeus.** The wording agrees with MA (1).
**2. Patricius.** In placing the saint in Britain, MDr agrees with the Commentary on MO and the *Antverp. Maj.* and *Rosweyd.* versions of MU, which assign him to Glastonbury. MA (2) and most of the *auctaria* of MU record on this day a Patricius of Nevers; see Grosjean, 'S. Patrice d'Irlande', pp. 153–6.

## [25 August] b UIII KAL.

1 Romae, sancti<sup>a</sup> Genessi martyris.<sup>b</sup>
2 <sup>c</sup>Eodem die, Audonii archepiscopi.<sup>c</sup>

<sup>a</sup>sancte MCh, *preceded by* natale MA. <sup>b</sup>*add more detail* MCh, MA. <sup>c–c</sup>Apud Rotomagum, depositio Sancti Audoeni, episcopi et confessoris MCh.

**2. Audoenus.** This saint, the patron of Rouen, is more properly commemorated on the previous day, where he is recorded in MCh, MA (2), and MU, none of which describes him as an archbishop.

## [26 August] c UII KAL.

1 Romae, natale<sup>a</sup> sancti Zephirini papae, qui annis<sup>b</sup> octo, mensibus<sup>c</sup> septem, et diebus<sup>d</sup> decem, <sup>e</sup>Romanam rexit cathedram.<sup>e</sup>

<sup>a</sup>*om.* MCh, MA. <sup>b</sup>annos MCh, MA. <sup>c</sup>menses MCh, MA. <sup>d</sup>dies MCh, MA. <sup>e–e</sup>rexit ecclesiam MCh, MA, *after* qui.

**1. Zepherinus.** This entry is absent from MA (2). Also, by the standards of MDr it is unusually detailed.

## [27 August] d UI KAL. SEP.

1 Apud Capuam, natale[a] sancti Ruphi martyris.[b]
2 Item,[c] sancti Siagrii episcopi et confessoris.

[a]*om.* MCh. [b] *add more detail* MCh, MA. [c]Apud Augustudunum MCh, (MA).

**2. Siagrius.** This is the last entry of the day in MCh, MA.

## [28 August] e U KAL. SEP.

1 Beatissimi Hermetis martyris.[a]
2 [b]Et eodem[b] die in Affrica, natale[c] sancti Augustini episcopi et confessoris.[a]

[a]*add more detail* MCh, MA. [b-b]ipso MCh, MA. [c]depositio MCh, MA.

**1, 2. Hermes, Augustinus.** The wording in both entries agrees with MA (1) against MA (2). Although probably composed by an Augustinian canon (Introduction, § 5), unlike its treatment of John the Baptist on the following day, MDr here evinced little interest in Augustine himself.

## [29 August] f IIII KAL.

1 Romae,[a] natale[b] beatissimae[c] Sabinae martyris.[d]
2 Eodem die quoque,[e] decollatio sanctissimi[f] Iohannis Baptizae.[g]

[a]*add* in Aduentino, oppido Uindinense, ad arcum Faustini MCh, (MA). [b]*om.* MCh. [c]*add* et illustrissime MCh, MA. [d]*add more detail* MCh, MA. [e]ueneratur MCh, MA. [f]sancti MCh, MA. [g]*add more detail* MCh, MA.

**1, 2. Sabina, Iohannes.** The wording in both entries agrees with MA (1) against MA (2). The use of the superlative *sanctissimi* to describe John may be a pointer to the involvement of the canons regular of St Augustine, who favoured this cult, in the production of MDr (Introduction, § 5).

## [30 August] g III KAL.

1 Romae,[a] natale[b] sanctorum[c] martyrum Felicis et Audacti.[d]
2 Eodem quoque die, natale sanctarum [e]uirginum Agappae cum suis sororibus.[e]

[a]*add* uia Ostiensi, mil(l)iario secundo ab urbe MCh, (MA). [b]*om.* MCh. [c]beatissimorum MCh, MA. [d]Adaucti MCh, MA, *add more detail* MCh, MA. [e-e]húag Agappa . . . cona sethraib, 'the virgin A. with her sisters' MO.

**2. Agape.** Of the manuscripts of MO, two, R1 and P, agree with MDr in reading *Agappa*; the others read *Agatha*.

## [31 August] a II KAL.

1  Treuiris, natale[a] sancti Paulini episcopi et confessoris.[b]
2  Et in Britania, natale sancti confessoris et episcopi Aedain.[c]

[a]*om.* MCh. [b]*add more detail* MCh, MA. [c]Aedán MO.

**2. Áedán.** Several manuscripts of the Commentary on MO, together with some *auctaria* of MU, place this saint among the *Saxain* (*in Anglia/in Britannia*). The entry was also in the Irish MA, with MCh reading: *Item, ipso die, sancti Edani, episcopi et confessoris.*

## [1 September] b KAL. SEPTIMBRIS

1  Natale[a] Iesu Naue et Gedeon profetarum.
2  Et[a] apud Capuam,[b] natale sancti Prisci martyris, qui unus fuit de illis antiquis Christi discipulis.
3  Item, apud Cessaream Capadociae, beati Longini militis,[c] quem tradunt illum esse qui lancea latus Domini Saluatoris[d] [e]in cruce pendentis[e] aperuit.[f]
4  Item, eodem die, [g]Ciciliam sanctam uirginem[g] quidam ferunt esse coronatam.
5  [h]Item, Sanctonas,[h] beati Lupi episcopi.[i]

[a]*om.* MCh, MA. [b]*add* uia Aquaria MCh, MA. [c]*add* et martiris MCh, (MA). [d](nostri) Ihesu Christi (MCh), MA. [e-e]*reversed* MCh, MA. [f]*add more detail* MCh, MA. [g-g]Cicilia . . . co núagi, 'the virgin C.' MO. [h-h](Item), eodem die, apud Senonas MCh, (MA). [i]*add more detail* MCh, MA.

**3. Longinus.** This entry, which is confined to MA (1), follows an entry on Lupus in MCh and MA.
**4. Caecilia.** This entry from MO interrupts the entries taken from MA.
**5. Lupus.** Perhaps because there was some space left on the last line of the manuscript page, the author of MDr returned to MA for this entry.

## [2 September] c IIII N.

1  Natale sancti Iusti Lugdunensis episcopi.[a]
2  Item, sanctarum uirginum [b]Molothae et Teathotae.[b]
3  Et apud Hiberniam, natale sancti confessoris Senain.[c]

[a]*add more detail* MCh, MA. [b-b]Molthae Theodotam MO. [c]Senán MO.

**2. Molotha, Theodota.** In common with most manuscripts of MO, which read either *Molatha* (R1, F) or *Molotha* (L, Lb), MDr took *Molthae*, 'praise thou', to be the name of a saint.

**3. Senán.** This saint is a hibernicised form of Zeno of Nicomedia, with MDr taking its cue, as usual, from the Commentary on MO. Cf. Ó Riain, 'Some Bogus Irish Saints', pp. 6–7.

### [3 September] d III N.

1 Romae, passio<sup>a</sup> sanctae<sup>b</sup> Serapiae uirginis.<sup>c</sup>
2 Et apud Hiberniam, natale sanctorum confessorum <sup>d</sup>Luin, Colman et Meicc Nissi.<sup>d</sup>

<sup>a</sup>*add* et natalis MA. <sup>b</sup>beatae MA. <sup>c</sup>*add more detail* MCh, MA. <sup>d–d</sup>Colmán . . . Lon . . . Macc Nisse MO.

**2. Lon etc.** Although also in MCh, which reads *Eodem die sanctorum Lomani et Colmani et Macnisi*, this entry is placed there on the previous day. However, in MCh for this day, we find the entry: *Et in Hibernia; sanctorum confessorum Colmani sotiorumque eius*. The agreement between MCh and MDr, against MO, on the order of the names probably goes back to the Irish MA. To be noted also is the vernacular genitive case provided for two of the names.

### [4 September] e II N.

1 Moysi<sup>a</sup> profetae.
2 Et in Hibernia, natale sancti prespeteri et confessoris Ultani,<sup>b</sup> admirandae uitae ac sanctitatis uiri.

<sup>a</sup>Moysis MA. <sup>b</sup>Ultan MO.

**2. Ultanus.** It seems that the Irish version of MA, rather than MO, was MDr's direct source here; MCh reads: *Et in Hibernia, sancti Ultani, episcopi et confessoris*. However, the final words, absent from MCh, were added by the author of MDr, possibly because of the reputation of the saint – who was attached to the church of Ardbraccan, Co. Meath – as a biographer of St Patrick. The *Grevenus* MU reads here: *In Hibernia, Vultani abbatis*.

### [5 September] f N. SEP.

1 Romae,<sup>a</sup> beati Uictorini martyris.<sup>b</sup>
2 Et apud Hiberniam, natale sanctorum confessorum <sup>c</sup>Eulaig et Bricin.<sup>c</sup>

<sup>a</sup>In suburbano Rome, (natale) MCh, (MA). <sup>b</sup>*add more detail* MCh, MA. <sup>c–c</sup>Brecc . . . Eolang MO.

**1. Victorinus.** The text of MDr agrees with that of MU.
**2. Eolang, Bricín.** Some manuscripts of MO read *Eolach* (whence the genitive *Eulaig* in MDr). Also, some manuscripts of the Commentary gloss *Brecc* as *Breccín* (R1), *Bricin* (L).

## [6 September] g UIII IDUS

1  Natale[a] Zachariae profetae.
2  Et in Hibernia, natale sanctorum confessorum [b]Meic Cuilinn, Columbae,[c] et sanctae uirginis Scethi.[b]

[a]*om.* MCh, MA. [b–b]Macc Cuilinn . . . Scéthe . . . Coluimb MO. [c]*corrected from* Colombae
MDr.
**1. Zacharias.** The text agrees with MA (1) against MA (2).
**2. Mac Cuilinn.** Although the Irish form of his name was no doubt taken, with
the other saints, from MO, the entry relating to Mac Cuilinn was in the Irish
MA, with MCh reading: *Eodem die, Maculini episcopi et confessoris.* According to MT, but not MO, Mac Cuilinn was a bishop. The *Grevenus* MU likewise
describes him, albeit under a corrupt form of his name, as a bishop, with the
words: *In Hibernia, Mastulini episcopi.*

## [7 September] a UII IDUS

1  [a]Apud Nicomediam,[a] natale sancti[b] Iohannis martyris[c] sub Diocletiano imperatore.[d]
2  Item sanctorum martyrum [e]Zenoti et Anathassi.[e]

[a–a]*after* Iohannis MCh, MA. [b]beati MCh, MA. [c]*om.* MCh, MA. [d]*add more detail* MCh,
MA. [e–e]Senoti . . . Anathais MO.
**1. Iohannes.** MDr, but not MCh, follows MA (2) and MU in the arrangement of
the opening words here.
**2. Sinotus, Anastasius.** The L version of the Commentary on MO also spells the
first name with initial Z-. All manuscripts of MO likewise have the incorrect
spelling *Anath-*.

## [8 September] b UI IDUS

1  Natiuitas sanctae Dei genetricis[a] Mariae.[b]
2  Et[c] eodem die, apud Nicomediam, natale sancti Adriani martyris.[d]

[a]*-c- corrected from -s-* MDr. [b]*om.* MA. [c]*om.* MCh, MA. [d]*add more detail* MCh, MA.
**1. Maria.** The wording of the entry agrees with MA (1) against MA (2).

## [9 September] U IDUS

1  Serigii[a] papae, qui [b]tredecim annis Romanam rexit cathedram.[b]
2  Et eodem die, in Hibernia, natale sancti prespeteri et eximi abbatis
Ciarani.[c]

<sup>a</sup>Sergi(i) (MCh), MA. <sup>b–b</sup>sedit annos tre(s)decim Rome (MCh), MA, *add more detail* MCh, MA. <sup>c</sup>Chiaráin MO.

**1. Sergius.** In common with many other papal entries, this is confined to the second recension of MA, where it is in final position.

**2. Ciaranus.** This is also in MU, which reads: *In Scothia, Quaerani abbatis.* However, it is absent both from MA and, strangely, given the importance of the saint, also from MCh. The description of Ciarán as *eximius*, 'outstanding', is perhaps due to the presence in Clonmacnoise, Ciarán's church, of an apparently Augustinian foundation (Gwynn, Hadcock, *Medieval Religious Houses*, p. 165; cf. Introduction, § 5).

## [10 September] D IIII IDUS

1 Apud Affricam, natale<sup>a</sup> sanctorum episcoporum Nemessiani, Felicis, Lucii.
2 Et in Hibernia, natale beatissimi episcopi et confessoris sancti Finniani.<sup>b</sup>

<sup>a</sup>*om.* MCh. <sup>b</sup>Findbarr MO.

**2. Finnianus.** The saint was better known as Finnian than as Findbarr, as is clear from several manuscripts of the Commentary on MO. The praise given him here, by means of the superlative *beatissimi*, is probably due to the presence at Movilla, Finnian's church, of a house of Augustinian canons (Introduction, § 5).

## [11 September] e III IDUS

1 Romae,<sup>a</sup> natale sanctorum Prothi et Iacinthi.<sup>b</sup>
2 Et in Hibernia, sancti Sillani<sup>c</sup> confessoris.

<sup>a</sup>*add* uia Salaria uetere in cymiterio Bassille MCh, (MA). <sup>b</sup>Hyacinthi MA, *add more detail* MCh, MA. <sup>c</sup>Sillán MO.

**1. Protus, Hyacinthus.** The spelling of the saints' names in both MDr and MCh agrees with MO for the same day, i.e. *Prothi, Iacinthi*, as well as with several *auctaria* of MU.

## [12 September] f II IDUS

1 Apud urbem Tycinium,<sup>a</sup> natale<sup>b</sup> sanctorum confessorum Siri et Iuuentii.<sup>c</sup>
2 Item, in Hibernia, natale sanctorum sacerdotum et confessorum <sup>d</sup>Lasren et Ailbi et sanctae uirginis Fleide.<sup>d</sup>

<sup>a</sup>*add* qu(a)e et (P)appia dicitur MCh, (MA). <sup>b</sup>*om.* MCh. <sup>c</sup>Yuencij MCh, *add more detail* MCh, MA. <sup>d–d</sup>Ailbi . . . Fleid . . . Laissréin MO.

**1. Syrus, Iventius.** Use of the word *confessorum* follows MA (2).
**2. Fled.** Both MG and the Commentary on MO likewise took *fleid*, 'feast', of the metrical text of MO to denote a saint.

[l3 September] g IDUS SEP.

1  Apud Aegiptum, ciuitate Alaxandriae, beati Pilippi episcopi.ᵃ
2  Et in Hibernia, sancti confessoris et prespeteri Dagain.ᵇ

ᵃ*add more detail* MCh, MA. ᵇDagán MO.

**1. Philippus.** The wording here agrees with MA (1) against MA (2).
**2. Dagán.** The saint is also described as a *presbyter* in MT.

[14 September] a XUIII SEP.

1  Romae,ᵃ natale sancti Cornilii papaeᵇ sub persecutione Decii.ᶜ
2  Item, ᵈeodem tempore,ᵈ apud Affricam, nataleᵉ beati Cipriani episcopi subᶠ ᵍGalliano imperatore.ᵍᶜ
3  ʰEodem quoqueʰ die, exaltatio sanctae crucis.ᶜ
4  Et in Hibernia, natale sancti confessoris Coemain.ⁱ

ᵃ*add* uia Appia, in cymiterio Calixti MCh, (MA). ᵇepiscopi, qui MA. ᶜ*add more detail* MCh, MA. ᵈ⁻ᵈ*om.* MA, eodem die MCh. ᵉ*om.* MCh. ᶠ*om.* MA. ᵍUaleriano et Gallieno imperatoribus MCh, (MA). ʰ⁻ʰ(item) eodem (MCh), MA. ⁱChóemáin MO.

[15 September] b XUII KAL. OCTIMBRIS

1  Natale sancti Nicomedis martyris.ᵃ
2  Item,ᵇ sanctiᶜ Appri Tulensisᵈ episcopi et confessoris.

ᵃ*add more detail* MCh, MA. ᵇEodem die MCh, MA. ᶜfestiuitas sancti, MCh, depositio beatissimi MA. ᵈ*add* ecclesie MCh.

**2. Aprus.** The wording agrees with MA (1).

[16 September] c XUI KAL. OC.

1  Calcidonia,ᵃ natale sanctae Eufemiae uirginis, quaeᵇ sub Diocletiano imperatore,ᶜ ᵈdiuersis examinata suppliciis, nouissime bestiarum morsibusᵉ ᶠmartyriy cursumᶠ compleuit.ᵈ
2  Et in Hibernia, natale sanctorum confessorum et sacerdotum ᵍLasren Monenn et Lasren.ᵍ

ᵃ*further on in the entry* MA. ᵇ*add* martyrizata est MA. ᶜ*add* proconsule (autem) Prisco MCh, (MA). ᵈ⁻ᵈ*much more detail* MA. ᵉmorsu MCh. ᶠ⁻ᶠmartyrium MCh. ᵍ⁻ᵍMoninn . . . Laissrén . . . Laissrén MO.

**2. Laisrén (bis), Moinenn.** The homonymous saints are usually distinguished as (1) an abbot of Iona (d. 605) and (2) the patron of Mundrehid, Offerlane p., Co. Laois. An entry in the *Grevenus* MU for the previous day, which reads: *In Scotia, Mereni episcopi*, may refer to Moinenn who was associated with the church of Cloncurry, now tl./p., Ikeathy and Oughterany b., Co. Kildare. However, *Grevenus* also refers to Ninian, who is often wrongly identified with Moinenn, with the words: *In Scotia, Niniani episcopis et confessoris.*

[17 September] d XU KAL.

1  In Britania,[a] natale[b] sanctorum[c] Socratis, Stefani.
2  Niuiduni,[d] Ualeriani, Marci[e] et Gordiani.[f]
3  Et in Hibernia, natale sancti confessoris [g]Brocain et sanctae uirginis Riaglae.[g]

[a]Britannis MCh, MA. [b]*om.* MCh, MA. [c]*om.* MCh. [d]Niuiduno MA, *add* (natale) sanctorum MCh, (MA). [e]Macrini MCh, MA. [f]Cordiani MA. [g-g]Broccán . . . Riaglae MO.

**2. Valerianus etc.** It would seem from the manuscript, which shows no break at this point, that MDr felt the placename *Niuiduni* to be another of the saints mentioned in the previous entry.

[18 September] e XIIII KAL.

1  Natale sancti Mothodii,[a] Olimpii Liciae.[b]

[a]Methodii MA. [b]*add* et postea Tyri episcopi *and more detail* MCh, MA.

**1. Lycia.** This is the name of a place, not of a saint.

[19 September] F XIII

1  In Neapoli[a] Campaniae,[b] sanctorum Ianuarii[c] [d]cum binis suis diaconibus, Sosio et Festo[d], et lectore suo Desiderio.[e]

[a]*add* ciuitate MCh. [b]*add* natalis MCh, (MA). [c]*add* Beneuentane ciuitatis episcopi MCh, MA. [d-d]cum Sotio diacono Messane ciuitatis, et diacono suo Festo MCh, (MA). [e]*add more detail* MCh, MA.

[20 September] g XII

1  Natale[a] sanctae[b] Faustae uirginis et Euilassi.[c]
2  [d]Et[e] eodem die, uigilia sancti Mattei apostoli.[d]

[a]In Cizico, natalis MCh, (MA). [b]sanctorum MA. [c]*add more detail* MCh, MA. [d-d]*om.* MA. [e]*om.* MCh.

**2. Vigilia sancti Matthaei.** Vigils had not yet become a regular feature of the celebration of the more important feasts by the ninth century, which would explain why this feast is neither in MA nor in the slightly later MU. All *auctaria* of MU have it.

### [21 September ] a XI

1 Mattei[a] apostoli et euangelizae [b]qui primum[c] in Iudea euangelium Christi Hebreico[d] [e]scripsit sermone.[be]

[a]natale sancti Matthei MA. [b-b]*om.* MA. [c]primus MCh, MA. [d]Hebraeo MA. [e-e]sermone conscripsit MCh, MA, *add more detail* MCh, MA.

**1. Matthaeus.** The text agrees with MA (2) against MA (1).

••••••••••••••••••••••••••••••

Here a leaf of the manuscript has been lost.

••••••••••••••••••••••••••••••

### [11 October]

1 Et apud Hiberniam, natale sancti confessoris et prespeteri [a]Cainnich.
2 Et item, in Hibernia, sanctorum confessorum Fortcheirn et Lommain.[a]

[a-a]Fortchern, Lommán . . . Cainnech MO.

**1, 2. Cainnech, Foirtchern, Lommán.** The text resumes with entries on Irish saints for 11 Oct. Of these, that on Cainnech, patron of the cathedral church of Kilkenny, was in the Irish MA, with MCh reading: *In Hibernia, natalis sancti Channiche abbatis et confessoris.* Cainnech was also among the few Irish saints to find their way into MU, which reads: *In Scotia, sancti Cainichi abbatis.*

### [12 October] a IIII ID

1 Apud Rauennam,[a] natale sancti Edistii.[b]
2 Et in Hibernia, natale sanctorum confessorum [c]Fiacc, Fiachraich, et beatissimi ac uenerabilis uiri Mobi, qui absque nasso et oculis plana facie natus de mortua, ut ferunt, femina et conceptus.[c]

[a]*add* uia Laurentina MCh, MA. [b]Hedistii MCh. [c-c]Fiacc . . . Fiachraig . . . Mobíi . . . in clárainech, 'F., F., M. the flatfaced one' MO.

**2. Mobí.** Several of the manuscripts of the Commentary on MO refer to the circumstances of the saint's birth from a dead woman, and to the shape of his face. The author's obvious interest in Mobí may derive from the saint's role as tutor of Colum Cille, whose church of Iona is regularly singled out for special mention (Introduction, § 4). The saint was also among those commemorated on this day in the *Grevenus* MU, which reads: *In Scotia, Movei abbatis.*

## [13 October] III ID.

1  Commemoratio[a] sanctorum confessorum et martyrum quatuor milium noncentorum et[b] septuaginta septem.[c]
2  Et apud Hiberniam, natale sancti confessoris [d]Comgain et sanctae uirginis Finsiche.[d]

[a]Apud Africam MA. [b]*om.* MCh, MA. [c]sex MCh, MA, *add more detail* MCh, MA. [d-d]Comgan . . . Findsiche MO.

**1. Commemoratio etc.** This entry is on the previous day in MCh, MA, and MU.

## [14 October] II ID. OC.

1  Toronis,[a] depositio sancti Uenantii abbatis et confessoris.
2  [b]Romae, pasio[b] sancti Calisti[c] papae.[d]

[a]Turonis MCh, MA. [b-b]natale MA. [c]Calixti MCh. [d]*add more detail* MCh, MA.

**1. Venantius.** This saint is on 11 Oct. in MA (2), and on 13 Oct. in MU. However, the *Bruxellensis* MU agrees with the Irish MA in placing him here.

## [15 October] ID. OC.

1  In Gallia,[a] natale[b] sanctorum Maurorum.[c]
2  [d]Romae, quoque[e] sanctae Furtunatae.[df]
3  Remis,[g] sancti Basolii[h] confessoris.[i]

[a]Galliis MCh, MA, *add* apud Coloniam Agrippinam MCh, MA. [b]*om.* MCh, MA. [c]*add more detail* MCh, MA. [d-d]*om.* MA. [e]*om.* MCh. [f]Fortunate MCh. [g]Remis ciuitate, depositio MCh, In territorio Remensi, natale MA. [h]Bausoli MA. [i] presbyteri et confessoris MA, *add more detail* MA.

**2. Fortunata.** Although absent from MA, this name is included, in its masculine form Fortunatus, in MU. In MCh, it is added by the main hand in the margin.
**3. Bausolus.** Of the two recensions of MA, this saint is in MA (2) only.

## [16 October] XUII KAL. NOVIMBRIS

1  In Affrica, pasio[a] sanctorum martyrum [b]Ceicrae et aliorum[b] ducentorum septuaginta pariter coronatorum.
2  Et in Hibernia, sanctorum confessorum [c]Cere, Riagla et Colmain.[c]

[a]natale MA. [b-b]*om.* MA. [c-c]Ciar . . . Riaguil, Colmán MO.

**1. Caera.** The words *Ceicrae*, alias *Caerae, et aliorum* derive here ultimately from MH, but they are also found in some *auctaria* of MU.

**2. Ciar.** Although treated here as an Irish name, with genitive *Cére*, in fact the saint intended by the metrical text of MO was the African *Caera*, who is thus unwittingly duplicated.

## [17 October] XUI KAL.

1 In Gallia,[a] natale[b] sancti Florentii episcopi, qui multis [c]uirtutibus clarus[c] in pace quieuit.
2 Et sancti [d]Nicodimi martyris.[d]

[a]Galliis, ciuitate Arausica, MCh, MA. [b]*om.* MCh, MA. [c-c]*reversed* MCh, MA. [d-d]in martir Necodimus MO.

**1. Florentius.** This is the third entry in MA.
**2. Nicodemus.** Most, but not all, manuscripts of MO spell the saint's name with initial *Ne-*

## [18 October] XU KAL.

1 Natale sancti Lucae euangelizae, qui natione Syrus fuit[a] Antiochensis, arte medicus, [b]apostoli Pauli discipulus,[b] usque ad confessionem eius seruiens Domino sine crimine.[c]

[a]*before* natione MCh, MA. [b-b]discipulus apostolorum, (postea) Paulum secutus (MCh), MA. [c]*add more detail* MA.

**1. Lucas.** The wording here corresponds to MA (2).

## [19 October] a XIIII KAL.

1 Apud Antiochiam,[a] natale sanctorum Beronici, Pelagae et aliorum quadraginta novem.
2 [b]Et aliorum.[b]

[a]*add* Sirie MCh, (MA). [b-b]*om.* MCh, MA.

**1. Beronicus, Pelagia.** Of the recensions of MA, this entry is in MA (1) only.
**2. Et alii.** It is not clear which saints are intended, unless they be the *et alii martyres* referred to at the end of the Roman section of MT. Interestingly, MCh records *sanctus Auxilius episcopus et confessor . . . in Hibernia,* who is otherwise unknown on this day.

## [20 October] XIII KAL.

1 In Gallia,[a] natale[b] sancti Caprassi martyris.[c]
2 Et in Hibernia, sancti confessoris Fintain.[d]

[a]Galliis, Aginno ciuitate MCh, (MA). [b]*om.* MA. [c]*add more detail* MA. [d]Fintan MO.

## [21 October] XII KAL.

1 Apud Nicomediam, natale sanctorum martyrum Damassi,[a] Zoticii, Gaii,[b] cum duodecim milibus.[c]
2 [d]Et[e] in Colonia, undecim milium[f] uirginum.[d]
3 Et in Hibernia, sancti confessoris Munnu,[g] in uirtutibus et miraculis clarissimi uiri.

[a]Dasii MCh, MA. [b]Caii MA. [c]militibus MA. [d–d]om. MA. [e]om. MCh. [f]milia MCh. [g]Fintan MO.

**1. Duodecim milia/milites.** Already in the transmission of MH there is confusion here between *milibus*, 'thousands', and *militibus*, 'soldiers'; see *AASS* Nov. II.2, p. 565.
**2. Undecim milia virginum.** This is last in MCh.
**3. Munnu (Fintan).** The name *Fintan* is glossed as *Munnu* in several manuscripts of the Commentary on MO. Since the saint was very closely connected with Colum Cille and Iona (*Vita Columbae*, I.2), we may assume that the high praise reserved for him had the same origin as that lavished on Mobí at 12 Oct. (Introduction, § 4). Munnu was also remembered here by the *Grevenus* MU, which reads, corruptly: *In Hibernia, Nummi confessoris.*

## [22 October] XI KAL. NOVIMB.

1 Apud Adrionopolim Traciae, natale sanctorum Pilippi,[a] Eusebii, et Hermetis.
2 [b]Et[c] sancti Seueri.
3 Et[d] passio sancti Leogati martyris.[b]

[a]add episcopi MA. [b–b]om. MA. [c]in Tracia MCh. [d]add alibi MCh.

**1. Philippus etc.** Although not so in MA, this is also the first entry in MU.
**2, 3. Severus, Leogathus.** These two saints follow each other in the Roman section of MT. However, the (erroneous ?) assignment of Severus to Thrace in MCh points to the use as source at some stage of a non-breviate version of MH, where the placename immediately preceded the name of the saint.

## [23 October] e X KAL. NOVIMB.

1 Apud Antiochiam,[a] natale sancti Teodoriti prespeteri [b]et martyris.[b]
2 Et[c] in Colonia,[d] sancti Seuerini episcopi [e]et confessoris.[e]

[a]add Sirie MCh, (MA). [b–b]om. MCh, MA, *which add much more detail*. [c]om. MCh, MA. [d]Colonia ciuitate, natale MA. [e–e]om. MA, *which adds more detail*.

**2. Severinus.** This is in MA (2) only, where, as in MCh, it is the last of three entries. The tradition that Severinus was one of the first to be made aware of the death of Martin of Tours, who was much favoured at Armagh (Introduction, § 4), may explain his inclusion here.

## [24 October] f IX KAL.

1 Apud Affricam, commemoratio sanctorum martyrum Marciani et Satiriani, cum duobus fratribus eorum, et egregiae Christi ancillae Maximae uirginis.[a]

[a]*add more detail* MA.

**1. Marcianus etc.** This entry is in MA (cf. MU) on the 16 Oct. However, the *Bruxellensis* MU agrees with the Irish MA in placing the saints on the 24 Oct.

## [25 October] g UIII KAL. NOVIMB.

1 In Gallia,[a] natale sanctorum Crispini et Crispiniani.[b]
2 Et in Hibernia, natale sancti confessoris Lasriani,[c] [d]et sancti Gormani confessoris et perigrini et sanctissimi uiri.[d]

[a]Gallis, ciuitate Suessionis MCh, (MA). [b]*add more detail* MCh, MA. [c]Laissrén MO. [d–d]*om.* MO.

**2. Gormanus.** This entry has arguably an important bearing on the authorship of MDr. Otherwise found in MG, but in no earlier martyrology, Gormanus (Gormán) – probably the *anamchara*, 'spiritual advisor', of that name who died in 1055 – is there attached in a note to Cell Gormáin, now Kilgorman tl./p., Gorey b., Co. Wexford. Of greater interest, however, is the saint's description in MG as 'of the metres', which is paralleled here by a reference to his status as a 'pilgrim'. The author of MG was the poet, Máel Muire Ua Gormáin, literally 'descendant of Gormán', and, as I argue above (§ 6), Máel Muire's probable brother, Flann Ua Gormáin, who had spent many years abroad, possibly had a hand in the production of MDr. In that case, it may not be fanciful to suggest that Máel Muire and Flann respectively used 'of the metres' and 'pilgrim' to emphasise their affinity with Gormán. The basis of this perceived affinity may have been purely onomastic. On the other hand, although incapable of proof, the possibility that Gormán (d. 1055) was progenitor of this ecclesiastical dynasty, whose first recorded representative, Óengus, abbot of Bangor, died at Lismore in 1123, cannot be ruled out entirely.

## [26 October] a UII KAL.

1 In Hispania,[a] natale sanctorum Uincentii, Sabinae et Cristetis.[b]
2 Et in Hibernia, natale sanctorum confessorum [c]Nasad, Beoain, et Mellain, et filiarum uirginum filii Iair.[c]

<sup>a</sup>Hispanniis, Alela ciuitate MCh, (MA). <sup>b</sup>*add more detail* MA. <sup>c–c</sup>Nassad, Beóán, Mellán . . . ingen Maicc Iair, 'N., B., M., daughters of the son of I.' MO.

**1. Vincentius etc.** This entry is on the following day in MA.

### [27 October] b UI KAL.

1 <sup>a</sup>Uigilia beatorum apostolorum Simonis et Iudae.<sup>a</sup>
2 Et in Hibernia, natale sanctorum confessorum <sup>b</sup>Ercci, Abban, Odran, et Colmain.<sup>b</sup>

<sup>a–a</sup>*om.* MA. <sup>b–b</sup>Erc . . . Abbán . . . Odrán . . . Colmán MO.

**1. Vigilia etc.** As already seen at 20 Sep., the celebration of vigils of important feasts had not yet become common practice in the ninth century, which explains the absence of the entry in MA. Most *auctaria* of MU refer to it. As can be seen from the first entry on the following day, Iudas was also known as Thaddeus.
**2. Odrán.** Of the saints listed here, only Odrán, who was the abbot of Iona of that name, merited inclusion in the *Grevenus* MU, which reads: *In Hibernia, Orani episcopi et confessoris.*

### [28 October] c U KAL.

1 <sup>a</sup>In Persidia,<sup>a</sup> natale sanctorum<sup>b</sup> apostolorum Simonis Cannanei<sup>c</sup> et Tathei.<sup>d</sup>
2 <sup>e</sup>Et eodem die, sancti Terentii episcopi et confessoris.<sup>e</sup>

<sup>a–a</sup>*om.* MA, in Perside MCh. <sup>b</sup>beatorum MA. <sup>c</sup>*add* qui et Zelotes scribitur MA. <sup>d</sup>*add more detail* MCh, MA. <sup>e–e</sup>*om.* MCh, MA.

**1. Simon, Thaddeus.** As in the cases of Matthaeus (21 Sep.) and Lucas (18 Oct.), the text of this entry agrees with MA (2) against MA (1).
**2. Terentius.** This is neither in MCh nor in MA but several *auctaria* of MU refer on this day to Bishop Terentius of Metz.

### [29 October] d IIII KAL.

1 Ciuitate Tingitana, pasio sancti Marcelli centurionis qui capitis decollatione<sup>a</sup> martyrium consummauit.<sup>b</sup>
2 <sup>c</sup>Et<sup>d</sup> sancti Feliciani martyris,<sup>e</sup> <sup>f</sup>cum suis sociis.<sup>cf</sup>

<sup>a</sup>abscisione MCh, MA. <sup>b</sup>*add more detail* MCh, MA. <sup>c–c</sup>*om.* MA. <sup>d</sup>*add* alibi, passio MCh. <sup>e</sup>*om.* MCh. <sup>f–f</sup>*reversed* MCh.

**1. Marcellus.** This entry is on the following day in MA and MU.
**2. Felicianus.** This saint is mentioned, *cum sociis suis*, in MH (cf. MT), in the list for 30 Oct., where he is also remembered, with his companions, in some *auctaria* of MU.

## [30 October] e III KAL.

1 Apud Affricam, natale sanctorum martyrum Rogationi prespeteri et Felicissimi.[a]
2 Et apud Hiberniam, natale sanctorum confessorum [b]Colmani et sanctae uirginis Ernach.[b]

[a]*add more detail* MCh, MA. [b-b]Ernach óg . . . Colmán, 'The virgin E., C.' MO.

**1. Rogatianus, Felicissimus.** In MA this entry is placed on 26 Oct. However, in Florus the feast falls on 31 Oct. Moreover, it falls on this day in the *Hagenoyensis* version of MU.

## [31 October] f II KAL.

1 In Gallia,[a] natale sancti Quintini martyris.[b]
2 [c]Et [d]eodem die,[d] uigilia omnium sanctorum.[c]
3 Et in Hibernia, natale sancti confessoris Faelani[e] et Aeda.[f]

[a]Galliis, oppido Uirma(n)densi MCh, (MA). [b]*add more detail* MCh, MA. [c-c]*om.* MA. [d-d]*om.* MCh. [e]Faelán MO. [f]*om.* MO.

**1. Quintinus.** This is the last entry in MA.
**2. Vigilia etc.** This feast was introduced by MU, which gave it first place.
**3. Faelanus, Áed.** The first saint, Fursa's brother, of Fosses in Belgium, was in the Irish MA, with MCh reading: *eodem die, passio sancti Foilani martiris*. He is also in several *auctaria* of MU. The second, Áed, is nowhere else attested on this day, but may be identical with the Áed son of Róe included in MG in the list for 1 Nov.

## [1 November] g KAL. NOVIMBRIS

1 [a]Romae, natale sancti Cessarii martyris.[a]
2 [b]Et eodem[c] die,[b] festiuitas [d]omnium sanctorum.[d]
3 Et apud Hiberniam, natale sanctorum confessorum [e]Lonani, Colmani et Cronani.[e]

[a-a]*om.* MA (see note 1). [b-b]*om.* MA. [c]ipsa MCh. [d-d]*reversed* MA, *add more detail* MCh, MA. [e-e]Lonán, Colmán, Cronán MO.

**1. Caesarius.** The deacon Caesarius mentioned further down in the list for this day in MA had no connexion with Rome. The MCamb version of MH leads off with *Romae, natale sancti Cessari*.

## [2 November] a IIII N.

1 Natale sancti Uictorini Pictauiensis[a] episcopi.[b]
2 Et apud Hiberniam, natale sancti episcopi et confessoris Ercci.[c]

[a]Pictauionensis (*with* c *added later above line*) MCh, Pitabionensis MA. [b]*add more detail* MCh, MA. [c]epscop Erc MO.

## [3 November] b III N. No.

1 Apud Cessariam Capadociae, natale sanctorum Germani, Teophili, Cessarii et Uitalis.[a]
2 Et in Hibernia, natale sanctorum confessorum [b]Muirdebuir, Curcunutain, et Coemain.[b]

[a]*add more detail* MA. [b–b]Muirdebar . . . Corcunutain . . . Cóemáin MO.

**1. Germanus etc.** This is the second entry in both MA and MU.
**2. Muirdebar etc.** Here MCh adds the feast of Malachy of Armagh (d. 1148), placing the saint at Clairvaux *in Galliis*. If, as I argue (Introduction, §§ 3–5), MDr is likely to have been compiled at Armagh, one might expect to find Malachy in it. Indeed, Schneiders ('The Drummond Martyrology', p. 137) uses the fact of his omission as evidence to date the text to before 1148. However, with the notable exception of Gormán at 25 Oct., the author of MDr appears to have had little interest in contemporary or near-contemporary saints. He likewise omitted to mention several other notable Armagh clerics, including Malachy's predecessor, Cellach. Several *auctaria* of MU also commemorate Malachy on this, or on the preceding, day or, most commonly, on the 5 Nov.

## [4 November] C II N.

1 In Gallia,[a] natale sancti Amantii episcopi.[b]
2 [c]Et[d] in Nicea,[e] sancti Dominini.[cf]

[a]Galliis, ciuitate Redenis (Rotenus) MCh, (MA). [b]*add more detail* MCh, MA. [c–c]*om.* MA. [d]*om.* MCh. [e]*add* natalis MCh. [f]Domnini MCh.

**1. Amantius.** This is the second entry in MA.
**2. Domninus.** This is the final entry in MCh. It appears to reflect an entry for this day in MH, which reads: *in Nicea Domnini.*

## [5 November] d N.

1 Zachariae profetae, patris Iohannis Baptizae.
2 Et in Hibernia, sancti confessoris Colmain.[a]

[a]Colmán MO.

105

## [6 November] UIII ID.

1 In<sup>a</sup> Affrica, natale sancti Felicis martyrys.<sup>b</sup>
2 <sup>c</sup>Et<sup>d</sup> in Gallia,<sup>e</sup> depositio sancti Melanii episcopi et confessoris.<sup>c</sup>

<sup>a</sup>Zoniza (Toniza) MCh, (MA). <sup>b</sup>*om.* MCh, MA, *add more detail* MCh, MA. <sup>c–c</sup>*om.* MA. <sup>d</sup>*om.* MCh. <sup>e</sup>*add* ciuitate Redenis MCh.

**2. Melanius.** This saint is in MA at 12 Nov. However, he is commemorated here in several *auctaria* of MU, as well as in MH.

## [7 November] f UII ID.

1 Natale sancti Amaranti martyris.<sup>a</sup>
2 Et<sup>b</sup> sancti Millibordi<sup>c</sup> episcopi <sup>d</sup>et confessoris.<sup>d</sup>

<sup>a</sup>*add more detail* MA. <sup>b</sup>Hasternaco monasterio depositio MCh, In Frisia, natale MA. <sup>c</sup>Willibrordi MCh, MA. <sup>d–d</sup>*more detail* MA.

**1. Amarantus.** This is the second entry in MA.
**2. Willibrordus.** Of the recensions of MA, this entry is confined to MA (2). It is also in MU.

## [8 November] g UI ID.

1 Romae, natale sanctorum <sup>a</sup>quattuor coronatorum,<sup>a</sup> Claudii, Nicostrati, Simforoniani,<sup>b</sup> et<sup>c</sup> Castorii, Simplicii.<sup>d</sup>
2 Et in Hibernia, sancti confessoris Barrinni.<sup>e</sup>

<sup>a–a</sup>martyrum MA. <sup>b</sup>Simphoriani MCh, (MA). <sup>c</sup>*after* Castorii MCh, MA. <sup>d</sup>*add more detail* MCh, MA. <sup>e</sup>Barrfind MO.

**1. Claudius etc.** The fifth person, Simplicius, although also martyred, had been a pagan until converted shortly before his martyrdom, whence, perhaps, the use of *quattuor* in the Irish MA. However, among the *auctaria* of MU, there is likewise confusion as to the exact number, with several also favouring the phrase *quattuor coronatum.*
**2. Bairrfhind.** Some manuscripts of MO also spell the name as *Barrinn-.*

## [9 November] a U ID.

1 Romae,<sup>a</sup> sancti Teodori martyris.<sup>b</sup>
2 Et in Hibernia, sanctae uirginis Sinche.<sup>c</sup>

<sup>a</sup>Natale MA. <sup>b</sup>*add more detail* MA. <sup>c</sup>Sinche MO.

**2. Sinche.** This saint was in the Irish MA, with MCh also reading: *Et in Hibernia, sancte uirginis Sinche.*

## [10 November] b IIII ID.

1 Natale$^a$ sanctorum martyrum, Tiberii, Modesti et Florentiae.$^b$
2 Et in Hibernia, natale sancti Aeda$^c$ episcopi et confessoris.

$^a$*preceded by* In territorio Agat(h)ensi, in Cesarione (MCh), MA. $^b$*add more detail* MCh, MA. $^c$Aed MO.

## [11 November] c III ID.

1 In Gallia,$^a$ Toronis$^b$ ciuitate, natale sancti Martini episcopi et confessoris $^c$qui tres mortuos suscitauit $^d$multisque uirtutibus ac miraculis refulsit.$^{cd}$
2 Item,$^e$ eodem die $^f$in Frigia$^f$, pasio sancti Mennae martyris.$^g$
3 Et in Hibernia, sancti Corbri$^h$ episcopi et confessoris.

$^a$Galliis MCh, MA. $^b$Turonis MCh, MA. $^{c-c}$*om.* MA. $^{d-d}$et multas uirtutes fecit MCh. $^e$*om.* MCh, MA. $^{f-f}$in Scicia metropoli Prigie Salutarie MCh, (MA). $^g$*add more detail* MCh, MA. $^h$Carbre MO.

**1. Martinus.** The reference to the resuscitation of the three dead is also in MU. The concluding part of the entry, absent from MA (1), may reflect an addition to MA (2), which speaks of the miracles performed at Martin's tomb.
**3. Coirpre.** One manuscript of MO, viz. R1, also spells the saint's name with initial *Cor-*.

## [12 November] d II ID.

1 Apud Affricam, natale$^a$ sanctorum Arcadii, Paschasii, Probi $^b$et Ethigiani,$^b$ qui ex Hispania oriundi.$^c$
2 Et in Hibernia, sancti Cummini$^d$ confessoris.

$^a$commemoratio MCh, MA. $^{b-b}$*om.* MCh, et Eutychiani MA. $^c$*add more detail* MCh, MA. $^d$Chummain MO.

**2. Cuimmíne.** At least one of the manuscripts of MO, viz. P, likewise spells the saint's name as a trisyllable.

## [13 November] e ID. NO.

1 Rauenna,$^a$ natale sanctorum martyrum Ualentini, Solutoris,$^b$ Uictoris.
2 $^c$In Italia, natale sancti Columbani Scoti.$^c$

$^a$Ravennae MA. $^b$*add* et MA. $^{c-c}$*om.* MCh, MA.

**2. Columbanus.** This entry belongs more properly at 21 Nov., where it is also entered, in much the same words. Of the *auctaria* of MU, only *Bruxellensis*, which reads: *In Ytalia, monasterio Bobio, sancti Columbani abbatis, Scotici generis*, records the feast on this day. But see Overgaauw, *Martyrologes manuscrits*, II, p. 1056, and Introduction above, § 10. For a survey of the liturgical witnesses to his feast, see Gougaud, *Les saints irlandais*, pp. 56–61.

## [14 November] f XUIII KAL. DECIMBRIS

1  Apud Traciam,[a] natale sanctorum martyrum Clementini, Teothoti, et Filumini.[b]
2  Et in Hibernia, natale sanctorum confessorum Colmani,[c] et trium fratrum Gabran, Eoil, et Fachtnae.

[a]*add* ciuitate (H)eraclea MCh, (MA). [b]Philumeni MA. [c]Colmán MO.

**2. Gabrán, Eól, Fachtna.** Why these three brothers, who are also in MG, were chosen for inclusion is not clear. The church attached to the saints in MG, and in Ó Riain, *Corpus*, § 305, was Kiltoom, now a tl. name, Faughalstown p., Fore b., Co. Westmeath. MCh and several *auctaria* of MU record here the feast of Lorcán Ua Tuathail (Laurence O'Toole).

## [15 November] g XUII KAL.

1  [a]Antiochiae, natale sanctorum Donati, Restituti, Ualeriani, Fructuosae cum aliis duodecim.
2  Et [b]in Colonia[b] sancti Benedicti.[a]

[a–a]*om.* MA (see note). [b–b]*after* Benedicti MCh.

**1. Donatus etc.** This feast had also been placed here by Florus, before being transferred by MA, followed by MU, to 23 Aug. However, some *auctaria* of MU, among them *Bruxellensis* and *Grevenus*, likewise place the saints here.
**2. Benedictus.** This is preceded in MCh by an entry commemorating the dedication of a church, which may also apply in this instance. The Irish monastery of Groß-Sankt-Martin in Cologne was Benedictine.

## [16 November] a XUI KAL.

1  Natale sancti Eucherii, episcopi Lugdunensis,[a] admirandae fidei, uitae ac[b] doctrinae uiri.[c]

[a]*om.* MA. [b]et MCh, MA. [c]*add more detail* MCh, MA.

## [17 November] b XU KAL.

1  <sup>a</sup>Apud Pontum, natale sancti Grigorii<sup>b</sup> episcopi et martyris.<sup>ac</sup>
2  Et in Hibernia, natale sanctorum confessorum <sup>d</sup>Buadbeo et Dulech.<sup>d</sup>

<sup>a–a</sup>*om.* MA (see note). <sup>b</sup>*add* Neocessariensis MCh. <sup>c–c</sup>*add more detail* MCh. <sup>d–d</sup>Buaidbeo . . . Duilech MO.

**1. Gregorius.** MA, followed by MU, transposed Gregorius to 3 July. However, several versions of MU refer to him here, including *Bruxellensis*, which has a similar wording to the Irish MA.
**2. Dúilech.** This saint was patron of St Doolagh's, now a tl. name, Balgriffin p., Coolock b., Co. Dublin. Dúilech is also in MCh, which reads: *Eodem die, sancti Dulech confessoris.*

## [18 November] c XIIII K.

1  Antiochiae,<sup>a</sup> natale sancti Romani martyris.<sup>b</sup>
2  Et in Hibernia, natale sancti confessoris Ronain.<sup>c</sup>

<sup>a</sup>Antiochiam MCh. <sup>b</sup>*om.* MCh, MA, *which add more detail.* <sup>c</sup>Rónáin MO.

## [19 November] d XIII KAL.

1  Romae,<sup>a</sup> natale sancti<sup>b</sup> prespeteri et martyris, qui <sup>c</sup>sub Maximiano imperatore pasus est.<sup>c</sup>
2  <sup>d</sup>Et<sup>e</sup> sancti Simplicii episcopi.<sup>df</sup>

<sup>a</sup>*add* uia Appia MCh, MA. <sup>b</sup>*add* Maximi MCh, MA. <sup>c–c</sup>persecutione Maximini passus MCh, MA, *add more detail* MCh, MA. <sup>d–d</sup>*om.* MCh. <sup>e</sup>Augustoduno, natale MA. <sup>f</sup>confessoris MA.

**1. Maximus.** MDr omitted the saint's name, Maximus, probably through confusion with the emperor's name, Maximianus.
**2. Simplicius.** This is omitted from MCh, possibly by an oversight, but is present in MA (2).

## [20 November] e XII KAL.

1  Romae, natale sancti Pontiani papae.<sup>a</sup>
2  Et in Hibernia, natale sancti confessoris Fraechani.<sup>b</sup>

<sup>a</sup>*add more detail* MCh, MA. <sup>b</sup>Froechán MO.

## [21 November] f XI KAL.

1 In Italia,<sup>a</sup> natale<sup>b</sup> sancti Columbani abbatis.<sup>c</sup>
2 Et in Hibernia, natale sanctorum confessorum <sup>d</sup>filii Commain et filii Congnaid.<sup>d</sup>

<sup>a</sup>*add* monasterio Euouio (Bobbio) MCh, (MA). <sup>b</sup>*om.* MA. <sup>c</sup>*add more detail* MCh, MA.
<sup>d–d</sup>Macc Commain . . . macc Congraid, 'Sons of C., sons of C.' MO.

**1. Columbanus.** This entry is in MA (1) only. Although assigned by MH to 23 Nov., Columbanus is usually placed on this day by the Irish martyrologies. For a previous entry of the feast, see above at 13 Nov.
**2. Filii Congnaid.** Most manuscripts of MO in fact spell the name with medial -*gr*-. However, one witness to the metrical text and another to the Commentary show medial -*gn*-, as in MDr.

## [22 November] g X KAL. DE.

1 Romae, passio<sup>a</sup> sanctae<sup>b</sup> Ceciliae uirginis <sup>c</sup>et martyris.<sup>c</sup>
2 <sup>d</sup>In Campadocia,<sup>d</sup> <sup>e</sup>natale sanctorum Longini,<sup>e</sup> <sup>f</sup>Leontii et Fausti.<sup>f</sup>

<sup>a</sup>natale MA. <sup>b</sup>sancti MCh. <sup>c–c</sup>*om.* MCh, MA, *which add more detail.* <sup>d–d</sup>In Capadocia MCh, Apud Caesaream Cappadociae MA. <sup>e–e</sup>beati Longini militis et martyris MA. <sup>f–f</sup>*om.* MA.

**2. Longinus etc.** Longinus is here only in MA (2), with MA (1) placing him at 1 Sep., where MDr and MCh also commemorate him. His two companions are also in MH for this day.

## [23 November] a IX KAL. DEC.

1 Romae,<sup>a</sup> natale sancti Clementis <sup>b</sup>episcopi et martyris.<sup>b</sup>
2 <sup>c</sup>Item, sancti Fateri prespeteri et sancti Trudonis confessoris.<sup>c</sup>

<sup>a</sup>*om.* MA. <sup>b–b</sup>*om.* MA, *add more detail* MCh, MA. <sup>c–c</sup>*om.* MCh, MA.

**2. Faterus, Trudo.** Both saints are in MH for this day, Trudo, who is also in MU, being added in one of the *codices pleniores*. Faterus is commemorated here in the *Bruxellensis* and *Grevenus* versions of MU.

## [24 November] b UIII KAL.

1 Romae,<sup>a</sup> sancti Crisogonii<sup>b</sup> martyris.<sup>c</sup>
2 Et in Hibernia, sanctorum confessorum <sup>d</sup>Ciannan, Colman, Meic Lenin.<sup>d</sup>

<sup>a</sup>*add* natalis MCh, (MA). <sup>b</sup>Grisogoni MCh. <sup>c</sup>*add more detail* MCh, MA. <sup>d–d</sup>Cianán . . . Macc Lenéni . . . Colmán MO.

**2. Colmán, Mac Léinín.** There is no stop between the names, which may mean that Colmán mac Léinín only was intended. However, the metrical text of MO also refers to a separate saint named Colmán.

## [25 November] c UII KAL.

1  Natale sancti Petri Alaxandrini episcopi.[a]
2  Et[b] in Hibernia, sancti confessoris Finchon.[c]

[a]*add more detail* MCh, MA. [b]*om.* MCh. [c]Findchú MO.

**2. Finnchú.** This saint was in the Irish MA, with MCh reading: *In Hibernia sancti confessoris Finnchua.* As usual, MDr gave the name a genitive form.

## [26 November] d UI KAL.

1  Natale sancti Lini papae [a]et martyris.[a]
2  Et in Hibernia, natale sanctorum confessorum [b]Banban et Sericii episcopi.[b]

[a–a]*om.* MCh, MA, *which add more detail.* [b–b]Banbán . . . epscop Siric MO.

**2. Siricius.** Intended is the Roman pope Siricius (d. 399) who, although he is so described in the Commentary on MO, and in MG, was not Irish. MCh correctly assigns 'Syricus' to Rome.

## [27 November] e U KAL. DE.

1  [ab]Apud Augustunam,[b] natale[c] Amatoris episcopi.[a]
2  In Gallia,[d] natale sancti Maximi episcopi, [e]qui tres mortuos suscitauit.[e]
3  Et in Hibernia, sancti episcopi et confessoris Secundini.[f]

[a–a]*om.* MA. [b–b]Augustuduno MCh. [c]depositio MCh. [d]Galliis MCh, MA, *add* ciuitate Reg(i)ensi MCh, (MA). [e–e]*om.* MCh, *much more detail* MA. [f]Sechnall MO.

**1. Amator.** This saint was introduced by Usuard, albeit on the previous day, from MH, which explains his absence from MA. Alone of the *auctaria* of MU, *Bruxellensis* includes Amator on this day.
**2. Maximus.** The omission in MCh of the reference to the raising from the dead was probably due to an oversight.
**3. Secundinus.** This saint was in the Irish MA, with MCh reading, very extensively: *Eodem die, sancti Secundi, episcopi et confessoris. Qui Longobardorum nobili genere ortus, beatum Patricium ad Hiberniam secutus, post eum primus episcopatum tenuit. Ibique recto morum tramite exempla illius perfecte complens, quieuit in pace.* The elaborate nature of the entry in MCh, and the obvious interest in Patrick, point to Armagh as the place of origin of the Irish MA (cf. Introduction, §§ 3–5). The Lombardian origin of the saint, and the spelling *Secundinus* as opposed to *Sechnall*, are also referred to in the course of a long note in the Commentary on MO.

## [28 November] f IIII KAL.

1  Natale sancti Sostenis,[a] [b]discipuli apostolorum.[b]
2  Et Hibernia, tres [c]filii Bochrai[c] perrexerunt ad Christum.

[a]Sostenes MCh. [b–b]*reversed* MA. [c–c]maicc Bochrai, 'sons of B.' MO.

**2. Tres filii Bóchrai.** The Commentary on MO provided MDr with the number of sons involved, which is not specified in the metrical text.

## [29 November] g III KAL. DECIM.

1  Uigilia sancti Andreae apostoli.
2  Et in Hibernia, natale sancti Braendini[a] confessoris.
3  [b]Eodem quoque die, sanctae uirginis Fiadnatae.[b]

[a]Brénainn MO. [b–b]*om.* MO.

**3. Fiadnat.** This saint is also in MG, which presumably drew her name from MT, whose November lists have been lost. The saint may be the eponym of Tech Fi[a]dnatan, now the tl. name Tippeenan, Fontstown p., Offaly W. b., Co. Kildare.

## [30 November] a II KAL.

1  In ciuitate Patras, prouinciae Achaiae, natale sancti[a] Andreae apostoli, qui etiam [b]euangelium Christi[b] [c]in Scithia[c] predicauit.[d]

[a]beati MA. [b–b]*om.* MCh. [c–c]apud Sichiam MCh, (MA). [d]*add more detail* MCh, MA.

**1. Andreas.** The wording of the entry agrees with that of MA (2).

## [1 December] b KAL. DECIMBRIS

1  [a]Romae, natale sanctorum Candidae, Lucii, Marinae, Ambonii, et[b] Filati.[a]
2  Et in Hibernia, natale sancti confessoris Nessain.[c]

[a–a]*om.* MA. [b]*before* Marinae MCh. [c]Nessáin MO.

**1. Candida etc.** These names are also found together in MH, whence they found their way, in full or in part, into many *auctaria* of MU, including *Bruxellensis* whose version is very similar to the text of the Irish MA.

## [2 December] c IIII N.

1  [a]Romae, natale sanctorum Primitii,[b] Potentiani, Uiuiani.[a]
2  Et in Hibernia, sancti confessoris [c]Mael Odráin.[c]

[a–a]*om.* MA. [b]Primi (*with* ti *erased*) MCh. [c–c]Mael Odrán MO.

**1. Primiti[v]us etc.** Of these saints, only Uiuianus, albeit in the feminine form Bibiana, is found in MA. Originally, the, much corrupted, names came from MH. The *Bruxellensis* MU is close to the text of the Irish MA.

## [3 December] d III N.

1  [a]In Mauritania,[a] natale sancti Cassiani martyris gloriosi.[b]
2  Et in Hibernia, sancti confessoris Macc Aige.[c]

[a–a]Tingi, metropoli Mauritannie Tingitane MCh, (MA). [b]*add more detail* MCh. [c]Macc Oige MO.

**1. Cassianus.** The text agrees with MA (1) against MA (2). It is most unusual to find additional detail in MCh, identifying Cassianus's persecutor as 'Aurelius Agricolanus', over and above that found in MA.

## [4 December] e II N.

1  [a]Commemoratio sanctorum confessorum,[a] Armogastis,[b] [c]Archinimi et Saturi.[c]
2  Et in Hibernia, natale sancti confessoris [d]Fir Da Lethi[d] seu Berchain.

[a–a]In Africa, natale sanctorum MA. [b]Armogasti MCh, MA. [c–c]Arthinimi et Satiri MCh. [d–d]Fer Dá Lethe MO.

**1. Armogastus etc.** The wording of the Irish MA here corresponds exactly to that of Florus and the *Grevenus* version of MU. The entry is in MA (2) only.
**2. Fer Dá Leithe.** The alias, Berchán, is drawn from the Commentary on MO.

## [5 December] f N. DE.

1  In Affrica,[a] natale[b] sanctae Crispinae uirginis.[c]
2  Et [d]Iustini episcopi, Umbani, Filadii.[d]

[a]*add* apud Coloniam, (apud) Tebestinam (MCh), MA. [b]*om.* MCh. [c]*om.* MCh, MA, *which add more detail.* [d–d]Iustini ind epscoip . . . Umbani, Filadi MO.

**2. Iustinus etc.** The two latter saints, Umbanus and Filadus, who are here taken directly from MO, have already been commemorated at 1 Dec.

## [6 December] g UIII ID. De.

1  Natale[a] sancti Necolai,[b] episcopi[c] Mirorum Liciae.
2  [d]In Rauenna, sancti Blassii episcopi et martyris.[d]
3  Et in Hibernia, sancti confessoris Gobbain.[e]

[a]*om.* MCh, MA. [b]Nic(h)olai (MCh), MA. [c]*after* Liciae MA. [d–d]*om.* MCh, MA. [e]Gobbáin MO.

**2. Blasius.** This saint would not appear to be attested elsewhere on this day.

## [7 December] a UII ID.

1  Commemoratio[a] sanctarum[b] Dionissiae, Datiuae, Leontiae.[c]
2  [d]Eodem die, octauae sancti Andreae apostoli.[d]
3  In Hibernia, sancti episcopi et confessoris Buti,[e] admirandae sanctitatis uiri.

[a]*preceded by* Apud Africam MA. [b]sanctorum MA. [c]*add* et Emiliani medici *and more detail* MCh, MA. [d–d]*om.* MA. [e]Buiti MO.

**1. Dionysia etc.** This entry was moved from here, where it is also found in Florus and in the *Bruxellensis* MU, to the previous day in MA.
**3. Buite.** This saint was attached to Monasterboice, a church supposedly founded by Colum Cille, whence, perhaps, the greater than usual interest in him here (Introduction, § 4). The saint is also commemorated here in the *Grevenus* MU, which reads: *In Hibernia, Boetii confessoris*.

## [8 December] b VI ID.

1  Romae, natale sancti Euticiani papae.[a]
2  Et in Hibernia, sancti Hichtbrichtain,[b] confessoris Angli natione.

[a]*add more detail* MCh, MA. [b]nIchtbrichtáin MO.

**2. Ichtbrichtán.** The reference to the saint's English nationality may have come either from the text of MO, which places his origins *tar romuir*, 'beyond the sea', or from its Commentary, which places him in churches associated with *Sachsain*, 'England' .

## [9 December] c U IDUS.

1  Natale sanctae Leocadiae uirginis.[a]
2  Et apud Hiberniam, natale sanctarum uirginum [b]Fedelmae et Mugaine.[b]

[a]*add more detail* MCh, MA. [b–b]dí ingein Ailella, 'the two daughters of A.' MO.

**2. Fedelm, Mugain.** The names of the two virgins are taken from the Commentary on MO.

## [10 December] d IIII IDUS.

1  ᵃIn Hispania,ᵃ natale sanctae Eulaliae uirginis ᵇet martyris.ᵇ
2  Et in Hibernia, natale sancti confessoris Modimoc.ᶜ

ᵃ⁻ᵃApud Emeritam, Hispannie ciuitatem MCh, (MA). ᵇ⁻ᵇom. MCh, MA, *which add more detail.* ᶜModímóc MO.

## [11 December] e III IDUS

1  Danielis profetae.
2  Et in Hibernia, natale sanctorum confessorum ᵃEllteni et Mosenoc.ᵃ

ᵃ⁻ᵃIam' Senóc . . . Melteóc, 'M. with M.' MO.

**2. Eiltín.** The Commentary on MO provided MDr with the alternative, non-hypocoristic form of the name *Melteóc*.

## [12 December] f II IDUS

1  ᵃIn Alaxandria, sanctorum Sammonii et Emeriti.ᵃ
2  Et in Hibernia, natale sancti Finnianiᵇ abbatis et confessoris et magistri.

ᵃ⁻ᵃom. MA. ᵇFindén MO.

**1. Sammon(i)us, Emeritus.** Neither saint is in MA, but both are in MH for the previous day, whence their presence in later copies of MU, such as *Bruxellensis* – whose text is the same as the Irish MA – and *Grevenus*.
**2. Finnianus.** This saint appears to have been in the Irish MA, with MCh adding in different ink: *Et in Hibernia sancti Finniani episcopi et confessoris.* The special interest shown in the saint by MDr, which adds *magister* to the other titles, is probably due to the fact that Clonard, the saint's church, was the site of a house of Augustinian canons (Introduction, § 5). The saint is also commemorated here in the *Grevenus* MU, which reads: *In Hibernia, Finniani abbatis et confessoris.* He is remembered on the following day in the same words by the *Bruxellensis* MU.

## [13 December] g IDUS DECIMBRIS

1  ᵃIn Sicilia,ᵃ natale sanctae Luciae uirginis et martyris, quae ᵇsub Diocletiano imperatore passa est.ᵇ
2  Et in Hibernia, natale sanctorum confessorum ᶜColumbae et Baethain.ᶜ

[a–a]Apud Siracusas, Sicilie ciuitatem MCh, (MA). [b–b]passa est persecutione Diocleciani et Maximiani sub Pascasio consulari MCh, MA, *which add more detail.* [c–c]Báethán . . . Colomb MO.

## [14 December] a XUIIII KAL. IAN.

1 Apud Antiochiam, natale sanctorum martyrum, Deusi,[a] Zosimi et Teodori.

2 Et[b] sancti Nicassi episcopi [c]et martyris.[cd]

[a]Eleusi MCh, Drusi MA. [b]Remis, (natale) (MCh), MA. [c–c]qui capite truncatus est MCh. [d]*add more detail* MA.

**2. Nicasius.** Of the recensions of MA, this entry is in MA (2) only.

## [15 December] XUIII

1 Apud Affricam, natale[a] sancti Auriliani[b] episcopi et confessoris.[c]

2 Et in Hibernia, sancti confessoris Flainn[d] prespeteri et abbatis.

[a]*om.* MCh, *after* confessoris MA. [b]Valeriani MA. [c]*add more detail* MCh, MA. [d]Flaind MO.

**1. Valerianus.** The corrupt form of the saint's name in the Irish MA may be due to the occurrence of the placename *Aurelianis* at the beginning of the entry that followed in the source text. Exactly the same corruption is found in the *Bruxellensis* MU.

## [16 December] XUII KAL.

1 [a]Rauenna, natale sanctorum Ualentini, Naualis, Agricolae[b] et Concordii.[a]

2 Et in Hibernia, sancti confessoris Mofioc.[c]

[a–a]*om.* MA. [b]ae *is written as ligature* MDr. [b]Mobeócc MO.

**1. Valentinus etc.** The text is in agreement with the opening words of MH, which are: *Ravenna, natale Valentini, Novalis, Agricolae, Concordiae* (v. l. *Concordi*). MU, which drew the entry from MH, omitted Concordus, but its *Bruxellensis* version includes him. Finally, the use of the ligature *-æ* in the spelling of *Agricolae* is unparalleled elsewhere in the text in names of non-Irish saints.

**2. Mobeóc.** A form of the name with medial *-ph-*, the equivalent of *-f-* here, occurs as a variant reading in the manuscripts of MO. The saint is also in the *Grevenus* and *(Molanus)* versions of MU, which read: *In Hibernia, Beani episcopi (primi Aberdonensis) et confessoris.*

## [17 December] d XUI KAL.

1 <sup>a</sup>In Antiochia,<sup>a</sup> natale<sup>b</sup> sancti Ignatii martyris et episcopi, qui tertius post beatum Petrum<sup>c</sup> Antiochenam rexit cathedram.<sup>d</sup>

<sup>a–a</sup>Translatio MA. <sup>b</sup>*om.* MA. <sup>c</sup>*add* apostolum MCh, (MA). <sup>d</sup>ecclesiam MCh, MA, *add more detail* MCh.

**1. Ignatius.** To be noted is the use of *cathedram* (for *ecclesiam*), which is usually reserved for the chair of Peter in Rome. Also of interest is the inclusion in the Irish MA – if it is represented here by the additional detail in MCh – of an account of the saint's martyrdom, which is usually reserved for the main feast at 1 Feb.

## [18 December] e XU KAL.

1 <sup>a</sup>Laodiciae ciuitate, natale sanctorum Teothotini,<sup>b</sup> Basiliani.<sup>a</sup>
2 Et apud Hiberniam, sanctorum confessorum <sup>c</sup>Magnenn et Diucolla<sup>c</sup>, et sancti Flannain uenerabilis clarique uiri.

<sup>a–a</sup>*om.* MA. <sup>b</sup>Theotini MCh. <sup>c–c</sup>[Flannán] . . . Magniu . . . Diucaill MO.

**1. Theotecnus, Basilianus.** The wording here is very close to MH, which reads: *In Laodicia civitate, natale Teotecni et Basiliani.* The *Bruxellensis* and *Grevenus* versions of MU likewise record these saints in much the same wording and spelling as the Irish MA.
**2. Maigniu, Dícuill, Flannán.** Maigniu was in the Irish MA, with MCh reading: *In Hibernia, sancti* (added in margin) *Maigneni confessoris.* Some manuscripts only of MO include Flannán here. Why MDr should have had a particular interest in this saint, describing him as *uenerabilis clarusque uir*, is unclear, unless it be due to Flannán's status as a diocesan patron. Flannán's feast is also in the *Grevenus* MU, which reads corruptly: *In Hibernia, Flamiani episcopi.*

## [19 December] f XIIII KAL.

1 Apud Affricam, natale sancti Moysitis<sup>a</sup> martyris.
2 Et in Hibernia, natale sanctae uirginis Samthainne.<sup>b</sup>

<sup>a</sup>Moysetis MA. <sup>b</sup>Samthann MO.

**1. Moyses.** This entry is on the previous day in MA.

## [20 December] g XIII KAL.

1 <sup>a</sup>Romae, natale<sup>b</sup> sancti Zeferini episcopi.
2 In Tracia,<sup>c</sup> sancti Iuliani.
3 Item,<sup>d</sup> sancti Liberati.
4 In Oriente, sanctae Teclae uirginis.

5 <sup>e</sup>Et sancti Ignatii.<sup>aef</sup>
6 Et in Hibernia, sancti prespeteri et confessoris <sup>g</sup>Cruimthir Fhraich.<sup>g</sup>

<sup>a–a</sup>*om.* MA. <sup>b</sup>deposicio MCh. <sup>c</sup>*add* Gildaba, natale MCh. <sup>d</sup>Et alibi MCh. <sup>e–e</sup>*om.* MCh. <sup>f</sup>Ignati MO. <sup>g–g</sup>*om.* MO.

**1–4. Zepherinus etc.** Of the saints mentioned here, two (Iuli(an)us, Liberatus) were introduced by MU from MH. The two others (Zepherinus, Tecla) are also found in much the same wording as here in the *Bruxellensis* MU.
**6. Cruimther Fráech.** This saint is not in MO, but is noted on the previous day in MT. MG agrees with MDr, and with the *Grevenus* MU – which reads: *In Hibernia, sancti Fregi abbatis* – in placing the feast here.

[21 December] a XII KAL.

1 Natale beati Tomae apostoli, qui Parthis et Mediis euangelium predicans passus est in India.<sup>a</sup>

<sup>a</sup>*add more detail* MCh, MA.

**1. Thomas.** The text of the entry agrees with MA (2) and MU against MA (1).

[22 December] b XI KAL.

1 Romae,<sup>a</sup> natale triginta martyrum.<sup>b</sup>
2 Et in Hibernia, sanctorum confessorum <sup>c</sup>Tuae, Hitharnaiss, et Emin.<sup>c</sup>

<sup>a</sup>*add* uia Lauicana inter duos lauros MCh, (MA). <sup>b</sup>*add more detail* MCh, MA. <sup>c–c</sup>Tuae, Itharnaisc . . . la hEméne MO.

**2. Itharnaisc.** I know of no other example in an Irish source of a spelling of the name with final *-s(s)*, but the saint found his way into the wider MU transmission in this guise, with the *Grevenus* version reading: *Ethernasii confessoris.*

[23 December] c X KAL. IA.

1 Romae, natale sanctae Uictoriae uirginis et martyris.<sup>a</sup>
2 Et in Hibernia, sancti confessoris Mothemnioc.<sup>b</sup>

<sup>a</sup>*add more detail* MCh, MA. <sup>b</sup>lamm' Themnióc, 'with M.' MO.

[24 December] d IX KAL.

1 Uigilia natalis<sup>a</sup> Domini.
2 Et in Hibernia, sancti confessoris Mochua.<sup>b</sup>

<sup>a</sup>nativitatis MA. <sup>b</sup>lamm' Chua, 'with M.' MO.

## [25 December] e UIII KAL.

1 Bethleem[a] Iudae, natiuitas Saluatoris Domini nostri Iesu Christi secundum carnem.[b]

2 Et[c] eodem die, natale sanctae Anastasiae martyris.[d]

3 [e]Et sancti Anastassi apud Constantinapolim.[e]

[a]In Bethleem MA. [b]*add more detail* MA. [c]*om.* MCh, MA. [d]*om.* MCh, MA, *which add more detail.* [e–e]Constantinopolim, sancti Athanasii MCh, *om.* MA.

**1. Iesus Christus.** Exceptionally in terms of MDr, the initial letters of *natiuitas* and *Domini* are written as capitals. The wording of the entry agrees with MA (2), with several *auctaria* of MU, and with MH.

**3. Anastasius.** Some versions of MH, including MT, likewise add Anastasius to Anastasia here. The *Grevenus* MU assigns him to the following day.

## [26 December] f UII KAL.

1 [a]In Hierusolimis,[a] pasio sancti Stefani protomartyrys,[b] [c]Leuitae diaconi, qui a Iudeis lapidatus Gamalielo sancto sepultus est.[c]

2 Et in Hibernia, natale sanctorum confessorum Iarlathae[d] et Commain.[e]

[a–a]In oppido Ierosolimitano, uia Gaphargamula MCh, Apud Hierosolymam MA. [b]martyris (*in later hand*) MCh. [c–c]diaconi, qui lapidatus a Iudeis, et a Gamalieno sancto sepultus MCh (*which adds more detail*), *much different wording* MA. [d]*om.* MO. [e]Mochommóc MO.

**1. Stephanus.** The text of the entry is closer to MA (2) than to MA (1). The elaborate character of the entry and the additional detail of the Irish MA, as represented especially by MCh, may be due to the particular interest in this saint at Armagh, where his relics were revered (Introduction, § 3).

**2. Iarlaithe, Commán.** The Commentary on MO, as represented by R1, like-wise adds Iarlaithe of Tuam to Commán.

## [27 December] g UI KAL.

1 Natale b[e]atissimi[a] Iohannis apostoli et euangelizae, [b]quem Iesus plurimum dilexit.[b]

2 [c]Eodem die, ordinatio episcopatus sancti Iacobi fratris Domini, qui ab apostolis primus ex Iudeis Hierusolimis est episcopus ordinatus, et [d]predicando populis in Pascha fuste fullonis percussus martyrio coronatus est.[cd]

[a]beati MCh, sancti MA. [b–b]quem Ihesus amauit plurimum MCh, *which adds more detail*, dilecti Domini MA. [c–c]*om.* MA (see note). [d–d]medio Pasca martirio coronatus MCh.

**1, 2. Iohannes, Iacobus.** Both entries follow the text of the *libellus* attached to MA (Dubois, *Le martyrologe d'Adon*, pp. 5–7, §§ 4, 5).

## [28 December] a U KAL.

1 Bethleem, pasio[a] sanctorum infantum,[b] [c]qui sub Herodis regis[d] per-
fidia pro Christo [e]fuso sangine coronati sunt, numero duorum milium
ducentorum.[ce]

[a]natale MA. [b]infantium et lactentium MCh, innocentium MA. [c-c]*different wording and
more detail* MA. [d]*om.* MCh. [e-e]passi sunt MCh.

**1. Sancti infantes.** The number of the slain innocents, omitted from MCh and
MA, reflects the Commentary on MO, which gives the number of *infantes* [*qui*]
*occisi sunt* variously as *duo milia .cc.xx.* or *duo milia .cc.xl.*

## [29 December] b IIII KAL.

1 Hierusolimis,[a] Dauid regis.
2 Et in Hibernia, sancti confessoris [b]Airerain, mirandae sanctitatis et
sapientiae uiri.[b]

[a]*om.* MCh, MA. [b-b]la hAirerán n-ecnae, 'with A. of the wisdom' MO.

**1. Dauid rex.** MA (2) and MU also preface the entry with a reference to
*Hierosolymis.*
**2. Airerán.** The particular praise reserved for Airerán may be due to his attachment to Clonard, the site of a house of Augustinian canons (Introduction, § 5),
where, according to the Commentary on MO, he was *fer léiginn* or teacher.

## [30 December] c III KAL.

1 Oia[a] insola, sancti Florentii, Serenii[b], Pauli, Stefani, Papiani, Cleti.

[a]Oina (*written with* n-*suspension above* i) MDr, Oya MCh. [b]*om.* MCh.

**1. Florentius etc.** This entry, which agrees very closely both with MH and with
the *Bruxellensis* and *Grevenus* versions of MU, is not in MA. It is followed in
MCh by the crossed out entry *pape donati.*

## [31 December] d II KAL. IANUARII

1 Romae, natale sancti Siluestri papae.[a]
2 Item,[b] pasio[c] sanctae Columbae uirginis [d]et martiris.[d]
3 Et in Hibernia, sanctorum confessorum [e]Lochan et Ennae.[e]

[a]episcopi et confessoris MA, *which adds more detail.* [b]*om.* MCh, Apud Senonas MA.
[c]*om.* MA. [d-d]*om.* MCh, MA, *which add more detail.* [e-e]Lóchán ocus Endae MO, *the
remainder of this leaf together with the top of the next is filled by a listing of the stages of
the moon entitled* Annalis martyrylogii circulus consummatus.

**1. Silvester.** The text agrees with MA (1).

120

# CHAPTER THREE

# THE MARTYROLOGY OF TURIN: INTRODUCTION

## 1 *The Manuscript*

In a joint article published in 1981–2, the two Irish martyrologies in manuscript D IV 18 of the Biblioteca Nazionale in Turin, which had hitherto escaped scholarly notice, were edited by A. Vitale Brovarone and F. Granucci.[1] Of the two texts, the one edited by Brovarone represents a unique Irish version of the so-called metrical Martyrology of York (IMY), which is presented here in a new edition in Chapter Six.[2] The other, which I term the Martyrology of Turin (MTur), is the subject of the present chapter.[3] Previously edited by Granucci, it lists on each day a small selection of saints, Irish and non-Irish.[4]

The manuscript, which is described in great detail by Brovarone,[5] is made up of two separate and originally independent sections. One of these – the martyrological section – consists of five unpaginated folios, the other – a copy of Pope Gregory's Homily on the Gospels – is made up of 155 folios, numbered, as follows, in a mixture of arabic and roman numerals: 1–4, v–lx, 61–155 (i–lxxxxiii).[6] Since the hand responsible for the arabic numbering differs from comparable hands in other Turin manuscripts, Brovarone concluded that the manuscript was numbered

---

[1]  Brovarone, Granucci, 'Il calendario'. Due to the loss of a folio, the text for November and December is lacking.
[2]  Brovarone, Granucci, 'Il calendario', pp. 33–54.
[3]  For the distinction between martyrology and calendar/calendario, as preferred by Brovarone and Granucci, see Dubois, *Les martyrologes*, pp. 16–17.
[4]  Brovarone, Granucci, 'Il calendario', pp. 55–88, 38–113. For stringent criticism of the linguistic treatment of the text by Granucci, see Campanile, 'Per l'interpretazione'. I wish to thank Dr Patricia di Bernardo-Stempel for having drawn my attention to the review by Campanile.
[5]  Ibid., pp. 33–8.
[6]  The numbering, none of which is early, was done by different hands. The recommencement of the roman numbering at f. 61 is due to the division of Gregory's Homily into books.

before it arrived in the Biblioteca Nazionale, where, on the evidence of a catalogue of 1713, it has been since at least the early eighteenth century.[7] The originally separate character of the martyrological and homiletic parts of the manuscript is reflected in the distinctive quality of their vellum, characteristically Irish in the first, certainly non-Irish in the second.[8] Yet the two sections appear to have been brought together at an early period, which Brovarone would place, at the latest, in the fourteenth century.[9] However, although regular entries and corrections in the margins show that the homiletic section was frequently consulted in the medieval period, there is no scribal evidence of this kind to indicate that readers of the Homily also made use of the martyrological section.[10] The non-Irish hand that wrote the copy of Gregory's Homily is dated by Brovarone to the late eleventh century.[11] William O'Sullivan and Bernard Meehan, who examined a specimen of this hand at my request, would place it in the late eleventh or early twelfth century, between 1075 and 1125.[12] Moreover, they would regard it as more French than English. Michael Gullick would also place the 'probably not English' hand in the second half of the eleventh century.[13] The characteristically Irish single hand of the martyrological section, for its part, appears to Brovarone to be datable to the period between about 1050 and 1150, but this is by no means certain. As we shall see, a date earlier than the 1170s is in fact ruled out by the textual evidence of the martyrology.

The two martyrologies, one on the right-hand margin of the page, the

---

[7] Ibid., p. 33n. The presence of the martyrology in the manuscript is first noted in a catalogue drawn up in 1739. A library stamp occurs at the bottom of the first folio of the martyrological section and 'no. 90' is written at the top in an eighteenth-century(?) hand.

[8] Ibid., p. 35. From the loss of text, and also from the still discernible remnant of a lost folio, it would seem that the first section was originally a gathering of six folios.

[9] Ibid., p. 35n. Either then, or more likely later, trimming of the folios of the martyrological section led to a very slight loss of text on the top margins.

[10] William O'Sullivan made the tempting suggestion that the martyrological section, no longer perhaps of interest to the users of the Homily, might have covered the manuscript, thus helping to explain why one folio is now lacking. However, the vellum of the first folio, although somewhat affected by rubbing at the right-hand margin, is not unduly black, retaining even the clearness of the colouring of its initials. Slight traces of preservation in damp conditions and traces of the effects of woodworm are spread throughout the manuscript.

[11] 'Il calendario', p. 36. Brovarone does not exclude the possibility of an insular origin, but states that the hand is 'certainly non-local'. Some later hands in the margins appear to him to reveal French features.

[12] Private communication dated 6 Nov. 1986.

[13] In a letter to William O'Sullivan who kindly enlisted M. Gullick's opinion on the subject.

other in the centre of the lower margin, frame for each month from January to October a very elaborate apparatus of tables divided vertically into nineteen columns, corresponding to the Dionysian cycle of nineteen years, and horizontally into thirty-one columns, corresponding to the maximum number of days in the month. Where horizontal and vertical columns intersect, boxes containing numbers indicate the lunar dates. The lunar positions are shown by the use of rhombs and coloured circles. Framing the Dionysian apparatus on the left-hand side are ten other columns similarly divided vertically and horizontally under such headings as the names of the months (calculated in Roman notation), *septimanae* (from letters *a* to *g*), *aleae* (the letters of the alphabet), *branduib* (letters *a* to *l*), and so on, all of which served to interpret or otherwise complement the Dionysian tables.[14]

At the lower end of the left margin for each month, indications of unlucky days as well as some quatrains in Irish are added.[15] Entered along the top margin for each month are zodiacal signs, Hebrew, Greek and Latin names of the months, and other miscellaneous pieces of calendrical information.

The overall presentation of the martyrological section is of a very high standard. In addition to parts of the calendrical apparatus, capital letters of both initial and occasional other entries are illuminated, predominantly in red and yellow, but also in other colours, including various shades of green.

## 2  Sources of the Martyrology of Turin (MTur)

A cursory glance at the entries for each day reveals that the principal source of MTur was the early ninth-century Martyrology of Óengus (MO). A comparison of entries for the month of January already makes this abundantly clear, and nowhere perhaps more forcibly than at 20 Jan. where the four names, *Molaca, Moeca, Sabaist et Oenu*, correspond exactly in form and order of entry to the four saints listed in MO – *Molaca, Moecu, Sabaist ocus Oenu* – one of whom *Sabaist*, although non-Irish, bears a thoroughly hibernicised version of his proper name, *Sebastianus*. Equally striking agreement between the two sources occurs

[14]  Brovarone, Granucci, 'Il calendario', p. 41.
[15]  For these see Brovarone, Granucci, 'Il calendario', pp. 51–4, 65–6, and Campinile, 'Per l'interpretazione'. See also below at pp.

123

at 2 Jan., where MTur reads *Essodori* (for more correct *Isiridonus*), *Manchine, Scothine*, for MO's *Esodir, Manchéne, Scothíne*. And, although not always quite as obviously, on ten other days in January (12, 17, 21, 23, 26–31) agreement obtains between the two texts at least in relation to choice and, where more than one entry is involved, often also with regard to order of entries. Furthermore, on several occasions in January, the two agree against all other martyrologies on the detail of their entries. At 16 Jan., for instance, both refer to 2300 martyrs, of whom no trace appears to have been preserved elsewhere. Similarly, at 30 Jan., each specifies 150 otherwise unknown martyrs and, at 28 Jan., it is only they that record the martyrdom of ten virgins.

On the evidence, then, of the month of January, there can be no doubt but that MO was the principal source. Evidence for the use of other sources, although less plentiful, is nonetheless also present, among them a version of the *Martyrologium Hieronymianum* (MH), which is repre-sented in breviate form by the Martyrology of Tallaght (MT).[16] For example, taking the entries for 5 Jan. as a guide, of the first two saints, *Felicis, Simoin*, only the second occurs in MO, whereas both are in MT and, in the same order, in the full Hieronymian text of MH. Similarly, at 9 Jan., where the text of MT is lacking, MH contains a reference to *Secundus*, who was probably the model ultimately for *Secundinus*, a saint not in MO. At 1 and 6 Jan., where the entries in MO are para-phrased in Irish, MT agrees with MTur in reading *circumcisio Domini* and *epifania Domini* respectively. Similarly, at 7 Jan., where MO again paraphrases, the phrase *initium ieiunii* is otherwise found – outside Irish sources – only in the Irish-influenced *secunda manus* entries of the MCamb list MH.[17] At 15 Jan., MT too has an entry on the prophet Abacuc, absent from MO, which, as in MTur, it spells in Irish fashion with initial *Amb-*. Elsewhere evidence for dependence on a martyrology like MT is equally discernible. At 8 August, the two texts agree on the name, spelling and description of the first, relatively unimportant, saint, *Darii uirginis*, who is not in MO, and on the previous day, of the two saints listed – Sophronius and Cronanus – none is in MO, whereas both are in MT. The fact that these concordances are on successive days sug-gests that where a text other than MO was consulted its influence might continue for more than one day. A similar cluster occurs at 27–28 Aug., where Faustus and Augustinus, who are not in MO, correspond to two

16 Best, Lawlor, *The Martyrology of Tallaght.*
17 Lawlor, *The Psalter and Martyrology of Ricemarch*, p. 5.

entries grouped together in MT on the second day.

Besides a Hieronymian-type source, an historical martyrology of the kind first compiled by the Venerable Bede was also consulted.[18] This can be seen, for instance, at 8 Jan., where Timotheus and Egemonus (spelt *Agmemnonus*), of whom only the latter is in MO, are otherwise grouped together in the Munich version of the Martyrology of Bede.[19] Similarly, at 10 Jan., the second entry concerns Paul the Hermit, who owes his inclusion in the martyrological record to Bede,[20] and this also applies to Anastasius, the second saint at 22 Jan. However, both saints are likewise mentioned in the Irish copy of the Martyrology of York (IMY) on the same folio of the Turin manuscript, which may explain their presence in MTur. The influence of IMY is almost certain at 5 June, where Tatberctus, who is otherwise known only from the Martyrology of York and the Life of Wilfrid – which identifies him as an abbot of Ripon – is listed.[21]

The most popular historical martyrologies of the later medieval period were those compiled by Ado of Vienne and Usuard of Paris, and, although none of the January entries points directly to the use of either of these, entries elsewhere in the text allow for this possibility. For example, at 9 July, Anatholia and Audax, who are lacking in MO, are otherwise grouped together in both MU and MA.[22]

In sum, the results of our examination of the January entries, which are paradigmatic for the whole text, shows that, although MO was clearly the principal source, occasional use was also made both of a Hieronymian-type text similar to MT, and of a historical martyrology of the kind first made popular by Bede, perhaps a copy of MU or MA. The Irish version of the Martyrology of York (IMY), which was also in the historical tradition, and which is found on the lower margins of the same manuscript pages, likewise appears to have served as an occasional source.[23]

I now propose to examine more closely the evidence for the use of MO, the main source of MTur, with a view to providing a more precise context and narrower date for the composition of the text.

[18] For Bede's martyrology, see Quentin, *Les martyrologes historiques*, pp. 17–119.
[19] Although also in MH and MT, they are not grouped together in these.
[20] Of the Hieronymian texts only MCamb's *secunda manus* assigns Paulus to this day (Lawlor, *The Psalter and Martyrology of Ricemarch*, p. 6).
[21] Colgrave, *The Life of Bishop Wilfrid*, pp. 2, 136, 138, 140, 142, 150–1.
[22] Only Anatholia is in MH.
[23] For the text of IMY, see Chapter 6 below.

## 3  Use of the Commentary on the Martyrology of Óengus (MO)

Alone in the month of January, there are three examples of the use of the annotated version of MO, which I term the Commentary.[24] For example, at 3 Jan., Findlug is assigned to a place called Dún *'Flesce, uel Blesce'*, now Doon in Co. Limerick. Whereas the regular form of this placename, as attested in MT, seems to be Dún Ble(i)sce,[25] the alternative form proposed here, with initial *F*, is otherwise found only in the Commentary.[26] At 13 Jan., the identification of Poitiers (*Pictauis*) as the name of a city – *.i. nomen ciuitatis* – corresponds to a gloss in some versions of the Commentary, which reads *.i. ciuitas*. At 31 Jan., use of the hypocoristic *Moedóc*, as against *Aed* of MO, may be due to the fact that the former is regular in the Commentary.

Of the many other instances of apparent dependence on the Commentary spread throughout the text, one of the more striking is at 1 March, where a gloss on the name Senán, reads: *.i. Senan salmchetlaid epscoip Moynend*, 'i.e. Senán, psalmist of Bishop Moinenn'. As it happens, there was no connexion between Senán and Moinenn, but a note added to the name Moinenn by the Commentator, which accurately states *.i. sailmchétlaid epscop Moinenn*, '.i.e. a psalmist was Bishop Moinenn', was misread here as a comment on the juxtaposed Senán. Similarly striking examples occur at 25 May, where only the Commentary otherwise expresses the view that John was the Evangelist of that name, at 26 July, where *transformatio*, a Latin calque on MO's *tarmchruthad*, 'transfiguration', is otherwise also found in the Commentary,[27] and at 5 Oct., where the enigmatic initials *e. m.* very probably reflect a gloss in the Commentary, which reads: *ergna .i. maith*, '*ergna*, that is good'.

## 4  The Line of Transmission of the Commentary Source

As I have shown elsewhere, the Commentary on MO breaks down into two separate lines of transmission, one, denoted *z* – represented by manuscripts R1, P, and L – the other, designated *y* – preserved in manu-

---

[24] For the Commentary, see Stokes, *Félire Oengusso*.
[25] In the Life of Fintan, Findlug's brother, it is written *Dun Lescy* corrected to *Dun [B]lescy* (Heist, *Vitae*, p. 116), and the Lb version of MO has much the same spelling.
[26] As in manuscripts P and C.
[27] The only other attestation is in MDr, which is likewise derived from MO.

scripts B, C, F, L1, Lb and R2.[28] That MTur used a manuscript belonging to the *y* line of transmission is clear from a substantial number of
entries. For example, at 7 Aug., where the the the number of years slept by
the seven sleepers of Ephesus is at issue, *z* opts for 150 years, whereas *y*
and MTur prefer 305. Similarly, at 28 June, MTur and the F version of
MO agree in rendering the name of the martyr Fabianus as *Flauianus*
(cf. Lb *Flovianus*), as against the more correct *Fabianus* of the manuscripts of the *z* line. And again, at 27 Aug., the spelling *Rufin* of the *y*
line of transmission contrasts with *Rufi* of MTur and the *z* line.

## 5  *Date of the Martyrology of Turin (MTur)*

Use of the Commentary on MO, which cannot have been compiled
before about 1168–70, when its principal source, the Martyrology of
Gorman (MG), was completed, implies that MTur cannot be dated any
earlier than this. And since the Commentary was itself probably complete before 1174, this may be taken as an absolute earliest possible date
for the composition of MTur.[29] Indeed, its use of the *y* line of transmission of the Commentary points to a still later date. Whereas the original Commentary was demonstrably compiled at Armagh, possibly by
Flann Ua Gormáin (d. 1174) – brother or close relative of the author of
MG, Máel Muire Ua Gormáin – its *y* manuscripts derive from a
common source edited in a Midlands church, possibly Clonmacnoise or
Seirkieran.[30]

Dependence on a revised Midlands version of the Commentary does
not necessarily imply a very much later date of composition. As we have
seen, MDr, which also used the Commentary, albeit in its original form,
appears to have been composed at Armagh for the church of Glendalough already by 1174.[31] The countrywide network of Augustinian
priories would have facilitated the production and diffusion of copies of
the Commentary in quick succession, possibly leading to the rapid
emergence of a Midlands version. Although there can be no certainty
about this, therefore, it is entirely possible that a Midlands version used
by the author of MTur was already in circulation by the mid- to late

---

[28] Ó Riain, 'The Martyrology of Óengus'; idem, 'Die Bibliothek des Verfassers'.
[29] Ó Riain, 'The Martyrology of Óengus'.
[30] Ibid.
[31] Above Chapter 1.

1170s. If so, then MTur would also reflect the perceived need for new martyrologies that appears to have already led to the composition, successively, of MG, the Commentary on MO, and MDr.

## 6  *Provenance of the Martyrology of Turin (MTur)*

Although assigning the manuscript to Ireland, Brovarone and Granucci made no attempt to locate its provenance more precisely. This is understandable because, beyond the use of a typical Irish hand in the martyrological section, and the presence in the main section of the manuscript of a non-Irish, possibly French, hand, there is no palaeographical or codicological evidence to indicate a more exact provenance. However, the deficiency in this kind of evidence is amply remedied by textual clues, beginning, as we have just seen, with the use of a Midlands version of the Commentary. As I show in Chapter 6, a provenance in ancient *Mide*, now roughly the counties of Meath and Westmeath, would best suit the metrical martyrology (IMY) accompanying MTur in the lower margins of the manuscript, which gives prominence to a number of saints belonging to west Midland churches.[32] But, more significantly, three entries in the text of MTur itself point directly to a particular church in the east Midland area.

The first piece of evidence lies in the mention at 24 October of *féil Masán*, 'the feast of Masán', a very minor saint, of whom little else is known. Not only is his feast otherwise unrecorded, his genealogy has not been preserved, and no mention is found of him in the Life of any saint. In fact, the only other literary mention of this saint that I know of is in the Middle Irish tale *Aided Muirchertaig Meic Erca*, 'the death-tale of Muirchertach mac Erca',[33] where he is one of three saints sent by Cairnech of Tuilén – now Dulane, near Kells – to succour Muirchertach at Newgrange, near the river Boyne in Co. Meath. In view of the tale's setting in an area redolent of Tara and its kingship, Masán can scarcely be other than the patron of the church of Kilmessan, *Cell Massáin*, in the parish of the same name, Lower Deece barony, Co. Meath, about two miles or so south-west of Tara.[34]

A provenance in the Tara area is also indicated by an entry at 12 June

[32]  Cf. O'Sullivan, 'Additional Medieval Meath Manuscripts', pp. 68–9.
[33]  Nic Dhonnchadha, *Aided Muirchertaig Meic Erca*, pp. 17–18, 27.
[34]  Hogan, *Onomasticon*, p. 200, hesitantly places the name under *Cell Messáin*.

which concerns Ciarán of Belach Dúin, now Castlekeeran, the name of a townland and parish in Upper Kells barony, Co. Meath. The entry on Ciarán was drawn neither from the metrical text of MO nor from its Commentary. Furthermore, in other martyrologies Ciarán's feast is placed two days later on 14 June, which suggests that both the choice of the saint and the day assigned to him were determined by local consider-ations. It is hardly a coincidence, therefore, that an ecclesiastical site named Templekeeran, *Teampall Ciaráin*, is located three miles or so north-east of Kilmessan, near Tara.

These two pointers to the area around Tara are underpinned by entries from 15 to 17 June, where the scribe, who was doubtless also the author, wrote the names and descriptions of the saints, one for each day, in majuscule. This would suggest that more than usual importance was attached to the three feasts in question, of which two were of the infants Vitus and Cyricus.[35] The third, and only Irish, feast was that of Moling of Luachair, who is best known as the patron of Tech Moling, now St Mullins in the parish and barony of the same name in Co. Carlow.[36] However, just north of Tara, within a few miles of Kilmessan, close to Templekeeran, was the ecclesiastical site of Lismullin, in the parish of the same name, barony of Skreen. The Irish form of the name is un-attested, but the most likely derivation is from *Les Moling*, 'the dwell-ing place of Moling'.[37] Lismullin was the site of a convent of Augustinian nuns 'founded' under English auspices c. 1240, very prob-ably to replace the adjacent convent of Skreen established for Augustin-ian canonesses possibly as early as 1144, which appears to have merged

[35] These were respectively patrons of sufferers from nervous diseases and children. They are written large very probably because they made up, with that of Moling, a triduum of feasts.

[36] An important early church in its own right, St Mullins later became attached as a dependency to the priory of the Augustinian canons at Ferns. Coincidentally, a church apparently dedicated to Messán/Massán was also located within the parish of St Mullins, at Kilmissan. However, given the other indications of a Meath provenance, this is unlikely to have had any connexion with MTur.

[37] The similarly-named 'Lismolyn', now Lismalin, a townland and parish in Co. Tipperary, is derived by Hogan, *Onomasticon*, p. 493, from *Lis Moling* or, less likely, *Lis Muilind*, 'enclosure of the mill'. The Ordnance Survey Name and Letter Books likewise opt for the reference to a mill, but the nature of the site and the presence on it of a church which gave its name also to the parish favour a derivation from the name of the saint. A further dedication to Moling in the Meath area, likewise obscured by the lack of an Irish attestation, is at Stamullin, from *Tech Moling*, now a townland and parish name in Upper Duleek barony.

with Lismullin.[38] MTur is likely to have been compiled for this convent some time between 1174 or so and 1240, when English interests officially began to dominate locally, in which case the text would represent the earliest surviving manuscript written for an Irish convent of nuns. How the Gregory Homily became attached to it is a matter for speculation. The head house of the canonesses in this area was St Mary's of Clonard, which would doubtless have had external connexions of a kind sufficient to explain the presence in this part of Ireland of a manuscript of probable French origin.[39]

## 7 Scribal Characteristics

If both writing and colouring of the manuscript were his responsibility, then the author was certainly a versatile and well equipped clerical scholar. His command of both Latin and Irish was on the whole quite good, as can be seen in the general competence of his translations of the vernacular wording of his main source, MO. Sometimes he extrapolated names only, but he also regularly rendered into Latin whole phrases or sentences, as at 24, 25, 27 Jan., and 13, 15, 27 Feb. Having said that, his preference occasionally was for a hybrid approach, involving the retention of some Irish of the source, as at 22 Feb., where the Irish word *geini*, genitive of *gein*, 'birth' of MO, is retained in the middle of an otherwise fully translated sentence, and again at 27 Feb., where *airec capitis*, which reflects *airec cinn*, 'finding of the head' of MO, contrasts sharply with the use of *inuentionis capitis* two days previously to paraphrase another entry in MO.[40] Similarly, at 19 March, and again at 28 May, the word *aite*, 'fosterer', is taken from MO in conjunction with two names. Retention of the vernacular of the source in full, although rare, is also attested, as at 25 Sep., where we find *féil Barre ó Chorcaich*, 'the feast of Bairre of Cork', precisely the wording of MO.

This is not to say that the author of MTur was altogether free from

---

[38] Gwynn, Hadcock, *Medieval Religious Houses*, pp. 311, 322, 324. After the English 'foundation' of Lismullin, Skreen is no longer heard of in this context.

[39] For this see also O'Sullivan, 'Additional Medieval Meath Manuscripts', p. 68. His suggestion of a Duleek involvement in the bringing of the Gregory manuscript to the area was predicated on its association with Llanthony in Wales, and predated the discovery that Lismullin was probably the convent for which the martyrology was intended.

[40] For essays on translation policy in medieval Irish texts, see now Poppe, Tristram, *Übersetzung, Adaptation und Akkulteration*.

serious error. On the contrary, he was prone to occasional lapses on points of detail, transforming, for example, one saint into two on several occasions. This might have been due to a failure to read his source properly, as at 6 July, where *Moninne et Darerca* is written in mistake for *Moninne .i. Darerca*, or to the omission of the filial marker *mac*, as at 4 May, where *Mochua, Cummeni* should read *Mochua mac Cummeni*, 'M. the son of C.'. Failure to distinguish a hypocoristic from a non-hypocoristic form might also have led to duplication, as at 13 July, where Moshilóc duplicates Sillán, or again at 7 June, where Docholmóc and Colum are the same saint. Different cognomina used of the same saint in the source occasionally also lead to duplication, as on 29–30 October, where Colmán of Camas and Colmán moccu Gualae are in fact one and the same. Nor is this kind of error confined to Irish saints. At 1 July, Iudas and Thaddeus, who were identical, masquerade as separate persons, and, at 5 May, Eutimus and Iustinus are presented as names of different saints instead of as optional forms of one saint's name. The reverse procedure, involving the reduction of two separate saints to one, also occurs at 12 May, where Erc and Ailithir are combined in the manuscript to produce the incorrect single name Erc ailithir, 'Erc the pilgrim'.

The following points may be made regarding the author's treatment of the vernacular. The genitive of nouns/names ending in *-ach* is almost invariably written *-aich*, as in *Moenaich, Muiredaich, Cainnich, Domnaich*. Genitives of names ending in *-én* often become *-eain*, as in *Lasreain, Temneain*.The diphthong *áe/óe* is frequently written *uí*, as in *Muil* for *Máel, Buíthíne* for *Bóethíne*, but compare *Faelanus* (31 Oct.). In Latin names, *Fau-* regularly becomes *Fu-*, as in *Fusti, Fustini*.

## 8 *Editorial Method*

In preparing the text for publication, I have worked both from the manuscript itself, which I consulted in 1986 and again in 2000, and from a microfilm copy, received from the Biblioteca Nazionale of Turin, and now in the Boole Library, University College, Cork. Punctuation and capitals are editorial. Abbreviations in the mansucripts are silently expanded, unless I am not altogether certain of my rendering, in which case italics are used. (For a rendering of all abbreviations in italics, Granucci's edition may be consulted.) The ligature *-æ* is written out as *-ae* throughout. Except where they relate to the date of the feast, Roman numerals are regularly expanded. Although treated here as scribal, the length-marks may have been added later. Parentheses are used to indicate barely legible letters or words; square brackets denote editorially restored lettters or words. Slashes are used to set off words or letters added above or, much more rarely, below the line. Almost always the superscript words or letters were rendered necessary by an estimated lack of space on the line below. In some cases, however, they represent glosses, which I have inserted, as required, after the glossed names.

In preparing the notes, I have collated the text as widely as possible. All the Irish martyrologies have been used, including some lesser known texts of Irish authorship preserved on the Continent, such as the Karlsruhe Calendar whose entries are given here whenever appropriate.[41] I have also used the main continental martyrologies, such as the *Martyrologium Hieronymianum*, which has been particularly helpful where the Martyrology of Tallaght is lacunose.[42] The main historical martyrologies, beginning with that of the Venerable Bede,[43] have also been consulted. In citing the relevant text of other martyrologies, especially that of MO, I have sometimes silently introduced length-marks, changed capitals, and emended translations.

[41] For the text of this calendar, see Schneiders, 'The Irish Calendar'.
[42] Delehaye, Quentin, 'Commentarius Perpetuus'.
[43] I have used the text in Quentin, *Les martyrologes*, pp. 17–119.

# CHAPTER FOUR

# THE MARTYROLOGY OF TURIN: TEXT

## 1–6 January

Enarius triginta et unus *secundum* solem. triginta *secundum* lunam.
soer a rrith, riaguil o kl- En*air* co .iii. (i.ì.) Feb(r)ai.*

[1] a Kl.        Circumcisio Domini nostri Iesu Christi.
[2] b iiii n.      Essodori, Manchine, Scothine.
[3] c iii.         Findlog Duna Flesce, uel Blesce.
[4] d ii.         Marciani, Cessari.
[5] e N.          Felicis, Simoin, Ciar ingen (D)ub R(ea).
[6] f uiii id.    Epifania Domini. Nox horarum sedecim, /(et dies) octo/.

---

### JANUARY

*    The addition in Irish states, 'noble their course, a measure from the calends of January
     to the third [. . .] of February'.

1.   The first entry of the Hieronymian tradition, as also in MT (*Circumcisio Domini*) and
     MO (*luid fo recht*, 'he underwent the Law'), concerns the Circumcision; the historical
     martyrological tradition, as in MDr (*Octavas Dominicae natiuitatis*), leads off with
     the octave of Christ's birth.

2.   The spelling of the first name in *Es-*, more usually *Is-*, is characteristically Irish, as
     reflected by *Esiridoni* (MT), *Esodir* (MO) and *Esudir* (MG). Both the order of the
     entries and the spelling of the Irish names reflect MO (*Esodir . . . Manchéne* (v.l.
     *Mainchine*) . . . *Scothíne*).

3.   The nominative *Findlog* (cf. gen. *Findlugo*, MT), indicates the use of MO (*Findlug
     . . . Dúin Blésce*). The form *Flesce* is found in several versions of the Commentary on
     MO.

4.   Despite Granucci, *Cessari* is not a saint's name, but the remnant of an entry on the
     Dolphin constellation. A fuller version is preserved in the Karlsruhe Calendar
     (*Caesari delfinus matutino exoritur*). Marcianus, who is not in MO, is in MT
     (*Marciani*), but well down the list.

5.   The order of the first two saints agrees with MH (reversed in MT: *Semionis <bis> . . .
     Felicis*). Felix is not in MO (*Semeoin . . . Ciar ingen Duib Rea*, 'S., C. daughter of D.
     R.').

6.   The wording of the first entry, which rarely varies, agrees with MT (*Epifania
     Domini*). In MO/MG *epiphania* is translated as *bathes/bastedh*, 'baptism', in keeping
     with the Eastern view of the feast. In the West, it came to be regarded as the showing
     of Christ to the Jews. The (boxed) computistical addition applies to the month of
     January as a whole, and is thus usually either at the beginning or, as in the Karlsruhe
     Calendar, at the end of the month.

## 7–16 January

| | | |
|---|---|---|
| [7] g uii. | Initium ieiunii. |
| [8] a ui. | Timothi et Agmemno(n)i. |
| [9] b u | Secundini, Felicis et Uitali(s). |
| [10] c iiii. | Diarmait Inse Clothrann, Pauli he/remit(ae)/. |
| [11] d iii. | Eductio Christi de Egipto. |
| [12] e ii. | Muscendi, Laidgneain. |
| [13] f id. | Helarii epis[copi] Pictauis /.i. nomen ciuitatis/. |
| [14] g xix kl. | Cluceri diaconi, Felicis. |
| [15] a xuiii. | Ambucuc profetae, Itae Cl*uana* Cr(e)*dail*. |
| [16] b xuii. | Fursai et viginti tres milia martirum. |

7. Other than the entry by *secunda manus* in MCamb, the *initium ieiunii*, 'beginning of fast/Lent', paraphrased as 'the beginning of Jesus's Lent' in MO (*tossach corgais Íssu*) and MG (*tossech . . . a charghais*), would appear to be confined to Irish sources. The tradition may be reflected in the so-called *centessima Pascha*, 'Easter hundreth', which began on the day after the Epiphany. It survived in Irish-speaking areas, where *Inid* (from *initium*), 'Lent', was said to begin on the day after *Lá Nollag Beag*, 'Little Christmas' (6 Jan.).

8. Although widely separated there, these two saints, one only of whom is in MO (*Egemoni*), are in MT (*Timothei . . . Egemoni*). Together, they head the list in the Munich version of the Martyrology of Bede. There is no trace in the manuscript of Granucci's third entry, *M[oliba]*.

9. Secundinus is not in MO (*Felix find, Uitális*) and, unfortunately, the beginning of the list in MT is illegible. However, the list in MH includes Secundus.

10. MTur and MO (*Diarmait Inse Clothrann*) agree fully on the first saint. The second saint, who is also in the Karlsruhe Calendar (*Pauli primi heremitae*), was first introduced by Bede. However, as in the case of Anastasius (22 Jan.), MTur may have taken him from IMY. He was added to the MCamb by *secunda manus*.

11. Although commonly on this day in Ireland (*a hEgipt . . . tánic Macc . . . Muire*, 'out of Egypt came the Son of Mary', MO, *Eductio Christi de Aegypto*, Karlsruhe Calendar), as well as in parts of Germany (*AASS* Ian. I, p. 355) the feast is at 7 Jan. in both the Hieronymian and – beginning with Florus – historical traditions.

12. The selection of saints is as in MO (*Muscenti . . . Laidcenn*). Some manuscripts of MO spell the latter name with medial *dg/dc*. No other source, to my knowledge, spells the first name with *-nd-*.

13. The added words correspond to the gloss *.i. ciuitas* in the Lb and C versions of the Commentary on MO, whose metrical text describes Hilarius as *abb Pictauis*, 'abbot of Poitiers'.

14. The deacon's name is usually spelt in Irish texts with initial *Gl-* (*Gliceri* MT, *Gluceri* MO, *Glucerus* MDr). The spelling with initial *Cl-* is found in some versions of MH, including MCamb. MO (*Felix*) also lists the second saint.

15. MTur and MO (*Íte Chluana Credal*) are in full agreement on the form of the second entry. The spelling of the first name, which is not in MO, reflects the usual Irish spelling with initial *Amb-*, as in MT (*Ambucuc . . . profetarum*).

16. Only MTur and MO (*Fursai . . . trí míli for fichit . . . míle*, 'F. and twenty-three thousand') appear to preserve the number of martyrs. The spelling *Fursai* is also in MO.

## 17–28 January

[17] c xui.      Antoni monachi.
[18] d xu kl.    Mariae uirguinis. Sol in Aq(*uarium*).
[19] e xiiii kl.  Mariae, Marthae.
[20] f xiii kl.   Molaca, Moeca, Sabaist /et Oenu/.
[21] g xii.       Natiui*tatis* Agnae, Fanche.
[22] a xi.        Colma/i/n meicc hui Birnn, Anath[assii], /(Ua)[lerii]/.
[23] b x.         Pasio Seueriani.
[24] c ix.        Babilli episcopi cum tribus paruulis.
[25] d uiii.      Conuersio Pauli apostoli ad fidem.
[26] e uii.       Policarpi.
[27] f ui.        Agnetis cum decem uirguinib(us).
[28] g u.         Accobrain, pasio octo uirg[uinum].

---

17. This important feast, which is also recorded in the Karlsruhe Calendar (*Antonii monachi*), is likewise the only one listed in MO (*Antóin manaig*).
18. The attachment here of *uirguinis* to Maria seems peculiar to MTur. Most MO manuscripts have *tásc*, 'tidings' of Mary, but one (Lb) refers to her *bás*, 'death'. The astronomical comment (cf. Bede, *De temporum*, XVI = *Wallis*, p. 57) is also in the Karlsruhe Calendar.
19. The Irish tradition, as reflected by MT (*Marii*), MG (*Marius*), MO (*Mairi*), and MDr (*Marii*), mostly preferred Marius to Maria, sister of Lazarus. However, MTur agrees with MH (*Marthae et Mariae sororum Lazari*). The confusion was due to a separate entry at 20 Jan. on the Roman saints Marius and Martha. The Karlsruhe Calendar opts here for the feast of *cathedra Petri in Roma*, which is more usually assigned to the previous day.
20. There is full agreement here with MO (*Molaca, Mo Ecu, Sabaist ocus Oenu*).
21. The choice, but not the order, of saints is as in MO (*Fuinche . . . Agna*). A genitive of *Agna* in *-ae* is usual in Irish martyrologies, with the exception of MDr (*Agnetis*), which agrees with MA.
22. Anastasius (*quod recte*) is neither in MT nor MO, but he is in IMY (*Anathassius*), which was doubtless the source here. Moreover, following the historical tradition, where the feast had been commemorated on this day since Bede, MG (*Anastais*) also records the saint. The Karlsruhe Calendar (*Anastasii*) likewise commemorates him. The two other saints are shared by MO (*Colmán maccu Béognai, Ualerius*), but the reading *Birnn* for *Beognai* is otherwise unattested.
23. MO (*césad Sevriani/Seueriani* R1, L), which also stresses the saint's martyrdom (*césad*), begins with this feast. The Karlsruhe Calendar has Cornelius, who is second in the list of MT.
24. MO (*Babill . . . cona thriúr dedblén*, 'B. and his three orphans') has the same entry, adding *epscop* in the Commentary.
25. As in MDr, the phrase *ad fidem* may reflect *i mbathis*, 'into baptism', of MO, which likewise lists only Paul's conversion.
26. Polycarpus is also the only saint in MO (*Policarpi*).
27. Otherwise only MO (*Agnetis deich n-uagaib*, 'of A. with ten virgins') specifies the saint's companions.
28. MTur agrees very closely here in substance and wording with MO (*La hAccobrán . . . páis ocht n-uag*, 'with A., the passion of eight virgins').

29 January – 6 February
[29] a iiii.   Hipoliti, Pauli, (pu)gilde (*cons*) . . . /tini/.
[30] b iii.   Enain Rois, centum quinquaginta ma(r)tir*es*.
[31] c ii.   Moedóc (Ferna et M)uile (Anf)[aid].

Februarius viginti et octo *secundum* sol*em*, viginti et
novem *secundum* lu*nam*.
[1] d Kl.   Brigitae uirguinis sanctae /et multi martires/.
[2] e iiii n.   Oblatio Christi ad templum.
[3] f iii.   Simfroni, Lurentii, Felicis /martirum/.
[4] g ii.   Germani martiris, Cuandai.
[5] a N.   Agathae uirguinis et Epscop Mel /et Lucia/.
[6] b uiii id.   Andreas apostolus et Lucais /euangelistae/.

---

29. The first two entries are in the same order as the saints in MO (*Hipolitus, Paulus*). The final words are almost illegible due to scrubbing of the manuscript. They may represent the third and fourth names in MO (*Gillas, Constantinus*), but this is far from certain.
30. Otherwise only MO (*Cóecae ar cét martir . . . Enán Roiss . . .*, 'one hundred and fifty martyrs . . . É. of R.') agrees on the (round) number of martyrs.
31. Despite Granucci's <*meicc*> *o[che]*, the final word appears to be *Anfaid*, as in MO (*Aed . . . Ferna, Mael Anfaid*). The use of the hypocoristic *Moedóc* for *Aed* of MO may have been due to the fact that the former is regular in the Commentary.

FEBRUARY
1. Other than MO (*fross martir már . . . Brigit . . .*, 'a great number (lit. shower) of martyrs, B.'), only MTur refers to many martyrs.
2. The usual wording is *in templo praesentare* (Hieronymian tradition) or *Hypapante* (historical tradition), if Christ is given prominence, or *purificatio*, if the emphasis is on Mary. MO has *Airitiu Maicc Maire hi Tempul*, 'the reception of Mary's Son in the Temple'. For *Oblatio*, 'presentation, offering', see also Migne, *Ephem.*, cc. 761–2. The Karlsruhe Calendar has exactly the same wording as MTur.
3. Apart from its order of entries, MTur follows MH (*Natale Felicis, in Foro Simfroni Laurenti*). Despite both MTur and MO (*Felicis, Simfróni*), Symphron(i)us was not a saint; he gave his name to the *forum*.
4. Otherwise only MO (*Germán martir . . . Cuannae*), mentions Germanus here. He probably represents a corruption of the name Geminus, which heads the list in MH.
5. Agatha is also in MO, whose Commentary describes her as *uirgo*. Mel and Lucia belong more properly on the following day, where they are both also in MO (*epscop Mel . . . Lucia*). MTur agrees with MO in placing, *hibernice*, the title *epscop* before Mel.
6. The feast of Luke the evangelist was 18 Oct., so that his presence here may be due to a deliberate (?) corruption of Lucia, whose feast, as we have seen in the previous note, properly falls on this day. Andrew the apostle is nowhere else commemorated on this day, except in MO (*Andreas*), which begins with him. However, he figures in MH at 10 Feb.

TEXT

7–18 February

| | |
|---|---|
| [7] c uii. | Lommán Locha hUair. Ortus Uir/giliar*um* medie die occas*us* (*autem*) media nocte. |
| [8] d ui. | Hua ind ecis. |
| [9] e u. | Mochuaroc, Cairech Derg/ain/. |
| [10] f iiii. | Grigorii /et/ Cronani. |
| [11] g iii. | Epscoip Étchein, Gobbnait. |
| [12] a ii. | Damiani militis. |
| [13] b Id. | Modomnoc qui transuexit ap[es] /ad Hiberniam/. |
| [14] c xui kl. | Ualentini. |
| [15] d xu. | Triumphum Christi de diabulo. |
| [16] e xiiii. | Iulianae uirguinis. |
| [17] f xiii. | Fintain Cluanae Eidnech. |
| [18] g xii. | Ioseppi, Colmain, Meicc Dergain /et Moliba/. |

7. MTur, MO (*Lommán . . . Locha Uair*) and MT (*Lomman Locha hUair*) agree on the name and place of this saint. For the (mostly boxed in) astronomical note, more appropriate to the 8 Feb., see Bede, *De temporum*, XXX (= *Wallis*, p. 87). Cf. 7 Aug. below.
8. MO also has *Haue . . . ind écis*, 'descendant of the poet'.
9. The form *Mochuaroc*, which is also in MO and MDr, is rendered *Cuaran(us)* in MT and MG.
10. This feast of Gregory is nowhere else attested, but the second pope of that name is commemorated on 13 Feb. Furthermore, the *Liber de romanis pontificibus* places Gregory's death on 11 Feb. Crónán is the only saint of the day in MO.
11. Although the order of the entries is more in keeping with MT (*Etchani episcopi, Gobnat*), their choice, together with the position of the title before Étchén's name, points to MO (*Mogopnat . . . epscop Etchen*) as the likely source. The form *Gopnat*, without the prefix of endearment *mo-*, 'my', is in some manuscripts of MO, as well as in its Commentary.
12. MO (*Damán mil*, 'D. the soldier') hibernicised the saint's name.
13. MO (*Modomnóc . . . dobert . . . síl . . . mbech nÉrenn*, 'Modomnóc . . . brought . . . the race of Ireland's bees'), agrees very closely with MTur here. The ending of *ap[es]* has been made illegible by a hole made for binding.
14. Although apparently treated as part of a placename by MO (*hi rroí Ualentini*, 'in Valentine's field'), this saint, who is also in IMY, heads the list in MH.
15. The – otherwise unattested – wording here may be a translation of MO (*buaid Maicc Dé dia námait*, 'the Son of God's victory over his enemy'), which MDr (*uictoria Christi de diabulo*) also translated. The usual wording in other sources is: *diabolus recessit a domino*.
16. MO (*óig Iulianae*, 'I. the virgin') likewise lists Iuliana only.
17. There is close agreement here with MO (*Fintain . . . Chluana Ednig*).
18. Colmán and Moliba are in other Irish martyrologies, including MO (*Colmán, Moliba*), but Meic (Mac?) Dergáin otherwise figure(s) only in the lists of homonymous and youthful saints (Ó Riain, *Corpus*, §§ 707.282 (with Colmán), 709.133). Likewise, Iosephus appears to be listed in no other source on this day.

## 19–28 February

| | | |
|---|---|---|
| [19] a xi. | Marcelli, passio Pilippi /uel Pauli/ /et Colmani/. | |
| [20] b x. | Gaii episcopi cum triginta martiribus. | |
| [21] c ix. | Iucundi, Fintain Corach /et Uiroli/. | |
| [22] d uiii. | Ordinationis Petri in Antiochi(a) /et gene Lurentii/. | |
| [23] e uii. | Madiani apostoli. | |
| [24] f ui. | Luciani. Locus bissexti; littera huius diei in quo/cumque alfabéto híc et in ciculis geminattur/. | |
| [25] g u. | Inuentionis capitis Pauli, /Teolessii/. | |
| [26] a iiii. | Alaxandrii qui idola distru/xit/. | |
| [27] b iii. | Comgain Glinne Ussen, airec ca/pitis Iohannis/. | |
| [28] c ii. | Sillain Bennchoir et decem uirguines. | |

---

19. Most manuscripts of MO also read both *Pauli* and *páis*, '*passio*'. However, MS R1 has the correcter form *Publi*, which may lie at the base of *Philipi* here. No other Irish source has Colmán.

20. Otherwise only MO (*Gaius in t-epscop . . . imma slecht tricha*, 'G. the bishop about whom were slain thirty') refers to thirty martyrs; other sources, such as MH, specify ten or twenty.

21. The same saints, in different order, are listed in MO (*Fintain Choraig . . . Uiruli, Iucundi*).

22. Dependence on MO (*i nAntóig a ordan Petair . . . gein Laurint*, 'in A., the ordination of P., the birth of L.') is clear not only from the choice of entries but also from the use of *gene*, 'of the birth'. Laurentius occurs here in MH only in connexion with the road on which his church lay in Rome.

23. Although also so spelt in IMY, the form *Madianus* for *Matthias* may again point to the use of MO, which has *Madianus* in most of its manuscripts. The apostle's more usual day is 24 Feb.

24. The *bisextus* fell on 24 Feb.; cf. Bede, *De temporum*, XL (= *Wallis*, p. 109).

25. MO (*Teolis*) also has a corrupt form of the second name, which may be from *Theon* (gen. *Theonis*), as in the list of the following day in MH (cf. Ó Riain, 'Some Bogus Irish Saints', p. 7). MO (*fofrith cenn Póil apstail*, 'The head of apostle Paul was found') also has the first feast.

26. MO (*Alaxandri*) does not refer to the saint's destruction of idols.

27. The use of *airec*, 'finding', again shows dependence on MO (*airec cinn Iohannis*, 'the finding of John's head'). MO also has both Comgán and, in the Commentary, the name of the church.

28. MH names a substantial number of virgins on this day. Otherwise, however, only MO (*Silláin Bennchoir, deich noébóga . . .*, 'S. of B., ten holy virgins') gives the number as ten.

## 1–11 March

Martius triginta et unus *secundum* sol*em*, triginta *secundum* lu*nam*.

| | |
|---|---|
| [1] d Kl. | Senan /.i. Senan salmchetlaid Epscoip Moynend/, Moynenn, Moysi, Dauid C*ille* M*uine*. |
| [2] e ui n. | Nati*uitatis* Pauli senis, Fergnae /Iae/. |
| [3] f u. | Floriani, Musacru. |
| [4] g iiii. | Lucii. |
| [5] a iii. | Ciarain Saigre. *Septimus* embo*lismus*. |
| [6] b ii. | Uictorini. *Tertius* embo*lismus*, ultimus dies /accensionis lunae initii/. |
| [7] c N. | Perpetuae. |
| [8] d uiii. id. | Senain Inse C*athaich*. Primus dies accen/sionis lunae primi mensis/. |
| [9] e uii. | Pasionis quadraginta miled. |
| [10] f ui. | Constantini filii Elenae. |
| [11] g u. | Constantini Rathin. |

---

### MARCH

1. The choice of saints is as in MO (*Senán, Moinenn, Moisi, Dauid Cille Muni*). Also, the added gloss, although inaccurate since Moinenn had no connexion with Senán, derives from the Commentary, which reads: *.i. sailmcetlaid epscop Moinenn*, 'a psalmist was Bishop Moinenn'. MO also refers here to *Moysi*, 'Moses', who, as Grosjean ('Une prétendue fête', p. 417) showed, is a misreading of *Mac Nisse*, written with abbreviated *mac*.

2. The wording agrees with MO (*gein senPhóil . . . Fergnai Iae*, 'the birth of old P. . . . F. of I.'). Old Paul was thought to be Paul the First Hermit, whose feast fell on 10 Jan., where he is also listed in MTur. His presence here is due to a deliberate (?) misreading of *Primitivi*, a separate saint, whose name is followed immediately by *Pauli* in MH.

3. None of the manuscripts of MO (*Floriani . . . Momacru*), which mostly read *Moacru*, spell the Irish saint's name with medial -*s*-. Likewise, MDr, which depends on MO, reads *Moacro*, whereas MC, which also depends on MO, agrees with MTur.

4. MO (*Lucius*) mentions this saint only.

5. MO has *Ciarán . . . Saigre*. For the addition, see Bede's *De temporum*, XLV (= *Wallis*, p. 123).

6. MO (*Uictorini*) likewise mentions this saint only. For the astronomical addition, see Bede's *De temporum*, XLV (= *Wallis*, p. 123) and Migne, *Ephem.*, cc. 763–4.

7. This saint is also in MO (*Perpetua*).

8. MTur agrees on name and place with MO (*Senán Inse Cathaig*). For the astronomical comment, see Bede, *De temporum*, XLV (= *Wallis*, p. 123) and Migne, *Ephem.*, cc. 763–4.

9. The retention of *míled*, 'soldiers' reveals direct dependence on MO (*Bás cethorchat míled . . .*, 'The death of forty soldiers'). Cf. Karlsruhe Calendar (*pasio .xl. milium* (for *militum*?)).

10. Constantine's feast in the East is 21 May, but here MO (*Constantín*) is followed, the name of the emperor's mother coming from its Commentary (*Consatin mac Elena*).

11. MO (*Constantín . . . Rathin*) is closest here. MT does not name the church.

## 12–24 March

| | | |
|---|---|---|
| [12] a iiii. | Grigorii Romae. |
| [13] b iii. | Mochoemoc Leith. |
| [14] c ii. | Dionissii /episcopi/ et Saluatoris. |
| [15] d Id. | Iacobi et Lucais et Filiorum Nessání. |
| [16] e xuii kl. | Abbain et Finain Lobair. |
| [17] f xui. | Quiés Patricii episcopi. |
| [18] g xu. | Tiamda /.i. martir/. Sol in Arietem. Primus dies mundi /in quo facta est lux et angeli et animae/. |
| [19] a xiiii. | Lactein, Ioseph aite Iesu. |
| [20] b xiii. | Policarpi. |
| [21] c xii. | Benedicht et Endai Árne. |
| [22] d xi. | Pasio Secundi. Primus dies Pas/chae/. |
| [23] e x kl. | Momedoc et Filiae Feradaich. |
| [24] f ix. | Cammeni et Mochtae. Locus con[c]ur/rentium/. |

---

12. The formulation is the same as in MO (*Grigoir Ruamae*).
13. Compare MO (*Mochóemóc . . . ó Liath*, 'M. from L.') and MT (*Mocháemóc Léith*).
14. Dionysius otherwise receives the title of bishop only in MT and MO (*Dionis in t epscop . . . Saluator*, 'Bishop D., S ') which also agrees on the choice of saints.
15. These are also the saints of the day in MO (*Iacóib . . . Lucas . . . Maicc Nessáin*). Moreover, although also given precedence in MT, there the second name is provided with a genitive *Lucae*.
16. Again, although MT (*Abbani . . . Finani Lobair*) also gives prominence to these saints, it renders their names in Latin, unlike MO (*Abbán . . . Fínán . . . Lobur*) and here.
17. The use here of *quies*, 'death', is peculiar to MTur, but *episcopi* is shared with MT (*Patricii episcopi*), and with the Karlsruhe Calendar (*Patricii episcopi et apostoli Hiberniae*). MO reads *apstal hÉrenn . . . Pátraic*, 'P. the apostle of Ireland'.
18. MO (*Tiamdae*) also uses the Irish form of *Timotheus*. For the astronomical/chronological comments, see Bede's *De temporum*, VI (= *Wallis*, p. 27) and Migne, *Ephem.*, cc. 763–4.
19. The description of Joseph is exactly the same as in MO (*aite . . . Íssu*, 'fosterer of J.'). Despite Auf der Maur ('Feste und Gedenktage', p. 156), who traces its earliest mention to the Martyrology of Rheinau (c. 950), Joseph's role as fosterer of Jesus was established in Ireland in the early ninth century. The preference for *Lactein*, as against MO's *Molachtóc*, may relate to the use of *Lachtain/Lacteine* in the Commentary.
20. Polycarpus is otherwise unknown on this day, but MT (*Policarpi*) has him on the following day, possibly in error for a saint named Filocalus/Filocarpus in MH. MO has Policron(i)us, who is also in both MT and MDr.
21. There is close agreement here with MO (*Benedicht . . . Éndae . . . Arne*).
22. The wording *pasio Secundi* probably reflects MO (*ardchésad Secundi*, 'the great suffering of S.'). For the computation, see Bede, *De temporum*, XXX (= *Wallis*, p. 88).
23. The choice of entries is the same as in MO (*Ingen . . . Feradaig . . . Momáedóc*).
24. Although here in MT, MG and MDr, Camméne is in the Commentary on MO for the 25th. The *a* of *-ae* in *Mochtae* is open, whence Granucci's *Mochtie*. For the computation, see Bede, *De temporum*, LIII (= *Wallis*, p. 136).

## 25 March – 3 April

[25] g uiii.    Conceptio Christi et pasio secundum quosdam.
[26] a uii.     Mochelloc et Sinchill Cille Aichid.
[27] b ui.      Resurrectio Domini secundum quosdam.
[28] c u.       Mariae Magdalenae.
[29] d iiii.    Grigorii Nazanseni, .i. Nazon /no*men* oppidis o
                n-anmnigther in Grigoir/.
[30] e iii.     Mochua Balla et Tola Craib*dig*.
[31] f ii.      Pilippi apostoli et Anissi /cruciati/.

Aprilis triginta *secundum* sol*em*, viginti et novem *secundum* luna*m*.
[1] g Kl.       Ambrosii et Mariae.
[2] a iiii n.   Ezechelis profetae.
[3] b iii.      Xisti papae.

---

25. The words *conceptio Christi* are also in IMY. The use of *pasio* for the more usual *crucifixus est* (MH, MT)/*crochad* (MO) may reflect a note in MO's Commentary (*pasus est eodem die*).
26. MO (*Mochellóc . . . in tSinchill . . . Cille Achid*) agrees on choice, order and description of the two saints.
27. Notice of the resurrection on this day, although regular in Hieronymian texts, is rare in the historical tradition, which may explain the use of *secundum quosdam*. MO reads: *asréracht Íssu*, 'J. has arisen'.
28. Maria is also the only saint in MO (*Maria*). See the note to MDr on this day.
29. The placing here of Gregory of Nazianzus, on what was a feast of Pope Gregory, seems to be confined to Irish martyologies, such as MO (*Grigoir Nazanzeni*). The note on the name, with the redundant -*s* of *oppidis* plainly legible, is found neither in MT nor in MO. However, the entry on Gregory at his proper day of 9 May in MU and MA refers to *Nazianzi oppidum*.
30. As against MT, which prefers here the non-hypocoristic *Crónán* for *Mochua*, MTur agrees with MO (*Mochuae Ballae . . . Tolai Chrabdig*).
31. Of the manner of Anesus's martyrdom nothing is known. However, MTur clearly follows MO (*Croch . . . Anissi . . .*, 'The cross of Anesus'), in his use of *cruciatus*, which is nowhere else attested. Likewise elsewhere unattested here, even in MO and its Commentary, is the feast of Philip the Apostle. However, on the previous day in Hieronymian texts, including MT, we find *Philopoli*, which might easily have given rise, by accident or design, to *Philippi apostoli*.

### APRIL

1. MO (*Ambrois . . . Maire*) has the same order and choice of entries. The inclusion of Ambrosius, whose feast fell on 4 April, accords with Irish tradition, as also in MT, MO and MDr. MG, which followed MU, and the Karlsruhe Calendar place him on the 4th. In MT, as also in MH, Maria is given precedence over Ambrosius.
2. Ezechiel's usual day is 10 April. No other source has him here.
3. As on the previous day, this feast, which normally falls on 6 Aug., is out of place here. However, it is also in some versions of MH (but not MT), as well as the *Liber pontificalis*.

## 4–15 April

[4] c ii.     Tigernaich Cluana Eóis.

[5] d N.     Becain meicc Culae, Cairech, incensio babtismi Patrici in Ibernia.

[6] e uiii id.     Herennii episcopi.

[7] f uii.     Fina/i/n Cam Chinn Ettich.

[8] g ui.     Enarii marteris.

[9] a u.     Quadrati marteris.

[10] b iiii.     Cuandai Ruis Eó.

[11] c iii.     Moedóc huae Dunlaing.

[12] d ii.     Iulii episcopi papae Romae.

[13] e Id.     Eufoniae et Pauli diaconi.

[14] f xuiii kl.     Tassaich/i/ epscoip/i/ qui dedit /euchari[s]tiam Patricio/.

[15] g xuii.     Ruadain Lothra. H*íc* ora auium aperi/untur et ciconia canunt/.

---

4.   MO (*Tigernach . . . Cluana hEuis*) also has only this saint and his church.

5.   There is general agreement here with MO (*maicc Cula Beccain . . . baithes Pátraic . . . adrannad i nhÉre*, 'Beccán mac Cúla . . . Patrick's baptism has been kindled in Ireland'). Both texts use the term 'kindle', which is nowhere else attested in this context. The perfectly legible *Cairech* may denote the saint of that name already commemorated at 9 Feb.

6.   MO (*Herenius int epscop*, 'H. the bishop') also mentions this saint only.

7.   This is close to MO (*Fínán Camm Cinn Etig*), with MT (*Finani Caimm*) omitting the church.

8.   To be noted here is the hibernicised form of the saint's name, more correctly Ianuarius. This reflects *Enair* of MO, which otherwise also describes the saint as a martyr (*in martir*).

9.   This saint, *plane ignotus* according to the editors of MH, is otherwise confined to MT, which adds *cuius sanguis adhuc remanet*, MO (*Chadrati*, v.l. *Quadrati*), and MDr.

10.   The spelling of the saint's name with medial -*nd*- is also found in the R1 manuscript of MO.

11.   MO (*Máedóc . . . huae . . . do Dúnlang*, 'M., grandson of D.') also mentions this saint only.

12.   The wording here points to the influence of the Commentary on MO, which in one manuscript reads: *papa et epscop*, in another, *.i. Romae*.

13.   Only the latter saint is in MO (*Pól deochain*), but Euphemia (sic. leg.) heads the list in MT.

14.   It seems that the scribe first wrote the name and title *hibernice* before latinising them. The gloss is clearly based on the text of MO (*epscop Tassach dobert . . . corp Críst la commainn do . . . Phátric*, 'Bishop Tassach gave the body of Christ at communion to Patrick'). Similar sentiments are expressed in MG, which was also occasionally influenced by MO. Ultimately, the tradition derives from Muirchú's seventh-century Life of Patrick (cf. Bieler, *The Patrician Texts*, p. 118).

15.   MO (*Ruadán* (sic. MSS) . . . *Lothrai*) also has this saint only. For the singing of the birds/storks, see Migne, *Ephem.*, cc. 761–2, 769–70.

## 16–27 April

[16] a xui.     Felicis diaconi.
[17] b xu.      Petri diaconi et Don[n]ain Ega. /Sol in Taurum/.
[18] c xiiii.   Molasse Lethglinne.
[19] d xiii.    Hermoginis.
[20] e xii.     Sollemnitas sanctorum Europae quorum /festiuitas incerta est et pasio Eradii marteris/.
[21] f xi.      Muil Rubai i nAlbain.
[22] g x.       Pilippi apostoli nati*uitatis*.
[23] a ix.      Epscoip Ibair.
[24] b uiii.    Giurgii pasionis.
[25] c uii.     Marci euangelistae et Epscoip Meicc Cailli. /Ultimus dies Paschae/.
[26] d ui.      Cirilli marteris.
[27] e u.       Alaxandri abbatis Romae.

---

16. The saint is also in MH, but his description as a deacon is peculiar to the Irish martyrologies MT (*Felicis diaconi*), which places him in Connacht, MO (*deochoin Felic*) and MDr.
17. These saints are also in MO (*Petair deochain . . . Donnán Ega* (sic. most of the MSS)). For the astronomical note, see Bede, *De temporum*, XVI (= *Wallis*, p. 56).
18. Although written non-hypocoristically in MO (*Laisrén . . . Lethglinne*), the saint's name is given the hypocoristic form *Molaisse* in both MT and the Commentary on MO.
19. MO (*Ermogin*) also mentions this saint only.
20. This feast of all saints is peculiar to Irish martyrologies (MT, MO, MDr), although none agrees with the comment here that it applied to saints of uncertain days (see Hennig, 'A Feast of All the Saints of Europe'). MO (*céssad Herodi . . . nóeb nEorpa uile*, 'passion of H., all saints of Europe') has the same choice of feasts, with two of its manuscripts, R1 and B, also spelling Herodius's name without initial *H-* as *Eradi*.
21. There is almost word-perfect agreement here with MO (*I nAlbain . . . Maelrubai*, 'M. in Alba').
22. Here the wording agrees with MT (*Pilippi apostoli natiuitas*) against MO (*Pilip apstal*).
23. This is the only saint mentioned in MO (*epscoip Ibair*), which has the same spelling.
24. MO (*páis Giurgi*, 'passion of G.') and IMY (*Giurgius*) have the same spelling of the name.
25. Although absent from the verse of MO (*Marc . . . epscop . . . Macc Caille*), the description of Mark as evangelist – also in MT (*Marci euangelistae*) – is in its Commentary (cf. Hennig, 'Studies in the Latin Texts', pp. 69–70). The computation is at 23 Apr. in the Karlsruhe Calendar (*finis paschae latinorum*); cf. Bede, *De temporum*, LXI (= *Wallis*, pp. 145–7).
26. The description of Cyrillus as a martyr, which is absent from all other martyrologies, is probably based on MO (*Cirillus . . . céssais*, 'Cyrillus . . . suffered').
27. Here there is near perfect agreement with MO (*Alaxander . . . abb Rómae*), the only other source to describe Alexander as an abbot/pope.

## 28 April – 5 May

[28] f iiii.    Cronain Rois Cré.
[29] g iii.    Germani marteris /et sacerdotis/ et Fachtnai.
[30] a ii.    Ronain Ruis Leith, Cirini *papae* in Roma.

Maius triginta et unus *secundum* sol*em*, triginta *secundum* luna*m*.
[1] b Kl.    Pilipi apostoli, cetpr*ai*cept Isu, /Iacobi fratris Domini/.
[2] c ui n.    Conceptio Mariae, Nectain daltai /Patraic/.
[3] d u.    Inuentio crucis Christi, Mariae /uirginis, Conlaid/.
[4] e iiii.    Anatheri, Mochua, Cummeni et /Sillani diaconi/.
[5] f iii.    Ascensio Domini, Elarii et Euticii /et Iustini diaconi/.

---

28. MT (*Cronain Ruis Cré*) and MO (*Crónán Roiss Chrée*) also add the name of the church in the genitive.
29. Otherwise only MO (*Martrae Germáin chruimthir . . .*, 'The martyrdom of Germanus the priest') draws attention to the saint's martyrdom. *Fachtnae* is usually written *Fiachnae*.
30. MO (*Rónán . . . Roiss . . . i rRóim . . . Ciríni*) has much the same spelling of Quirinus, whom it also places in Rome. The Commentary on MO (*.i. Cirinus papa*) gives him the title of pope. *Ros Liath* here is for the more usual *Liathros*.

### MAY

1. MT, which places Christ's preaching first, has the same three initial entries. MO (*gein Pilipp . . . praicept . . . Íssu*, 'the birth of P., J.'s preaching') refers to Philip's apostolate only in its Commentary, where it also mentions James's feast. Schneiders, 'The Irish Calendar', p. 69, claims that 'the Irish did not celebrate both apostles on May 1', but they are both in MT and IMY.
2. The second entry clearly derives from MO (*Nechtain daltai Pátric*). The peculiarly Irish feast of the conception of Mary has been much discussed (Grosjean, 'La prétendue fête', Hennig, 'The Feasts of the Blessed Virgin', pp. 165–6, O'Dwyer, *Mary*, p. 59). MT (*Mariae uirginis conceptio*) has it on 3 May, as does MO (*Maire huage*, 'Virgin Mary'), without reference to conception, which may explain the second entry in MTur on 3 May, i.e. *Mariae uirginis*.
3. MTur is very close to both MT (*Crucis Christi inuentio, Mariae uirginis conceptio . . . Conlaid*) and MO (*Prímairec crainn chroiche Críst . . . Conlaíd . . . Maire huage*, 'The first finding of Christ's cross, C., V. M.'). Usually spelt *uirguinis*, the word is here written out correctly.
4. If Pope Anteros is intended, then, although also here in MT (*Antherii*) and MO (*Anatheri/Anteri(ni)*), his feast falls more properly on 3 Jan. (cf. Hennig, 'The Notes', p. 139). As MO (*mo Chuae . . . mac Cummíni*) shows, Mochua was Cumméne's son. MO (*Siluain dechain*) also describes Silvanus, more correctly a bishop, as deacon. Moreover, the spelling *hibernice* of the deacon's name here corresponds to some manuscripts of MO, as well as MDr.
5. This feast of the ascension is also in MT (*ascensio prima Domini*), MO (*laithe . . . frisrócaib ar Fiada*, 'the day our Lord ascended'), and the Karlsruhe Calendar (*ascensio Domini*). The spelling *Elarii* for *Hilarius* reflects *hElair* of MO, and *non* should be added before *Iustini* in the entry *Euticii* (sic. leg. *Eutimus*) *et Iustini*, as in both MT and the Commentary on MO.

## 6–16 May

| | |
|---|---|
| [6] g ii. | Natiuita/ti/s Mathae. |
| [7] a N. | Mochuarocc et Breccain. |
| [8] b uiii id. | Uictoir et Maxim. |
| [9] c uii. | Mich/i/elis manifes*tationis*, pasionis /Cirilli et episcopi Sanctani/. |
| [10] d ui. | Comgaill Bennchoir. Finis primus Pentecostes. |
| [11] e u. | Ioib, Mochrito/i/c, Cormaic cr*um*/thir/. |
| [12] f iiii. | Ciriaci crucifixi et Eirc, Aili/thir/. |
| [13] g iii. | Tiriaci et Probáci mar*tirum* et *seser* ar *sé cétaib* mar*tir*. |
| [14] a ii. | Mochutu Rathin, Coronae et Uictoir. |
| [15] b Id. | Sáráin et Dublitir, Spiritus Sancti super /apostolos/. |
| [16] c xuii kl. | Broendini Cluana Ferta. |

---

6. MO (*gein*, 'birth') also refers to Matthew's physical rather than spiritual birth, which is in other authorities. The spelling of the evangelist's name also agrees with MO (*Matha*).

7. MO (*Mochuaróc la Breccán*) has the same choice and order of saints.

8. The Irish forms of the names agree with MO (*Uictor ocus Maxim*), which also has these two saints only.

9. The word *manifestationis* is more likely to be a translation of MO's *foillsigud*, 'manifestation', or a reflection of *manifestus est* in the Commentary than a paraphrase of MT's *reuelatio*. The spelling *Cirilli* accords with MO (*Cirill*), which also has the same choice of entries.

10. MO (*Comgall . . . Bennchuir*) also refers only to this saint. The computistical addition usually relates to the middle of the month (Migne, *Ephem.*, cc. 767–8).

11. MO (*Ioib . . . Mochritóc . . . Cruimther Cormacc*) has the same choice and order of saints. Job is on the previous day in MH.

12. MO (*Ciriacus crochthae*, 'C. was crucified') also attributes crucifixion to Cyriacus. Furthermore, MO (*Ailithir . . . la hErc*, 'A. with E.') appears to attach the personal name *Ailithir* to Erc, whence the confusion in MTur which took it to be the word for pilgrim. Cyriacus, whose day is otherwise 1 May, is supposed to have found the true cross, as MT (*qui crucem Domini inuenit*) relates.

13. This is clearly based on MO (*Teraci . . . Propaci* F, Lb) which, possibly due to its being surrounded by names ending in *-ci*, added this ending also to *Probi*. Similarly, the number of martyrs specified, written, Irish style, as *.ui. ar .dc.*, reflects MO's *seser ar sé cétaib*, 'six hundred and six'.

14. Although accorded precedence here, Mochutu of Rahan is last in MO (*Corona . . . Victor . . . Charthaig Rathin*), whose Commentary also uses the hypocoristic form of the saint's name.

15. MO (*in Spirto . . . Sárán . . . Duiblitir*) has all three entries. Furthermore, although a similar text is found in several *auctaria* of MU, the entry on the Holy Spirit is probably a translation of MO (*rath in Spirto . . . for cléir*, 'the grace of the Spirit on the company [of apostles]').

16. MO (*Brénainn*) adds two other saints. The irregular spelling here of the saint's name (cf. MDr), more usually *Brendini* (MT), may have been influenced by the belief, as expressed in the Commentary on MO, that the name derived from *bróen*, 'drop'.

## 17–26 May

| | | |
|---|---|---|
| [17] d xui. | Adrionis et Uictoris et Bas/sille/. | |
| [18] e xu. | Momedóc et Modomnóc. Sol in /Geminos/. | |
| [19] f xiiii. | Urbani. | |
| [20] g xiii. | Gerbassi et Protassi et Marcel/losi/. | |
| [21] a xii. | Tiamdai marteris, Colmain Lobair. | |
| [22] b xi. | Boithine meicc Finnaig, Ronain /Find/. | |
| [23] c x kl. | Epactaci cum multis martiribus. | |
| [24] d ix. | Augustini episcopi et Hermis et Coloim /Tiri Da Glas/. | |
| [25] e uiii. | Iohannis euangelistae, Dionisii, Dunchaid /Iae/. | |
| [26] f uii. | Colmain et Bécáin et Bedae. | |

17. These three saints correspond to the entries for the day in MO (*Adrionis, Uictoris, Basille*).

18. MO (*Momáedóc* (*Momedóc* R1) . . . *Modomnóc*) has both saints. For the computistical addition, see Bede, *De temporum*, XVI (= *Wallis*, p. 56), and Migne, *Ephem.*, cc. 767–8.

19. MO (*Urbain*) also has Urbanus only.

20. Although also in MO (*Gerbassi, Protassi*), these two saints belong more properly at 19 June, where they are again in both texts. According to the editors of MH, their inclusion here is due to notational confusion. Most manuscripts of MO also decline the final name – more correctly *Marcellosae*, as in manuscript R1 – in the same way as here.

21. MO (*Tiamdae . . . Colmán Lobor*) has the same spelling of Timotheus, and also adds *martir*.

22. These are also the two saints in MO (*Rónáin Find . . . Baíthéne macc Findach*), whose Commentary twice uses the genitive form *Finnaig*.

23. The reference to *multi martyres* may reflect *findshluag Epectiti*, 'the fair host of E.', of MO. The form of the saint's name here is interesting because it differs from the Hieronymian form Epictetus (*Epectiti* MO), but agrees, at least in its ending, with the form of the Roman Martyrology (*Epitacii*), which, according to the editors of MH, *delendum est*.

24. Most Irish martyrologies (MO, MDr and MTur) place Augustinus, apostle of the English, on this day, rather than two days later as in other sources, including MG which follows MU. Apart from MO (*Hermes/Ermes*), whose Commentary describes him as (an otherwise unknown) *papa Romae*, Hermes is rarely assigned to this day (*AASS* Maii V, p. 270). It is worth noting that the names Augustinus and Hermes are again brought together at 28 Aug., both here and in other martyrologies. The attachment of *Tíri Da Glas*, 'Terryglass', to *Colum*, more correctly *Colmán* (in fact, it belongs to a saint named Aidbe in MT and MO), may be due to a note in the Commentary, as in R1, which speaks of *Colmán .i. o Thír Dá Glas*.

25. Some manuscripts of MH commemorate John the Apostle here. However, only the Commentary on MO otherwise identifies him as the evangelist. MO (*Iohannis . . . Dionis . . . Dúnchad hIae*) has the same choice and order of saints.

26. The first two saints are also in MO (*Colmáin . . . Béccán*), but mention of Bede on this day is neither in MO nor in any Hieronymian source. However, he is in several English calendars dating to before 1000, and also in *auctaria* of MU, including the one that served as source of MG (*Beda*); some such source was doubtless used here.

## 27 May – 6 June

[27] g ui.    Aculei prespeteri.
[28] a u.    Germain aite Patraicc.
[29] b iiii.    Colmáin et Ingeni Áildeain, Polli/onis/.
[30] c iii.    Gein/i/ Tomais /et/ pasionis Eutici.
[31] d ii.    Pasio/nis/ Crisogini et pasionis /Patronioli/.

Iunius triginta *secundum* sol*em*, viginti et novem *secundum* lu*nam*
[1] e Kl.    Teclae uirguinis.
[2] f iiii n.    Erasm/i/ episcopi et Lurentii et trecentorum m*ilium*.
[3] g iii.    Coemgein Glinne Da Locha.
[4] a ii. n.    Apollinaris marteris, translationis /Martini/.
[5] b N.    Pasionis Marciani, Tatbercti.
[6] c uiii id.    Pasionis Amanti, Muil Aid/chein/.

---

27. This is also the only entry in MO (*Aculius cruimther*, 'A. the presbyter').
28. MO (*Germán . . . aite Pátraicc*, 'G., tutor of P.') is clearly the source here. Germanus is one of the few saints listed in the Karlsruhe Calendar.
29. Although based on MO (*Pollionis . . . Cummain . . . ingen Allén* (v.l. *Ailden* F), 'P., C. daughter of A.), MTur seems to have misread its source, taking *Cummain* of MO to be *Colmán* and treating *ingen Aildeáin* as a separate name.
30. The entry as a whole is very close to MO (*gein Tomáis . . . páis Eutaic*, 'The birth of T., the passion of E.'). Thomas's *natale* is otherwise recorded in MH at 3 June and again at 30 June. Accordingly, it may have become attached to 30 May through notational confusion.
31. There is considerable agreement here with MO (*céssad Crisogini la páiss Petronellae*, 'passion of C. with the passion of P.'), whose manuscripts vary greatly in their spelling of the final name.

### JUNE

1. Both MO (*Teclae*) and the Karlsruhe Calendar also mention this saint only. Furthermore, the Commentary on MO, as in manuscripts F, Lb, describes her as a *uirgo*.
2. Although mainly based on MO (*Erasmus int epscop . . . trí chét . . . míle*, 'E. the bishop . . . three hundred thousands'), Laurentius, who is in MH on the following day, came from another source.
3. Both MO (*Cóemgen . . . i nGlinn Dá Lind*, 'C. in G.') and the Karlsruhe Calendar (*Cóemgeni Uallis*) likewise mention this saint only.
4. Stokes, *The Martyrology*, p. 401, suggests, plausibly, that MO's *Apollinaris* on this day was a mistake for Apollonius of Egypt, who is commemorated in MH on the following day. The translation of Martin's remains, which is also in MO (*tarmbreith Martini*, 'the translation of M.'), more properly belongs at 4 July.
5. The first entry reflects MO (*martrae Marciani*, 'the martyrdom of M.'). The second saint is otherwise found in the June section of IMY (l. 34), and has been identified as an abbot of Ripon otherwise known from the *Vita Wilfridi* (Wilmart, 'Un témoin', p. 49n).
6. MO (*ógchéssad Amanti, Máel Aithgin*, 'the perfect martyrdom of A., M.') likewise mentions these two saints only. None of the witnesses to MO has a spelling close to *Muil Aidchein*.

## 7–16 June

[7] d uii id.    Pasionis Furtinati, Pauli marteris /et Dacholmoc et Coluim m*eicc* hu Altai/.

[8] e ui.    Sancti Ioib et Medrain et Murchon.

[9] f u.    Coluim Chille et Buithine.

[10] g iiii.    Marci et Barnabi.

[11] a iii.    Meicc Tháil et Basillae et Fur/tinati marteris/.

[12] b ii.    Coemain et Torannain et Ciarain /Belaich Duin/.

[13] c Id.    Partholoin et Meicc Nisse Cluan/a/. /Ultimus dies Pentecostes/.

[14] d xuiii kl.  Ném meicc u Birnd et Benedicti et /Heleisii profetae/.

[15] e xuii.    UITUIS MACCAIN.

[16] f xui    CÍRIC MACCAIN.

---

7.    Fortunatus follows Paulus at the head of the list here in Hieronymian texts, but is absent from MO, except at 9 June in version P of the Commentary. Two of the other three saints are in MO (*Póil in martir, Coluimb*). The third, *Dacholmoc*, may derive from the Commentary, which glosses *Colum* as *Mocholmóc*. No manuscript of MO (*maccu Artai*) has a form like *meicc hu Altai* (with *h* written as aspiration mark).

8.    The choice, order, and spelling of the names are exactly as in MO (*Ioib . . . Medráin . . . Murchon*). Medardus is also in the Karlsruhe Calendar.

9.    Although in reverse order, MO (*Báethíne, Colomb Cille*) also has these two saints only.

10.  MO (*Mairc, Barnaip*) likewise has these two saints only.

11.  MO (*Basilla . . . Maicc Tháil . . . . Fortunati*) has the same choice and number of saints.

12.  The first two entries are the same in MO (*Cóemáin, Torannán*). However, the final entry, on Ciarán of Castlekieran, U. Kells b., Co. Meath, is absent from MO. Moreover, it is found in other martyrologies (MT, MG) two days later, at 14 June. See also Introduction, § 6.

13.  MO (*Partholón* (most MSS), *Mac Nissi . . . Cluana*) agrees on the choice, order and description of the two saints. For the computistical addition, see Migne, *Ephem.*, cc. 769–70.

14.  The first two feasts are in MO (*Nem maccu Birn, Benedicht*), which is the only other authority for the latter. The Commentary describes it as the feast of the enshrining of Benedict's relics, more regularly 11 July. The feast of Heliseus, although absent from Hieronymian texts on this day, is given pride of place in MA and MU, and is already present in Bede.

15.  Apart from the provision of an Irish genitive ending to both words, the entry accords perfectly with MO (*Uitus maccán*, 'V. the child'). Judging by the use of capitals here and on the following two days, the saints or days in question had a particular importance for the author of MTur (Introduction, § 6). Vitus was patron of sufferers from epilepsy, various nervous diseases, and rabies.

16.  Cyricus, patron of children, was widely venerated, especially among the Celts (cf. Grosjean, 'Un quatrain irlandais', p. 270). The entry is close to MO (*Ciric* (MS F only) . . . *do maccaib domain*, 'C. of the world's sons').

17–28 June

| [17] g xu | MOLING LUACHAIR. Sol /in Cancrum/. |
|---|---|
| [18] a xiiii. | Boithine, Furudrain meicc /Moenain/. |
| [19] b xiii. | Gerbassi et Protassii. |
| [20] c xii. | Pauli, Ciriaci et Faelain /Amlabor/. |
| [21] d xi. | Cormaic hui Liathain. |
| [22] e x kl. | Iacobi Alfei, Cronain Fer/na/. |
| [23] f ix. | Mochoe Noi[n]dromma. |
| [24] g uiii. | Geini /uel natiuitatis/ Iohannis Baptistae et reuersionis Iohannis /euangelistae ad Effesum/. |
| [25] a uii. | Sinchill et Telle et Moluoc /Lis Moir/. |
| [26] b ui. | Gallicani et Iohannis et Pauli. |
| [27] c u. | Passio septem fratrum in Roma. |
| [28] d iiii. | Crummine Lecna et Flauiani /marteris/. |

17. The wording here, the third in capitals, reflects MO (*Moling Luachair*). For the possible significance of the use of capitals for Moling's name, see Introduction, § 6. For the astronomical addition, also in the Karlsruhe Calendar, see Bede, *De temporum*, XVI (= *Wallis*, p. 56).
18. MO (*Baíthín* [*Baithine* F] . . . *Furudrán* . . . *maicc Moínáin*, 'B. [and] F., sons of M.') correctly describes the first two saints as sons of Móenán, whereas MTur seems to have three separate entries, 'B., F., [and] the sons of M.'.
19. This entry, which duplicates that of 20 May, again agrees closely with MO (*Geruassi* [*Gerbassi* R1], *Protassi*). The feast is also in the Karlsruhe Calendar.
20. There is general agreement here with MO (*Póil, Ciriaci, Fáelán . . . int amlabar*, 'P., C., F. the mute').
21. MO (*Cormacc . . . haue Liatháin*) likewise has this entry only.
22. MO (*Iacob nAlphaei . . . Crónán . . . Fernae*) has much the same text.
23. The scribe omitted the suspension over the -*i*- of *Noidromma*. This is also the only entry in MO (*Mochóe . . . ó Óendruimm*), whose Commentary, as in F, Lb, has the form *Mochóe Noíndromma*.
24. The wording is very close to MO (*ríggein Iohain Baptaist . . . tathchor Iohain . . . do Effis*, 'the royal birth of J. B., the return of J. to E.'). The use of *reuersio* for the more usual *receptio* (MH) reflects MO's *tathchor*, 'return'. The feast of John is also in the Karlsruhe Calendar.
25. There is near perfect agreement with MO (*Sinchill, Telli, M'Luóc* [*Moluóc* F] . . . *Liss Móir*).
26. MO (*Gallicanus, Iohannes, Paulus*) has the same choice and order of saints. Gallicanus, who is on the previous day in MU, and who is not in MH, is an associate of Iohannes and Paulus.
27. MO (*martrai . . . secht nderbbráthir . . . i rRóim*, 'martyrdom of seven brothers in Rome'), gave rise here to Latin *fratres* in place of the more usual *germani* (MH).
28. MO's *y* line of transmission, as in F (cf. Lb), also has *Flauiani* for the more correct *Fabiani*.

## 29 June – 8 July

[29] e iii.  Pasio Petri et Pauli in Roma.
[30] f ii.  Ioib et pasio Timothei et Zoli.

Iulius triginta et unus *secundum* sol*em*, triginta *secundum* lunam.

[1] g Kl.  Iudae fratris Iacobi, Simonis et /Tathei/.
[2] a ui n.  Ordinationis Martini episcopi, Da/massi et Processi/.
[3] b u n.  Translatio Tomae apostoli, Cirio/nis/.
[4] c iiii.  Finnbarr Inse Doimle.
[5] d iii.  Agathae uirguinis translat*ionis*.
[6] e ii.  Moninne et Dare[r]ca.
[7] f N.  Heleae, Parmeni, Moel Ruain /Tamlactan/.
[8] g uiii id.  Comgain Glinne Uissen et Brocain /scriptoris/.

---

29. In MO (*Féil Phóil ocus Phetair*, 'feast of P. and P.') the order is reversed, *metri causa*. Neither *passio* nor *Roma* is reflected by MO. The saints are also in the Karlsruhe Calendar.
30. These three only are in MO, albeit in different order, and Job is not at this day in any other source.

### JULY

1. The names of the apostles Simon and Jude are rendered *Simon* and *Tathae* in the metrical text of MO, whence *Tathei* here, and the Commentary explains that *Tatha* was also called *Iudas . . . frater Iacobi*. The entry here is an inaccurate conflation of MO and its Commentary.
2. Processus and Martinianus were the main saints in MH, *Damasi* being part of the name of the cemetery they were buried in. However, in MO (*Damasi co n-áni*, 'D. with splendour'), Damasus is treated as a saint, whence the entry here. Moreover, perhaps because his eye wandered to the first line of MO at 4 July (*Dagordan . . . Martain*, 'The good ordination of Martin'), the author transformed Mart(in)ianus of his source into the feast of Martin's ordination. The third saint is also in MO (*Processi*).
3. The order of entries in MO (*Cirionis . . . tarmbreith Tomais*, 'C., the translation of T.'), which omits to designate Thomas an apostle, is different.
4. Having already noticed the ordination of Martin at 2 July – at 4 July in MO – the author contented himself here with the remaining entry of MO (*Findbarr Inse Doimle*).
5. Among the manuscripts of MO, some (F, L, Lb) read *Agatha*, which is probably why the saint is treated here, possibly more correctly (*AASS* Nov. II.2, pp. 353–4), as a female. A gloss on MO in Lb also uses *uirgo*. There is no other authority for *translatio*.
6. Although taken here to be separate names, Darerca, as is pointed out in the Commentary on MO, was in fact an alias of Moninne.
7. Although not in MO (*Parmeni, Máel Ruain*), Helias is in the Hieronymian tradition for this day. A reference to Tamlachta (Tallaght) is contained in the Commentary.
8. MO (*Broccán scríbnid, Diarmait Glinne hUissen*) has only one of these saints. Comgán, may derive from the Commentary, as in F, Lb, which affirms that Diarmait was in Glenn Uisen 'before Comgán'.

## 9–17 July

| | |
|---|---|
| [9] a uii. | Anathaliae et Audacis /et Onchon et Moronoc et Garbain Cind Shale/. /Turcbail cen (f)uiniud *uero* dont shectarreu ó *secht* id Iúil co k*alendae* Decimbris .i. *sé* lathe *dachait* ar *chét*/. |
| [10] b ui. | Pilipi et Uitalis /et pasionis septem fratrum/. |
| [11] c u. | Eufen/i/ae uirguinis et Benedi/ct et pasionis Moysi/. |
| [12] d iiii. | Nazari et Felicis /cum magno exercitu/. |
| [13] e iii. | Moshiloc et Sillain et Euangeliae /.i. nomen uirginis/. |
| [14] f ii. | Iacobi episcopi et decem infantes. |
| [15] g Id. | Misio /duodecim/ apostolorum ad predicandum. |
| [16] a xuii kl. | Mammetis et Helarii. |
| [17] b xui. | Slo/i/g Scillitarum et Marcelli. |

---

9. Two only of these feasts are in MO (*Onchon . . . Garbán . . . Cinn Sáli*). Morónóc may be the saint of Druim Samraid, now Drumsawry or Summerbank, Loughcrew p., Fore b., Co. Meath, who is in MT at 22 July. He may be here because of local preference (Introduction, § 6). The two non-Irish saints, Anatholia and Audax, are otherwise in MU and MA, whence their inclusion in MG and MDr. The astronomical/ computistical addition, alongside the entries from 9–12 July, is boxed. It translates: 'rising without setting then for the Great Bear from 9 July to 1 December, that is 146 (sic!) days'.

10. In both the Hieronymian (MH) and historical traditions (MA, MU), Philip and Vitalis are included among the seven brothers, nonc of whom is named in MO (*céssad secht mbráthre*, 'the passion of the seven brothers').

11. Both saints are in MO (*Eufemiae* (*Eufenia* F, Lb) . . . *Benedicht*). Moreover, the Commentary on MO describes Euphemia as a *uirgo*. There is no authority, that I know of, for the inclusion of 'Moses the martyr' here.

12. This is a calque on MO (*Nazair . . . Felix . . . cona shluag mór*, 'N. and F. with his large host'). Otherwise only MDr (*cum aliis sanctis tam plurimis*), which likewise derives from MO, specifies a large host. *Nazair* (MO), whence *Nazari* here, a corruption of *Nabor* (MH), is also in MDr (*Nazarii*). MO's source, MT (*Nazair*), placed the saint among its Irish saints.

13. *Euangeliae* is a misreading of *Euangeli* in MO (cf. MDr), which also refers to *lam' Shílóc*, 'with Moshílóc'. Evangelus is glossed .i. *nomen* in the Lb Commentary on MO. The form *Sillain*, which reflects *Moshiloc* ('my Sillán'), probably derives from a no longer extant gloss in the source.

14. Although also in both MO (*in t-epscop Iacob . . . co ndechenbur noíden*, 'Bishop J. . . . with ten infants') and its derivative MDr, these two feasts belong more properly on the following day, where, in line with MU, they are found in MG.

15. The use of *misio* (cf. MDr) for the more usual *divisio* of MO (*In dá apstal déac . . . fos-dáil . . . Íssu*, 'J. divides up the twelve apostles'), is probably due to the Commentary, which begins: *In hoc die missi sunt apostoli ad praedicandum*. See Hennig, 'Studies in the Latin Texts', p. 77; idem, 'The Notes', p. 146.

16. MO (*Mammetis*) has the first saint only. *Helarii*, more usually *Hilarini*, heads the list in MH. MT (*Hilarmi*) places the saint in its Irish section.

17. The use of *sloig*, 'of the host', reflects MO (*la slóg Scillitarum*, 'with the host of S.'). Marcellus, who is not in MO, is second in MH.

## 18–26 July

| | |
|---|---|
| [18] c xu. | Cristinae uirguinis cum septem fratribus. |
| [19] d xiiii. | Sussenni cum turba martirum. |
| [20] e xiii. | Sabine et Romulae et Curfin. /Sol in Leonem/. |
| [21] f xii. | Heleae marteris et Danielis /profetae et Fraxidis/. |
| [22] g xi. | Mariae Magdalenae, Mobiu Inse /Cuscraid/. |
| [23] a x kl. | Uincenti et undeviginti milia, Iacobi /fratris Domini/. |
| [24] b ix. | Iohannis euangelistae, Declain Ardae /More/. |
| [25] c uiii. | Iacobi fratris Iohannis. |
| [26] d uii. | Transformationis Domini in Monte Tabor, ul/timus finis transformationis Christi/. |

18. The seven brothers (*germani* MH) are also in MO (*co mmórfessiur bráthre in Christina*, 'with the seven brothers of C.'). Christina, who is also in MDr, is more commonly found on 24 July. However, several English calendars before 1100 (Wormald, *English Calendars*, pp. 8, 78, 204, 218, 246) place her on 19 July. See also Hennig, 'The Notes', p. 146.

19. Sisennius is also the only saint in MO (*Sisenni*), whose added words, *co mmórbuidin*, 'with a great troop', inspired *cum turba martyrum* both here and in MDr. The spelling in *Sus-* is not shared by any manuscript of MO.

20. MO (*Sabina . . . Romula . . . Curufin*) has the same saints. Sabina, who is also in MDr and some English calendars (Wormald, *English Calendars*, pp. 50, 78), is a mistake for Sabinus (MH). Romula, likewise in MDr, may be the saint otherwise commemorated on 23 June. Cur(i)fín is treated in the martyrologies as an Irish saint. For the, boxed, astronomical addition, which is usually at the 18th, see Bede, *De temporum*, XVI (= *Wallis*, p. 57), Migne, *Ephem.*, cc. 771–2.

21. With the exception of Daniel the prophet, who is already in Bede and is taken here from an historical martyrology, the entries more or less agree with MO (*Heli martir . . . Fraxidis*). Already in MH there is confusion regarding the gender and identity of Helia. See also MDr.

22. Other than having a third saint (Apollinaris), who is also in the Karlsruhe Calendar, MO (*Magdalena Maire . . . Mobiu Inse Cúscraid*) agrees with MTur.

23. MO (*Uincenti . . . dá noí míled* (v.l. *míle*), 'V. eighteen soldiers/thousand') has a different number, which seems in any case to be a misinterpretation of the distance measurement *miliario xviii/xviiii* of MH. Iacobus, who is not in MO, may be the same as the apostle listed at 25 July, in which case he was not the brother of the Lord.

24. MO (*Déclán Arde Máre*) lists the second saint only. John the evangelist, whose day was 27 Dec., is placed here probably because he was a brother of James.

25. MO (*Iacob . . . bráthar Iohannis*, 'J. brother of J.') has the same description. See previous note.

26. As Hennig pointed out ('The Notes', p. 147), MO (*tarmchruthud . . . Íssu i Sléib Thaboir*, 'transfiguration of J. on Mount Tabor') contains one of the earliest Western notices of this feast, which, very much later, became attached to 6 Aug. In line with MO, the feast is also here in MDr and MG. The word *transformatio* (cf. MDr), a calque on *tarmchruthad*, literally 'trans-formation', probably came from the Commentary, which, in MSS F, Lb, reads: *transformatio Christi in monte Tabor . . .* Some *auctaria* of MU note the feast on the following day, with one only, *Bruxellensis*, placing it here. The reference to *ultimus finis* may reflect the specification of *dedól*, 'daybreak', in MO.

27 July – 3 August

[27] e ui.     Semionis mon/a/chi. /Domnach as nesam *secht déc* esce
Iuil, is e domnach samchasc in sein/.
[28] f u.      Teofili et Panta/leo/.
[29] g iiii.   Pauli heremitae /et Lumbi et Simplicis/.
[30] a iii.    Abdoní et Senni/s/.
[31] b ii.     Dionis  et  Colmain  meicc  Darane.  /Locus  saltus
Egiptiorum/.

Augustus triginta et unus *secundum* solem, viginti et
novem *secundum* lunam.
[1] c KL.      Machabeorum septem cum matre /et Aron/.
[2] d iiii n.  Teothotae cum tribus filiis. *Sextus* emb*olismus*.
[3] e iii.     Iohannis Metrapolis inuentio*nis*.

---

27. Of the manuscripts of MO (*Semeoin manaig*) – which likewise lists this saint only – F
and R1 also spell the name with medial *-mi-*. The computistical addition, which is
boxed alongside the entries for 27–30 July, reads in translation: 'the nearest Sunday to
the seventeenth July moon is the Sunday at the end of Summer-lent'.

28. MO (*Theophil, Pantaleo*) has the same choice and order of saints.

29. Paul the (First) Hermit, whose feast generally fell on 10 Jan., where he has already
been noted, appears to be peculiar to MTur on this day. The word *Lumbi* may be compared to *Lumbus* of manuscripts F and Lb of MO (*Lupus . . . Simplicc*).

30. MO (*Abdon ocus Sennis*, 'A. and S.') also has these companion saints only.

31. Dionisius, who is absent from MO (*Colmán macc Daráne*), is the last name in MU,
which may have been the source here. For the computistical addition, which is boxed
in orange, see Bede, *De temporum*, XLII (= *Wallis*, p. 115), and Migne, *Ephem.*, cc.
771–2.

## AUGUST

1. The wording of the first entry is close to the Commentary on MO, which reads:
*septem filii cum matre sua . . .* The Hieronymian texts prefer *fratres* to *filii*, as does the
Karlsruhe Calendar (*Machabeorum septem fratrum cum matre*). Aron (from *Aaron*?),
who is absent from MO (*macc Mochabae*, 'of the sons of M.'), is assigned to the
church of Cluain Caín in MT (*Arun*). He may be the *Aoron sapiens* whose death in
783 is recorded in AU.

2. MO (*Teothota . . . na trí maccáin*, 'T., the three children') likewise has this entry only.
Moreover, the Commentary, as in MSS R1 and Lb, uses the phrase *cum tribus filiis*,
which is also in MT. Theodota is the more correct form of the mother's name. For the
computistical addition, which is boxed in ink, see Bede, *De temporum*, XLV (=
*Wallis*, p. 123), and Migne, *Ephem.*, cc. 773–4.

3. Although the name of a bishop in MH, Metropolis came to be associated with
Iohannes in the Irish tradition, apparently in the sense of the metropolis Jerusalem.
This would seem to be the usage in MO (*Metropoil ind Eoin*, 'John's metropolis'),
which locates there the finding of Stephen's relics. The attachment of *inventio* to
Iohannes Metropolis adds to the confusion.

## 4 15 August

| | |
|---|---|
| [4] f ii. | Molua m*ei*c Choche. |
| [5] g N. | Osualt ri Saxan et Heren/tii/. |
| [6] a uiii id. | Mochua Cluana D*olcain*. |
| [7] b uii. | Sufroni et Cronani /et trecentorum quinque /annorum sanctorum septem/ dormitauerunt in Effessu*m*. Ortus Uirgiliarum media nocte occassus autem media die/. |
| [8] c ui. | Darii uirguinis /et Beoain meic Nessain/. |
| [9] d u. | Antoni et Nathíi. |
| [10] e iiii. | Blaáin Cinn Garad. |
| [11] f iii. | Sussannae et Airerain sapien*tis* /et Ualeriani et Tiburtii/. |
| [12] g ii. | Molaisse Inse Muiredaich /et Segeni/. |
| [13] a Id. | Momedóc Feda Duin et Hipo/liti marteris/. |
| [14] b xix kl. | Furtinati et Factnai meic Mong*aich*. |
| [15] c xuiii. | Sanctae Mariae obitus. |

---

4.   MO (*Molua macc Oche*) also has this entry only.

5.   Although the order is reversed in MO (*IIerenti . . . hOsualt . . . ardrí Saxan*, 'H., O. highking of the Saxons'), the entries here are otherwise very similar.

6.   MO also has Mochua *ó Chluain Dolcain*, 'from C. D.'.

7.   Although present in MT, Sophronius and Cronanus are absent from MO, which in some manuscripts only – F (*chóic ar thrí chétaib*, '305') , Lb and L – agrees with the number of years slept here by the seven sleepers. Other manuscripts, including R1 (*cóic ar thríb cóectaib*), have 155. The computistical addition, which is boxed in orange alongside 7–9 August, corresponds to the addition at 7 Feb. above.

8.   The second entry only is in MO (*Beoáin meicc Nessáin*). As on some previous days (1, 7 Aug.), the source of the additional entry in MTur may have been MT (*Darii uirginis*).

9.   Both saints are in MO (*Antoni . . . Nathí*).

10.  MO (*Blaan . . . Cinn Garad*) adds here Laurence the deacon, who is also in the Karlsruhe Calendar.

11.  The first entry is otherwise in MT (*Susannae*), with the others also in MO (*Airerán n-ecnai . . . Ualerán . . . Tiburtius*, 'A. of the wisdom, U., T.). Tiburtius is in the Karlsruhe Calendar.

12.  MO (*Lassréin Inse Muredaig . . . Ségéni*) has the same choice of saints, but the preference here for the hypocoristic form *Molaisse* may reflect either MT or the Commentary on MO.

13.  MO (*Hipolitus martir*) also describes the second saint as a martyr. Unlike MT (*Momedoc Feda Dúin*), MO (*Momáedóc*) does not add this saint's church, but its Commentary does.

14.  MO (*Fortunati . . . Fachtnai maicc Mongaig*) has the same choice and order of saints, and several of its manuscripts spell the first name with initial *Fu-*.

15.  This feast of Mary is also in MO (*fírmáthir ar n-athar*, 'true mother of our father'), whose Commentary uses the words *dormitatio Marie* to describe it. The wording of the Karlsruhe Calendar (*obitus sanctae Mariae uirginis*) is close to MTur.

## 16–29 August

| | | |
|---|---|---|
| [16] d xuii. | Arionis. |
| [17] e xui. | Mammetis marteris et Temneain man/aich/. |
| [18] f xu. | Moernoc et Daig *meic* Cairill. |
| [19] g xiiii. | Magni marteris et Enain Dromma Rathe. |
| [20] a xiii. | Samuelis profetae. |
| [21] b xii. | Epscoip Senaich. |
| [22] c xi. | Timothi. |
| [23] d x. | Eogain Aird Sratha. |
| [24] e ix. | Senpatraicc. |
| [25] f uiii. | Bartholomei apostoli. |
| [26] g uii. | Quintini marteris. |
| [27] a ui. | Rufin et Fusti. |
| [28] b u. | Augustini episcopi et Hermis. |
| [29] c iiii. | Decollationis Iohannis Babtistae. |

---

16. The spelling is closer to MT (*Arionis*) than to MO (*Adrionis*).
17. Choice, order and wording of the entry agrees with MO (*Mammes martir . . . Temnéin manaig*).
18. MO (*Mernóc . . . Daig . . . macc Cairill*) has the same choice and order of entries, and only it otherwise gives preference to the hypocoristic *Moernóc* over the more regular *Ernine*.
19. Both MO (*martir Magni . . . Énán Dromma Ráthe*) and MT (*Magni martiris . . . Enani Dromma Rathi*) agree with MTur here.
20. There may have been a switch here to an historical martyrology like MU or MA. In line with Bede, these give Samuel, who is absent from MO, MT and MH, pride of place. However, the Commentary on MO, as in MS Lb, also lists *Samuel prop[h]eta*.
21. This is the second entry in MO (*epscop Senach*).
22. Unlike the entries at 18 March and 21 May, where MO's spelling *Tiamda* is followed, here, and again at 8 Sept., *Tiamdai* of MO is rendered *Timoth[e]us*.
23. MO (*Eogain Aird Sratha*) has this entry. MT adds *episcopus* to *Eogan*.
24. Otherwise only MO (*Senphátric*) prefixes *sen-*, 'old, senior', to the saint's name.
25. Although absent from the metrical text, which reads *Bartholom*, the title *apostolus* is attached to Bartholomeus in the Lb version of the Commentary on MO.
26. Most manuscripts of MO have this saint, albeit under the more regular form of *Quinti*. Both *Quinti* and *Quintini* are in MH on this day.
27. With both *Rufi* and *Rufini* attested in MH (cf. MT), the manuscripts of MO divide in their spelling (*Ruf(f)i* (R1), P, *Rufin* L, (Lb, F)) along the two main lines of their transmission (Introduction, § 4). Faustus is doubtless the bishop listed in MT (*Fausti episcopi*) on the following day.
28. MT (*Hermis . . . Augustini episcopi*) rather than MO (*Hermes . . . in t-airdirc a hAfraic*, 'H., the conspicuous one out of Africa') seems to be the source here. The Karlsruhe Calendar also has Augustine, adding *Hipponensis*.
29. The metrical text of MO (*céssad*, 'passion') and MT (*passio*) omit to refer to the beheading, which, in line with MU (*decollatio vel potius inventio capitis*), is mentioned only to be questioned in the Commentary.

## 30 August – 8 September

[30] d iii.   Agathae uirguinis cum sororibus /suis tribus/.
[31] e ii.   Paulini uiduae.

September triginta *secundum* sol*em*, triginta *secundum* lu*nam*.

[1] f Kl.   Constantini et Candidae et Pan/crati et Nessain Ulad/.
[2] g iiii n.   Teothotae et Zenoni. *Secundus* emb*olismus*.
[3] a iii.   Colmain /Dromma/ Ferta et Meicc Nisse /et Longaraid/.
[4] b ii.   Ultain Arddae Breccain.
[5] c N.   Ercalini et Eolaing Aichid /Bo *uel* Aigthi Bolg/.
[6] d uiii id.   Meicc Cuilind Luscai et Scéthe /et Coluim Ruis Gil/.
[7] e uiii.   Pasio*nis* Zenoti marteris.
[8] f ui.   Nati*uitatis* sanctae Mariae et Timothei cum tricentibus marteribus.

---

30. The manuscripts of MO divide along the two main lines of transmission (Introduction, § 4) as regards the name of the virgin, one (R1, P) preferring *Agappa*, in line with MT and MH, the other (L, Lb, F) adopting *Agatha*. MO (*cona sethraib*, 'with her sisters') also mentions sisters, but nowhere else is the number three attached to them. See also Hennig, 'The Notes', p. 151.
31. This appears to be a direct translation of MO (*Paulin na fedbae*, 'P. of the widow').

### SEPTEMBER

1. None of these saints is in MO. Constantinus, who is also in the Karlsruhe Calendar and in MT, is among the additions to MH. Neither Candida nor Pancratius is elsewhere assigned to this day, and the regular feast of Nessán Ulad is 29 Sept.
2. MO (*Teothotham* (v.l. *Teothota*) . . . *Senan*) has the same choice and order of saints, but the latter has been hibernicised, and is identified in the Commentary with Senán of Láthrach Briúin (cf. Ó Riain, 'Some Bogus Irish Saints', pp. 6–7). For the computistical addition, see Bede, *De temporum*, XLV (= *Wallis*, p. 123), Migne, *Ephem.*, cc. 775–6.
3. These saints are also in MO (*Colmán Dromma Ferta, Longarad . . . Macc Nisse*).
4. This is also the only entry in MO (*Ultán Aird Breccáin*).
5. Only the second saint is in MO (*Eolang . . . Achid Bó*), with the Lb version spelling the name in *-ng*. The alternative, more correct, name of the church is peculiar to MTur (Ó Riain, 'To be Named is to Exist', pp. 50–2). Herculanus is among the saints commemorated here in MH (cf. MT).
6. Both saints and church point clearly to dependence on MO (*Luscai la Mac Cuilinn . . . Scéthe . . . Coluimb Roiss gil Glandai*, 'M. C. of Lusk, S. C. of bright Ross Glanda'). MO's *gil* from *gel*, 'bright', is wrongly taken to be part of the name of the church.
7. Only the L version of MO has initial Z-. The more correct form, as in MH, MT, is *Sinotus*.
8. Although absent from the metrical text of MO (*Maire . . . la Tiamdae . . . co tríb cétaib martir*, 'M. with T. with 300 martyrs'), Mary's *natiuitas* is mentioned in its Commentary. The Karlsruhe Calendar also notices Mary's birth. Only MO otherwise specifies 300 martyrs.

## 9–20 September

| | |
|---|---|
| [9] g u. | Ciarain meicc int Shaír. |
| [10] a iiii. | Finnia Maige Bile. |
| [11] b iii. | Pasionis Protí, Iacinti et Sillain Imblech/a/ /Ibair/. |
| [12] c ii. | Molasse Daminse et Ailbe Imlech/a/ /Ibair/. |
| [13] d Id. | Dagain Inbir Duile /et/ viginti duorum martires. |
| [14] e xuiii kl. | Cornilii et Cipriani et Coemain Bricc. |
| [15] f xuii. | Dedicationis basilicae Mariae. |
| [16] g xui. | Monenn Cluana Conaire. |
| [17] a xu. | Brócain Ruis Tuirc et Regulae. /Sol in Libram/. |
| [18] b xiiii. | Enáin Dromma Rathe. |
| [19] c xiii. | Dimetri, Castoris et Enarii /marteris/. |
| [20] d xii. | Doromae uirguinis et alterae uirg/uines/. |

9. Both MO (*Mac int Shair . . . Clarán*) and the Karlsruhe Calendar (*Ciarani maic ind Sair*) also have this one entry only.

10. MO (. . . *Findbarr Maige Bili*) also has this saint only. Its Commentary supplied the hypocoristic form *Finnia(n)* favoured here and in MDr.

11. Otherwise only MO (*páiss Prothi Iacinthi . . . Sillán . . . i nImbliuch*), which has the same choice of saints, uses the term *passio/páiss*. The attachment of *Ibair* to *Imblecha*, in place of the more correct *Cassáin*, was due to the entry of the following day, which is directly below in the manuscript.

12. MO (*Ailbi . . . Laissréin . . . ó Daiminis*, 'A., L. from D.'), which has the same entries, adds both the name of Ailbe's's church and the hypocoristic *Molaisse* in its Commentary.

13. Otherwise only MO (*díis ar fichit martir . . . Dagán Indbir Doíle*, '22 martyrs, D. of I. D.') refers to twenty-two martyrs.

14. MO (*Cóemáin Bricc . . . Cipriain . . . Cornaill* v.l. *Cornil*) has the same saints, and the Latin forms of the names – likewise spelt *Cornilius, Ciprianus* – are in the F and Lb versions of its Commentary. These two saints are also in both the Karlsruhe Calendar and IMY.

15. The wording reflects either MT (*Dedicatio basilicae Mariae*) or, in translation, MO (*cosecrad mbaslicc Maire*, 'consecration of the basilica of M.').

16. Although absent from the metrical text of MO (*Moninn*), the name of Moinenn's church is in its Commentary. It is also in MT (*Monenn Cluana Conaire*).

17. These two are also in MO (*Broccán Roiss Tuirc . . . Riaglae*), with MO's *Riaglae* rendered here in the Latin form *Regulae*. For the astronomical addition, see Bede, *De temporum*, XVI (= *Wallis*, p. 57), and Migne, *Ephem.*, cc. 775–6.

18. This entry is also in MO (*Énán Dromma Ráthe*).

19. The third entry, the only one in MO (*Enair*), is provided here with a Latin ending. The description of this saint as a martyr is both in the Commentary on MO and, together with the other two saints, in MT (*Ianuarii martiris, Dimetri, Castoris*).

20. A construe mark (*x*) below the line separates *Daroma* from *uirguinis*. The entry is clearly a paraphrase of MO (*na hóga . . . Daroma cona slóg*, 'the virgins, D. with her host').

## 21 September – 2 October

[21] e xi.  Mathei euangelistae.
[22] f x kl.  Pantaleonis.
[23] g ix.  Adamnain Iae.
[24] a uiii.  Conceptio Iohannis Babtistae.
[25] b uii.  Iosebi, féil Barre ó Chor*caich*.
[26] c ui.  Colmain Ela.
[27] d u.  Cosmae et Damiani.
[28] e iiii.  Marcialis.
[29] f iii.  Michielis archangeli.
[30] g ii.  Hironim/i/ sapientis obit[us].

October triginta et unus *secundum* sol*em*, viginti et
novem *secundum* lu*nam*.

[1] a Kl.  Lucae euangelistae, Germani /et Prisci/.
[2] b ui n.  Eusebii, Iuliter marteris.

---

21. Matthew – described as *euangelista* in the Commentary – is the only entry in MO (*Mathae*).
22. This saint is the first entry of MO (*Pantaleo*).
23. This is also the only entry in both MO (*Adamnán Iae*) and the Karlsruhe Calendar (*Adomnani sapientis*).
24. The wording is the same in MT, the Karlsruhe Calendar, and, albeit in Irish, in MO (*Compert Iohain . . . Babtaist*, 'The conception of J. B.').
25. Both entries are clearly drawn from MO (*Eusebi* (*Iosebi* R1, F) . . . *féil Barri ó Chorcaig*, 'E., the feast of B. from C.').
26. This is also the only entry in MO (*Colmán ó Laind Elo*, 'C. from L. E.').
27. These two names only are in MO (*Cosmas, Damianus*).
28. MO (*Marcill*) also has this saint, with its Commentary spelling the name as *Marcialis*.
29. This is likewise the only entry in MO (*Michéll* v.l. *Michiél*). The entry is also both in IMY (*Michielis*) and in the Karlsruhe Calendar (*Michaelis archangeli basilicae dedicatio*).
30. The final *i* of *Hironimi* is below the line. *Sapiens* reflects *suí*, 'sage', of MO (*suí . . . Ciríne*, 'Jerome the sage'), which replaces *presbyter* of other sources, including MT. The Commentary on MO renders Ciríne *Hironimus*. This saint is also in both the Karlsruhe Calendar and IMY.

### OCTOBER

1. The three saints are also in MO (*Prisci . . . Lucais* (v.l. *Lucae*) . . . *Germáin*), whose Commentary adds *euangelista[e]* to *Lucae*. The latter saint is also in the Karlsruhe Calendar.
2. The two saints are also in MO (*Eleuther* (*Iuliter* F, L, Lb) *in martir . . . Eusébi*). The description of Eleutherius as a martyr is otherwise a feature of historical martyrologies only.

## 3–15 October

| | | |
|---|---|---|
| [3] c u. | Geini Mairc, gein Colmain /Ela/. | |
| [4] d iiii. | Marcelli episcopi, Babíní. | |
| [5] e iii. | Sinche Cruachain e.m. | |
| [6] f ii. | Luceill ap Cluana /et epscop Lugid/, Boi/thine/. | |
| [7] g N. | Mathae episcopi et Marc et Cel/laich/. | |
| [8] a uiii id. | Pasionis Fustini et Dauid regis et multarum /uirg*uinum*/. | |
| [9] b uii. | Eusebi, ducentorum septuaginta, Marc, Dio/nis, et Meic Thail/. | |
| [10] c ui. | Fintain Dromma Ing, trecentorum septuaginta mart*irum*. | |
| [11] d u. | Cainnich, Fortcheirn, Lomman. | |
| [12] e iiii. | Mobi clarainech. | |
| [13] f iii. | Comgain et Marcill et Finsigi. | |
| [14] g ii. | Pasio Paulini. | |
| [15] a Id. | Pasio Murorum. | |

3. Here the wording clearly reflects MO (*Sóergein Mairc . . . gein . . . Colmáin Ela*, 'noble birth of M., birth of C. E.'). The latter saint is also in the Karlsruhe Calendar (*Colmáin Alo*).

4. MO (*Marcellum n-epscop . . . Baluíne* (v.l. *Balline/Ballbine*)) has the same saints.

5. This is also the saint of the day in MO (*Sínech . . . Cruachan*). Although expanded by Granucci to read *e(rgna). m(aige)* – reflecting the name of the saint's father, Fergna, and the location of Cruachan in Mag Abna – I suspect that the two letters derive from the Commentary on MO which has: *ergna .i. maith*, '*ergna*, .i.e. good'.

6. MO (*Abb Cluana in Lucell . . . Baíthíne . . . epscop Lugdach*) has much the same text.

7. The title of bishop belongs to Mark, as in MO (*Mathae, Marc n-epscop . . . Cellaich*).

8. Only MO (*trét ingen co n-ógi . . . páiss . . . Faustini*, 'a group of virginal girls, the passion of F.') otherwise specifies both the many virgins and the passion of Faustinus. The entry on King David corresponds to a note in the Commentary on MO, as in Lb, F, which reads: *Dauid meic Iese hic*.

9. Despite the variation in the number, very common in the transmission of Roman numerals, the first two entries correspond to MO (*Eusebi . . . coícae ar tríb cétaib*, 'E., 350'). The third entry, Marc – presumably the same as at 3 Oct. – is otherwise unknown. The other two entries are in MT (*Dionisii, Meic Tail*). The Karlsruhe Calendar reads: *Dionisii cum suis sociis*.

10. MO (*Trí chét ar thríb dechib* (v.l. *secht ndeichib* L, Lb, F, P) . . . *Fintan . . . Dromma Ing*, '330 (v.l. 370) F. of D. I.') has much the same text.

11. MO (*Fortchern, Lommán . . . Cainnech*) has the same saints. The Karlsruhe Calendar has *Cainnich*.

12. This entry is also in MO (*Mobíi . . . clárainech*, 'M. the flatfaced one').

13. MO (*Comgan . . . Marcill . . . Findsiche*) has the same choice and order of saints.

14. Otherwise only MO (*céssad . . . Paulini*, 'suffering of P.') asserts that Paulinus, who died a natural death, was martyred.

15. Most manuscripts of MO (*prímchéssad Maurorum*, 'principal suffering of M.'), which has this entry only, also read *Murorum*.

## 16–26 October

[16] b xuii kl.  Colma/i/n Cille Ruaid.

[17] c xui.  Necodimi *passio*? et Alaixandri /et Moenaich, M*eic* Clarin/.

[18] d xu.  Nati*uitatis* Lucae et Tri*m*ponia et Pilip*i*. /Sol in Scorpionem/.

[19] e xiiii.  Austin et Sussi.

[20] f xiii.  Pasionis Euticii.

[21] g xii.  Mundu /uel *Munnu*/ meicc Tulchain.

[22] a xi.  Mathei euangelistae, Pilipi episcopi.

[23] b x kl.  Longiní.

[24] c ix.  Seueri cum quadraginta martiribus.

[25] d uiii.  Maxim/i/ et Lasreain, centum nonaginta, /feil Masan/.

[26] e uii.  Beoain m*eic* Meldáin.

---

16. This saint is also in MO (*Colmán ón Chill Ruaid*, 'C. from C. R.'), and its Commentary adds the name of the church, as here, in the genitive.

17. Nicodemus is shared by MO (*Ro céss . . . in martir Necodimus*, 'The martyr N. suffered'), whose description supports the expansion of *p*. as *passio*. The other two entries, the first of which is attached, albeit as a place, to Nicodemus in MH, are in MT (*Nicodimi martyris, Alexandrini . . .. Noínachi* (recte *Moínachi*)). The only other source to record Mac Cláirín here is MG. Móenach is also in the *Grevenus* MU, which reads: *in Hibernia, Monachi confessoris*.

18. The two latter saints are also in MO (*Pilipp . . . Trifoniae*), but only the F version of its Commentary refers to Lucas, whose feast is also in both MT and the Karlsruhe Calendar. For the computistical addition, which is also in the Karlsruhe Calendar, see Bede, *De temporum*, XVI (= *Wallis*, p. 57) and Migne, *Ephem.*, cc. 779–80.

19. These two saints are also in MO (*Auster . . . Susi*), but the form of Asterius's name in MT (*Austini*) is closer to the form here.

20. The reading reflects MO (*Páiss Eutaicc*).

21. This is also the only entry in MO (*Fintan . . . macc Telcháin*), which prefers the non-hypocoristic form of the saint's name, with its Commentary opting for the hypocoristic *Munnu*.

22. Matthew, whose regular feast has already been noted at 21 Sep., appears otherwise to be confined to MT (*Mattei apsotoli*) and MO (*Mathae*), which also has *Pilipp . . . epscoip*.

23. MO (*Longini*) also has this entry only.

24. MO (*Seuir . . . co cethorchait chréssen*, 'S. with forty pious ones') agrees on the choice of entries, and also on the number involved in the second entry, which MT gives as twelve.

25. Although differing in the number involved, more correctly 120 (MH), this and the two saints are also in MO (*Cethir deich dá choícait . . . Maxim . . . Laissrén*, 'Four tens, two fifties, M., L.'). The last entry, 'feast of Masán', is nowhere else recorded, which points to local preference. See Introduction, § 6.

26. MO (*Beoán, Mellán*) and other sources treat these names separately, attaching them to two saints from Britain.

27–31 October

[27] f ui.    Erc Domnaich Moir, Abbain, Od/rain/.
[28] g u.     Tathei et Simonis.
[29] a iiii.  Quinti marteris et Colmain Camsa.
[30] b iii.   Colmain meic hui Gualae.
[31] c ii.    Quintíní martiris et Faelani.

(The months of November and December are lacking due to a lacuna in the manuscript.)

27. MO (*Erc Domnaig Móir . . . Abbán . . . Odrán*) has much the same entry.
28. MO (*Tathae . . . Simón*) has the same order and choice of saints.
29. The second entry relates to the saint commemorated on the following day, who is glossed *abbatis Camsa* in MT and also assigned to Camas in the Commentary on MO. Both the Commentary (*Quinti .i. martir*) and MT (*Quinti martiris*) also agree on the description of the first saint.
30. This is very close to MO (*Colmán maccu Gualae*), with MT preferring the hypocoristic *Mocholmóc*. See note to the previous day.
31. MO (*Quintinus . . . Fáelán*) has the same order and choice of entries.

# CHAPTER FIVE

# THE MARTYROLOGY OF CASHEL: INTRODUCTION AND TEXT

## 1 *Background to the Text*

Alone of the four martyrologies edited in this volume, the Martyrology of Cashel, henceforth MC, now depends for its text almost exclusively on printed rather than manuscript evidence. Although it was apparently still extant in the early seventeenth century, when either its original manuscript or, as seems more likely, a copy, was used extensively by John Colgan in the notes to his two monumental volumes on the Irish saints, *Acta Sanctorum Hiberniae* and *Trias Thaumaturga*, it has since been lost.[1] Consequently, Colgan's quotations, although invariably in Latin translation, are now as close as one can get to the original text, which appears to have been mainly in Irish.[2] Moreover, the edition which Colgan was preparing for publication – according to a document in his hand found among the papers of James Ware – which has also been lost, would doubtless have likewise contained a Latin translation only.[3]

In his description of the text, Colgan stated that it had been copied *ex Psalterio Casselensi vel alio codice qui Hibernice Psaltar Naran dicitur*, thus providing two possible titles for its manuscript source.[4] In fact, neither the Psalter of Cashel, which I have dated to the beginning of

---

[1]  Colgan, *Acta Sanctorum*; idem, *Triadis Thaumaturgae*. These volumes are indicated below by the abbreviations A and T. A very small number of entries also survive in note-books in Colgan's hand in the Franciscan Library, Killiney, indicated below by the abbreviation KF.

[2]  Confirmation of the original Irish character of the text is found, firstly in the comment by Colgan at 13 Feb. that his source was now turning to Latin, secondly in the variations, however slight, in the translation he provides on more than one occasion of such entries as 4 Feb. (Cuanna), 20 Ian. (Molaggius), 21 Mar. (Endeus), and 24 Aug. (Patricius Senior).

[3]  McNeill, 'Report on Recent Acquisitions', p. 144.

[4]  Ibid. Neither title would appear to be appropriate but, however inappropriate, Colgan's use of them suggests that the martyrology then formed part of a manuscript containing other materials.

the eleventh century,[5] nor *Saltair na Rann*, which had assumed many guises by the beginning of the seventeenth century, is likely to have been the correct title.[6] But Colgan's further comment that the text was composed of *soli et pauci sancti Hibernici* is indeed borne out by the paucity of the saints, all of them Irish, assigned to MC.[7] The scarcity of its entries may also explain why Colgan often referred to the text as a *calendarium* which typically contains much fewer entries than a *martyrologium*.

## 2 *Date of the Martyrology of Cashel (MC)*

Colgan proposed a date of circa 1030, which he justified by the omission of any reference to Malachy (d. 1148), Laurence (d. 1180), or any other of the *viri sanctitate conspicui* living later than Gormgal of Ardailén (5 Aug.), who died in 1018.[8] However, this argument takes no account of the fact that the entry on Gormgal is itself quite exceptional, all other entries, subject to one possible exception,[9] concerning saints who belonged to the so-called Age of Saints between about 500 and 650. Moreover, a date in the early eleventh century would be at variance with other aspects of the surviving text, including the location of a church at 21 Jan. *in diaecesi Lismorensi*, 'in the diocese of Lismore', which would not have been appropriate before the establishment of dioceses in 1111.

The most telling ground for rejecting Colgan's dating lies in the very extensive use by the author of MC of an annotated version of the Martyrology of Óengus (MO) as his main source of entries. A very large percentage of the entries can be traced directly to a – no longer extant – version of the Commentary, reflective in the main of the manuscripts now belonging to the *y* line of transmission of this text. This means, as

---

[5]  For a discussion of the Psalter of Cashel, see Ó Riain, 'The Psalter of Cashel'. There is, as I argue below (§ 4), some slight evidence to show that the Psalter of Cashel may have served as a source of pedigrees.

[6]  For the different applications of the title *Saltair na Rann* in the early seventeenth century, see Ó Riain, 'Rawlinson B 502 alias Lebar Glinne Dá Locha', pp. 143–5.

[7]  Colgan's failure to publish more than the acts of the saints venerated during the first three months of the year automatically sets a limit to the number of surviving extracts from MC.

[8]  A 5 § IV.

[9]  A possible exception, ignored by Colgan in his statement of the case for a date c. 1030, is the subject of the entry at 24 Dec., Marianus Scotus the Chronicler, who died in 1082/3.

we have already seen,[10] that MC cannot be dated to earlier than the mid-1170s, when MO was first provided with a Commentary.

## 3 *Provenance of the Martyrology of Cashel (MC)*

Colgan took the view that MC was compiled at Cashel,[11] on the grounds that its saints seem to have been selected for the use of the church or diocese of that name.[12] Unfortunately, the fragmentary character of MC prevents us from knowing what other evidence Colgan might have had to hand, but both church and diocese of Cashel were first established a hundred years later than the date he proposed for the text.[13] Although this is nowhere stated, Colgan's view may have been influenced by his mistaken belief that the manuscript containing the text was possibly the Psalter of Cashel. There is no independent evidence to show that the Psalter ever contained a martyrology, and, although Colgan did have access to it, this would have been in the form of transcripts, probably by Mícheál Ó Cléirigh, to which his copy of the martyrology could well have been attached, whence the confusion on his part.

In fact, the available textual evidence, however sparse, indicates a greater concern with Lismore than with any other church. For example, the placing of Bríg of *Killbrige* at 21 Jan. – rather than on her more usual, if also spurious, feast of 31 Jan.[14] – may indicate Lismore preference, since Bríg's church is said to have been in the 'diocese of Lismore'. Similarly, at 4 Jan., an otherwise unknown *Corman* (*Cormania*) of Lismore is said to have been mother of both Cuanna and the local patron, Mochuta,[15] and, although this conflicts with the more

---

[10] See above at p. 127.

[11] *quod Casselense vocamus*, 'which we call of Cashel' (A 5 § IV).

[12] A 5 § IV: *Hoc . . . opus malumus Calendarium quam Martyrologium appellare; quod videatur potius ad instar Calendarij ad vsum Ecclesiae vel Dioecesis Casselensis collectum, quam ad modum Martyrologij compilatum; cum plurimos ex Hiberniae sanctis . . . silentio praeterierit.*

[13] Cashel was first presented to the Irish church in 1101, and the synod of Rathbrassil in 1111 marked the inauguration of the Irish diocesan system.

[14] Ó Riain, 'Bogus Saints', p. 3.

[15] Despite Colgan (A 251), who supplied two other variant forms of the name, *Coirmfhin* and *Comania*, attributing them respectively to a scholiast of MO, whom I have been unable to locate, and to an *anonymus*. Moreover, he attempted to reconcile the name with the more usual *Fínmed* by drawing attention to the shared semantic associations of *fín* (wine), *med* (mead) and *coirm* (beer) with alcohol!

orthodox record of these saints' maternal descent from Fínmed,[16] it nonetheless reveals a particular interest in the church of Lismore. The inclusion of Gormgal of Ardailén in Co. Galway, at 5 Aug. may also point, indirectly, to a Lismore author, since Colgan attributed his copy of a text on Gormgal's 'sacred relics and miracles' to Corcrán the Cleric, 'head of the piety of Ireland', who died at Lismore in 1040.[17] Finally, a Lismore provenance would explain the local knowledge displayed at 6 Dec., where the church of *Kill-lamruidhe*, now Killamery, is placed near the celebrated hill of Sliabh na mBan, which overlooks the town of Clonmel, on the northern boundary of the diocese of Lismore.

## 4 *Sources of the Martyrology of Cashel (MC)*

The – almost exclusive – source used by the author of MC was an already annotated copy of MO, which, as in the case of MTur, belonged to the *y* line of transmission, as reflected by the bulk of the surviving manuscripts, comprising B, C, F, L1, Lb and R2.[18] This line appears to have originated in a church in the Irish Midlands – possibly either Saigir, now Seirkieran, or Clonmacnoise – where much local material was added to a copy of the original Commentary.[19] From the evidence of MTur, which also used a copy of *y*,[20] this Midland edition would appear to have been produced at an early stage in the transmission of the text.

A number of entries in MC are drawn directly from the metrical text of MO, sometimes with rather unhappy consequences, especially for Iona, two of whose abbots were provided in this way with unhistorical names. At 24 Feb., *cruimthir*, 'priest', which relates to a separate entry in MO, is put forward as an alternative name for Cuimmíne Find, and, at 2 Mar., *Finnius* (from *find*, 'fair') of the metrical text, is substituted for Fergnae. A ghost placename also resulted from a misreading of the metrical text at 27 Feb., where the words *cen dinnis*, 'without reproach', are taken to reflect the *nomen loci* 'Ceann Ionnais'. Similarly, at 10 (recte

[16] Ó Riain, *Corpus*, § 722.62, Plummer, *Vitae*, I, p. 170.
[17] AI 1040; cf. AFM 1040, AClon. pp. 173, 176 (AU and ALC do not mention Lismore). Corcrán is said to have governed Ireland, with Cúán Ua Lothcháin, for some twenty years.
[18] For a detailed discussion of the transmission of MO, see Ó Riain, 'The Martyrology of Óengus'.
[19] Ibid.
[20] Chapter 3, § 4.

11) Apr., an otherwise unrecorded *Mumonius*, 'of Munster', attached to Máedóc Ua Dúnlaing of Leinster, may have less to do with local bias than with the mistaking of the adjective *maínech*, 'treasurous', of MO for the similarly-pronounced *Muimhneach*, 'of Munster'.[21] More straightforwardly, the use of *mionn*, 'diadem', at 23 Mar. and 13 Aug. as a term of praise seems to have appealed to the author of MC, who reproduced it on both days together with its respective dependent words, *Alban*, 'of Scotland', and *Gaoidhel*, 'of the Gaeil'.

Unfortunately, there is not sufficient evidence to show what other martyrological sources, if any,[22] the author of MC had to hand. Examples of agreement with MT or MG against MO, as at 9 Mar., 10 Oct., 21 Oct., 21 Dec., are too sporadic to allow any firm inference concerning dependency. Moreover, the three latter entries concern saints named Sillán, culminating in a bishop attached to Lismore, which may imply a particular interest not only in the church but also in the name. An unknown source or sources, not necessarily martyrological, supplied MC with additional information at 15 Jan. (*prius Derthrea sive Dorothaea*), 29 Mar. (*Finegallia*), 8 June (*Medranus et Tomanus in Britannica Arcluidensi*), 21 Aug. (*Patricii discipulus*), and 27 Oct. (*Inis-mhureadhaigh in Connacia*).

Some of the additional information may have derived from the author's wider reading in ecclesiastical and secular literature. Lives of the saints concerned may lie behind the information on authorship of Lives of Columba (24 Feb.) and Patrick (24 Nov.), as well as the reference to Brigit's reception of the veil (25 Apr.). For the assertion at 3 Mar. that Mo-Sacru, abbot of Clonenagh, lived in the time of Niall Glúndub (d. 919), there is, alas, no support, either in the annals or elsewhere.[23]

An interest in pedigrees is evident throughout, with most of the twenty-six cases in point otherwise shared by one or other version of the Commentary on MO.[24] Moreover, while close agreement between those

---

[21] Both words have the same pronunciation in Munster Irish.

[22] The copy of MO used by him could have been fuller than any of the surviving versions, thus accounting for entries not now traceable to it or to its Commentary.

[23] Some examples of confusion with regard to place- and personal names have already been cited. For others, see 30 Mar., where Dísert Tola is placed in *Media*, 11 May and 16 May, where separate entries are amalgamated, 14 June, where Benedictus is transformed into an Irish saint, and 13 Aug., where Radegundis becomes an Irish mother!

[24] 2 Jan. (Finnloga), 10 Jan. (Diermitius), 15 Jan. (Ita), 16 Jan. (Fursaeus), 20 Jan. (Fechin), 9 Feb. (Carecha), 15 Feb. (Berachus), 17 Feb. (Fintanus), 19 Feb. (Baithenus), 5 Mar. (Kieranus), 8 Mar. (Beoaedus), 13 Mar. (Mochoemocus), 16 Mar. (Finnanus), 21 Mar.

shared is generally more the exception than the rule, four of the pedi-grees are not found in any other martyrology.[25] From these, and from ten entries relating to the mothers of the saints,[26] it would appear that a manuscript containing a version of the corpus of saints' pedigrees was available to the author.[27] Indeed, the pedigrees provided for Maccarthenus at 24 Mar. and Tola at 30 Mar. are in such close agree-ment with the pedigrees attributed by Colgan to the Psalter of Cashel – which is known to have contained a version of the corpus of saints' pedigrees[28] – that one is tempted to regard this manuscript, or a manu-script dependent on it, as the likely source.[29]

## 5  *Editorial Policy*

Most often Colgan presented the text of MC in direct quotations, albeit in Latin translation. These are reproduced here in italic form. However, where Colgan referred to MC simply as a source among others without quoting directly from it, entries are presented here within square brack-ets. Since Colgan did not use the Roman notation, arabic numerals only are used here for the days of the months. The pages of A (*Acta Sanctorum Hiberniae*), T (*Trias Thaumaturga*) and, very rarely, KF (manuscripts in the Franciscan Library, Killiney) and MG (Martyrology of Gorman), containing the separate entries are cited in the textual notes, which are otherwise designed to identify the relationship between MC and its sources. Since, in effect, the source used is almost always the

(Endeus), 24 Mar. (Domangartus), 24 Mar. (Schiria), 24 Mar. (Maccarthenus), 30 Mar. (Tola), 4 Apr. (Tigernachus), 10 Apr. (Muidocus), 9 June (Columba Kille), 14 June (Benedictus), 18 Aug. (Dagaeus), 11 Nov. (Carbreus), 24 Nov. (Kienanus), 12 Dec. (Finnianus).
[25] 16 Jan. (Fursaeus), 24 Mar. (Maccarthenus), 11 Nov. (Carbreus), and 24 Nov. (Kienanus).
[26] 10 Jan. (Editua), 16 Jan. (Gelgesia), 4 Feb. (Cormania), 21 Mar. (Brigh), 4 Apr. (Derfraichia), 2 May (Liemania), 13 Aug. (Radegunda), 30 Oct. (no name), 10 Nov. (no name), 27 Nov. (Liemania). Of these, the entries at 10 Jan., 16 Jan., 4 Feb., 13 Aug. and 10 Nov. are unique to MC.
[27] For an edition of the saints' genealogies, see Ó Riain, *Corpus*.
[28] Ó Riain, 'The Psalter of Cashel', pp. 123–6.
[29] For the Psalter's versions of these pedigrees, see A 740, § II, 794 § 3. However, that of Féichín at 20 Jan. differs both in the initial of the paternal name and in its length from the Psalter's version quoted by Colgan at A 143, § 1. Moreover, at A 402, § I, Colgan draws attention to an omission in Finnian's pedigree in MC vis-à-vis the Psalter. In both cases, the differences could be due to scribal preference or carelessness.

Commentary on the Martyrology of Óengus, this is here called simply the Commentary. In the indexes, forms of personal and placenames are kept as close as possible to the spellings adopted by Colgan in his indexes, with some modifications, such as the provision of capitals.

# MARTYROLOGIUM SEU CALENDARIUM CASSELENSE

1–12 January

Januarius
1. [Mobeocus (Dobeocus) de Glean Geirg, filius Bracani].
2. [Scothinus].
3. [Finnluga . . . discipulus et frater S. Fintani de Dunblesque, et . . . exijt in Albanionem; estque Sanctus qui colitur in Tamlact-Finnlogain in regione Kiennachtae de Glenngemin. Finnloga et Fintanus duo filij Demani, filij Fingenij, filij Demani, filij Carelli, filij Muredacij, Muinderg].
5. [Cera in Ecclesia . . . Kilcherensi . . . e Conurij Regis stirpe].
8. [Molibba . . . a Calendario Casselensi infra vocatur Libba].
9. [[Faelanus] quia eius natalis seruatur in Hibernia . . . in Ecclesia de Cluain-mhaoscna in Regione de Feratulach].
10. [S. Diermitius de Inis Clothrann filius Lugnae, filij Lugadij, filij Finbarrij, filij Fraici, filij Cathchuonis, filij Angussii (quem alij Becchuonem cognominant), filij Dauidis, filij Fiachrij, filij Eochudij Cognomento Moimedonij . . . de stirpe Aengussij cognomento Becchuonis, qui fuit filius Dauidis ut supra . . . matrem vero . . . *Edituam*].
12. *S. Laidgennus filius Baithi Bannaigh nomen patris eius Buadhach quod idem est ac bannach .i. victoriosus; et in Cluainferta Molua quiescit.*

---

## JANUARY

1. T 182, § 188, A 314, § 22. In T, the feast is assigned both to 1 Jan. and 16 Dec., whereas A's wording would suggest that it was on the latter day only.
2. A 10, § 13.
3. T 383, § 23. Versions C and F of the Commentary also contain the saint's pedigree.
5. A 15, §§ 4, 13; 16, § 14.
8. A 43, § 2. Unfortunately, the printer omitted the note referred to by Colgan as *infra*.
9. A 50, §§ 2, 10; 104, § 1.
10. A 52, §§ 2, 3, 17. The name *Editua* for Diarmait's mother is not in any of the surviving manuscripts of MO, several of which, including C, F, Lb and P, also have versions of the saint's pedigree.
12. A 58, § 9. The text reflects most versions of the Commentary.

## 15–21 January

15. *S. Ita siue Mida filia Kennfoeladij, filij Conchorbi, filij Comor-burij, filij Conalli, filij Aengussi, filij Artcorbi, filij Fiachi suigde, filij Felimij legiferi. Ita prius Derthrea siue Dorothaea: et in Cluain-chredhuil in regione Conalliae Gaura in Mamomia colitur.*

16. *S. Fursaeus Filius Finnlogae, Filij Dergrogae, Filij Locani, F. Lagae, F. Conallij, F. Eochadij de Vltonia oriundus, quiescit Peronae. Nomen matris eius erat Gelgesia: et habuit sibi deuinctos S. Magnennum de Kill-Magnenn, et S. Meldanum filium Hua Cuinn, de Inis-mac-hy-chuinn in lacu Connaciae, Loch Oirbsen dicto nunc vero Loch Coirb.*

17. [Vltanus].

20.1. *S. Mo-acca vel Mo-ecca, et idem est qui Fechin, filius Mael-charna, filij Killini, de stirpe mhic-airtchoirb, discipulus sancti Kyerani.*

   2. *S. Molaggius (filius Dubdligij) colitur in Lan-beachuir, in regione Breghensium, (et in Tulach-min-molaga in Momonia) originem ducens ex regione Feara muighe in Momonia.*

21. *S. Brigidae (Briga) de Killbrige in diaecesi Lismorensi; et prope etiam Killdariam est eius ecclesia.*

---

15. A 73, § 3. Both versions of the saint's pedigree in the Commentary (L, C) read *Chind Fhaelad meic Cormaic*. Also, both have *Conchobair* for *Comorburij* of MC. Neither *Derthrea* nor *Dorothea* are recorded in the surviving versions of MO. For *Déirdri*, see MD at 15 Jan., and for *Dorythy*, see Procter, Dewick, *The Martiloge*, p. 10 (15 Jan.).

16. A 95. None of the extant versions of the Commentary contains either Fursa's pedigree or the name of his mother. However, the names and churches of his *devincti* are in manuscripts L, Lb and F, representing the *y* line of transmission.

17. A 109, § 1.

20.1. A 140, §§ 2, 8; 143, § 1. Of the extant versions of MO, only R2, which has the more correct *mac Caelcarna mic Grilline*, contains the pedigree. A fuller version, apparently from the Psalter of Cashel, is quoted by Colgan at 143, § 1. The account of the saint's role as a disciple of Ciarán's is based on an anecdote in the Commentary.

   2. A 150, § 24; 151, §§ 32–4; 540, §§ 31–4. The bracketed words reflect the note at A 540, §§ 31–4. A slightly different version of the text is quoted at A 151, §§ 32–4. The detail of the entry reflects most versions of the Commentary.

21. T 543, § 18; 612. Although based on most versions of the Commentary at 31 Jan., the saint's usual day, both mentions of the feast place it on the 21st. Having regard to the probable Lismore provenance of MC, reflected here by a unique reference to the diocese of Lismore, the variation may reflect local preference. The saint's church is otherwise named only in the Lb version of the *y* line of transmission of the Commentary. The bracketed form is from the slightly different second quotation of the entry.

22 January – 7 February

22. *S. Colmanus filius Hua-Beogna in Lismora Mochuddae.*

31. *S. Aidus alias Moedocus Fernensis, de Hy Luirg iuxta Lacum Ernensem.*

Februarius

1. [Brigida].

3. [Colmanus filius Duach].

4. *Natalis S. Cuannae (Cuannani), cuius Ecclesia est in Occidentali plaga (parte) Connaciae, et alia de Kill-chuanna in regione de Tir-briuin: Cormana (Corman) nomen matris. Est de Lismoro, et ex eadem matre frater S. Mochuddae.*

6. *Sanctus Mel filius Darercae sororis S. Patricij, quae fuit mater septemdecim Episcoporum; quorum vnus fuit Sanctus Mel Episcopus Ardachadensis in Teffia, et sanctus Maccarthinn de Clohar. Sanctus vero Mel est, qui sacram Confirmationem B. Brigidae contulit. Darerca insuper habuit duas sanctas filias virgines, Acheam et Lallocam.*

7. *S. Mellanus de Insula filiorum Hua-Cuinn in Lacu Orbsen, in regione de Hibh-(Oirb)sen in Occidentali Connacia.*

---

22. A 155, § 12. Although Colgan referred the text both to MD and to MC, it is not close to the wording and spelling of the former text. I take it, therefore, to reflect MC, which regularly attaches the name of its saint to Lismore. The entry derives from a combination of the metrical text of MO and its Commentary.

31. A 220, § 54. This entry agrees with most versions of the Commentary.

FEBRUARY

1. T 622.

3. A 247, § 15.

4. A 250; 251, § 6; 252, § 11; 338, § 9. The words within brackets are from the slightly different text of p. 338, § 9. The name *Corman(a)* given here to his mother, whom he allegedly shared with Mochutu, was said by Colgan (A 252, § 10) to be confirmed by a note in the Commentary at 17 Sep., but I cannot find this in any of the extant versions.

6. A 263, §§ 20–1. Cf. A 260, § 6; 261, § 2; 263, §§ 26, 29; 717, § 4; T 227, § 7; 231. The detail of the entry relating to the saint's tenure of the see of Ardagh in Teffia is shared by the two main lines of transmission of the Commentary. The remainder reflects manuscripts of the *y* line, the names of the two daughters of Darerca being in L, Lb and F only.

7. A 271, § 12; 691, §§ 7–8; T 378, § 71. Printer's errors *Obrsen* and *rehione* have been silently corrected. The bracketed letters are from p. 691, §§ 7–8. Apart from the tribal name *Hi Oirbsen*, which probably reflect the name of the lake, the detail corresponds to the Commentary.

171

## 8–15 February

8. *Sanctus Onchuo singularis poeta, de Connacia oriundus; et Cluainmoriae in Lagenia quiescit.*

9. *Hac die S. Carecha Dergamensis filia Conalli Deirg filij Damenij filij Carbrei Damhairgid, qui separauit lacum Erne a Connacia, et Dubthor a Lagenia, et expulit Vlidios [. . .]tra Gleannrighe ad orientem. Et hac sunt tria heroica eius acta. Huius ergo Conalli filia fuit S. Carecha Derganiensis et Soror S. Endei Aranniensis, et ipsa quiescit in Cluainboireann in regione Imania ad ripam flumenis Sinennij.*

10. *Sanctus Cronanus filius Mellani; de Lismoria in Desiis Momoniae; et iuxta Surdum S. Columbae ad austrum quiescit.*

11.1. *S. Episcopus Etchanus, qui ordinem Praesbyteratus dedit S. Columbae Kille.*

2. *Sancta Gobnata Monialis de vico Boirne siue Bairnigh in Momonia et fuit de stirpe Conarij.*

13. *Hodie natalis S. Modomnoci (Dominicus) de Tobar Fachtna, inter Ossraighios et Desios ad ripam fluminis Siuirij* (et addit Latine) *Ipse est qui apes primo tulit in Hiberniam: hac autem est dies obitus eius, aut dies quo cum apibus appulit.*

15. *Berachus de Cluaincoirpthe, filius Nemnagij, filij Nemangani, F. Fintani, F. Malii, F. Dobtha, F. Aengusii, F. Erci Deirg, F. Briani, F. Eochadii Moimedonii, F. Muredacii Tirigh, F. Fiachi etc.*

---

8. A 277, § 18. Apart from his assignment to Connacht, which is also in R1, the name and description of the saint reflect the *y* line of transmission of the Commentary.

9. A 3, § 6. Colgan asserts that the entry is in MC at 9 Mar., but I take this to be an error for the 9 Feb., the saint's usual day. Apart from her assignment to Cluain Boirenn, which is also in R1, the detail concerning the saint corresponds closely to that of the manuscripts of the *y* line of transmission of the Commentary.

10. A 304; cf. 304, §§ 1, 6, 14. Only the L version of the Commentary agrees with MC in reading Lis Mór for the more usual Glas Mór; the Lb version combines the names.

11.1. A 306, § 17. The reception by Colum Cille of priestly orders from Etchén is mentioned only in the manuscripts of the *y* line of transmission of the Commentary.

2. A 315, §§ 7–10. Although most manuscripts of the Commentary assign Gobnat to Bairnech, I cannot find any reference to the variant *Boirne*.

13. A 150, § 25; 327, § 4; cf. 328, §§ 17–18. Of the extant manuscripts of the Commentary, only P includes the Déise and the bank of the river Suir. The Latin addition to MC reflects the metrical text of MO, but its gist, in Irish, is also in the C manuscript of the Commentary.

15. A 347, § 32. The pedigree is in several manuscripts of the *y* line of transmission of the Commentary, all of which have *Nemnann* for *Nemnagij* here.

## 17 February – 1 March

17.1. *Natalis S. Fintani, filij Gaureni, filij Corcrani, filij Echach, filij Bressalij, filij Denij etc. qui iacet in Cluain-edhnech in Laghisia [in] regione Lageniae.*

2. *Co[r]macus Episcopus de Athtruim in regione de Hy-Laogaire in Media, et comorbanus* (id est successor) *S. Patricij.*

18.1. *S. Molibba in regione de Hibh-Et[h]ach Vltoniae.*

2. [Colmanus] *in Ard-Bo in regione de Cinel-eoguin.*

19. *S. Baithenus filius Cuanachi, filij Ennij, filij Conalli Deirg, episcopus de Tegh-Baithein in occidentali Media vel in Airteach.*

21. *Fintanus Corach quiescit in Leamchuill, inter Hy duach et Laighis, vel in Cluainaithchin, vel in Cluainferta Brendani. Dicitur autem Corach, quia peregrinaturus, sponsores dedit, se aut viuum aut mortuum reuersurum.*

24. *Cruimthir .i. Sacerdos, Abbas Hiae S. Columbae hoc est Comineus Abbas Praesbyter, author vitae S. Columbae.*

27. *S. Comganus de Gleann vssen; et Ceann ionnais nomen loci vbi eius est Ecclesia.*

28. [Sillanus] *Abbas Bennchorensis et comorbanus Sancti Comgalli.*

Martius

1.1. *S. Moennius siue Mainennius Episcopus de Cluainferta; et comorbanus .i. Successor S. Brendani.*

---

17.1. A 356, § 5. The pedigree is in both lines of transmission of the Commentary. The saint's connexion with Cluain Eidnech is asserted in the metrical text of MO.

2. A 359, § 21. The text reflects the Commentary fairly closely.

18.1. A 368, §§ 6–7. This text is in almost all manuscripts of the Commentary.

2. A 368. Manuscripts of both lines of transmission of the Commentary place Ard Bó in Cenél Eogain.

19. KF 3, [5]; cf. A 361 (caput V); 369, § 7; 370, § 21. The full text, in Colgan's hand, is only in the Killiney manuscript. If we except the omission here of Baíthíne's grandfather, Cian (Cóem), the detail of the entry corresponds to the Commentary.

21. A 385, § 14. Both lines of transmission of the Commentary contain similar detail.

24. A 411, § 26. This is partly based on the metrical text of MO, where *cruimther*, 'priest', refers to a totally different saint. The reference to his authorship of a Life of Columba is not in MO.

27. A 418, § 15. Both lines of transmission of the Commentary assign Comgán to Glenn Uissen. *Ceann Ionnais* is a ghost name, derived from *cen dindis*, 'without reproach', of the metrical text of MO.

28. A 424, §§ 8–9. The entry corresponds to both lines of transmission of the Commentary.

### MARCH

1.1. A 439, § 7. The variant *Mainenn*, whence *Mainennius*, is not attested in any version of MO, the Commentary of which accounts for the bulk of the entry.

## 1–9 March

1.2.   *Sanctus Senanus de Inis-cathuigh hac die obiit: eius autem festiuitas celebratur octauo huius.*

2.   *S. Finnius .i. Candidus Abbas Hiae S. Columbae.*

3.   *S. Mo-sacra filius Senani Abbas de Cluain-edhneach: et tempore Nielli Glanduibh vixit.*

5.1.   [S. Kieranus Sagirensis] *de familia Dal-mb[i]rn oriundus, Kieranus nempe filius Luagni, filij Rumundi, filij Conaldi, filij Corprei Niadh, filij Buanij, filij Eochadij Lamdoid, filij Amalgadij, filij Leogarij Birn, filij Aengussij Ossergij.*

2.   *S. Carthacus alumnus Kierani Sagirensis, et filius Regis Eoganachtae Casselensis: et in Carbria Medensi iacet eius Ecclesia vel in insula de Inis Uachtuir in Lacu de Loch-Sileann. Fuit Carthacus institutor S. Mochudae; eique [de]dicata est Ecclesia de Inis-Carthach apud Lismorum.*

8.   *Aedus viuidus, siue Beoaedus Episcopus, filius Olcani, filij Comini, filij Manij, filij Trenij filij Buani, filij Lugadij Macconij.*

9.1.   *S. Sedna de Druim macublai in regione Chrimthannorum.*

2.   *Sanctus Sedna de Kill-aine in monte Bregh.*

3.   [Carecha] vid. 9 Feb.

---

1.2.   A 440; cf. 543, § VI. Two versions of the Commentary (R1, Lb) specify Senán's obit on this day.

2.   A 454, §§ 10–11. This ghost name of an abbot of Iona derives from the metrical text of MO, which reads: *féil find Fergnai Iae*, 'fair (taken here as a personal name) feast of Fergna of Iona'.

3.   A 454, §§ 9–11. The spelling of the saint's name is at variance with all extant manuscripts of MO (*Moacru/Momacru*). However, it agrees with MTur, which likewise depends on a manuscript of the *y* line of transmission. The reference to Niall Glúndub is also absent from all versions of the Commentary.

5.1.   A 471. Both pedigree and reference to Dál mBirn are otherwise attested in manuscripts of the *y* transmission of the Commentary. Of the two manuscripts containing the pedigree, F and R2, the former agrees closest with MC.

2.   A 476, §§ 14–15. The bulk of the information provided by the entry corresponds closely to most versions of the Commentary. The reference to *Inis Carthach* (recte *Cathrach?*) is otherwise confined to the F version.

8.   A 563, § 8. Almost all manuscripts of the Commentary contain much the same detail.

9.1.   A 565 [recte 569], § 2; cf. T 188, §§ 110–11. Of the manuscripts of the Commentary, only F, which cites MG as its source at this point, contains material similar to 9.1 and 9.2. Unless it was using a no longer extant version of the Commentary, therefore, it may be that MC turned here either to MT – which also assigns Cell Áine of 9.2 to Sliab Breg – or to MG.

2.   A 565 [recte 569], § 4. See previous note.

## 11–22 March

11.    *S. Constantinus ex Britannia ortus: Abbas de Cul Rathen Mochuddae in regione de Delbhna Ethra in Media.*

13.1.  [S. Mochoemocus, filius Beoani, filij Mellani, F. Nessanij, F. Erci, F. Cuinnedij (alijs Caredij), F. Finnchoemy, F. Coemscragij etc.].

2.    *Cuangussius mac dall* (.i. filius caecus) *de Lethmor.*

14.    [Vltanus].

15.    *S. Dichullus Derg, filius Nessani, de Inis-Nessani in Bregijs.*

16.    *S. Finanus Lobhra filius Conalli, filij Eochodij, filij Tadgaei, filij Kieni, filij Alildi Olom, de Surdo et de Cluainmor Maidoci in Lagenia, et de Inis faithlenn in lacu Lenensi, de Ard finain.*

17.1.  [S. Patricius].

2.    *Nessanus Corcagiensis.*

19.    *Lactocus, alias Lactinus de Achadh ur.*

21.    *S. Endeus de Arannia filius Conalli Deirg* (.i. rubei), *filij Damanij, filij Carbreij Daimhairgid Regis Orgelliorum: et Brigh seu Aibhfinn filia Anmirij, filij Romani (Ronani) Regis Firardiorum fuit eius mater.*

22.    [S. Falueus abbas Hiensis, comorbanus S. Columbae Kille].

---

11.    A 578, §§ 1–2. Other than the insertion of *Cul*, perhaps due to confusion with the well known Cúil Rathain (Coleraine), the detail of this entry accords with most manuscripts of the Commentary.

13.1.  A 598, § II. Colgan took the text from *Gen. Reg. SS. Hib.*, with a cross-reference both to MC and to the Psalter of Cashel. Of the manuscripts of the Commentary, only R2 contains the pedigree.

2.    A 607, § 5. The Latin translation of *mac dall* was added by Colgan. Otherwise, the entry agrees closely with the Commentary.

14.    A 109, § 1. Although assigned to it in a general statement at p. 109, Ultán's presence in MC is not confirmed by Colgan's notes to his feastday.

15.    A 609, §§ 10–14. Both lines of transmission of the Commentary name Dícuill Derg as one of the children of Nessán.

16.    A 629, § 14. Of the manuscripts of the Commentary, only F – which also adds a reference to Ard Fínáin – has the pedigree.

17.1.  T 232, § V.

2.    A 630, § 5. Both lines of transmission of the Commentary likewise attach Nessán to Cork.

19.    A 657, § [9]; cf. A 299, § 12; A 597, § 13. Both lines of transmission of the Commentary assign the saint to Achad Úr.

21.    A 3, § 5; 711, § I; 713, § III. The bracketed words are from A 711, 713. Some of the detail, but not the first name(s) of the saint's mother, is in the Commentary, which also lacks the name of the maternal great-grandfather.

22.    A 720, §§ 8–11.

175

23–30 March

23. *Maidocus, Mionn Alban.*

24.1. *S. Domangartus de Sliebh-Slanga, filius Eochadij, F. Muredacii, F. Forga, F. Dallani, F. Lugadii, F. Aengussii Finnii, F. Fergussii Dubdedii etc.*

  2. *S. Schiria de Kill-Schire in Media filia Eugenij, filij Canannani, filij Alildi, filij Fergussij, F. Eochadij Moimedonij etc.*

  3. *Mocteus Episcopus Lugmagensis.*

  4. *Episcopus Maccarthennus filius Cannechi, filij Fethlimij, filij Eochadij, filij Clodhchuonis, filij Aredij, filij Mailedij, filij Bressalij, filij Buanij de Clocharia filiorum Damenij in Orgiellia.*

  5. *S. Caminus siue Canius de Inis-Keltra.*

26. *S. Mochellocus de Kill odhrain, de Cathuir mac Conchuidh.*

29. *Sanctae filiae baiae de Cella filiarum baithe in Finegallia ad Surdum in campo Bregh.*

30.1. *S. Mochua de Balla in Connacia.*

  2. *S. Colmanus de Lanmocholmoc in Vltonia.*

  3. *S. Tola de Disert-tola in Media. Tola hic fuit filius Dunchadi, filij Ernini, F. Garuani, F. Senani, F. Muredacij, F. Tailgluin, F. Brogani, F. Corbmaci Galengij* [a quo Galengarum populi], *F. Tadgaei, F. Kieni etc.*

---

23. A 727, § 7. The description of the saint as 'Scotland's diadem' is drawn from the metrical text of MO.

24.1. A 744, § 9; cf. 328, § 15; T 187, §§ 94–5. Although both saint and church are noted in the Commentary, none of its extant versions contains the pedigree.

  2. A 339, § 31. Manuscripts F and Lb of the *y* line of transmission of the Commentary likewise contain Scíre's pedigree in a version very close to MC.

  3. A 732, § I. Mochta is noted in the same way in the Commentary.

  4. A 740, § I; cf. T 181, § 174. Although among the saints of the day in manuscripts L and Lb, Mac Caírthinn is not provided with a pedigree in the Commentary. The version here agrees closely with Ó Riain, *Corpus*, § 95.

  5. A 747, §§ [8–10]. Some manuscripts of the *y* line of transmission of the Commentary (R2, F, Lb) mention Caimmíne on the following day.

26. A 749, §§ 10–11. None of the extant manuscripts of the Commentary agrees with the corrupt *Kill Odhrain*, which MC derived from the personal name *Cillín mac Tulodráin.*

29. A 786, § 9. MC differs here from the extant versions of the Commentary, none of which specifies *Finegallia* and *campus Bregh.*

30.1. A 792, § 19. The detail here corresponds to the R1 version of the Commentary, which also adds the precise region in Connacht.

  2. A 793, §§ 10–11. The Lb version of the Commentary likewise attaches Colmán to Lann Mocholmóc in Ulster.

  3. A 794, § 7; cf. T 180, § 135. The words in square brackets were added by Colgan. Of the extant versions of the Commentary, only R1 places Dísert Tola in Mide and only

## 4 April – 11 May

Aprilis

4.  S. *Tigernachus filius (Cairbrei, filij) Fergussij, filij Sednae, filij Labani, filij Briuini, filij Eochadij, filij Darij cognomento Barrich, filij Caitherij Magni, Hiberniae regis. Et de Hi-Barrche oriundus, id est, filius Regis Hu Barche fuit. Derfraichia etiam filia Eochodij, f. Carthennij, Orgielliae Regis, Rath-Moriae iuxta Clocharium habitantis; fuit eius mater: et ipse in Cluain-Eoais quiescet.*

10. *Muidocus, Mumonius, filius Midnae filij Medi* [f. Ninnedij, f. Nazarij, f. Aengussij, f. Crimthanni, f. Cathiri Magni] *de Lageniis.*

25. S. *Maccaleus, qui colitur in Cruachan Brighele in regione de Iffalgia, ipse dedit velum Sanctae Brigidae.*

Maius

2.  S. *Nectanus de Kill-unche in regione Conalliae, alumnus S. Patricij: et Mac-Leamna* [id est filius Liemaniae] *ibi nominatur, a Liemania filia Calphurni eius matre: et iacet Finnauariae, ad ripam Boindi fluuij, in regione Bregiorum.*

11. [S. Cormacus Praesbyter de Achadh-finnigh iuxta fluuium Dothra, in Lagenia 11 Maij; quiescet in quadam Tirconalliae insula, Inis-Caoil nuncupata].

---

R2 supplies a pedigree, albeit a very different one from that of MC, which, although much longer, otherwise agrees with the version of the Psalter of Cashel quoted by Colgan at p. 794, § 3.

### APRIL

4.  KF 3, [12]. The bracketed words were added above the line. The pedigree is much longer than that of the *y* line of transmission of the Commentary, which has three generations only. Ráith Mór near Clochar is in the *y* line, as against *Rigraith* of R1. The saint's maternal great-grandfather is named Crimthann in both the Commentary and Ó Riain, *Corpus*, § 722.42.

10. A 727, § 8. The entry more properly belongs at 11 Apr. The bracketed names from p. 727, § 7 are inserted in response to Colgan's *etc. ut supra* at this point. For a possible explanation of the use of the word *Mumonius* in place of *maínech*, see § 4 of the Introduction. Both lines of transmission of the Commentary likewise record the saint's descent.

25. T 525, § 11; cf. p. 526, § 11. The saint's giving of the veil to Brigit is mentioned in both lines of transmission of the Commentary (MSS Lb, F and P).

### MAY

2.  A 263, § 18; 659, § 2; 717, § III; T 226, § 6. The bracketed words were added by Colgan. The detail here corresponds closely to the Commentary.

11. A 360, § I. It is not clear whether the whole or part of the entry was in MC. The detail is drawn from notes on three separate saints in the Commentary.

16 May – 14 June

16. [Carnechus cognomento Moel . . . in Ecclesia Tulenensi in Media
 . . . et Calend. Cassel. addit ipsum fuisse origine Britannum,
 iacere sepultum in Ecclesia de Inis-Baithin in Lagenia].

18. *S. Maidocus de Fedh-duin in Ossoria.*

Iunius

8.1. *SS. Medranus et Murchu, duo fratres, filij Hua Macten coluntur
 in Kill murchu in regione de Hi Garrchon.*

 2. *SS. Medranus et Tomanus in vna Ecclesia in Britannica
 Arcluidensi.*

9. *Nono Iunij S. Columba Kille, Crimthann prius appellatus, filius
 Fedhlimidij, filij Fergussij, filij Conalli, filij Corprei
 cognomento File, filij Alildi Magni, filij Darij Barrigh, filij
 Caithirij Magni etc.*

11. *Mac Tail de Kill-cuilin de Mag-laigean; Pater eius fuit Eugenius
 filius Dergani, et fuit Faber: et Mac Tail .i. filius Fabri dicitur.
 Aengussius autem fuit primum eius nomen.*

12. [Natalis autem S. Coemani celebratur in ecclesia Ardnensi prope
 Wexfordiam].

14. *S. Benedictus filius Luagnei, filij Leth-triuni, filij Birn de Dal-Birn
 Ossoriae, Comorbanus siue successor Endei Arannensis; et frater
 Kierani Sagirensis: ipse est Papa, quem ferunt esse in insula
 Araniensi.*

---

16. A 473, § IV. Colgan paraphrased here the entry on Cairnech in MC. The mistaken
 reference to Inis Baíthín reflects a note in the Commentary, as in the F version,
 which relates to a separate saint.
18. A 727, § 9. Both lines of transmission of the Commentary provide the same detail.

JUNE

8.1.2. A 465, §§ 31–2; cf. KF 3, [9]. None of the extant versions of the Commentary
 assigns the saints to the otherwise unattested Cell Murchon in Uí Garrchon; nor, to
 my knowledge, is there is any reference elsewhere to the saints placed in the
 Dumbarton area of Scotland.
9. T 477, § I; cf. 483, § 4. Colgan described the pedigree, which amalgamates the
 saint's paternal and maternal descents, as *confuse nimis et mendose.* What probably
 gave rise to the confusion was the juxtaposition of the two descents in the version of
 the Commentary used by MC, as is also the case in L, Lb and F.
11. T 185, § 32. The entry corresponds to both lines of transmission of the Commentary.
12. A 281, § 3.
14. A 472, § III; 711, § 32; cf. T 182, §§ 199–200. Here Benedictus stands for the more
 correct Nem, the confusion being due to a misinterpretation of the metrical text of
 MO, which reads: *Nem maccu Birn . . . la Benedicht . . .*, 'Nem of Moccu Birn with

178

TEXT

## 17 June – 12 August

17.1. [S. Molingus . . . eius [Moedoci] discipulus].

2. *S. Colmanus filius Luachain de Lann-micluachain in Media.*

22. [Cronanus Abbas Fernensis].

25.1. [S. Tellius de Tegh Telle in Occidentali Media].

2. *S. Moluocus de Lismoro in Albania, seu Albione.*

## Iulius

9. [S. Garbhanus . . . qui prope Dubliniam colitur].

12. [S. Nazarus Episcopus . . . in hoc monasterio (Liathmorum)].

25.1. *S. Colmanus filius Hua-Beogna in Lismora Mochuddae.*

2. [S. Nessanus diaconus de Mungarett].

## Augustus

5. [S. Gormgalius Abbas de Ard-oilen].

8. [Beoanus filius Nessani in Fidh Cuilenn in regione de Hi Faelain].

10. [Blaanus].

12. [Sigenius (Segenus) Abbas Hiensis].

---

Benedict'. The remainder of the detail corresponds to both lines of transmission of the Commentary.

17.1. A 219, § 36. Only the L version of the *y* line of transmission of the Commentary attests to Moling's position as disciple (*daltae*) of Máedóc.

2. A 793, § 2; T 453, § 21. Although not in the metrical text of MO, Colmán is included in manuscripts L, F, Lb of the *y* line of transmission of its Commentary.

22. A 219, § 36.

25.1. A 15, §§ 9–10.

2. T 481, § 34. The same detail is provided by the Commentary.

### JULY

9. A 751, § 4.

12. A 598, § IV.

25.1. A 155, § 12. The saint's descent from *Hua-Beogna* is not recorded in any of the extant versions of the Commentary.

2. A 630, § 2.

### AUGUST

5. A 5, § IV; 141, § 13; 206, § 3; 715, § 3; MG, p. xvii. Gormgal, 'chief confessor of Ireland', died in 1018 (AU) and this was one of the factors that encouraged Colgan (A 5) to date MC to c. 1030. None of the extant versions of the Commentary refers to him.

8. A 609, § 9.

10. A 234, § 9.

12. A 45, § 4; T 374, § 30. The variant form of the abbot's name is at T 374.

## 13–24 August

13. *Maidocus, dictus Mionn Gaoidhel, abbas Fedh-dunensis in Ossoria, et filius Radegundis sancte Reginae.*

14. *S. Fachtdani, Episcopi de Ros alethir in occidentali plaga Momoniae fuit etiam Abbas de Dar inis Moelanfaidh in regione Desiorum in Momonia, dictusque Fachtna Mongach, quia cum caesarie natus.*

15. *S. Ferdachrichus Episcopus de Clochar, post Episcopum Maccarthennum. Clochar vero dicitur a Cloch-oir, id est lapis aureus , in quo Gentilos habebant idola aurea , et argentea.*

18.1. *S. Dagaeus filius Carelli, filij Lasreni, filij Dallani, filij Eugeni, filij Nielli Naoigiallach. Hic Dagaeus fuit faber tam in ferro quam aere; et Scriba insignis. Fabricauit enim trecentas campanas, trecenta peda pastoralia: et scripsit trecentos libros Euangeliorum. Fuitque primarius S. Kierani faber.*

2. *Erneneus, id est Mernocus filius Gresseni, de Rath naoi in Hi-Garchon in Lagenia, et de Kill-Droigneach, in Hi-Drona.*

21. [Senachum Episcopum Cluanerardensem fuisse Patricii discipulum dicit].

24. *Patricius Senior de Ros-dela, in Mag-lacha quiescit sed secundum aliquos, et verius, Glastiberiae (Glastoniae) Scotorum (Hibernorum) quiescit Patricius senior. Haec est ciuitas in occidentali (Aquilonari/Boreali) parte Angliae (Saxonum) et Hiberni (Scoti) habitant eam. Reliquiae tamen eius quiescunt Ardmachiae in Lipsanis, Patricij Senioris (in reliquiario/scrinio S. Patricij) appellatis.*

---

13. A 727. His description as *Mionn Gaoidhel*, 'diadem of the Irish', derives from the metrical text of MO. The suggestion that he was Radegund's son is explained by Colgan as *non corporalis procreationis sed spiritualis amicitia*. The feast of Radegund, foundress of a convent at Poitiers, also fell on this day.

14. A 596, § 7. The entry more or less agrees with the Commentary, which locates Dairinis, however, in Uí Cheinselaig.

15. A 740, § I. The etymology of Clochar is not found in any version of the Commentary.

18.1. A 374. Of the several versions of the Commentary, Lb is closest to MC, agreeing with it on the form of name of Daig's grandfather *Lasreni/Laisrein* and on the addition of *insignis/togaide* to *Scriba/scribnid*.

2. T 373, § 30. This entry is also in the Commentary.

21. T 178, § 118. None of the extant versions of the Commentary describes Senach as a disciple of Patrick's.

24. A 366, §§ 6–7; 431, § 21; T 7, § 22; 10, § 48; 229, § 14; 262. The bracketed variants are from A 431 and T 10. Although MC is here very similar to the Commentary,

## 24 August – 20 October
31.    [Aidanus Lindisfarnensis].

September
3.    [Lonius ... in Ecclesiis de Killagaura in monte Margio, in Magtuathad, et deserto Garadh in Boreali parte Ossoriae].
10.    *Finnianus Fionn de Magbile; ipse est qui primo legem Moysaicam ... et totum Euangelium in Hiberniam portauit.*
13.    [Daganus de Inber-Daoile] *Bellatorem qui et in regione de Dalmocorb in Lagenia.*
14.    [Coemanus ... Breac ... Abbas de Ros Each].
17.    [Broganus ... in Ecclesia de Ros-tuirck, in Ossoria].

October
10.    *Sillanus Abbas.*
12.    *Fiachrius filius Fieci, et ambo quiescunt in Minbeag, id est sylua, quae est inter Cluain-mor Maodhoc et Achadh-abhall.*
13.    [Finsecha in Monte Guarij, in regione Galengae].
16.    [Cera in Ecclesia ... Kilcherensi ... e Conurij Regis Hiberniae stirpe].
20.    *S. Fintanus Moeldubh de regione Eoghanacht Cassil, et institutor S. Fechini.*

---

only F, Lb and R2 of the *y* line of transmission allude to the presence of the saint's relics in a shrine at Armagh.
31.    A 47.

### SEPTEMBER
3.    T 565, § 12.
10.    A 643, § II. The entry corresponds to the Commentary, with the Lb version deriving the saint's name from *find*, 'fair', whence *Fionn* here.
13.    A 586, §§ 18–19. The use of *bellator*, 'warrior', to describe Dagán reflects the metrical text of MO which uses the words *cingid mbáge*, 'champion of battle'.
14.    A 140, § 15.
17.    T 518, §§ 1–2.

### OCTOBER
10.    T 381, § 3. Although absent from both MO and its Commentary on this day, Sillán the abbot is listed in MT, MG and MD.
12.    T 185, § 37. The detail of the entry agrees closely with both lines of transmission of the Commentary.
13.    A 367.
16.    A 15, §§ 4, 13; 16 § 14.
20.    A 355, § 27. Although much abbreviated here, the entry agrees in substance with the Commentary, as in manuscripts R2, F, Lb.

21 October – 11 November

21. *Sillanus Hua Gairbh, cognomento Magister, Abbas Magbilensis.*

26. [Festum Sanctorum Nassadij Beoani et Mellani: tres sancti de Britannia, et in una Ecclesia . . . in Tamhlachta umhail, in regione Iuechiae in Vltonia iuxta lacum Bricreann].

27.1. *Natalis Colmani Hua Fiachra, qui colitur in Inis-mhureadhaigh in Connacia: et iuxta eius Ecclesiam sunt anates aues illaesae semper manentes.*

2. [S. Odranus, abbas Hiensis, et de Tegh-Ererain in Media].

3. [S. Abbanum] *filium Hua Corbmaic de Kill-Abbain, in Hi Murredhaigh* [appelet].

30. *S. Colmanus filius Hua Gualann de Vltonia: et quiescit in Lann-mocholmoc: et est filius matris S. Mocholmoci de Lann.*

31. [S. Foilanus frater S. Fursaei, abbas et martyr in Gallia].

November

3. [S. Coemhanus de Enach Truim] . . . [dicunt ipsum esse Fratrem S. Coemgini Abb. de Gleandalach et S. Natchomij Abbatis de Tyrdaglass].

10. *S. Aidus filius Brecij de stirpe Fiachi filij Neill: mater autem eius, erat de regione Muscraighethire. Colitur Kill-ary, in occidentali Media, et in Sliebh lieg, in valle de Senghlenn in Vltonia.*

11. *Sanctus Carbreus Episcopus de Cuil-raithen, filius Degilli, filij Natsluagij, filij Coelbadii, filii Crunnii Badhraoi etc.*

---

21. T 381, § 3. Absent from both MO and its Commentary, Sillán Magister is commemorated on this day in other martyrologies, including MG which has the same detail as MC.

26. A 90, § 19.

27.1. A 141, § 19; T 384, §§ 34–5. Although otherwise in agreement with MC, the Commentary assigns Colmán to a church in south Leinster.

2. A 372, § 16; T 377, § 65; 452, § 10.

3. A 624, § I. The wording corresponds closely to the Commentary.

30. A 793, §§ 10–11. The reference to the saint's relationship with Mocholmóc of Lann is also in manuscripts F and Lb of the *y* line of transmission of the Commentary.

31. A 104, § I (with 13 by mistake for 31).

NOVEMBER

3. A 597, §§ 15–16.

10. A 423, § 31. Since Colgan mentioned several other authorities at this point, it is not certain that the text of MC is intended. Neither the saint's mother nor his church in 'Senglenn' is mentioned in the Commentary.

11. T 183, § 227. Again, since Colgan also cites *Sanctilogium Genealogium*, it is not

18 November – 9 December

18. [Sanctus Ronanus filius Berachi ... Abbas de Druim-ineascluinn].

24.1. [S. Colmanus cognomento Mitine, (Leninij filius) ... in Ecclesia de Cluain-uamhach, in regione de uibh-Liathain].

2. *Sanctus Kienanus de Damliag, filius Sednae, filij Trenij, filij Tiguernachi, filij Finchuonis (Finnchaemij), filij Tiehij (Feicii), filij Finchadij, (filij Conlae) filij Tadgaei, etc. Et in regione Bregarum est Damliegum, in Orientali Media. Huius Sancti Kierani (Kienani) remanet incorruptum, et illaesum corpus. Scripsit vitam Sancti Patricij.*

27. *Secundinus filius Liemaniae sororis S. Patricij: et Restitutus Pater eius. Colitur in Domnach-sechnaill: estque de Longo-bardis: et Finus nomen eius ibi.*

December

1. *Nessanus de Corcagia, qui et de Vltonijs oriundus.*

6. *S. Gobanus de Kill-Lamruidhe iuxta montem Sliabh na mBhan bFionn dictum: vel Gobanus de Teg-Da-Goba ad ripam Bannii fluminis in Ibh-Echach [in] regione Vltoniae. Quisquis horum est, fuit pater mille monachorum.* [requiescat in monasterio de Cluain Ednech in Lagenia].

9. [Mugenia ... filia Alilli, filij Dunlaing Regis Lageniae, ... cum sorore sua Felimia ... in Ecclesia de Kill naningen in regione Lageniae, quae Magh liffe nuncupatur].

certain that the text of MC is meant here. None of the manuscripts of the Commentary contains Cairpre's pedigree.

18. A 141, § 17.
24.1. A 104, § II; 310, § 14. The bracketed words are from p. 310.
2. T 217; KF 3, [9]; cf. A 413, § 2; 443, § 11. The bracketed variants/additions are from KF. The incorrupt state of the saint's body is also specified in the Commentary, which omits, however, both the pedigree and the reference to Cianán's authorship of Patrick's Life.
27. A 263, § 18; 659, § 2; 716, § III; T 226, § 6; cf. A 262, § 17; T 230. Most of this information is also in the Commentary, which has *Secundinus nomen eius* for *Finus nomen eius* here.

DECEMBER

1. A 630, § 9. Nessán of Cork is also listed here in the Commentary.
6. A 750; cf. A 92, § 6. The bracketed addition is from p. 92. The detail of the entry is reflected most fully in the F manuscript of the Commentary, which likewise alternatively locates the saint in the Ulster church. The reference to Sliabh na mBan bhFionn, the name of a hill near Clonmel, is unique to MC.
9. A 340, § 40; T 185, § 29.

## 11–29 December

11. [Meoltecus].
12. *Finnianus Fionn, .i. candidus Abbas de Cluain-eraird, nempe Finnianus filius Fintani, filij Conchradij, filij Darchelli, filij Senachi, filij Fergussij, filij Olildae, filij Cheltcharij, filij Vthecharij.*
13. [S. Baitanus de Cluain-andobhair].
16. [S. Dabeocus].
21. *Sillanus Lismorensis Episcopus.*
23. [S. Mothemnogus seu Temneogus, Coquus S. Moluani Cluainfertensis].
24. [Maolmuire ... B. Marianus Scotus Chronographus, de quo quod in Martyrologio Casselensi deest (?) Martyrologio Tamlactensi].
26. [S. Hierlatius].
29. [Aleranus ... Cluain Erairdiae in Media].

---

11. A 573, § 4.
12. A 402, § I; cf. 397, § 2. *Fionn* is taken from the metrical text of MO (*Findén find*, 'F. the fair'). As Colgan pointed out (p. 403), two generations are omitted from the body of the pedigree vis-à-vis the Commentary and other sources.
13. A 437, § 2.
16. A 314, § 22; T 182, § 188.
21. T 381, § 3. Although in MT and MG, Sillán is neither in the metrical text of MO nor in its Commentary. This also applies to the other entries on Sillán at 10, 21 Oct.
23. A 104, § II. There follow in A several generations of Motheimneóc's pedigree but it is not possible to say that these were taken from MC.
24. MG 246. Somewhat enigmatically, Colgan added a note in the right margin of the Martyrology of Gorman, then in Louvain, at 24 Dec., stating that the Maol Muire noted by Gorman may have been the same as Marianus Scotus of MC. However, the Irish form of the chronicler's name was Máel Brigte. Moreover, his day, according to the necrology of the Schottenkloster of Regensburg (Ó Riain-Raedel, 'Das Necrolog', p. 78) was 22 Dec., the 24th being reserved for another Marianus. And finally, the chronicler died in 1082/3; yet, when discussing MC (A 5, § IV), Colgan used the obit of Gormgal of Ardoilén in 1018 to date it to about 1030.
26. A 310, § 23.
29. A 140, § 12.

CHAPTER SIX

# THE IRISH VERSION OF
# THE MARTYROLOGY OF YORK:
# INTRODUCTION AND TEXT

## 1 *Background to the Text*

Along with the Martyrology of Turin (MTur), there survives on the
lower margins of the first five folios of Biblioteca Nazionale, Turin, MS
D IV 18, a unique, if fragmentary, Irish version of the metrical
Martyrology of York (MY).[1] First published in 1671 from a single,
since lost, ninth-century Reims manuscript by Luc d'Achery, who
attributed it to Bede,[2] MY was edited critically in 1908 from seven
manuscripts by Henri Quentin, who showed that the attribution to Bede
was baseless, and that the martyrology was compiled 'either at the
church of York or Ripon'.[3] Quentin also drew on the occurrence in the
text of the feast of Wilfrid II, archbishop of York, who died in 745, to
date the text to the middle of the eighth century.[4] Subsequently, following his discovery and edition in 1934 of a fragment of the text in an early
ninth-century Vespasian (V) manuscript of English provenance,[5] André

---

[1]   This Irish version has previously been edited by A. Vitale Brovarone (Brovarone,
Granucci, 'Il calendario irlandese', pp. 33–54). The metre is based on the dactyllic hexame-
ter, which, in its classical form consists of five dactyls (one long syllable, two short) and a
trochee (one long, one short syllable). Neither the original poem nor its Irish version adheres
strictly to these requirements. For the manuscript, see Chapter 3, § 1.
[2]   For Migne's reprint of d'Achery's edition, see *PL* xciv.603–6.
[3]   The seven manuscripts, with date and provenance, are: A (Paris, Bibliothèque Nationale
9432, 9th c., Amiens); B (Milan, Bibliotheca Ambrosiana S. 33 sup., 11th c., Bobbio); C
(Brussels, Bibliothèque Royale 10470–10473, 10th c., St Riquier); M (Venice, Biblioteca
San Marco LV, IX, late copy); O (Oxford, Bodleian Library Canonici Misc. 560, 11th c.,
Milan?); R (text of lost Saint-Remi MS used by d'Achery, 9th c., Reims); S (British Library,
Sloane MS 263, 11th c., Lyon?).
[4]   Quentin, *Martyrologes historiques*, pp. 120–30; at p. 130. In the same year, Edmund
Bishop, working from d'Achery's edition, likewise began to use the name 'metrical York
calendar' for the text (Gasquet, Bishop, *The Bosworth Psalter*, cited in Wilmart, 'Un témoin
anglo-saxon', p. 41, which summarises the history of the text's editions).
[5]   Wilmart, 'Un témoin anglo-saxon'. This manuscript is one of only two extant English

Wilmart argued from its entries on St Boniface (d. 755) and the November feast of All Saints – which is unattested on the Continent before the early ninth century – that the martyrology should be dated at the earliest to about 800.[6] Since then, Michael Lapidge, in his 1984 edition of a tenth-century metrical calendar from Ramsey, which contains a considerable number of extracts from MY, has gone back to a somewhat earlier date in the second half of the eighth century.[7]

## 2  The Irish Version of the Martyrology of York (IMY)

As Wilmart noted, the text of MY, which in its original form consisted of over 80 lines, has never been stable, almost all its redactors striving to make it more relevant to their audiences by including local feasts.[8] This complicates considerably the task of establishing a manuscript stemma, which has been described by both Wilmart and Lapidge as well-nigh impossible.[9] Wilmart was nonetheless prepared to identify two main manuscript groups, which, using Quentin's sigla, he designated AB and CRS.[10] The latter group, although comprising solely continental manuscripts, reveals what Wilmart described as 'Celtic influence', two of its manuscripts, R and S, containing lines in honour of Patrick.[11] Interest-

copies, all others, excepting the Irish version, being of continental origin. As recently described by Michael Lapidge, 'A Tenth-Century Metrical Calendar', p. 328, the two English manuscripts are: British Library, Vespasian B. VI (9th c., Mercia), and Cambridge, Trinity College O.2.24 (1128) (12th c., Rochester/Canterbury).

[6]  Wilmart, 'Un témoin anglo-saxon', pp. 46–57, 64–5; perhaps as early as 805–14. (Wilmart's article, which also presented additional evidence for a provenance in York, was not taken into consideration by Dubois, *Les martyrologes*, p. 59.) An equally late, if not later, date is implicit in the view expressed in 1954 by John Hennig, 'Studies in the Literary Tradition', pp. 205, 212, that MY may originally have been 'an imitation' of the Martyrology of Óengus (MO). In Hennig's day a date of about 800 was accepted for MO, but this has since been replaced by a new date of c. 830 (Ó Riain, 'The Tallaght Martyrologies').

[7]  Lapidge, 'A Tenth-Century Metrical Calendar', pp. 330–1. Lapidge (pp. 331–2) drew attention to the similarity between the choice of Northumbrian/York saints in MY and a poem by Alcuin on the saints of York, and wondered whether the martyrology might not be an early work of this author.

[8]  Wilmart, p. 44. The original number of lines is given by Wilmart as 82 (cf. Lapidge, p. 327), but allowance is made for the possibility of one or two more.

[9]  Wilmart, 'Un témoin anglo-saxon', p. 45; Lapidge, 'A Tenth-Century Metrical Calendar', pp. 332, 342.

[10]  Above note 3. Lapidge (pp. 332–42) groups the manuscripts according to their countries of origin.

[11]  Wilmart included Samson of Dol (manuscript R only), and Brigit (manuscript O) among his examples of Celtic influence.

ingly, the R version – the now lost St-Remi manuscript used by d'Achery – is said to have been compiled between 816 and 846, a period of intense Irish martyrological activity.[12] However, if there was Irish influence, this is likely to have occurred on the Continent. The English version, V, which appears closer to CRS than to AB, does not contain the entry on Patrick, and the line commemorating the saint in the Irish version of the martyrology (IMY) reveals no affinity to that of the continental manuscripts. If we except a few isolated examples of particular agreement between IMY and R,[13] it is as part of the group comprising also C, S, and the English manuscript V that these versions reveal most affinity to one another. This group has in common an entry on the presentation of Christ in the Temple (11), and its manuscripts agree on the reading *festi pl[a]udente corona* (39) against AB's *festi lautus coronatus*. IMY also agrees with V against all others on a number of occasions, as at 33 (*adem(p)tam/adeptam*), 36 (*Gerb-/Gerv-*), 56 (*consecrat et/consecrant*), 64 (*Octimbris/Octobris*) and 68 (*metet/tenet*).

On at least three occasions – at 28 and 46, where IMY joins all other manuscripts in preferring *frater* and *almum* to V's *seruus* and *aptum*, and at 35, where IMY agrees with the continental versions against V in omitting all reference to Bonifatius – the Irish and English versions disagree significantly. The omission by IMY of Bonifatius could mean that the entry on the Apostle of Germany, who died in 754, belongs rather to the archetype of the English line of transmission than to the 'original poem', as asserted by Wilmart and Lapidge.[14] In that case, the archetype of the versions circulating in Ireland and on the Continent would already have broken away before the English archetype was formed. Against this, the Irish and English versions join one continental copy (A) in transposing lines 20–21, and the entry on John of Beverly (d. 721) – at 7 May in the continental SR manuscripts, but omitted from the English archetype – is absent from the Irish version.[15]

---

[12] For Irish martyrological activity during this period, see Ó Riain, 'The Tallaght Martyrologies'.

[13] For example, both read *fratrem* (44) and *qua* (53) for *fratremque* and *quis* of all other manuscripts.

[14] Wilmart, p. 50, Lapidge, pp. 329–30. For the English archetype, see Lapidge's comments at p. 329; he allows for some loss of lines and corruption of the text on the way between York and Mercia, where V was copied (p. 331n).

[15] For comments on the omission in the English archetype, see Lapidge, pp. 327n, 329n. Wilmart, pp. 50, 66n.

## 3  The Provenance and Date of the Irish Martyrology of York (IMY)

As Wilmart and Lapidge have shown, the textual history of the Martyrology of York presents unusually intricate problems that are best left to a future editor using all extant versions. In the meantime, attention may be drawn to the peculiarities of the Irish text, some of which allow scope for deduction regarding its provenance. Most of the unique readings are trivial verbal variants in the spelling of words or names, which involve well-attested Irish spelling preferences, as at 14 (*Madian* for *Mathias*) and 15 (*Grigorius* for *Gregorius*). In certain cases, including the two names just mentioned, the spelling peculiarities may have been influenced by the choice of the same forms by the same scribe on the same manuscript page in his copy of MTur, as may also have been the preference for *epifania* (2) rather than *theophania*. Less likely to have been influenced by the accompanying text, however, is the addition of the names of three local saints, Carthach (31) of Rahan, Ciarán (54) of Clonmacnoise, and Énán (58) of Drumrath alias Drumraney, whose churches lay in close proximity in the western part of the Irish Midlands. Two of these churches, Clonmacnoise and Rahan, lay within the territory of Delbna Ethra, effectively an 'ecclesiastical state' ruled by the abbots of Clonmacnoise;[16] the third, Drumrath, was located in a neighbouring kingdom about 14 miles north-east of Clonmacnoise. Since Clonmacnoise was pre-eminent in this area, there can be little doubt but that IMY was given its extant Irish form there. Indeed, by attaching *Clonensis* (54) to *Ciaranus*, its author, no doubt deliberately, gave Clonmacnoise the privilege of being the only church named in the text.

Unfortunately, there is no obvious internal dating evidence for the Irish version of the martyrology. The York text could have reached Ireland, either from England or the Continent, at any stage between the late eighth and twelfth centuries. The presence of the text in the Turin manuscript, which was most probably compiled in the East Midlands in the late twelfth century, at least provides a date for the copy edited here.

---

[16]  Byrne, *Irish Kings and High-Kings*, p. 221.

## 4 *Editorial Method*

As in Brovarone's edition, the text is presented here in semi-diplomatic form, with extensions of abbreviations indicated in italics and the ligature *æ* written *ae*. Unlike Brovarone's edition, which takes account of the line numbers in Wilmart's edition of MY, indicating gaps or additions as they occur, the numbering here is based on the Irish version only. Parentheses indicate barely legible words or letters; square brackets are used for the restored letter at 34. Capitals, punctuation and word division are editorial, but, with the exception of the one restored letter (*tran[s]* for *tran*), no attempt is made to provide more correct spellings or grammatical forms. Idiosyncrasies and the more important variants from other manuscripts, as noted in the editions of Quentin and Wilmart, are listed in the notes.

# Text of the Irish Version of the Martyrology of York (IMY)

1 January – 5 February

Ianuarius
1. [Kl]        Prima dies Iani qua circumciditur Agnus.
2. [uiii id.]  Octauas idús colitur Epifania Christi,
3. [iiii id.]  Diserti quartas primus capit acula Paulus.
4. [xui kl.]   Sedecimas Antonius obtinet aeque kalandas.
5. [xiii kl.]  Tres decimas Sabastianus tenuisse fertur.
6. [xii kl.]   Bis senas meritis mundo (fulg)entibus Ag(nes),
7. [xi kl.]    Martirio undecimas et Anathassius auctor.
Februarius
8. [Kl.]       O felix Februarii te furtuna decorat,
9.             Brigitae nanque tuis motatur uita kalandís.
10.            Prima dies Februarii qua patitur Policarpus,
11. [iiii n.]  Et quartas nonás Christus templo ferebatur
12. [N.]       Nonarumque die festa celebramus Agathae,

---

(Forms after the stroke / are from the editions of MY by Wilmart (mainly) and Quentin)

1.    1 Jan. *Iani/Iani est.*
2.    6 Jan. *Epifania/Theophania.* Cf. *Epifania* MTur.
3.    10 Jan. IMY and VSR read *primus* for *et primus* of AB.
4.    17 Jan.
5.    20 Jan. *fertur/refertur. Sabastianus* (recte *Sebastianus*) may be compared to *Sabaist* of MTur, which took the spelling from MO (*Sabaist*), which in turn had taken it from MT (*Sabastianus*). It is also so spelt in two manuscripts of MH.
6.    21 Jan.
7.    22 Jan. *Anathasius/Anastasius; auctor/memoratur.* The spelling *Anathasius* corresponds to MTur (*Ana[thasii]*). The use of *auctor* for *memoratur* suggests that the Irish compiler may have been reminded of Athanasius, author of a well known Life of Anthony of Egypt.
8.    1 Feb. This and the following line are peculiar to IMY.
9.    1 Feb. *Brigitae* (wrongly read as *Brigitie* by Brovarone). The saint is also commemorated in manuscript O of MY, which reads: *et Brigide festum celebramus virginis almum.*
10.   1 Feb. *Februarii/Februi est iam.*
11.   2 Feb. *ferebatur/offerebatur.* This line is absent from the AB version of MY.
12.   5 Feb. *die festa/diem festum.*

190

## 14 February – 29 April

| | |
|---|---|
| 13. [xui kl.] | Atq*ue* Ualentini sédenís sorte kalandís. |
| 14. [uii kl.] | Septenas meriti Madian uirtute dicabat. |

Martius

| | |
|---|---|
| 15. [iiii id.] | Hinc ídús Martis quartas Grigorius aurat. |
| 16. [xui kl.] | Sedecimas Patricii Aprilis uenerare kalandas. |
| 17. [xiii kl.] | Eub*erctus* denas tenuit terrasq*ue* kalandas. |
| 18. [xii kl.] | Bis senas s*anctus* post *quem* seq*uitur* Benedictus, |
| 19. [uiii kl.] | Octauis merito gaudet *c*onceptio *Christi*. |

Aprilis

| | |
|---|---|
| 20. [ix kl.] | Atq*ue* Giurgi*us* hinc euecht*us* ad astra uolauit, |
| 21. | Carnifices non*í*s Maiae uincendo kalandís. |
| 22. [uiii kl.] | Eutb*erctus* digna uirtutu*m* laude corr*uscus*, |
| 23. | Astriferu*m* octauis uenerant*er* scandit Olimpu*m*. |
| 24. | Quoq*ue* die p*r*esul penetrauit Ulfrad*us* alma, |
| 25. | Anguelico gaudens uect*us* t*r*ans culmi*na* coetu. |
| 26. [iii kl.] | Ulfrid*us* t*er*nís s*u*p*er*am penetrauit in aulam, |
| 27. | Te*m*pore post*er*ior, mor*um* n*on* flore secund*us*. |

---

13.     14 Feb. A line commemorating Iuliana (16 Feb.) follows in the other manuscripts.

14.     23 Feb. *Septenas/Ac senas; Madian/Mathias*. The change from sixth to seventh in IMY reflects Irish preference for the 23rd rather than the more common 24th as the feast of Matthew. The form *Madian* for *Mathias* is regular in Irish usage; it is so written in MTur, and all but one of the manuscripts of MO read *Madian* on this day.

15.     12 March. *Grigorius/Gregorius*. As reference to both MTur and MDr shows, the spelling of the pope's name is typically Irish.

16.     17 March. This addition to IMY is not shared by any other manuscript. However, two lines are devoted to the saint in manuscripts S and R, which read: *Doctor apostolicus sanctorum lumen ad astrum/Patricius Domini servus conscendit ad aulum*.

17.     20 March. *Euberctus/Cuthbertus*; *terrasque/ternasque*. Although the name is also mangled in other manuscripts, nowhere else is *E* substituted for *C*.

18.     21 March. *senas/senis*.

19.     25 March. Brovarone adds *[ma . . ae]* at the end of the line, but this is not supported by the manuscript.

20.     23 April. *Giurgius/Georgius*. Most manuscripts more correctly place line 20 of IMY after line 21. However, IMY agrees with V and A in placing it here.

21.     *uincendo/vincente*. See previous note.

22/23. 24 April. *Eutberctus/Egbertus*.

24/25. 24 April. *Ulfradus/Uilfridus, Wilfridus*. As the text of ll. 26/27 makes clear, this Wilfrid (d. 709), who advocated the case for the Roman party at Whitby in 663/4, is to be distinguished from Wilfrid II (d. 744), bishop of York, who is commemorated in the following lines. IMY joins V and ABO in omitting at this point three lines commemorating both the 'great litany' procession in Rome on the feast of St Mark (25 April). and the dedication of a church (27 April).

26/27. 29 April. *Ulfridus/Uilfridus, Wilfridus*. An *et*, subsequently erased, was added to *Uilfridus* in V. See previous note.

## 1 May – 29 June

Maius
| | |
|---|---|
| 28. [Kl.] | Iacob*us* frate*r* Dom*i*ni pius atque Pilippus |
| 29. | Mirifico Maias uenerantur honore kalandas. |
| 30. [iiii id.] | Bis binis sequitur Pancratus idib*us* insons. |
| 31. [ii id.] | Carthagus etherias binis adit idibus insons, |
| 32. [xu kl.] | Ter quínís Marcus meruit paurare kalandís. |

Iunius
| | |
|---|---|
| 33. [N.] | Iuni*us* i*n* no*n*ís mundo mirat*ur* ademptam, |
| 34. | Ad su*m*mos Tatb*er*cti anima*m* tran[s] sidera uectam, |
| 35. [iiii id.] | Inq*ue* su*i*s quadris Barnaban idib*us* aequat. |
| 36. [xiii kl.] | Gerbassius denis patit*ur* te*r*nisq*ue* kalandis, |
| 37. | P*r*otassius simul i*n* regnu*m*q*ue* p*er*enne uocatur. |
| 38. [uiii kl.] | Estq*ue* Iohannes bis q*u*adris Bab*t*ista colendus, |
| 39. | Natalis pulcre festi pludente corona. |
| 40. [ui kl.] | Mart*i*rio *et* Paul*us* senis ouat atq*ue* Iohan*n*es. |
| 41. [iii kl.] | Doctores Petrus *et* Paulus, |
| 42. | Maxima q*uo*s palma claret sibi lum*i*na mundi. |

---

28/29.   1 May. The English tradition, as represented by V, reads *seruus* here for *frater* of IMY and most other manuscripts. Although not in MH itself, the phrase *frater Domini* occurs in its breviate version in MT and also in the Martyrology of Bede. In some continental versions of MY, but – as at ll. 24–5 – not in ABO, a line is added here commemorating John of Beverly, bishop of York (d. 721).

30.   12 May. *Pancratus/Pancratius*.

31.   14 May. The feast of Carthage of Rahan and Lismore is one of several local Irish additions to IMY. The wording is clearly modelled on that of the previous line.

32.   18 May. For *paurare* – recte *pausare* (cf. V, O) – the other manuscripts have the less appropriate *pulsare*.

33/34.   5 June. Brovarone wrongly read *Tatberti*. IMY agrees with V (*ademtam*) against *adeptam* of other manuscripts. Most other manuscripts read *et summi(s)* at l. 34. The saint is otherwise known only from the Life of Wilfrid (Wilmart, 'Un témoin anglo-saxon', p. 49), but his feast is also in MTur. At this point, the English recension (V) adds two lines on Bonifatius (d. 754).

35.   10 June. Brovarone incorrectly expanded cicumflexed *ss* (= *suis*) to read *spiritus*.

36/37.   19 June. IMY and V agree here in spelling the first syllable of the saint's name *Gerb-* against *Gerv-* of all others. However, V reads *uocati* for *uocatur* of line 37, which IMY shares with most others.

38/39.   24 June. At line 39, IMY agrees with all others except V (*feste*) in reading *festi*, and joins VOSR against AB (*lautus coronatus*) in having *pl[a]udente corona*.

40.   26 June. Brovarone incorrectly expanded the final name as a genitive form *Iohannis*.

41/42.   29 June. The last two words of 41 in most other manuscripts, viz. *ternis sociantur*, are omitted in IMY. At 42, IMY reads *claret . . . mundi* for *clarat . . . mundus* of all other manuscripts.

## 25 July – 16 September

Iulius

| | |
|---|---|
| 43. [iiii kl.] | Iulius in quadris bis gaudet ferre kalandís |
| 44. | Iacobum fratrem Iohannis more colendum. |
| 45. [iii kl.] | Sanctificant Abdon *et* Sennis ternas uenerando. |

Augustus

| | |
|---|---|
| 46. [uiii id.] | Augustus Xixtum octauís tenet idibus almum. |
| 47. [iiii id.] | Bis binis uictor superat Lurentius hostes. |
| 48. [xuiii kl.] | Sancta Dei genetrix senas ter constat adire |
| 49. | Anguelicos uecta inter coetus uirgo kalandás. |
| 50. [uiii kl.] | Octauis sanctus sortitur Bartholomeus. |
| 51. [iiii kl.] | Bis binis pasus colitur Babtiza Iohannes. |

September

| | |
|---|---|
| 52. [ui id.] | Idús Septimbris senás dedicatur honore |
| 53. | Qua meruit nasci felix iam uirgo Maria, |
| 54. [u id.] | Et quinís sequitur Ciaranus scandere Clonensis. |
| 55. [xuiii kl.] | Octauas decimas Cornilius inde kalandas |
| 56. | Consecrat *et* Ciprianus simul ordine digno. |
| 57. [xui kl.] | Eufemia ac sextas decimas tenet intemerata, |

---

43/44.  25 July. IMY agrees with R only in reading *fratrem* for *fratremque* of all other manuscripts.

45.  30 July. *Abdon /Abdo*. Only IMY and V read *Sennis* rather than *Sennes* of all other manuscripts.

46.  6 August. *Xixtum/Xystum*. Despite Brovarone, who read *Xistum*, the second *x* is quite clear. The English recension, as in V, stands alone in reading *aptum* for *almum*.

47.  10 August. *Lurentius/Laurentius*.

48/49.  15 August. The *u* of *Anguelicos* is added above the *g*.

50.  25 August. *Octauis/Octonas* (*Octonos* V).

51.  29 August. If we except the various feasts of Christ and his mother Mary, John the Baptist (ll. 38, 51) and the apostle Matthew (ll. 14, 59) are the only saints twice commemorated in the text.

52/53.  8 September. *dedicatur?dedicabat*. At line 53, IMY joins OR in rending *qua* in place of *quis* of other manuscripts.

54.  9 September. The entry on Ciarán of Clonmacnoise, an Irish addition to the text, contains the only placename in the text. It is written as *clos* with a suspension above the *o*, whence Brovarone's impossible *Clonnois*. I take the reading to be *Clon(o)ensis* (from *Cluain*, gen. *Cluana/Clóna*), a short, adjectival form of the name, which is already attested in relation to Clonmacnoise in Adamnán's *Vita Columbae* (Anderson and Anderson, *Vita Columbae*, pp. 144, 214, 218).

55/56.  14 September. IMY agrees with V and OSR at l. 56 in reading *consecrat et* for *consecrant* of AB.

57.  16 September. *sextas/sex*.

## 18 September – 10 October

| | |
|---|---|
| 58. [xiiii kl.] | Dénís *et* q*u*adrais Enan *tr*ans astra uolauit, |
| 59. [xi kl.] | Undecimas capit *et* Matheus doctor amoen*us*, |
| 60. [x kl.] | Muriac*us* decimas martir *cum* milibus úna, |
| 61. [u kl.] | Q*ui*ntas sortít*ur* Cosmas sibi *cum* Damiano. |
| 62. [iii kl.] | Michielis *te*rnas templi, |
| 63. [ii kl.] | Atq*ue* bon*us* p*r*idias micat *inter*p*re*s Hironim*us*. |
| October | |
| 64. [ui n.] | Sextas Octimbris n*on*ás Bosa optat h*abe*re, |
| 65. [u n.] | At gemini q*u*inis Eoualidi sorte colunt*ur*. |
| 66. [xu kl.] | Doctor t*er* q*u*inis *et* Iudae uota feramus. |
| 67. | Sollemnis *te*rris su*m*mo qui gaudet Olimpho. |
| 68. [ui id.] | Paulinus senas metet id*us* iure magistro. |

---

58.  18 September. Énán of Drumrath (Drumraney) is the least important of the added Irish saints.
59.  21 September. The saint's name, originally spelt *Matheuus*, was corrected via a *punctum delens* added under the second *u*.
60.  22 September. *Muriacus/Mauricius*.
61.  27 September.
62.  29 September. The last two words of the line, which read *dedicatio sacrat* in the other manuscripts, are omitted from IMY.
63.  30 September. *Hironimus/Hieronymus*. This line is omitted from AB.
64.  2 October. IMY and V agree in reading *Octimbris (Octembris)* rather than *Octobris* of other manuscripts. Bosa (d. 705) was bishop of York. Except for O, which omits it altogether, the other manuscripts add line 67 here in commemoration of Bosa.
65.  3 October. *Eoualidi/H(a)euualdi* is treated as two words (*eo ualidi*) by Brovarone). The twins Hewald, who are commemorated on the following day in MT, are also here in the Martyrology of Bede.
66.  18 October/28 October. Here, through haplography, IMY conflates two lines of the original poem, which, mainly following the V and OSR versions, read: *Doctor ter quinis Lucas succurre kalendis, Simonis quinis et Iudae uota feramus.*
67.  See the note above to line 64.
68.  10 October. The commemoration of Paulinus of York (d. 644), wrongly placed here in IMY, is correctly placed after line 65 in the other manuscripts. The other manuscripts read *tenet* for *metet* of IMY, V, and C, and *magister* for *magistro*.

# APPENDICES

## 1

The following lunar observations are appended to the final list of saints in MDr (fol. 17v):

Annalis martyrylogii circulus consummatus est

| | | | |
|---|---|---|---|
| Luna prima | Luna .uii.ª | Luna .xiii.ª | Luna nonadecima |
| Luna secunda | Luna .uiiii.ª | Luna .xiiii.ª | Luna uigissima |
| Luna .iii.ª | Luna nona | Luna .xu.ª | Luna uigissima prima |
| Luna .iiii.ª | Luna .x.ª | Luna .xui.ª | Luna .xx.ª secunda |
| Luna .u.ª | Luna .xi.ª | Luna .xuiii.ª | Luna .xx.ª tertia |
| Luna .ui.ª | Luna .xii.ª | Luna .xuiii.ª | Luna .xx.ª .iiii.ª |

*Luna .xx.ª u.ª Luna .xx.ª .ui.ª Luna .xx.ª .uii.ª Luna .xx.ª .uiiii.ª Luna .xx.ª nona Luna .xxx.ª

*These are added at the top of fol. 18r.

## 2

Accompaning the two martyrologies of the Turin manuscript, on the top and lower margins of the folios, are various Latin and Irish notes which, for completeness, are edited here and, when in Irish, written in bold and, if possible, translated:[1] As a rule, the notes leading up to the lists of unlucky days (*dies infelices*) are written from the left along the top margins, whereas the notes beginning with, or concerning, the unlucky days are on the bottom margins, again written from the left. However,

---

[1] For a previous edition of these notes, see Brovarone, Granucci, 'Il calendario', pp. 51–4, 65–6. The notes relating to the signs correspond mainly to Bede's *De temporum ratione* (Chapter 16), and *De natura rerum* (Chapter 17). Those relating to the Hebrew, Greek and Latin names of the months may be compared to *De temporum ratione* (Chapters 11, 14) and, more especially, as D. McCarthy pointed out to me, to the Irish *De ratione conputandi* (Chapter 22), edited by Walsh and Ó Cróinín, whose versions of the Hebrew names are remarkably similar to those of the Turin text.

the bottom left margin of the lists for February is given over to notes 4 and 5, followed in the right lower margin by the unlucky days. In the case of May, which has no list of unlucky days, the two notes are on the top margin. Barely legible letters/words are placed between round brackets. Illegible letters/words are indicated by dots between brackets. Unless there is doubt, in which case italics are used, expansions are normally done silently.

## January

1. Capram iouis nutricem. Dies posteriore(m) corporis i(n) efigiam piscis ideo f(in)auerunt (in templum) eisdem mensibus designarent q(ua)s solet idem mensis habere in extremis plerumque.

2. Primus mensis secundum latinos ianuarius. decimus mensis secundum ebreos tibeth. secundus mensis secundum grecos edimos.[2]

3. Ianua*rius* .Ø. ianua*rius* .B. .i. nb(?) .i.ii.iii.iiii.u.uii.uii.ix.xi.[3]

4. Infelices dies enarii .i.ii.iiii.u.ix.xu.xx. (. . .) dies periculosos auc(. . .)es grecorum nucupauerunt. Quia (. . .)lis dolore opremitur non resurget et qui nascitur diu non ir(. . .).[4] Qui coniugem ducit non (. . .)ge habebit eam. Qui per uiam graditur non reuertetur. Qui negotium exigit sibi prodesse.

5. F(. . .) autem omnes .xxx.u. Ianuarius enim .iiii. Februarius .iii. Martius .iiii. Aprilis .ii. Maius .iii. Iunius .i. Iulius .ii. Augustus .ii. Septimber .ii. Octimber .ii. Nouimber .ii. Decimber .ii.

## February

1. Porro aquarium et pisces ab imbribus temporum uocauerunt quod hieme in his signis sol uenit. Maiores pluuiae profunduntur et miranda gentilium dementia quia non solum pisces sed etiam arietes et hircos et tauros et ursos et scorpiones et cancros in celum transtulerunt.

2. Undecimus mensis secundum ebreos sabath tertius mensis secundum grecos peritos secundus mensis secundum latinos febrarius.

3. Haec est aetas quae insolitam adiectionem recipit id est denariam quia quamuis omnes decinouenales peragras aetates nullam tamen aliam .xx.am in his sex milibus .ii. centis .xl. aetatibus denariam adiectionem assumere reperies.

4. Bisextus lunaris .iiii. annis sequitur solarem id est .iii.o et .ui.o et

---

[2] Read edunos?

[3] The second .uiii. is probably a mistake for .uiii.

[4] Brovarone, Granucci, 'Il calendario', reads uiuit.

.xi.o et .xiiii.o uno autem anno id est .xui. solaris pene continet bisextum lunarem. In ceteris autem .xiiii. lunaris precedit solarem.

5. Infelices dies februarii .xui.xuii.xu.

## March
1. Procedunt[5] duplices in martia tempora pisces.
2. Martius grecum nomen id est uirilis .i. quia **comprit na lossa**[6] **and** [the herbs/plants bring forth in it] . Uel martius a marte a patre romuli qui fuit rex romanorum et qui per .x. menses annum ordinauit et primum patri dedicauit.
3. .xii. mensis secundum ebreos adar .iiii. mensis secundum grecos distrios. .iii. secundum latinos martius.
4. Infelices .dies martii .xu.xui.xuiii.xuiii.[7]
5. **Aile huathad mar*ta* mís**[8]
   **for se la*the* .xx. bís**
   **cuic cuic lath*e* comol gle**
   **fo aile na hinite**.

   **Aile martai ocus a prim**
   **cid rodoscar ri comlín**
   **da la fon prim bés ní ró**
   ***ocus* aile for oenlo**.

6. **Noi laithe dec is fír fasc**
   **fo .xiiii. na casc**
   **cúic cúic laithe comol ngle**
   **fó aile na hinite**.

## April
1. Respicis aprilis aries frixee kalandas. Arietem primum signum dicunt cui uero librae mediam mundi lunam tradunt propter ammon iouem ideo uocauerunt in cuius capite cornua fingunt qui simulacra iouis faciunt. Ideo autem hoc signum[9] uel signa posuerunt primum. Quia in martio mense qui est anni principium solem in eo signo cursum suum agere dicunt.

---

5 Ibid. reads Concidunt.
6 Ibid. reads *losse*.
7 The scribe may have intended to write .xuiii.
8 Since I cannot make satisfactory sense of these quatrains, I leave them untranslated.
9 There are two dots under the n of signum.

2. Primus mensis secundum ebreos nisan .u.tus mensis secundum grecos canticos .iiii.tus mensis secundum latinos aprilis.
3. Infelices dies aprilis .uii.xu.

## May

1. Taurum inter sidera collocant et ipsum in honorem iouis eo quod in bouem sit conuersus fabulose quando Eoropam (. . .asu)exit.[10] Maius agenori miratur cornua tauri. Maius a maiore flore **.i. ar is uilliu blath and** [because flowering is greater in it] quam in aprilem.
2. Sextus mensis secundum grecos arthimesios. Quintus mensis secundum latinos maius. Uel Maius a maia et reliqua.

## June

1. Castorem et pullucem post mortem inter notissima signa posuerunt quod signum gemini uocauerunt. Iunius aquatos celo uidet ire laconas.
2. Tertius mensis secundum ebreos siban. septimus secundum grecos dios. sextus secundum latinos iunius.
3. Infelices dies iunii .ui.
4. **Esca iuin trath tert adannaither** [The June moon is lit up at terce].

## July

1. Cancrum quoque dixerunt quia cum sol ad id signum uenerit retro graditur in modum cancri[11] breuiores dies facere incipit. Hoc animal incertam habet primam partem quia ad utriusque gresum dirigit ita ut prior sit posterior et posterior prior. Solstitio ardentis cancri fert iulius astrum. Iulius ab iulio cesare dictus. Quartus mensis secundum ebreos tamni. Octauus mensis secundum grecos parmeneos. Septimus mensis secundum latinos iulius.
2. Infelices dies iulii .xu.xix.
3. **Esce iuil medon laithi adannaither** [The July moon is lit up at midday].

## August

1. Leonem in grecia ingentem hercoles occidit et propter uirtutem suam hunc inter .xii. signa constituit hoc signum cum sol attegirit nimium calorem mundo reddit et bestias facit. Augustum mensem leo feruidus igne perurit.

---

[10] Brovarone, Granucci, 'Il calendario', reads transuexit.
[11] The first three letters are added above the line.

2. Quintus mensis secundum ebreos ebus. Nonus mensis secundum grecos laos. Octauus secundum latinos augustus.

3. Infelices dies .xix.xx.

4. **Esce aguist eter medon lai et nonai adannaither** [The August moon is lit up between midday and nones].

## September

1. Uirginis etiam signum idcirco inter astra collacauerunt quod hisdem diebus sol ad id signum decurrit terra exusta solis ardore nihil pariat. Est enim hoc tempus canicularium dierum. Sidere uirgo bachum septimber opimat.

2. Sextus mensis secundum ebreos ellil. Decimus mensis secundum grecos gorpeos. Nonus mensis secundum latinos septimber.

3. Infelices dies .xui.xuii.

4. **Esce septimb*er* im nónai adannaither** [The September moon is lit up about nones].

## October

1. Libram uocauerunt ab aequalitate mensis ipsius quia ab .uiii. kalendarum octimbrium sol per id signum currens equinoctium facit. Aequat et octimber sementis tempore libram.

2. Septimus mensis secundum ebreos tesseri. Undecimus secundum grecos iberbaritos. Decimus secundum latinos october.

3. Infelices dies .ui.uii.

# BIBLIOGRAPHY

Anderson, A. O., and M. O. Anderson, eds/trs, *Adomnan's Life of Columba* (Edinburgh 1961; rev. ed. Oxford 1991).

Auf der Maur, H., 'Feste und Gedenktage der Heiligen', in P. Harnoncourt and H. Auf der Maur, *Gottesdienst der Kirche* (Handbuch der Liturgiewissenschaft 6.1; Regensburg 1994), pp. 65–358.

Best, R. I., and H. Lawlor, eds, *The Martyrology of Tallaght* (Henry Bradshaw Society 68; London 1931).

Bieler, L., ed./trs., *The Patrician Texts in the Book of Armagh* (Scriptores latini Hiberniae 10; Dublin 1979).

Bolland, J. *et al.*, eds, *Acta Sanctorum quotquot toto orbe coluntur* (Antwerp/Brussels 1643– ).

Brovarone, A. V., and F. Granucci, 'Il calendario irlandese del codice D IV 18 della Bibliotheca Nazionale di Torino', *Archivio Glottologico Italiano* 66.1–2 (1981–2), pp. 33–88, 38–113.

Byrne, F. J., *Irish Kings and High-Kings* (London 1973).

Campanile, E., 'Per l'interpretazione del calendario irlandese di Torino', in idem, *Problemi di lingua e di cultura nel campo indo-europeo* (Pisa 1983), pp. 23–8.

Colgan, J., ed., *Acta Sanctorum Veteris et Majoris Scotiae seu Hiberniae . . . Sanctorum Insulae*, I (Louvain 1645; repr. Dublin 1947).

Colgan, J., ed., *Triadis Thaumaturgae seu Divorum Patricii, Columbae et Brigidae, Trium Veteris et Maioris Scotiae seu Hiberniae, Sanctorum Insulae, Communium Patronorum Acta* (Louvain 1647; repr. Dublin 1997).

Colgrave, B., ed./trs., *The Life of Bishop Wilfrid by Eddius Stephanus* (Cambridge 1927; repr. 1985).

Colker, M. L., *Trinity College Library Dublin: Descriptive Catalogue of the Medieval and Renaissance Manuscripts* (London 1991).

Cross, F. L., and E. A. Livingstone, eds, *The Oxford Dictionary of the Christian Church*, 3rd ed. (Oxford 1997).

Crosthwaite, J. C., and J. H. Todd, eds, *The Book of Obits and Martyrology of the Cathedral Church of the Holy Trinity, commonly called Christ Church, Dublin* (Irish Archaeological Society for 1843; Dublin 1844).

Davies, W., *Wales in the Early Middle Ages* (Leicester 1982).

Delehaye, H., *Les origines du culte des martyrs* (Brussels 1912).

Delehaye, H., and H. Quentin, eds, 'Commentarius Perpetuus in Martyrologium Hieronymianum', *Acta Sanctorum Novembris*, II (Pars Posterior).

Delehaye, H., P. Peeters, M. Coens, B. de Gaiffier, P. Grosjean, F. Halkin, eds, *Propylaeum ad Acta Sanctorum Decembris* (*Martyrologium Romanum*) (Brussels 1940).

Dubois, J., ed., *Le Martyrologe d'Usuard* (Brussels 1965).

Dubois, J., *Les martyrologes du moyen âge latin* (Turnhout 1978).

Dubois, J., ed., *Le Martyrologe d'Adon* (Paris 1984).

Farmer, D. H., *The Oxford Dictionary of Saints* (Oxford 1978).

Forbes, A. P., ed., *Kalendars of the Scottish Saints* (Edinburgh 1872).

Forbes, G. H., ed., *The Ancient Irish Missal in the Possession of the Baroness Willoughby de Eresby, Drummond Castle, Perthshire* (Edinburgh 1882).

Gasquet, F. A., and E. Bishop, *The Bosworth Psalter. An Account of a Manuscript . . . now Addit. MS 37517 at the British Museum* (London 1908).

Gibbs Casey, S., ' "Through a Glass Darkly": Steps towards Reconstructing Irish Chant from the Neumes of the Drummond Missal', *Early Music* (May 2000), pp. 205–15.

Gougaud, L., *Les saints irlandais hors d'Irlande* (Louvain and Oxford 1936).

Grosjean, P., ed., 'Édition du Catalogus Praecipuorum Sanctorum Hiberniae de Henri Fitzsimon', in J. Ryan, ed., *Féil-sgríbhinn Eóin Mhic Néill* (Dublin 1940), pp. 335–93.

Grosjean, P., 'La prétendue fête de la Conception de la Sainte Vierge dans les Églises celtiques', = 'Notes d'hagiographie celtique 1', *Analecta Bollandiana* 61 (1943), pp. 91–107; at pp. 91–5.

Grosjean, P., 'S. Patrice d'Irlande et quelques homonymes dans les anciens martyrologes', *The Journal of Ecclesiastical History* 1 (1950), pp. 151–71.

Grosjean, P., 'Une prétendue fête de Moïse au 1er mars', = 'Notes d'hagiographie celtique 44', *Analecta Bollandiana* 76 (1958), pp. 413–18.

Grosjean, P., 'Un quatrain irlandais dans un manuscrit anglo-saxon', = 'Notes d'hagiographie celtique 54', *Analecta Bollandiana* 81 (1963), pp. 269–71.

Gwynn, A., *The Twelfth-Century Reform* (A History of Irish Catholicism 2; Dublin 1968).

Gwynn, A., and R. N. Hadcock, *Medieval Religious Houses: Ireland* (London 1970).

Hawkes, W., 'The Liturgy in Dublin, 1200–1500: Manuscript Sources', *Reportorium Novum* 2.1 (1957–8), pp. 33–67.

Heist, W. W., ed., *Vitae Sanctorum Hiberniae e Codice olim Salmanticensi* (Subsidia Hagiographica 28; Brussels 1965).

Hennessy, W. M., ed., *The Annals of Loch Cé . . . to A.D. 1590*, 2 vols (London 1871, repr. Dublin 1939).

Hennessy, W. M., and B. Mac Carthy, eds, *Annals of Ulster*, 4 vols (Dublin 1887–1901).

Hennig, J., 'A Feast of All the Saints of Europe', *Speculum* 21 (1946), pp. 49–66.

Hennig, J., 'The Feasts of the Blessed Virgin in the Ancient Irish Church', *Irish Ecclesiastical Record*, 5th Series, 81 (1954), pp. 161–71.

Hennig, J., 'Studies in the Literary Tradition of the *Martyrologium Poeticum*', *Proceedings of the Royal Irish Academy* 56 C 2 (1954), pp. 197–226.

Hennig, J., 'Studies in the Latin Texts of the *Martyrology of Tallaght*, of *Félire Oengusso* and of *Félire Húi Gormain*', *Proceedings of the Royal Irish Academy* 69 C 4 (1970), pp. 45–112.

Hennig, J., 'Zu Anfang und Ende der liturgischen Tradition der Divisio Apostolorum', *Archiv für Liturgiewissenschaft* 12 (1970), pp. 302–11.

Hennig, J., 'Grundzüge der martyrologischen Tradition Irlands', *Archiv für Liturgiewissenschaft* 14 (1972), pp. 71–98.

Hennig, J., 'The Sources of the Martyrological Tradition of Non-Irish Saints in Medieval Ireland', *Sacris Erudiri* 93 (1972–3), pp. 407–34.

Hennig, J., 'The Notes on Non-Irish Saints in the Manuscripts of *Félire Oengusso*', *Proceedings of the Royal Irish Academy* 75 C 7 (1975), pp. 119–60.

Henry, F., *Irish Art in the Romanesque Period* (London 1970).

Henry, F., and G. L. Marsh-Micheli, 'A Century of Irish Illumination (1070–1170)', *Proceedings of the Royal Irish Academy* 62 C 5 (1961–3), pp. 101–66.

Herbert, M., *Iona, Kells, and Derry: the History and Hagiography of the Monastic Familia of Columba* (Oxford 1988).

Hogan, E., *Onomasticon Goedelicum Locorum et Tribuum Hiberniae et Scotiae: an Index, with Identifications, to the Gaelic Names of Places and Tribes* (Dublin/London 1910).

James, J. W., *Rhigyfarch's Life of St David* (Cardiff 1967).

Jones, C. W., *Bedae opera didascalica*, 3 vols (Corpus Christianorum series latina 123A–C, Turnhout 1975–80), pp. 241–544.

Kenney, J., *The Sources for the Early History of Ireland (Ecclesiastical)* (Records of Civilization 11; Cornell 1929, repr. Dublin 1979).

Lapidge, M., 'A Tenth-Century Metrical Calendar from Ramsey', *Revue Bénédictine* 94 (1984), pp. 326–69.

Lawlor, H. J., *The Psalter and Martyrology of Ricemarch* (Henry Bradshaw Society 47; London 1914).

Mac Airt, S., ed., *The Annals of Inisfallen (MS. Rawlinson B 503)* (Dublin 1951).

Mac Airt, S. and G. Mac Niocaill, eds/trs, *The Annals of Ulster (to A. D. 1131)* (Dublin 1983).

McNeill, C., 'Report on Recent Acquisitions in the Bodleian Library, Oxford', *Analecta Hibernica* 1 (1930), pp. 1–178.

Migne, J.-P., ed., *Computus vulgaris qui dicitur ephemeris*, in *Patrologia Latina* 90, cols 727–87.

Murphy, D., ed., *The Annals of Clonmacnoise . . . to A.D. 1408* (Dublin 1896).

Nic Dhonnchadha, L., *Aided Muirchertaig Meic Erca* (Medieval and Modern Series; Dublin 1964).

O'Donovan, J., ed., *Annals of the Kingdom of Ireland by the Four Masters* (Dublin 1848–51, repr. Dublin 1990).

O'Dwyer, P., *Mary: a History of Devotion in Ireland* (Dublin 1988).

Ó Riain, P., ed., *Corpus Genealogiarum Sanctorum Hiberniae* (Dublin 1985).

Ó Riain, P., 'Some Bogus Irish Saints', *Ainm* 3 (1988), pp. 1–8.

Ó Riain, P., 'The Psalter of Cashel: a Provisional List of Contents', *Éigse* 23 (1989), pp. 107–30.

Ó Riain, P., 'The Tallaght Martyrologies, Redated', *Cambridge Medieval Celtic Studies* 20 (1990), pp. 21–38.

Ó Riain, P., 'A Misunderstood Annal: a Hitherto Unnoticed *Cáin*', *Celtica* 21 (1990), pp. 561–6.

Ó Riain, P., 'Adamnán's Age at Death: Fact or Symbol', *Studia Celtica Japonica* 5 (1992), pp. 7–17.

Ó Riain, P., 'Anglo-Saxon Ireland: the Evidence of the Martyrology of Tallaght', in *H. M. Chadwick Memorial Lectures* 3 (Cambridge 1993).

Ó Riain, P., 'To be Named is to Exist: the Instructive Case of Aghabulloge', in P. O'Flanagan and C. G. Buttimer, eds, *Cork History and Society* (Dublin 1993), pp. 45–62.

Ó Riain, P., 'Die Bibliothek des Verfassers des kommentierten *Félire Óengusso*', in E. Poppe, and H. L. C. Tristram, eds, *Übersetzung, Adaptation und Akkulteration im insularen Mittelalter* (Münster 1999), pp. 87–104.

Ó Riain, P., 'Rawlinson B 502 alias Lebar Glinne Dá Locha: a Restatement of the Case', *Zeitschrift für celtische Philologie* 51 (1999), pp. 130–47.

Ó Riain, P., 'The Martyrology of Óengus: the Transmission of the Text', *Studia Hibernica* 31 (2000–01), pp. 221–42.

Ó Riain, P., 'The Martyrologies of Flann Ua Gormáin' (forthcoming).

Ó Riain-Raedel, D., 'Das Nekrolog der irischen Schottenklöster', *Beiträge zur Geschichte des Bistums Regensburg* 26 (1992), pp. 7–119.

Oskamp, H., 'The Irish Quatrains and Salutation in the Drummond Missal', *Ériu* 28 (1977), pp. 82–91.

O'Sullivan, W., 'Medieval Meath Manuscripts', *Ríocht na Midhe* 7.4 (1985–6), pp. 3–21.

O'Sullivan, W., 'Additional Medieval Meath Manuscripts', *Ríocht na Midhe* 8 (1987), pp. 68–70.

Overgaauw, E. A., *Martyrologes manuscrits des anciens diocèses d'Utrecht et de Liège*, 2 vols (Hilversum 1993)

Plummer, C., *Vitae Sanctorum Hiberniae*, 2 vols (Oxford 1910; repr. 1968).

Plummer, C., *Irish Litanies* (Henry Bradshaw Society 62; London 1925).

Poppe, E., and H. L. C. Tristram, eds, *Übersetzung, Adaptation und Akkulteration im insularen Mittelalter* (Münster 1999).

Procter, F., and E. S. Dewick, *The Martiloge in Englysshe after the Use of the*

*Chirche of Salisbury . . . with Addicyons* (Henry Bradshaw Society 3; London 1893).

Quentin, H., *Les martyrologes historiques du moyen âge: étude sur la formation du martyrologe romain* (Paris 1908).

Robinson, F. N., 'The Irish Marginalia in the Drummond Missal', in U. T. Holmes and A. J. Denomy, eds, *Medieval Studies in Honor of J. M. D. Ford* (Cambridge Mass. 1948), pp. 193–208.

Schneiders, M., 'The Irish Calendar in the Karlsruhe Bede', *Archiv für Liturgiewissenschaft* 31 (1989), pp. 33–78.

Schneiders, M., 'The Drummond Martyrology and its Sources', *Analecta Bollandiana* 108 (1990), pp. 105–45.

Sollerius, J. B., ed., *Martyrologium Usuardi Monachi . . .*, in *Acta Sanctorum* Iunii vi, vii (Antwerp 1714–17).

Stokes, W., 'On the Calendar of Oengus', *The Transactions of the Royal Irish Academy* 1 (1880), pp. 1–32, i–ccclii.

Stokes, W., ed./trs., *Félire hÚi Gormáin: the Martyrology of Gorman* (Henry Bradshaw Society 9; London 1895).

Stokes, W., ed./trs., *Félire Oengusso Céli Dé: the Martyrology of Oengus the Culdee* (Henry Bradshaw Society 29; London 1905).

Wade-Evans, A. W., *Vitae Sanctorum Britanniae et Genealogiae* (History and Law Series 9; Cardiff 1944).

Wallis, F., trs., *Bede: the Reckoning of Time* (Liverpool 1999).

Walsh, P., *Genealogiae regum et sanctorum Hiberniae* (Maynooth/Dublin 1918).

Walsh, M., and D. Ó Cróinín, eds, *Cummian's Letter 'De controversia paschali' and the 'De ratione conputandi'*, Studies and Texts 86 (Toronto 1988).

Webster, B., *Medieval Scotland: the Making of an Identity* (London 1997).

Wilmart, A., 'Un témoin anglo-saxon du calendrier métrique d'York', *Revue Bénédictine* 50 (1934), pp. 41–69.

Wormald, F., *English Kalendars Before A. D. 1100* (Henry Bradshaw Society 72; London 1934).

# INDEX OF SAINTS

(Dates and variant readings are indicated as follows: regular = MDr, italics = MTur, underline = MC, brackets with line numbers = IMY. Latin and Irish names are standardised, with those of MC following, as far as possible, the spelling of Colgan's indexes to A and T)

Aaron
  sacerd. primus, in Monte Or 1 Iul.
Abacuc (Ambacuc)
  filius Marii et Marthae, Roma 19 Ian.
Abacuc (Ambacuc)
  propheta 15 (*15*) Ian.
Abbán
  filius Corbmaci, Kill Abbain, Hibernia 16 (*16*) Mar., 27 (*27*, 27) Oct.
Abdon
  m., Roma 30 (*30*) Iul. (IMY 45)
Abibon
  inventio corporis, Hierosolyma 3 Aug.
Accobrán
  *28 Ian.*
Acculus (*Aculeus*)
  pr. 27 (*27*) Mai.
Achea
  filia Darercae 6 Feb.
Achilleus
  frater Nerei et m., Roma 12 Mai.
Adamnán
  Ia *23 Sep.*
Adauctus
  m., Roma 30 Aug.
Adrianus
  m., Nicomedia 8 Sep.
Adrio
  see Ario.
Áed (Máedóc/*Móedóc*/Maidocus/Mom(á)edóc/Muidocus)
  ep., *Ferna*, Hibernia 31 (*31*, 31) Ian., Moling discipulus eius 17 Iun.
  filius Radegundis, mionn Gaoidheal, ab., *Fid Dúin*, Hibernia 18 (*18*, 18) Mai., 13 (*13*, 13) Aug.
  filius Breci, ep., Kill Ary, Sliabh Lieg, Hibernia 10 (10) Nov.

  Hibernia 8 Mar., 31 Oct.
  mionn Alban, Hibernia, 23 (*23*, 23) Mar.
  filius Midnae, *Ua Dúnlaing*, Lagenia, Hibernia, 10 Apr., 11 (*11*) Apr.
  vividus see Beoaedus
Áedán (Aidanus)
  ep., Lindisfarnensis, Britannia 31 (31) Aug.
Aengussius
  see Mac Tail
Agabus
  propheta 13 Feb.
Agape
  v., cum sororibus 30 Aug.
  v. et m., Thessalonica 3 Apr.
Agapitus
  diac. et m., Roma 6 Aug.
  m., Praeneste 18 Aug.
Agatha
  v. et m., Catana, Sicilia 5 (*5*) Feb. (IMY 12)
  v., cum sororibus tribus *30 Aug.*
  see Aglahes.
Agatho (Agathus/*Agatha*)
  m., *v., translatio* 5 (*5*) Iul.
Aggeus
  propheta 4 Iul.
Aglahes (Agatha)
  5 Iun.
*Agmemnonus*
  see Egemonus
Agnes (*Agna*)
  m., Roma, *natiuitas* 21(*21*) Ian. (IMY 6), 27–8 Ian.
Agricola
  Ravenna 16 Dec.

(MDr, *MTur*, <u>MC</u>, (IMY))

Aibhinnia
  see Briga
Ailbe
  sacerd., *Imlech Ibair*, Hibernia 12 (*12*)
    Sep.
Ailithir
  *12 Mai.* (see note)
Airerán (<u>Aleranus</u>)
  sapiens, <u>Cluain Eraird</u>, Hibernia 11(*11*)
    Aug., 29 (<u>29</u>) Dec.
Aithbe
  Hibernia 24 Mai..
Albanus
  m., Britannia 22 Iun.
Alexander
  *17 Oct.*
  abbas Romae *27 Apr.*
  ep. et m. 18 Mar.
  filius Felicitatis, m., Roma 10 Iul.
  m., Eumenia 10 Mar.
  m., Lugdunum Galliae 24 Apr.
  qui idola destruxit *26 Feb.*
Amantius
  ep., Gallia 4 Nov.
Amantus
  passio *6 Iun.*
Amarantus
  m. 7 Nov.
Amator
  ep., Augustodunum 27 Nov.
Ambacuc
  see Abacuc
Ambrosius
  ep., Mediolanum 1(*1*) Apr.
Ammonius (Ambonius, Umbanus)
  Roma 1 Dec., 5 Dec. (see note).
Amphianus
  Caesarea Lyciae 5 Apr.
Anacletus
  papa et m. 26 Apr.
Ananias
  Damascus 25 Ian.
  24 Apr.
Anastasia
  m. 25 Dec.
Anastasius *(Anathasius)*
  *22 Ian.* (IMY 7)
  Constantinopolis 25 Dec.
  m. 7 Sep.
  m., Salona 21 Aug.
  papa, Roma 27 Apr.

Anatholia
  v. et m., Tyrus 9 (*9*) Iul.
Andreas
  apostolus, Patrae Achaiae, *6 Feb.*, 30
    Nov., octavae 7 Dec., vigilia 29 Nov.
  m., Lamosacus 15 Mai.
  see Magnus.
Anesus
  cruciatus *31 Mar.*
Anteros (Anatherus)
  *4 Mai.*
Anteros,
  papa et m. 3 Ian.
Anthimus
  Roma 11 Mai..
Antonius
  *9 Aug.*
  mon., Thebais 17 (*17*) Ian. (IMY 4)
Aper
  ep., Tullensis 15 Sep.
Apollinaris
  ep. et m., Ravenna 23 Iul.
  m. 4 (*4*) Iun.
Apostoli
  4 Ian., 28 Nov., divisio (*missio
    duodecim*) ad praedicandum 15 (*15*)
    Iul., octavae 6 Iul., Spiritus Sanctus
    super *15 Mai.*
Appollonia
  v. et m., Alexandria 9 Feb.
Aquilinus
  m. Scillitanus, Carthago 17 Iul.
Arcadius
  Africa 12 Nov.
Archillaus
  Roma 23 Aug.
Archinimus
  4 Dec.
Ario
  see Orion
Ario (Adrio)
  *17 Mai.*
Aristarchus
  discipulus Pauli 4 Aug.
Armogastus
  4 Dec.
Arnulfus
  ep., Mettis 16 Aug.
Aron
  *1 Aug.*
Asterius (Austin)
  *19 Oct.*

(MDr, *MTur*, <u>MC</u>, (IMY))

Braendinus (*Broendinus*, <u>Brendanus</u>)
    ab., *Cluain Ferta*, Hibernia <u>1 Mar.</u>, 16
    (*16*) Mai.
    Hibernia 29 Nov.
Bran
    Hibernia 18 Mai.
Brancius
    see Bonifatius.
Brecán
    Hibernia 7 (*7*) Mai.
Brendinus
    see Braendinus.
Bricín
    Hibernia 5 Sep.
Bríg
    v., ghost saint  31 Ian. (see note).
Briga (Aibhinnia)
    filia Anmirii, mater Endei <u>21 Mar.</u>
    Kill Brige <u>21 Ian.</u>
Brigida
    v., Hibernia 1 (*1*, <u>1</u>) Feb. (IMY 9),
    confirmatio <u>6 Feb.</u>, velum <u>25</u>
    <u>Apr.</u>
Brocán
    *Ros Tuirc*, Hibernia 17 (*17*, <u>17</u>) Sep.
    *scriptor*, Hibernia 8 (*8*) Iul.
Broendinus
    see Braendinus.
Buaidbeo
    Hibernia 17 Nov.
Buite
    ep., Hibernia 7 Dec.
Buíthíne
    see Baíthíne

Caecilia
    v. 1 Sep.
    v. et m., Roma 22 Nov.
Caera
    see Ceicra.
Caesaria
    Palestina 1 Iun.
Caesarius
    Caesaria Cappadociae 3 Nov.
    m., Roma 1 Nov.
Caimín (*Camméne*, <u>Caminus/Canius</u>)
    <u>Inis Celtra</u>, Hibernia 24 (*24*, <u>24</u>) Mar.
Cainnech
    pr., Hibernia 11 (*11*) Oct.
Cairech
    *5 Apr.*

Cairech Dergáin
    <u>filia Conalli Deirg, soror Endei, Cluain</u>
    <u>Boirenn</u> 9 (<u>9</u>) *Feb.*
Cairnech
    <u>Inis Baithin, Tulen</u>, Hibernia 16 (<u>16</u>)
    Mai.
Caius (Gaius)
    m., Eumenia 10 Mar.
    m., Nicomedia 21 Oct.
Callistus
    cum aliis septem mm., Corinthus 16
    Apr.
    papa et m., Roma 14 Oct.
Camméne
    see Caimín
Candida
    *1 Sep.*
    Roma 1 Dec.
Canius
    see Caimín
Caprasius
    m., Gallia 20 Oct.
Carbreus
    filius Degilli, ep., Cuil Rathen <u>11 Nov.</u>
Carilephus
    8 Iun.
Carisa (recte Carisius)
    16 Apr.
Carisius
    cum aliis septem mm., Corinthus 16
    Apr. See Carisa.
Carthach
    <u>filius regis Casselensis, Inis Uachtair,</u>
    <u>Inis Carthach, institutor Mochuddae,</u>
    <u>alumnus Kierani</u>, Hibernia 5 (<u>5</u>) Mar.
Carthachus (*Mochutu*)
    ep., *Rathan*, Hibernia 14 (*14*) Mai.
    (IMY 31), Carthach institutor eius <u>5</u>
    <u>Mar.</u>, Cuannanus (Cuanna) frater
    eius? <u>5 Feb.</u>
Cassianus
    ep. 5 Aug.
    m., Mauritania 3 Dec.
Cassius
    m., Damascus 20 Iul.
Castor
    *19 Sep.*
Castorius
    m., Roma 8 Nov.
Cathedra Petri
    Antiochia 22 Feb.
    Roma 18 Ian.

(MDr, *MTur*, <u>MC</u>, (IMY))

Ceicra (Caera)
  m., Africa 16 Oct.
Céile
  Hibernia 3 Mar.
Cellach
  *7 Oct.*
Celsius
  m., Mediolanum 12 Iun.
Celsus
  m. 27 Iul.
  puer et m., Mediolanum 19 Iun.
Cenn Fáelad
  Hibernia 8 Apr.
Chionia
  v. et m., Thessalonica 3 Apr.
Christeta
  Hispania 26 Oct.
Christina
  *v.*, cum septem fratribus 18 (*18*) Iul.
  v. et m., Italia 24 Iul.
Christophorus
  28 Apr.
  m., Lycia 25 Iul.
Chrysantus
  Roma 12 Aug.
Chrysogonus (*Crisogonus*)
  m., Roma, *passio 31 Mai.*, 24 Nov.
Cianán
  v., <u>filius Sednae, Damliag</u>, Hibernia 24
  (<u>24</u>) Nov.
Ciar (<u>Cera</u>)
  *ingen Duib Rea*, v., <u>Kill Chere, Mag
  Ascad</u>, Hibernia 5 (*5*, <u>5</u>) Ian., 16 (16)
  Oct.
Ciarán (Ciaranus, <u>Kieranus</u>)
  Belach Dúin *12 Iun.*
  *macc int Shaír* (Clonensis IMY 54), ab.
  et pr., Hibernia 9 (*9*) Sep., Dageus
  faber eius 18 Aug., Fechinus
  discipulus eius <u>20 Ian.</u>
  <u>filius Luagni</u>, *Saigir*, Hibernia 5 (<u>5</u>)
  Mar., Benedictus frater eius <u>14 Iun.</u>,
  Carthachus alumnus eius <u>5 Mar.</u>
Ciaróc
  Hibernia 7 Mai.
Ciriacus
  see Quiriacus.
Ciric
  see Cyricus
Cirillus
  see Cyrillus

Cirinus (*Ciríne*)
  see Quirinus
Cirio
  *3 Iul.*
Claudius
  m., Roma 8 Nov.
Clemens
  ep. et m., Roma 23 Nov.
Clementinus
  m., Tracia 14 Nov.
Cletus
  Oia insula 30 Dec.
Clucerus
  see Glucerus
Cóemán
  <u>Airdne</u>, Hibernia, 12 (*12*, <u>12</u>) Iun.
  *Brecc*, <u>Ros Each</u>, 14 (*14*, <u>14</u>) Sep.
  <u>frater Coemgeni, Enach Truim</u>,
  Hibernia, 3 Nov.
Coemginus (*Cóemgen*)
  <u>frater Coemani, *Glenn Dá Locha*</u>,
  Hibernia 3 (*3*) Iun., <u>3 Nov.</u>
Coiningen
  Hibernia 29 Apr.
Coirpre
  ep., Hibernia 11 Nov.
Colmanus (Colmán, Mocholmóc)
  *19 Feb., 29 Mai.*
  Camas *29 Oct.*
  *Cell Ruaid*, Hibernia 16 (*16*) Oct.
  *Druimm Ferta*, Hibernia 3 (*3*) Sep.
  Ela *26 Sep.*, gein *3 Oct.*
  <u>ep., Ard Bo</u>, Hibernia 18 (*18*, <u>18</u>) Feb.
  ep., Hibernia 8 Aug.
  filius Duach <u>3 Feb.</u>
  filius Luachan, <u>Lann Mic Luachain</u> 17
  (<u>17</u>) Iun.
  filius Hua Beogna, Lismorum
  Mochuddae <u>22 Ian., 25 Iul.</u>
  Hibernia, 24 Mai., 26 (*26*) Mai., 1 Nov.,
  5 Nov., 14 Nov.
  <u>Hua Fiachrach, Inis Muredhaich</u>,
  Hibernia 27 (<u>27</u>) Oct.
  <u>Lann Mocholmoc</u>, Hibernia 30 (<u>30</u>)
  Mar.
  *Lobar*, Hibernia 21 (*21*) Mai..
  *macc Darane*, Hibernia 31 (*31*) Iul.
  <u>Mitine, filius Lenini, Cluain Huamha</u>,
  Hibernia 24 (<u>24</u>) Nov.
  (Mocholmóc) Hibernia 7 Iun., 25 Iul.
  (<u>Mocholmocus</u>) *moccu (mac hui)
  Gualae*, <u>filius matris Mocholmoci</u>,

(MDr, *MTur*, <u>MC</u>, (IMY))

de Ultonia, Lann Mocholmoc,
Hibernia 30 (*30*, <u>30</u>) Oct.
*moccu Birn*, Hibernia 22 (*22*) Ian.
Columba (*Colum*)
  *Cille*, prius Crimthann, filius
    Fedhlimidii, ab., Hibernia 9 (*9*, <u>9</u>)
    Iun., Comineus author vitae eius <u>24</u>
    Feb., Falueus comarbanus eius <u>22</u>
    <u>Mar.</u>, ordo <u>11 Feb.</u> See also Í,
    Surdum
  Hibernia 13 Dec.
  moccu Altai *7 Iun.* (see note)
  *Ros Gel* (sic) (see note), Hibernia 6 (*6*)
    Sep.
  Tír Dá Glas *24 Mai.* (see note)
  v. et m. 31 Dec.
Columbanus (Columbanus Scotus)
  ab., Italia 13 Nov., 21 Nov.
Comgallus
  ab., *Bennchor*, Hibernia 10 (*10*) Mai.,
    comarbanus eius <u>28 Feb.</u>
Comgán
  *Glenn Uissen*, Hibernia, 27 (*27*, <u>27</u>)
    Feb. (see note), *8 Iul.*
  13 (*13*) Oct.
Comineus
  see Cuimmíne
Commán
  Hibernia 26 Dec.
Concordius (recte Concordia?)
  Ravenna 16 Dec.
Conláed
  Hibernia 3 (*3*) Mai.
Conna
  Hibernia 8 Mar.
Constantin (Constantinus)
  *1 Sep.*
  ab., ex Britannia, *Rathan* (Cuil Rathen
    Mochuddae), Hibernia 11 (*11*, <u>11</u>)
    Mar.
  ep. 29 (*29*) Ian. (*see note*)
  filius Helenae *10 Mar.*
Corconutan
  Hibernia 3 Nov.
Cormac
  *cruimther* (<u>pr.</u>), Achadh Finnigh, Inis
    Caoil, Hibernia 11 (*11*, <u>11</u>) Mai.
  ep. et successor Patricii, Ath Truim,
    Hibernia, 17 (<u>17</u>) Feb.
  pr., *Ua Liatháin*, Hibernia 21 (*21*) Iun.
Corman (Corman(i)a)
  mater Cuannani (Cuanna) <u>4 Feb.</u>

Cornelius
  papa et m., Roma 14 (*14*) Sep. (IMY
    55)
Corona
  *14 Mai.*
Cosmas
  et Damianus *27 Sep.* (IMY 61)
Crescentia
  m., Sicilia 15 Iun.
Crescentianus
  31 Mai.
Crimthann
  see Columba Cille
Crisogonus
  see Chrysogonus
Crispina
  v., Africa 5 Dec.
Crispinianus
  Gallia 25 Oct.
Crispinus
  Gallia 25 Oct.
Critóc
  Hibernia 11 Mai.
Cronanus (Crónán)
  *7 Aug.*
  <u>ab.</u>, *Ferna*, Hibernia 22 (*22*, <u>22</u>) Iun.
  filius Mellani, Lismorum, Surdum S.
    Columbae, Hibernia 10 (*10*, <u>10</u>) Feb.
  Hibernia, 1 Nov.
  *Ros Cré*, Hibernia 28 (*28*) Apr.
Cruimmín (*Cruimmíne*)
  *Lecain*, Hibernia 28 (*28*) Iun.
Cruimther
  see Cuimmíne
Cruimther Fráech
  pr., Hibernia 20 Dec.
Crux (sancta crux)
  exaltatio 14 Sep., inventio 3 Mai.
Cuán
  Hibernia 10 Iul.
Cuangus
  mac dall, Liethmorum, Hibernia 13 (<u>13</u>)
    Mar.
Cuanna (Cuanda)
  v., Corman mater eius, Kill Chuanna,
    Hibernia 4 (*4*, <u>4</u>) Feb.,
  v., *Ros Eó*, Hibernia 10 (*10*) Apr.
Cucufas
  m., Hispania 25 Iul.
Cuimmíne (*Cuimméne*, <u>Comineus</u>,
  Cummain)
  *4 Mai.*

(MDr, *MTur*, <u>MC</u>, (IMY))

Cuimmíne (*Cuimméne*, <u>Comineus</u>,
    Cummain) *cont.*
  ab. <u>et pr.</u>, <u>Cruimther</u>, I (<u>Ia</u>, Iense
    monasterium), <u>author vitae</u>
    <u>Columbae</u> 24 (<u>24</u>) Feb.
    Hibernia 12 Nov.
Cummain
  v., Hibernia 29 Mai.
Curfin
  *20 Iul.*
Cuthbertus (Gubertus)
  Britannia 20 Mar. (IMY 17)
Cyprianus
  ep. et m., Africa 14 (*14*) Sep. (IMY 56)
Cyriacus
  *20 Iun.*
  m., Roma 16 Mar., 8 Aug.
  cruxifixus *12 Mai.*
Cyricus (*Ciric*)
  *maccán*, m., Antiochia 16 (*16*) Iun.
Cyrillus (Cirillus)
  m. *26 Apr.*
  passio *9 Mai.*
Cythinus
  m. Scillitanus, Carthago 17 Iul.

Dabeocus
  see Mobeóc
Dacholmoc
  *7 Iun.*
Dagán
  pr., *Inber Doíle*, Hibernia 13 (*13*, <u>13</u>)
    Sep.
Daig
  *mac Cairill*, <u>faber Kierani et scriba</u>,
    Hibernia 18 (*18*, <u>18</u>) Aug.
Damasius
  see Dasius.
Damassus
  *2 Iul.*
Damianus
  et Cosmas *27 Sep.* (IMY 61)
  m. et *miles* 12 (*12*) Feb.
Daniel
  propheta *21 Iul.*, 11 Dec.
Darerca (Moninne)
  <u>soror Patricii, mater Mel et</u>
    <u>septemdecim episcoporum</u>, <u>6 Feb.</u>, *6*
    *Iul.* (see note)
Daria
  Roma 12 Aug.

Darii
  v. *8 Aug.*
Dasius (Damasius)
  m., Nicomedia 21 Oct.
Dativa
  7 Dec.
David
  *Cell Muine*, archiep. insulae Britanniae
    1 (*1*) Mar.
  rex, Hierosolyma *8 Oct.*, 29 Dec.
Déclán
  *Aird Mór*, Hibernia 24 (*24*) Iul.
Derfraichia
  filia Eochodii, mater Tigernaci <u>4 Apr.</u>
Derthrea (Dorothaea)
  see Ita
Desiderius
  ep. et m., apud Lingones 23 Mai.
  lector, Neapolis Campaniae 19 Sep.
Deusus
  see Drusus
Diaconi
  septem primi 19 Apr., 6 Iun.
Diarmait
  <u>filius Lugna, mater eius Editua</u>, *Inis*
    *Clothrann*, Hibernia 10 (*10*, <u>10</u>) Ian.
  Hibernia, 8 Iul.
  pr., Hibernia 21 Iun.
Dícuill (<u>Dichullus</u>)
  Derg, filius Nessani, Inis Nessani <u>15</u>
    <u>Mar.</u>
  Hibernia 18 Dec.
Dimetrus
  *19 Sep.*
Dionysia
  7 Dec.
  m., Lamosacus 15 Mai.
Dionysius (Dionis)
  *25 Mai., 31 Iul., 9 Oct.*
  ep. *14 Mar.*
Dioscorus
  m. 20 Aug.
Díraid
  Hibernia 27 Iul.
Domangart
  <u>filius Eochadii</u>, pr., <u>Sliebh Slanga</u> 24
    (<u>24</u>) Mar.
Dominus
  see Iesus Christus
Domitius
  m., Syria 5 Iul.

(MDr, *MTur*, <u>MC</u>, (IMY))

Domninus
Nicea 4 Nov.
Domnóc
Hibernia 18 Mai.
Donata
m. Scillitana, Carthago 17 Iul.
Donatus
Antiochia 15 Nov.
ep. et m., Tuscia 7 Aug.
Donnán
m., *Eig*, Britannia 17 (*17*) Apr.
Dormientes see Sancti
Doroma
v. *20 Sep.*
Drusus (Deusus)
m., Antiochia 14 Dec.
Dubliter
Hibernia 15 (*15*) Mai.
Dúilech
Hibernia 17 Nov.
Dúnchad
pr. et ab., I (Iensis, *Ia*) 25 (*25*) Mai.

Edistius
Ravenna 12 Oct.
Editua
mater Diermitii filii Lugna <u>10 Ian.</u>
Egemonus (Agmemnonus)
*8 Ian.*
Egbertus
(IMY 22)
Eilténe (<u>Meoltocus</u>)
Hibernia 11 (<u>11</u>) Dec.
Éimín
Hibernia 22 Dec.
Elarius
see Hilarius
Eleutherius (Iuliter)
m. *2 Oct.*
Eleutherus
papa, Roma 25 Mai.
Emerentiana
v. et m., Roma 23 Ian.
Emeritus
Alexandria 12 Dec.
Emilianus
see Iulianus.
Énán
*Druimm Ráthe*, Hibernia 19 (*19*) Aug.
(IMY 58), *18 Sep.*
*Ros*, Hibernia 30 (*30*) Ian.

Enarius
see Ianuarius
Énna (*Éndae*, <u>Endeus</u>)
<u>filius Conalli Deirg, Brigh seu Aibhfinn
mater eius</u>, *Árainn*, Hibernia 21 (*21*,
<u>21</u>) Mar., frater Carechae 9 Feb.,
Benedictus successor eius <u>14 Iun.</u>
Hibernia 31 Dec.
Eogan
ep., *Ard Sratha*, Hibernia 23 (*23*) Aug.
Eol
frater Gabráin et Fachtna, Hibernia 14
Nov.
Eolang
*Achad/Aigthe Bó/Bolg*, Hibernia 5 (*5*)
Sep.
Eoualidi
see Heuualdi
Epactacus
*23 Mai.*
Eradius
see Herodius
Epimachus
m., Roma 10 Mai.
Erasmus
ep. et m., Campania *2 Iun.*, 3 Iun.
Ercalinus
see Herculanus
Erccus (Ercc)
*Domnach Mór*, Hibernia 27 (*27*) Oct.
ep., Hibernia 12 (*12*) Mai. (*see note*).
ep., Hibernia 2 Nov.
Ercnat,
v., Hibernia 8 Ian.
Ernach
v., Hibernia 30 Oct.
Erníne (<u>Mernocus</u>)
<u>filius Gresseni, Kill Droignech, Rath
Naoi</u>, Hibernia 18 (<u>18</u>) Aug.
Esdras
propheta 13 Iul.
Essodorus
see Isiridonus
Etchén
ep., <u>qui ordinem Columbae dedit,</u>
Hibernia 11 (*11*, <u>11</u>) Feb.
Eucherius
ep., Lugdunum 16 Nov.
Eulalia
v. et m., ciuitas Barcinona, Hispania 12
Feb.
v. et m., Hispania 10 Dec.

(MDr, *MTur*, <u>MC</u>, (IMY))

Euphemia *(Eufenia/Eufonia)*
   *13 Apr.*
   v. *11 Iul.*
   v. et m., Calcedonia 16 Sep. (IMY 57)
Eusebius
   *2 Oct., 9 Oct.*
   Adrianopolis Traciae 22 Oct.
   ep., Italia 1 Aug.
   pr. 14 Aug.
Eusebus (Iosebus)
   *25 Sep.*
Euthychianus
   Africa 12 Nov.
   papa 8 Dec.
Euthychius (Euticius)
   passio *30 Mai.*
   passio *20 Oct.*
Euthymius *(Eutimus/Euticius)*
   diac., Alexandria 5 (*5*) Mai. (*see note*)
Evangelius *(Evangelia)*
   *v.*, 13 (*13*) Iul.
Evilasius
   20 Sep.
Ezechiel *(Ezechelis)*
   propheta *2 Apr.*, 10 Apr.

Fabianus
   ep., Roma 20 Ian.
Fabius
   m., Caesaria 31 Iul.
Fachtna
   *29 Apr.*
   frater Eoil et Gabráin, Hibernia 14 Nov.
   *mac Mongaig*, <u>Ros Alithir, Darinis</u>
     <u>Moelanfaidh</u>, Hibernia 14 (*14*, <u>14</u>)
     Aug.
Faelanus (Fáelán)
   Amlobar *18 Iun.*
   <u>Cluain Maoscna</u>, Hibernia 9 (<u>9</u>) Ian.
   Hibernia 20 Iun.,
   <u>frater Fursaei, ab. et m., Gallia,</u>
     Hibernia 31 (*31*, <u>31</u>) Oct.
Fáilbe
   ab. <u>et comarbanus Columbae</u>, I (Iense
     monasterium) 22 (<u>22</u>) Mar.
Fainche,
   v., Hibernia 21 (*21*) Ian.
Faterus
   pr. 23 Nov.
Fausta
   v. 20 Sep.

Faustinus *(Fustinus)*
   m. 29 Iul.
   passio *8 Oct.*
Faustus *(Fustus)*
   *27 Aug.*
   Cappadocia 22 Nov.
Féichín *(Moeca,* <u>Moacca</u>)
   <u>filius Maelcharna, discipulus Kierani,</u>
     Hibernia 20 (*20*, <u>20</u>) Ian., institutor
     eius <u>20 Oct.</u>
Feidelm
   <u>filia Alildi</u>, v., <u>Kill na nIngen</u>, Hibernia
     9 (<u>9</u>) Dec.
Feimme
   v., Hibernia, ghost saint 21 Ian. (see
     note).
Felicianus
   m., cum sociis 29 Oct.
Felicissimus
   Africa 30 Oct.
   diac. et m., Roma 6 Aug.
Felicitas
   m., Tuburbo 7 Mar.
   mater septem fratrum, Roma 10 Iul.
Felicula
   v. et m., Roma 13 Iun.
Felix
   *5 Ian., 9 Ian.*, 12 (*12*) Iul.
   diac. 16 (*16*) Apr.
   ep., Africa 10 Sep.
   filius Felicitatis, m., Roma 10 Iul.
   m. *3 Feb.*
   m. Scillitanus, Carthago 17 Iul.
   m., Africa 6 Nov.
   m., Roma 30 Aug.
   papa et m., Roma 30 Mai.
   pontifex et m., Roma 29 Iul.
   pr., Nola Campaniae 14 (*14*) Ian.
Fer Dá Chrích
   <u>ep., Clochar</u>, Hibernia 15 (<u>15</u>) Aug.
Fer Dá Leithe
   seu Berchán, Hibernia 4 Dec.
Fergna
   (<u>Finnius Candidus</u>), ab., I (monasterium
     Iense, *Ia*) 2 (*2*, <u>2</u>) Mar. (see note)
Festus
   diac., Neapolis Campaniae 19 Sep.
Fiacc
   <u>pater Fiachrii, Min Beag</u>, Hibernia 12
     (<u>12</u>) Oct.
Fiachnae
   Hibernia 29 Apr.

INDEX OF SAINTS

(MDr, *MTur*, <u>MC</u>, (IMY))

Fiachra
  <u>filius Fieci, Min Beag</u>, Hibernia 12 (<u>12</u>)
    Oct.
  Hibernia 8 Feb.
Fiadnat
  v., 29 Nov.
Filatus (Filadius)
  Roma 1 Dec., 5 Dec. (see note).
Filia(*e*) Feradig
  v., Hibernia 23 (*23*) Mar.
Filiae Baite
  vv., <u>Kella Filiarum Baithe</u>, Hibernia 29
    (<u>29</u>) Mar.
Filiae Comgaill,
  vv., Hibernia 22 Ian.
Filiae Filii Iair
  vv., Hibernia 26 Oct.
Filii Bochrai
  tres, Hibernia 28 Nov.
Filii Nessáin
  Hibernia 15 (*15*) Mar.
Filius Commáin
  Hibernia 21 Nov.
Filius Congnaid
  Hibernia 21 Nov.
Filumenus
  see Philumenus.
Fínán
  *Cam, Cenn Étig*, Hibernia 7 (*7*) Apr.
  leprosus (*Lobor*), <u>filius Conalli, Ard
    Finain, Cluain Mor Maedoc, Inis
    Faithleann, Surdum</u>, Hibernia 16 (*16*,
    <u>16</u>) Mar.
Findech
  v., Hibernia 2 Feb.
*Findlug*
  <u>filius Demani</u>, *Dún Blesce (Flesce)*,
    <u>Tamlacht Finlagain</u> *3* (<u>3</u>) *Ian.*
Finguine
  Hibernia 16 Mai.
Finnbarr
  *Inis Doimle*, Hibernia 4 (*4*) Iul.
Finnchú
  Hibernia 25 Nov.
Finnianus (*Finnia*)
  <u>Fionn, filius Fintani</u>, ab. et magister,
    <u>Cluain Eraird</u>, Hibernia 12 (<u>12</u>) Dec.
  ep., *Mag Bile*, Hibernia 10 (*10*, <u>10</u>)
    Sep.
Finnius
  Candidus see Fergna

Finnsech
  v., <u>Mons Guairii</u>, Hibernia 13 (*13*, <u>13</u>)
    Oct.
Fintan
  *Corach*, <u>peregrinaturus, Cluain
    aithchin, Cluain Ferta Brendani,
    Leamchoill</u>, Hibernia, 21(*21*, <u>21</u>)
    Feb.
  Druimm Ing *10 Oct.*
  filius Demani, Dun Bleisce <u>3 Ian.</u>
  <u>filius Gabhreni</u>, *Cluain Eidnech*,
    Hibernia 17 (*17*, <u>17</u>) Feb.
  <u>Moeldubh, institutor Fechini</u>, Hibernia,
    20 (<u>20</u>) Oct.
Flann
  ab. et pr., Hibernia 15 Dec.
Flannán
  Hibernia Dec. 18.
Flauianus
  m. *28 Iun.*
Fled
  v., Hibernia 12 Sep. (see note).
Florentia
  m. 10 Nov.
Florentius
  Gallia 17 Oct.
  Oia insula 30 Dec.
Florianus
  *3 Mar.*
Focas
  see Phocas.
Foirtchern
  Hibernia 11 (*11*) Oct.
Forfirius
  see Porphirius.
Fortunata
  Roma 15 Oct.
Fortunatus (*Furtinatus*)
  14 (*14*) Aug.
  m. *11 Iun.*
  passio *7 Iun.*
Fraechanus
  Hibernia 20 Nov.
Fratres
  septem, cum Christina *18 Iul.*
  septem, passio *10 Iul.*
  septem, passio in Roma *27 Iun.*
Fraxides
  see Praxides
Fructuosa
  Antiochia 15 Nov.

216

(MDr, *MTur*, <u>MC</u>, (IMY))

Furseus Scotigena (*Fursu*)
 <u>filius Finnlogae et Gelgesiae, frater</u>
  <u>Faelani</u>, ab., <u>Perona</u>, 16 (*16*, <u>16</u>) Ian.,
  <u>31 Oct.</u>
Furudrán
 *mac Móenáin*, Hibernia 18 (*18*) Iun.
  (*see note*)
Fustinus
 see Faustinus
Fustus
 see Faustus

Gabrán
 frater Eoil et Fachtna, Hibernia 14 Nov.
Gabriel
 angelus 25 Mar.
Gaius
 ep., 20 (*20*) Feb.
 see Caius.
Gallicanus
 *26 Iun.*
Gamaliel
 cum Stephano, Hierosolyma 26 Dec.,
  inventio, Hierosolyma 3 Aug.
Garbán
 *Cenn Sáile*, <u>prope Dubliniam</u>, Hibernia
  9 (*9*, <u>9</u>) Iul.
Gedeon
 propheta 1 Sep.
Gelgesia
 mater Fursaei <u>16 Ian.</u>
Generosa
 m. Scillitana, Carthago 17 Iul.
Genesius
 m., Roma 25 Aug.
Georgius (*Giurgius*)
 m., Diospolis 23 Apr., *24 Apr.* (IMY
  20)
Germanicus,
 m., Smyrna 19 Ian.
Germanus (*Germán*)
 *1 Oct.*
 aite Pátraic *28 Mai.*
 Caesaria Cappadociae 3 Nov.
 pr., *m. et sac.*, 29 (*29*) Apr.
 m. *4 Feb.*
Gervasius (*Gerbassus*)
m., Mediolanum *20 Mai.*, 19 (*19*) Iun.,
 (IMY 36)
Gildas
 ep. 29 (*29*) Ian. (*see note*)

Glucerus (*Clucerus*)
 diac. et m. 14 (*14*) Ian.
Gobbán
 <u>Cluain Edhneach, Kill Lamruidhe, Teg</u>
  <u>Da Goba</u>, Hibernia 6 (<u>6</u>) Dec.
Gopnat
 v., <u>Bornech (Boirne)</u>, Hibernia 11 (*11*,
  11) Feb.
Gordianus
 m., Roma 10 Mai.
 Nividunum 17 Sep.
Gormanus
 peregrinus, Hibernia 25 Oct.
Gormgalius
 abbas, Ardoilen <u>5 Aug.</u>
Gregorius
 *10 Feb.*
 ep. et m., Pontus 17 Nov.
 Naziansenus *29 Mar.*
 papa, apostolus Anglorum, Roma 12
  (*12*) Mar. (IMY 15), 21 Mar., 24
  Mai.
 pr. 14 Aug.
Guaire
 Hibernia 27 Iul.
Gubertus
 see Cuthbertus.

Helena
 mater Constantini 10 Mar., regina,
  Hierysolyma 3 Mai.
Helia (*Helea*)
 m. 21 (*21*) Iul.
Helias
 *7 Iul.*
 26 Iul.
Heliseus
 propheta, Samaria Palestinae 14 (*14*)
  Iun.
Herculanus (Ercalinus)
 *5 Sep.*
Hereneus
 *ep.* 6 (*6*) Apr.
Herentius
 m. 5 (*5*) Aug.
Hermenegildus
 Hispania 13 Apr.
Hermes
 *24 Mai.*
 Adrianopolis Traciae 22 Oct.
 frater Teodosiae, m. 1 Apr.
 m. 28 (*28*) Aug.

(MDr, *MTur*, <u>MC</u>, (IMY))

Hermogoras
  ep., Aquileia 12 Iul.
Hermogenis
  *19 Apr.*
Herodius (Eradius)
  m., passio *20 Apr.*
Heuualdi
  gemini (IMY 65)
Hichtbrichtan
  see Ichtbrichtan.
Hieremias
  propheta 1 Mai.
Hieronymus (Hironimus)
  *sapiens, obitus 30 Sep.* (IMY 63)
Hilarinus
  m., Ostia 16 Iul.
Hilarius (Elarius)
  *5 Mai.,16 Iul.*
  episcopus Pictauis *13 Ian*
Hippolytus
  ep. 29 (*29*) Ian.
  m., Roma 13 (*13*) Aug.
  Roma 23 Aug.
Hitharnaiss
  see Itharnaisc.
Hyacinthus (Iacinthus)
  m. 26 Iul.
  Roma 11 (*11*) Sep.

Iacobus
  *15 Mar.*
  Alfeus *22 Iun.*
  [filius] Zebedei, *frater Iohannis,*
    apostolus 25 (*25*) Iul. (IMY 44), 26
    Iul.
  filius Mariae et apostolus et m., frater
    Domini et ep., Hierosolyma 1 (*1*)
    Mai. (IMY 28), *23 Iul.*, 27 Dec.
  ep., Nisibis 14 (*14*) Iul., 15 Iul.
  frater Iudae *1 Iul.*
Ianuaria
  m. Scillitana, Carthago 17 Iul.
Ianuarius (*Enarius*)
  filius Felicitatis, m., Roma 10 Iul.
  m. *8 Apr.*
  m., Roma 10 Mai.
  *m.*, Neapolis Campaniae 19 (*19*) Sep.
Iarlaithe
  Hibernia 26 (<u>26</u>) Dec.
Ibar
  ep., Hibernia 23 (*23*) Apr.

Ichtbrichtán (Hichtbrichtan)
  Anglus, Hibernia 8 Dec.
Ieiunium
  initium *7 Ian.*
Iesus Christus (Christus, Deus, Dominus,
  Dominus Salvator, *Iesu, Ísu*)
  24 Iun., 3 Aug., 15 Aug., 1 Sep., 8 Sep.,
    27 Dec., Bethleem Iudae 25 Dec.,
    annuntiatio/*conceptio*, crucifixio/
    *passio* 25 (*25*) Mar. (IMY 19),
    ascensio *5 Mai.*, *cétphraicept* 1 (*1*)
    Mai., circumcisio 1(*1*) Ian. (IMY 1),
    crux 10 Mar., discipulus eius 1 Sep.,
    epiphania 6 (*6*) Ian. (IMY 2),
    evangelium 21 Sep., Iacobus frater
    Domini *1 Mai.* (IMY 28)*, 23 Iul.*,
    ieiunium 7 Ian., inventio crucis *3
    Mai.*, Ioseph aite eius *19 Mar.*,
    *oblatio ad templum 2 Feb.* (IMY 11),
    octavae 1 Ian, reversio (*eductio*) de
    Aegypto 11 (*11*) Ian., resurrectio 27
    (*27*) Mar., transformatio 26 (*26*) Iul.,
    victoria (*triumphum*) de diabolo 15
    (*15*) Feb., vigilia 24 Dec.
  Nave
    propheta 1 Sep.
Ignatius
  20 Dec.
  ep. et m., Antiochia 1 Feb., 17 Dec.
Infantes
  decem *14 Iul.*
  2200 mm., Bethleem 28 Dec.
Ingen Áildéin
  *29 Mai.*
Iob
  *8 Iun., 30 Iun.*
  amicus Dei 11 (*11*) Mai.
Ioel
  propheta 6 Iul., 13 Iul.
Iohannes
  apostolus et evangelista 26 Ian., 28
    Mar., *25 Mai., 24 Iul.*, 26 Iul., 27
    Dec., airec capitis *27 Feb.*, ante
    Portam Latinam 6 Mai., frater Iacobi
    *25 Iul.* (IMY 44), reuersio ad
    Effessum *24 Iun.*
  Baptista, filius Zachariae et Elisabeth 5
    Nov., *conceptio 24 Sep.,*
    *gein/nativitas* 24 (*24*) Iun. (IMY 38),
    decollatio 29 (*29*) Aug. (IMY 51),
    vigilia 23 Iun.

(MDr, *MTur*, MC, (IMY))

Iohannes *cont.*
    Chrysostomus, Constantinopolis, 27 Ian.
    frater Pauli, m. 26 (*26*) Iun. (IMY 40)
    m., Nicomedia 7 Sep.
    Metropolis, *inventio* 3 (*3*) Aug. (*see note*)
    papa 28 Mai.
Iosebus
    see Eusebus
Ioseph
    iustus 19 Iul.
Ioseph (Iosephus)
    *18 Feb.*
    aite Iesu *19 Mar.*
Isaias
    propheta 6 Iul.
Isiridonus (Essodorus)
    *2 Ian.*
Ita (<u>Mida</u>)
    prius Derthrea (Dorothea), filia
    <u>Kennfoeladii</u>, v., *Cluain Credal*,
    Hibernia 15 (*15*, <u>15</u>) Ian.
Itharnaisc (Hitharnaiss)
    Hibernia 22 Dec.
Iucundus
    *21 Feb.*
Iudas
    frater Iacobi *1 Iul.* (see note)
    (Thaddeus) apostolus see Thaddeus
Iulia
    v. 22 Mai.
Iuliana
    v., Cumae 16 (*16*) Feb.
Iulianus
    m., Antiochia 9 Ian.
    ep., Vienna 22 Apr.
    m., Damascus 20 Iul.
    Tracia 20 Dec.
    (recte Emilianus), cum sociis 22 Aug.
Iulita
    mater Cyriaci et m., Antiochia 16 Iun.
Iuliter
    see Eleutherius
Iulius
    ep. *et papa*, Roma, via Aurelia 12 (*12*)
        Apr.
Iusta
    m., Hispania 18 Iul.
Iustinus
    diac. *5 Mai.* (see note)
    ep. 5 Dec.
Iustus
    ep., Lugudunum 2 Sep.

Iventius
    Ticinum 12 Sep.

Kienanus
    see Cianán
Kieranus
    see Ciarán

Laetatius
    m. Scillitanus, Carthago 17 Iul.
Laichtín (<u>Lactocus</u>)
    <u>Achadh Ur,</u> Hibernia 19 (*19*, <u>19</u>) Mar.
Laidcend (*Laidgnén*)
    <u>filius Baithi Bannaigh, Cluain Ferta</u>
    <u>Molua</u>, Hibernia 12 (*12*, <u>12</u>) Ian.
Laisrén (Lasrianus, *Molaisse*)
    ep., *Lethglenn*, Hibernia 18 (*18*) Apr.
    *Inis Muiredaig*, Hibernia 12 (*12*) Aug.
    Hibernia 25 (*25*) Oct.
    sacerd., *Daminis*, Hibernia 12 Sep.
    sacerd., Hibernia 16 Sep. (bis)
Lalloca
    filia Darercae <u>6 Feb.</u>
Laurentius (*Lurentius*)
    *2 Iun.*
    archidiac. et m. 10 Aug. (IMY 47),
        octavae 17 Aug., vigilia 9 Aug.
    gein *22 Feb.*
    m. *3 Feb.*
Lazarus
    28 Mar.
Leo
    papa 28 Iun.
Leocadia
    v. 9 Dec.
Leogathus
    m. 22 Oct.
Leontia
    7 Dec.
Leontius
    Cappadocia 22 Nov.
Libba
    see Molipa
Liberatus
    20 Dec.
Librén
    Hibernia 11 Mar.
Liemania
    filia Calphurni, soror Patricii, mater
        Secundini <u>27 Nov.</u>, mater Nectani <u>2</u>
        <u>Mai.</u>

(MDr, *MTur*, <u>MC</u>, (IMY))

Linus
   papa et m. 26 Nov.
Litania Maior
   Roma, ad Sanctum Petrum 25 Apr.
Lóchán
   Hibernia 31 Dec.
Lommán
   Hibernia 11 (*11*) Oct.
   *Loch Uair*, Hibernia 7 (*7*) Feb.
   (Tomanus), Britannia Arcluidensis <u>8
   Iun.</u>
Lon (*Longarad*)
   <u>Desertum Garadh, Kill Garadh,</u>
   Hibernia 3 (*3*, <u>3</u>) Sep.
Lonanus
   Hibernia 1 Nov.
Longinus
   miles, Cappadocia/Caesarea
   Cappodociae 1 Sep., *23 Oct.*, 22
   Nov.
Lucas
   evangelista *6 Feb.*, 15 (*15* ) Mar., *1
   Oct.*, discipulus Pauli, Syrus,
   Antiochia, *nativitas* 18 Oct.
Lucell
   ap Cluana *6 Oct.*
Lucia
   v. *5 Feb.*, 6 Feb.
   v. et m., Sicilia 13 Dec.
Lucianus
   *24 Feb.*
   pr., Hierosolyma 3 Aug.
Lucius
   ep., Africa 10 Sep.
   ep., Cyrene 6 Mai.
   papa et m. 4 (*4*) Mar.
   Roma 1 Dec.
Lugid
   ep. *6 Oct.*
Lupus
   ep. 29 (*29*) Iul.
   ep., Sanctonas 1 Sep.
Lurentius
   see Laurentius

Mac Aíge
   Hibernia 3 Dec.
Macarius
   ab. 2 Ian.
Mac Caille (Maccaleus)
   ep., <u>Cruachan Brigh Ele,</u> Hibernia 25
   (*25*, <u>25</u>) Apr.

Mac Caírthinn
   <u>filius Cannechi, Clocharia,</u> ep. 24 (<u>24</u>)
   Mar., Darerca mater eius <u>6 Feb.</u>,
   successor eius <u>15 Aug.</u>
Mac Clárín
   *17 Oct.*
Mac Conloga
   Hibernia 11 Iul.
Mac Cuilinn
   *Lusca*, Hibernia 6 (*6*) Sep.
Mac Dall
   see Cuangus
Machabei
   *septem, cum matre*, Antiochia 1 (*1*)
   Aug.
Mac Leamna
   see Nechtán
Mac Léinín
   Hibernia 24 Nov.
Mac Nisse
   *Cluain*, Hibernia 13 (*13*) Iun.
   Hibernia 3 (*3*) Sep.
Macra
   v. et m. 6 Ian.
Macrobius
   m., Damascus 20 Iul.
Mac Táil
   <u>prius Aengussius, filius Eugenii,</u> ep. <u>et
   faber,</u> Hibernia 11 (*11*, <u>11</u>) Iun., *9
   Oct.*
Madianus
   see Mattheus
Máedóc
   see Áed.
Máel Aithgen (*Aidchein*)
   Hibernia 6 (*6*) Iun.
Máel Anfaid
   Hibernia 31 (*31*) Ian.
Máel Doid
   24 Mar.
?Máel Muire (Marianus Scotus)
   <u>24 Dec.</u>
Máel Odráin
   Hibernia 2 Dec.
Máel Ruain
   ep., *Tamlachta*, Hibernia 7 (*7*) Iul.
Máel Rubae
   cum matre, *Alba*, Britannia 21 (*21*) Apr.
Magnus
   seu/et Andreas m. 19 (*19*) Aug.
Maigniu
   <u>Kill Magnenn, Hibernia 16 Ian.</u>, 18 Dec.

Mainchíne
  Hibernia 2 (*2*) Ian.
Mainennius
  see Moinenn
Mammes
  16 (*16*) Iul.
  m., Caesarea Cappadociae 17 (*17*) Aug.
Manchanus Conchenn
  Hibernia 24 Ian.
Mandregisilus
  see Wandregisilius.
Marcellianus
  [filius] Tranquillini, m., Roma 18 Iun.
Marcellinus
  pr. et m., Roma 2 Iun.
Marcell[in]us
  papa et m. 26 Apr.
Marcellosus
  20 (*20*) Mai.
Marcellus (*Marcell*)
  14 Feb., *19 Feb., 17 Iul., 13 Oct.*
  ep. *4 Oct.*
  m., Tingis 29 Oct.
  papa et m., Roma 16 Ian.
Marcia
  m., Sicilia 21 Iun.
Marcialis
  *28 Sep.*
Marcianus (*Martianus*)
  *4 Ian.*
  m., cum duobus fratribus, Africa 23
    Oct.
  passio *5 Iun.*
Marcus (*Marc*)
  *9 Oct.*
  [filius] Tranquillini, m., Roma 18 Mai.
    (IMY 32)
  ep. *7 Oct.* (see note)
  evangelista 25 (*25*) Apr., *10 Iun.*, gein *3
    Oct.*
  Nividunum 17 Sep.
Margarita
  v. et m. 13 Iul.
Maria
  v. et genetrix Dei, *1 Apr., 3 Mai.*,
    nativitas 8 Sep. (IMY 53), soror
    Mariae et mater Domini 1 Mai.,
    annuntiatio 25 Mar., annuntiatio
    assumptionis 18 (*18*) Ian.,
    assumptio/*obitus* 15 (*15*) Aug. (IMY
    48), conceptio *2 Mai.*, dedicatio
    basilicae *15 Sep.*, nativitas *8 Sep.*,

purificatio 2 Feb., vigilia
    assumptionis 14 Aug., ad Martyres
    13 Mai.
Magdalena, soror Marthae et Lazari *19
    Ian.*, 28 (*28*) Mar., 22 (*22*) Iul.
  soror matris Domini 1 Mai.
Marianus Scotus
  see Máel Muire
Marina
  Roma 1 Dec.
Marius
  m., Roma 19 Ian.
Martha
  m., Roma 19 Ian.
  soror Lazari *19 Ian.*, 28 Mar.
Martialis
  filius Felicitatis, m., Roma 10 Iul.
Martinianus
  m., Roma 2 Iul.
Martinus
  ep., Turones Galliae 11 Nov., ordinatio
    *2 Iul.* (see note), translatio *4 Iun.*, 4
    Iul., vita eius 13 Ian.
Martyres anonymi
  et vv., plurimi 1 Ian.
  iii discipuli et mm. 24 Ian.
  vii germani et mm. 29 Mai.
  xxi mm, Roma 8 Aug.
  xxii mm. *13 Sep.*
  xxx mm. *4 Feb.*
  xxx mm., Roma 22 Dec.
  xxxiv mm., Lugdunum Galliae 24 Apr.
  xl mm. *24 Oct.*
  xlviii mm., Roma 14 Mar.
  xc mm. 4 Mar.
  cl mm. *30 Ian.*
  cclxx mm. 16 Oct.
  ccc mm. *8 Sep.*
  cccx mm. 9 Mai.
  ccclxx mm. *10 Oct.*
  dcvi mm. *13 Mai.*
  mmccc mm. *16 Ian.*
  mmdxcvii 19 Aug.
  mmmmdccccxxvii mm. 13 Oct.
  octoginta milia 1 Aug.
  multitudo/turba 1 Ian., *1 Feb.*, 12 Feb.,
    14 Feb., 20 Feb., 20 Mar., 6 Apr., 13
    Apr., 17 Apr., 28 Apr., 29 Apr., 27
    Mai., 4 Iun, 16 Iul., 5 Iul., 19 (*19*)
    Iul.
Masán
  *25 Oct.*

(MDr, *MTur*, <u>MC</u>, (IMY))

Mater
    Machabeorum *1 Aug.*
Matthaeus
    apostolus et evangelista, 21 (*21*) Sep.
       (IMY 59), *7 Oct.* (see note), nativitas
       *6 Mai.*, vigilia 20 Sep.
Matthias (Madian, *Madianus, Mathae*)
    apostolus et m. 23 (*23*) Feb. (IMY 14),
       24 Feb., 19 Iul.
    ep., Hierosolyma 30 Ian.
Mauri
    *passio*, Gallia 15 (*15*) Oct.
Mauricius
    (IMY 60)
Maurinus (Maurus)
    ab. et m., Colonia 10 Iun.
Maurus,
    ab. et discipulus Benedicti 15 Ian.
Maxima
    v. et m., Africa 24 Oct.
Maximinus
    m., Damascus 20 Iul.
Maximus
    *25 Oct.*
    ep., Gallia 27 Nov.
    m. 8 (*8*) Mai.
    pr. et m., Roma 19 Nov. (see note).
Medardus
    ep., Gallia 8 Iun.
Medrán
    <u>frater Murchon, filii Hua Macten, Kill</u>
       <u>Murchu, Britannica Arcluidensis,</u>
       Hibernia 8 (*8*, <u>8</u>) Iun.
Meicc/Mac Dergáin
    *18 Feb.*
Mel
    <u>filius Darercae, ep., Ardachadh,</u>
       Hibernia *5 Feb.*, 6 (<u>6</u>) Feb.
Melanius
    ep., Gallia 6 Nov.
Mellán (*Meldán*)
    <u>filius hUa Cuinn, Inis Mac-hy Chuinn,</u>
       Hibernia <u>16 Ian.</u>, 7 Feb.
    <u>Tamlachta Umhail</u>, Hibernia 26 (*26*, <u>26</u>)
       Oct. (*see note*)
Meoltecus
    see Eiltíne
Mennas
    m., Phrygia 11 Nov.
Mernocus
    see Erníne.

Methodius
    18 Sep.
Michael
    archangelus *29 Sep.* (IMY 62),
       manifestatio *9 Mai.*
Mida
    see Ita
Micheas
    propheta 15 Ian.
Milites
    x 10 Feb.
    xii mm. 21 Oct. (see note).
    xii mm. 24 Iul.
    xl mm. 9 (*9*) Mar.
    xl mm., Roma, via Lavicana 13 Ian.
    xl, Sebaste 11 Mar.
Millibordus
    see Willibrordus.
Misael
    24 Apr.
Mo-acca
    see Féichín
Mobeóc (Mofioc, <u>Dabeocus</u>)
    filius Bracani, et fratres eius, Gleann
       Geirg <u>1 Ian.</u>
    Hibernia 16 (<u>16</u>) Dec.
Mobí
    *clárainech*, Hibernia 12 (*12*) Oct.
Mobíu
    *Inis Cúscraid*, Hibernia 22 (*22*) Iul.
Mochellóc
    <u>Cathair Mac Conchuidh, Kill Odhrain</u>
       <u>(see note)</u>, Hibernia 26 (*26*, <u>26</u>) Mar.
Mochóe
    *Noíndruimm*, Hibernia 23 (*23*) Iun.
Mochóeme
    Hibernia 1 Mai.
Mochóemóc
    *Liath*, <u>filius Beoani</u>, Hibernia 13 (*13*,
       <u>13</u>) Mar.
Mocholmóc
    see Colmán
Mochritóc
    *11 Mai.*
Mochtae
    ep., <u>Lugmagh</u>, Hibernia 24 (*24*, <u>24</u>)
       Mar., 19 Aug.
Mochua
    *Balla*, Hibernia 30 (*30*, <u>30</u>) Mar.
    Hibernia 4 (*4*) Mai., 24 Dec.
    ep., *Cluain Dolcain*, Hibernia 6 (*6*)
       Aug.

(MDr, *MTur*, MC, (IMY))

Mochuaróc
9 (*9*) Feb., *7 Mai.*
Mochutu
see Carthachus
Modestus
m. 10 Nov.
m., Sicilia 15 Iun.
Modímóc
Hibernia 10 Dec.
Modomnóc
*18 Mai.*
Tobar Fachtna, qui apes tulit in
Hiberniam, Hibernia 13 (*13*, 13) Feb.
Moeca
see Féichín
Móedóc
see Áed
Móenach
*17 Oct.*
Moernóc
*18 Aug.*
Moinenn (*Moynend*, Mainennius)
ep. (comarbanus Brendani), Cluain
Ferta, Hibernia 1 (*1*, 1) Mar. (*see
note*)
sacerd., *Cluain Conaire*, Hibernia 16
(*16*) Sep.
Molaca (Molocus)
filius Dubdligii, Lann Bechuire, Tulach
min Molaga, Hibernia 20 (*20*, 20) Ian.
Molaisse
see Laisrén
Moling
discipulus Moedoci, *Luachair*, Hibernia
17 (*17*, 17) Iun.
Molipa (*Moliba*, Libba)
8 Ian.
Hi Ethach Ultoniae, Hibernia 18 (*18*,
18) Feb.
Molotha
v. 2 Sep. (see note).
Molua
*macc Oche*, Cluain Ferta, 4 (*4*) Aug.,
Mothemnogus coquus eius 23 Dec.
Moluóc
*Les Mór*, Britannia (Albania) 25 (*25*,
25) Iun.
Momacru (Moacru, *Mosacru*)
filius Senani, ab., Cluain Eidhneach,
Hibernia 3 (*3*, 3) Mar.
Momáedóc (Momedóc)
see Áed

Monegundis
v. 1 Iul.
Moninne (*Darerca*)
v., Hibernia 6 (*6*) Iul. (*see note*)
Morónóc
*9 Iul.*
Mosacru
see Momacru
Moshenóc
Hibernia 11 Dec.
Moshilóc (*Sillán*)
Hibernia 13 (*13*) Iul. (*see note*), 25 Iul.
Mothairén (Mothoreas)
Hibernia 12 Iun. See also Torannán
Motheimnióc
coquus Molua, Cluain Ferta, Hibernia
23 (23) Dec.
Mothoreas
see Mothairén.
Mothuu
Hibernia 1 Aug.
Moynend
see Moinenn
Moyses (*Moysi*)
*1 Mar.* (see note)
m., Africa 19 Dec.
passio *11 Iul.*
propheta 26 Iul., 4 Sep., lex eius Ian. 1.
Mugain
filia Alilli, v., Kill na ningen, Hibernia
9 (9) Dec.
Muirdebar
Hibernia 3 Nov.
Muirgeilt
v., Hibernia 27 Ian.
Munnu
*mac Tulcháin*, Hibernia 21 (*21*) Oct.
Murchú
frater Medrani, filii Hua Machten,
Hibernia 8 (*8*, 8) Iun.
Muri
see Mauri
Muscentus (Muscendus)
*12 Ian.*

Nabor (Nazarius/*Nazarus*/Nazarus)
Liathmorum 12 (*12*, 12) Iul.
Narthalus
m. Scillitanus, Carthago 17 Iul.
Násad
Tamlachta Umhail, Hibernia 26 (26)
Oct.

223

(MDr, *MTur*, <u>MC</u>, (IMY))

Natchomius
  ab., Tir Da Glass, frater Coemhani <u>3</u>
    <u>Nov.</u>
Nathí
  1 Aug.
  pr., Hibernia 9 (*9*) Aug.
Navalis
  see Novalis.
Nazarius (*Nazarus*)
  m. 27 Iul.
  m., Mediolanum (*12*) 12 Iun.
Nazar(i)us
  see Nabor
Nechtan
  Britannia 8 Ian.
  (<u>Mac Leamna</u>), *daltae Pátraic*,
    <u>Liemania mater eius, Finnabhuir,</u>
    <u>Kill Unche</u>, Hibernia 2 (*2*, <u>2</u>) Mai.
Nem
  *Moccu Birn*, <u>filius Luagnei, de Dal Birn</u>
    <u>Ossoriae, comarbanus Endei, frater</u>
    <u>Kierani, Ara</u>, Hibernia 14 (*14*, <u>14</u>)
    Iun. (<u>see note</u>).
Nemesianus
  ep., Africa 10 Sep.
Nereus
  frater Achillei et m., Roma 12 Mai.
Nessán
  diac., <u>Mungared</u>, Hibernia 25 (<u>25</u>)
    Iul.
  de Ultoniis, Corcagia, Hibernia 17
    Mar., 1 (<u>1</u>) Dec.
  Ulad *1 Sep.*
Nestor
  ep., Perge 26 Feb.
Nicasius
  ep. et m. 14 Dec.
Nicetius
  ep., Lugdunum 2 Apr.
Nicodemus
  inventio corporis, Ierosolyma 3 Aug.
  m./*passio* 17 (*17*) Oct.
Nicolaus
  ep., Myra Lyciae 6 Dec.
Nicomedes
  m. 15 Sep.
Nicostratus
  m., Roma 8 Nov.
Novalis (Naualis)
  Ravenna 16 Dec.

Odrán
  <u>ab., Iensis, Tegh Ererain</u>, Hibernia 27
    (*27*, <u>27</u>) Oct.
Óengus
  Hibernia 11 Mar.
Óenu,
  Hibernia 20 (*20*) Ian.
Oisíne
  1 Ian.
Olympius
  Lycia (see note) 18 Sep.
Omnes sancti
  1 Nov., vigilia 31 Oct.
Omnes sancti Europae
  20 Apr.
Onchú
  <u>poeta, Cluain Mor</u>, Hibernia 8 (<u>8</u>) Feb.
    See also Ua ind Écis
  Hibernia 9 (*9*) Iul.
Orion (Adrio, *Ario*)
  m. 16 (*16*) Aug.
Oseas
  propheta 4 Iul.
Osvaldus (*Osualt*)
  rex Anglorum/*rí Saxan* 5 (*5*) Aug.

Pachomius
  mon. 14 Mai.
Pamphilius
  m. 20 Aug.
  pr., Caesaria Palestinae 1 Iun.
Pancratius
  12 Mai. (IMY 30)
  *1 Sep.*
Pantaleon
  *22 Sep.*
  m., Nicomedia 28 (*28*) Iul.
Papa
  see Benedictus
Papianus
  Oia insula 30 Dec.
Parmenius
  *7 Iul.*
Partholón
  see Bartholomeus
Parvuli
  tres *24 Ian.*
Paschasius
  Africa 12 Nov.
Patricius (*Pátraic*)
  *ep.*, archiepiscopus et apostolus
    Scottorum 17 (*17*, <u>17</u>) Mar.

(MDr, *MTur*, <u>MC</u>, (IMY))

Socrates
  Britannia 17 Sep.
Solutor
  m., Ravenna 13 Nov.
Sophronius (Sufronus)
  *7 Aug.*
Sorores
  Agathae, tres *30 Aug.*
Spiritus Sanctus
  super Apostolos *15 Mai.*
Sosius
  diac., Neapolis Campaniae 19 Sep.
Sosthenes
  discipulus apostolorum 28 Nov.
Soter
  papa 21 Apr.
Speratus
  m. Scillitanus, Carthago 17 Iul.
Stephanus
  Britannia 17 Sep.
  Oia insula 30 Dec.
  papa et m., Roma 2 Aug.
  protom., Hierosolyma Dec. 26, inventio
    corporis, 3 Aug.
Stolius
  see Zoilum.
Sulpicius,
  et vita Martini 13 Ian.
Susanna
  *11 Aug.*
Sussennus
  see Sisennius
Sussus?
  *19 Oct.*
Symphorianus
  m., Roma 8 Nov.
Symphron(i)us (Simfronus)
  m., *3 Feb.* (see note)
Syrus
  Ticinum 12 Sep.

Tassach
  ep., Hibernia, *dedit eucharistiam
    Patricio* 14 (*14*) Apr.
Tatberctus
  *5 Iun.* (IMY 34)
Teille (<u>Tellius</u>)
  <u>Tegh Telle</u>, Hibernia 25 (*25*) Iun.
Teimnén
  manach *17 Aug.*
Telesphorus
  papa et m., Romae 5 Ian.

Temneogus
  see Motheimnióc
Teolis (Theonas, *Teolessius*)
  25 (*25*) Feb. (see note).
Teophilus
  28 Iul.
Terentius
  ep. 28 Oct.
Thaddeus (Iudas)
  et Simon apostoli *1 Iul.*, 28 (*28*) Oct.
  (IMY 66), vigilia 27 Oct.
Thecla
  v. et m., 1 (*1*) Iun.
  v., Oriens 20 Dec.
Theodoritus
  pr. et m., Antiochia 23 Oct.
Theodorus
  m., Antiochia 14 Dec.
  m., Roma 9 Nov.
Theodosia
  soror Hermetis, Roma 1 Apr.
Theodota
  m., cum tribus filiis, Bithynia 2 (*2*)
    Aug.
  v. 2 (*2*) Sep.
Theodotus
  m., Tracia 14 Nov.
Theophilus
  *28 Iul.*
  Caesaria Cappadociae 3 Nov.
Theonas/Theon
  see Teolis.
Theotecnus (Teothotinus)
  Laodicia 18 Dec.
Thomas
  apostolus et m., India 21 Dec., gein *30
    Mai.*, translatio, Edessa 3 (*3*) Iul.
Tiamdae
  see Timotheus
Tiberius
  m. 10 Nov.
Tiburtius
  m., Roma 11 (*11*) Aug.
Tigernach
  anch., Hibernia 13 Mai.
  <u>filius Cairbrei et Derfraichiae</u>, ep.,
    *Cluain Eois*, Hibernia 4 (*4*, <u>4</u>) Apr.
Timo
  diac., Corinthus 19 Apr.
Timotheus (*Tiamdae*)
  *8 Ian.*, *8 Sep.*

(MDr, *MTur*, <u>MC</u>, (IMY))

Zacharias
    pater Iohannis Baptistae et propheta 6
        Sep., 5 Nov.
Zeno
    Roma 8 Iul.
Zenon
    *2 Sep.*
Zenotus
    see Sinotus
Zepherinus
    ep., Roma 20 Dec.

Zephirinus
    papa, Roma 26 Aug.
Zoilus
    Corduba in Hispania 27 Iun.
Zoilus (Stolius)
    30 (*30*) Iun.
Zosimus
    m., Antiochia 14 Dec.
Zoticus
    m., Nicomedia 21 Oct.

# INDEX OF PLACE AND TRIBAL NAMES

(Dates and variant readings are indicated as follows: regular = MDr, italics = MTur, underline = MC, brackets with line numbers = IMY. Latin and Irish names are standardised, with those of MC following, as far as possible, the spelling of Colgan's indexes to A and T)

Achad (g. Aichid) Bó
  uel Aighti (g.?) Bolg *5 Sep.*
Achadh Abhla
  <u>12 Oct.</u>
Achadh Finnigh
  in Lagenia, iuxta fluuium Dothra <u>11 Mai.</u>
Achadh Ur
  <u>19 Mar.</u>
Achaia
  12 Ian., 30 Nov.
Adrianopolis
  Tracia 22 Oct.
Aegyptus (Egiptus)
  11 (*11*) Ian., 17 Ian., 13 Sep.
Africa
  4 Ian., 28 Aug., 10 Sep., 14 Sep., 16 Oct., 24 Oct., 30 Oct., 6 Nov., 12 Nov., 5 Dec., 19 Dec.
Aigthi (g.?) Bolg
  see Achad Bó
Aird (g. Arddae) Breccáin
  *4 Sep.*
Aird Mór (g. Ardae Móre)
  *24 Iul.*
Airdne
  prope Wexfordiam <u>12 Iun.</u>
Airteach
  Tegh Baithin <u>19 Feb.</u>
*Alba* (<u>Albania</u>)
  <u>3 Ian., 23 Mar.</u>, *21 Apr.*, <u>25 Iun.</u> (Lismorum)
Alexandria
  9 Feb., 25 Apr., 5 Mai., 25 Nov., 12 Dec.
Angli
  12 Mar., 24 Mai., 5 Aug., 8 Dec.

Anglia
  Glastonia Scotorum <u>24 Aug.</u>
Antiochia
  9 Ian., 24 Ian, 1 Feb., 22 (*22*) Feb., 5 Mar., 16 Iun., 1 Aug., 18 Oct., 19 Oct., 23 Oct., 15 Nov., 18 Nov., 14 Dec., 17 Dec.
Aquileia
  12 Iul.
Arabia
  12 Ian.
Árainn (g. *Árne*)
  *21* (<u>21</u>) *Mar.*, <u>14 Iun.</u>
Ardachadh
  Teffia <u>6 Feb.</u>
Ard Bo
  Cinel Eoguin <u>18 Feb.</u>
Ard Finain
  <u>16 Mar.</u>
Ard Macha
  <u>24 Aug.</u>
Ardoilen
  <u>5 Aug.</u>
Ard (g. Aird) Sratha
  *23 Aug.*
Armenia
  11 Mar.
Ath Truim
  Hi Laoghaire <u>17 Feb.</u>
Augustodunum
  27 Nov.

Bairnech (Bornech)
  Momonia <u>11 Feb.</u>
Balla
  <u>Connacia</u> *30* (<u>30</u>) *Mar.*
Bannius
  flumen in Ibh Echach <u>6 Dec.</u>

(MDr, *MTur*, <u>MC</u>, (IMY))

Barcinona
  Hispania 12 Feb.
Belach Dúin
  *12 Iun.*
Bennchor
  <u>28 Feb.</u>, *10 Mai.*
Bethleem
  Iudae 25 Dec., 28 Dec.
Bithynia
  2 Aug.
Boind
  fluuius <u>2 Mai.</u>
Bornech
  see Bairnech
Bregae/Bregii/Breghenses/Campus Bregh
  regio in orientali Media <u>20 Ian.</u>, <u>15 Mar.</u>, <u>29 Mar.</u>, <u>2 Mai.</u>, 24 Nov.
Britannia/<u>Britanni</u>
  8 Ian., <u>11 Mar.</u>, 20 Mar., 17 Apr., 21 Apr., <u>16 Mai.</u>, 24 Mai., 22 Iun., 25 Iun., 10 Aug., 24 Aug., 31 Aug., 17 Sep., <u>26 Oct.</u>, insula 1 Mar.
Britannica Arcluidensis
  <u>8 Iun.</u>

Caesarea
  Cappadociae 17 Aug., 1 Sep., 3 Nov.
  Lyciae 5 Apr.
  31 Iul.
Calcedonia
  16 Sep.
Camas (g. Camsa)
  *29 Oct.*
Campania
  14 Ian., 3 Iun., 22 Iun., 19 Sep.
Cappadocia
  17 Aug., 1 Sep., 3 Nov., 22 Nov.
Capua
  27 Aug., 1 Sep.
Carbria
  Media <u>5 Mar.</u>
Carthago (Kartago)
  17 Iul.
Casinum
  21 Mar.
Castra
  3 Feb.
Catana
  5 Feb.
Cathuir Mac Conchuidh
  <u>26 Mar.</u>

Ceann Einnis
  ghost name <u>27 Feb.</u> (see note)
Cell Aichid
  *26 Mar.*
Cell
  see also Kill
Cell Muine
  *1 Mar.*
Cell (g. Cille) Ruaid
  *16 Oct.*
Cella Filiarum Baithe
  in Finegallia ad Surdum in Campo Bregh <u>29 Mar.</u>
Cend Sále (g. Cind Shále)
  *9 Iul.*
Cenn Étig
  *7 Apr.*
Cenn Garad (g. Cinn Garad)
  *10 Aug.*
Cinel Eoguin
  <u>18 Feb.</u>
Cinel Fiachach
  <u>10 Nov.</u>
Cinel Mhic Airtchoirb
  <u>20 Ian.</u>
Clochar/Clocharia
  (= Cloch-oir), Ferdachrichius, Maccarthenus <u>15 Aug.</u>, Orgiellia <u>6 Feb.</u>, <u>24 Mar.</u>, <u>4 Apr.</u>
*Cluain*/Clonoensis
  9 Sep. (IMY 54), *6 Oct.*, *12 Iun.*
Cluain Aithchin
  <u>21 Feb.</u>
Cluain Andobhair
  <u>13 Dec.</u>
Cluain Boireann
  ad ripam Senennii, Imania <u>9 Feb.</u>
Cluain Coirpthe
  <u>15 Feb.</u>
Cluain Credail
  <u>Conallia Gaura, Momonia</u> *15* (<u>15</u>) *Ian.*
Cluain Dolcain
  *6 Aug.*
Cluain Eidhneach
  Laghisia, Lagenia <u>17 Feb.</u>, <u>3 Mar.</u>, <u>6 Dec.</u>
Cluain Eois
  *4* (<u>4</u>) *Apr.*
Cluain Eraird
  Media <u>21 Aug.</u>, <u>12 Dec.</u>, <u>29 Dec.</u>
*Cluain Ferta*/ <u>Cluain Ferta S. Brendani</u>
  <u>21 Feb.</u>, <u>1 Mar.</u>, *16 Mai.*

(MDr, *MTur*, <u>MC</u>, (IMY))

(MDr, *MTur*, <u>MC</u>, (IMY))

# INDEX OF PLACE AND TRIBAL NAMES

# INDEX OF PLACE AND TRIBAL NAMES

(MDr, *MTur*, <u>MC</u>, (IMY))

Leamchuill
  inter Hy Duach et Laighis <u>21 Feb.</u>
Lecain (g. Lecna)
  *28 Iun.*
*Les Mór*/<u>Lismorum</u>
  <u>Albaniae</u>, *25 (25) Iun.*
Lethglenn
  *18 Apr.*
*Liath*/<u>Lethmorum</u>
  *13 (13) Mar.*, <u>12 Iul.</u>
Lindisfarnensis
  <u>31 Aug.</u>
Lingones
  23 Mai.
Lismorum/Lismorum Mochuddae
  Desii Momoniae <u>22 Ian., 31 Ian., 4
    Feb., 10 Feb., 5 Mar., 25 Iul., 21
    Dec.</u>
Lismorum
  Albaniae see Les Mór
Loch Bricreann
  iuxta Iuechiam <u>26 Oct.</u>
Loch Coirb
  see Loch Orbsen
Loch Erne
  <u>31 Ian., 9 Feb.</u>
Loch Len
  <u>16 Mar.</u>
Loch Orbsen (Coirb)
  Connacia <u>16 Ian.</u>
Loch Sileann
  <u>5 Mar.</u>
Loch Uair
  *7 Feb.*
Longobardi
  <u>27 Nov.</u>
Lothra
  *15 Apr.*
Luachair
  *17 Iun.*
Lugdunum
  Galliae 28 Feb., 2 Apr., 24 Apr., 2 Sep.,
    16 Nov.
Lugmagh
  <u>24 Mar.</u>
Luscae
  *6 Sep.*
Lycia
  5 Apr., 25 Iul., 18 Sep. (see note), 6
    Dec.

Mag Ascad
  <u>5 Ian.</u>
Mag (g. Maige) Bile
  *10 (10) Sep.*, <u>21 Oct.</u>
Mag Lacha
  <u>24 Aug.</u>
Mag Laigean
  <u>11 Iun.</u>
Mag Liffe
  Lagenia <u>9 Dec.</u>
Mag Tuathad
  <u>3 Sep.</u>
Mauritania
  7 Mar., 3 Dec.
Medi
  21 Dec.
Media
  <u>17 Feb., 19 Feb., 5 Mar., 11 Mar., 24
    Mar., 30 Mar., 16 Mai., 17 Iun., 25
    Iun., 27 Oct., 10 Nov., 24 Nov., 29
    Dec.</u>
Mediolanum
  20 Ian., 1 Apr., 8 Mai., 12 Iun., 19 Iun.
Mesopotamia
  3 Iul.
Metropolis
  *3 Aug.* (see note)
Mettis
  16 Aug.
Min Beag
  silva inter Cluain Mor Maodhoc et
    Achadh Abhall <u>12 Oct.</u>
Moccu Altai
  *7 Iun.* (see note)
Moccu Birn
  *22 Ian., 14 Iun.*
Moccu Gualae
  *30 Oct.*
Momonia
  <u>15 Ian., 20 Ian., 10–11 Feb., 14 Aug.</u>
Mons Tabor
  *26 Iul.*
Mungared
  <u>25 Iul.</u>
Muscraighe Thire
  <u>10 Nov.</u>
Myra
  Lycia 6 Dec.

Nazareth
  Galileae 25 Mar.

236

(MDr, *MTur*, <u>MC</u>, (IMY))

Ros Each
 <u>14 Sep.</u>
Ros Eó
 *7*
Ros Gel (sic) (g. Ruis Gil)
 *6 Sep.* (see note)
Ros Liath (g. Ruis Leith)
 *30 Apr.* (see note)
Ros (g. Ruis) Tuirc
 <u>Ossoria *17* (<u>17</u>) *Sep.*</u>
Sagirensis
 <u>5 Mar., 14 Iun.</u>
Salona
 21 Aug.
Samaria
 Palestina 14 Iun.
Sanctonas
 1 Sep.
Saxain (g. Saxan)
 *5 Aug.*
Scoti
 17 Mar., 19 Mar.
Scythia
 30 Nov.
Sebaste
 Armenia 11 Mar.
Senghlenn
 vallis in Ultonia, Sliabh Lieg <u>10 Nov.</u>
Sicilia
 5 Feb., 15 Iun., 21 Iun., 13 Dec.
Sinennius
 flumen <u>9 Feb.</u>
Sirmium
 9 Apr.
Siuirius
 flumen <u>13 Feb.</u>
Sliabh Bregh
 <u>9 Feb.</u>
Sliabh Guarij
 Galenga <u>13 Oct.</u>
Sliabh Lieg
 Senghlenn, Ultonia <u>10 Nov.</u>
Sliabh Mairg
 Mag Tuathad <u>3 Sep.</u>
Sliabh na mBan bhFionn
 <u>6 Dec.</u>
Sliabh Slanga
 <u>24 Mar.</u>
Smyrna
 19 Ian., 23 Feb.

Surdum/Surdum S. Columbae
 <u>10 Feb., 16 Mar., 29 Mar.</u>
Syria
 5 Iul., 18 Oct.
Tabor
 mons 26 Iul.
Tamlachta (g. Tamlachtan)
 *7 Iul.*
Tamlacht Finnloga
 Kiennachta de Glenn Gemin <u>3 Ian.</u>
Tamhlacht Umhail
 Iuechia <u>26 Oct.</u>
Teffia
 <u>6 Feb.</u>
Tegh Baithin
 occidentalis Media, vel Airteach <u>19 Feb.</u>
Tegh Da Goba
 ad ripam Bannii in Ibh Echach <u>6 Dec.</u>
Tegh Ererain
 Media <u>27 Oct.</u>
Tegh Telle
 <u>25 Iun.</u>
Thebais
 10 Ian., 17 Ian.
Thessalonica
 3 Apr.
Ticinum
 12 Sep.
Tingis
 29 Oct.
Tir Briuin
 <u>4 Feb.</u>
Tirconallia
 <u>11 Mai.</u>
Tobar Fachtna
 ad ripam fluminis Siuirii inter Ossoria et Desios <u>13 Feb.</u>
Tír Dá Glas
 *24 Mai.* (see note), <u>3 Nov.</u>
Tracia
 22 Oct., 14 Nov., 20 Dec.
Treviri
 31 Aug.
Tuburbo
 Mauritania 7 Mar.
Tulach Min Molaga
 Momonia <u>20 Ian.</u>
Tulen
 Media <u>16 Mai.</u>
Tullum
 15 Sep.

# INDEX OF OTHER PERSONAL NAMES

(Dates and variant readings are indicated as follows: regular = MDr, italics = MTur, underline = MC, brackets with line numbers = IMY. Latin and Irish names are standardised, with those of MC following, as far as possible, the spelling of Colgan's indexes to A and T)

Aengussius
  Becchuo filius Dauidis 10 Ian.
  filius Artcorbi 15 Ian.
  filius Crimthanni 10 Apr.
  filius Erci Deirg 15 Feb.
  Finnius filius Fergussii Dubdedii 24 Mar.
  Ossoriae 5 Mar.
Áildén
  *29 Mai.*
Alildus
  filius Celtcharii 12 Dec.
  filius Dunlaing 9 Dec.
  filius Fergussii 24 Mar.
  Magnus filius Darii Barrigh 9 Iun.
  Olom 16 Mar.
Amalgadius
  filius Leogarii Birn 5 Mar.
Anmirius
  filius Romani/Ronani 21 Mar.
Anna
  sacerd. 25 Mar.
Antoninus
  princeps 10 Iul.
Antonius (Antoninus) Uerus
  imperator 11 Apr.
Aredius
  filius Mailedii 24 Mar.
Artcorbus
  filius Fiachi Suigde 15 Ian.
Aurelianus
  imperator 18 Aug.

Baithus Bannach (Buadhach)
  12 Ian.
Baithe
  29 Mar.

Bassus (Bascus)
  consul 29 Iun.
Beoanus
  filius Mellani 13 Mar.
Berachus
  18 Nov.
Bern
  de Dal Birn 14 Iun.
Bracanus
  1 Ian.
Brecus
  10 Nov.
Bressalius
  filius Buanii 24 Mar.
  filius Denii 17 Feb.
Brianus
  filius Eochadii Moimedonii 15 Feb.
Briuinus
  filius Eochadii 4 Apr.
Broganus
  filius Corbmaci Galengii 30 Mar.
Buanius/Buanus
  24 Mar.
  filius Eochadii Lamdoid 5 Mar.
  filius Lugadii Maccon 8 Mar.

*Cairell*/Carellus
  filius Lasreni *18* (18) *Aug.*
  filius Muredacii 3 Ian.
Caipha
  sacerd. 25 Mar.
Calphurnus
  2 Mai.
Canannanus
  filius Alildi 24 Mar.
Cannechus
  filius Fedhlimii 24 Mar.

240

(MDr, *MTur*, <u>MC</u>, (IMY))

Carbreus
  Daimhairgid, rex Orgelliorum <u>9 Feb.</u>,
    21 Mar.
  File, filius Alildi Magni <u>10 Iun.</u>
  filius Fergussii <u>4 Apr.</u>
  Niadh, filius Buanii <u>5 Mar.</u>
Caredius
  see Cuinnidius
Carthennius
  <u>4 Apr.</u>
Cathchuo
  filius Aengussii <u>10 Ian.</u>
Catheirus
  Magnus, rex Hiberniae <u>4 Apr.</u>, <u>10 Apr.</u>,
    <u>9 Iun.</u>
Celtcharius
  filius Uthecharii <u>12 Dec.</u>
Clodhchuo
  filius Aredii <u>24 Mar.</u>
Coche
  see Oche
Coelbadius
  filius Crunnii Badhraoi <u>11 Nov.</u>
Coemscragius
  <u>13 Mar.</u>
Cominus
  filius Manii <u>8 Mar.</u>
Coelbadius
  filius Crunnii Badhraoi <u>11 Nov.</u>
Coemscragius
  <u>13 Mar.</u>
Cominus
  filius Manii <u>8 Mar.</u>
Commodius
  imperator 11 Apr.
Comorburius
  filius Conalli <u>15 Ian.</u>
Conallus
  Derg <u>19 Feb.</u>
  filius Aengussi <u>15 Ian.</u>
  filius Carbrei File <u>9 Iun.</u>
  filius Carbrei Niadh <u>5 Mar.</u>
  filius Dameni <u>9 Feb.</u>, <u>19 Mar.</u>
  filius Eochadii <u>16 Ian.</u>
  filius Eochadii <u>16 Mar.</u>
Conarius
  rex <u>5 Ian.</u>
Conchorbus
  filius Comorburii <u>15 Ian.</u>
Conchradius
  filius Darchelli <u>12 Dec.</u>

Conlae
  filius Tadgaei <u>24 Nov.</u>
Constantinus
  imperator 10 Mar., 3 Mai.
Corbmacus
  Galengius filius Tadgaei <u>30 Mar.</u>
Corcranus
  filius Echach <u>17 Feb.</u>
Crimthannus
  filius Catheiri Magni <u>10 Apr.</u>
Crunnius
  Badhraoi <u>11 Nov.</u>
Cuanachus
  filius Ennii <u>19 Feb.</u>
Cuinnedius (Caredius)
  filius Finnchoemy <u>13 Mar.</u>
Cúlae
  *5 Apr.*
Cyrinus
  pater Balbinae 31 Mar.

Dallanus
  filius Eugeni <u>18 Aug.</u>
  filius Lugadii <u>24 Mar.</u>
Damenus
  filius Carbrei Daimhairgid <u>9 Feb.</u>, <u>19
    Mar.</u>
Daráne
  *31 Iul.*
Darchellus
  filius Senachi <u>12 Dec.</u>
Darius
  Barrech filius Catheiri Magni <u>4 Apr.</u>, <u>9
    Iun.</u>
Dauid
  filius Fiachrii <u>10 Ian.</u>
Decius
  imperator 5 Feb., 9 Iul., 30 Iul., 6 Aug.,
    10 Aug., 13 Aug., 14 Sep.
Degillus
  filius Natsluagii <u>11 Nov.</u>
Demanus
  filius Carelli <u>3 Ian.</u>
  filius Fingeni <u>3 Ian.</u>
Denius
  <u>17 Feb.</u>
Derganus
  <u>11 Iun.</u>
Dergroga
  filius Locani <u>16 Ian.</u>

# INDEX OF OTHER PERSONAL NAMES

(MDr, *MTur*, <u>MC</u>, (IMY))

Diocletianus
  imperator 3 Apr., 2 Iun., 2 Aug., 29 Iul.,
    16 Aug., 7 Sep., 13 Dec.
Domitianus
  26 Apr.
Dobtha
  filius Aengusii <u>15 Feb.</u>
Duach
  <u>3 Feb.</u>
Dubdligius
  <u>20 Ian.</u>
Dubreus
  <u>16 Oct.</u>
Dunchadus
  filius Ernini <u>30 Mar.</u>
Dunlaing
  *11 Apr.*, <u>9 Dec.</u>

Echus
  filius Bressalii <u>17 Feb.</u>
Elizabeth
  mater Iohannis Baptistae 24 Iun.
Ennius
  filius Conalli Deirg <u>19 Feb.</u>
Eochodius
  <u>16 Ian.</u>
  filius Carthennnii, rex Orgelliae <u>4 Apr.</u>
  filius Clodhchuonis <u>24 Mar.</u>
  filius Darii Barrich <u>4 Apr.</u>
  filius Muredacii <u>24 Mar.</u>
  filius Tadgaei <u>16 Mar.</u>
  Lamdoid filius Amalgadii <u>5 Mar.</u>
  Moimedonius filius Muredacii Tirigh
    <u>10 Ian., 16 Feb., 24 Mar.</u>
Ercus
  Derg, filius Briani <u>15 Feb.</u>
  filius Cuinnedii (Caredii) <u>13 Mar.</u>
Erninus
  filius Garuani <u>30 Mar.</u>
Eugenius
  filius Canannani <u>24 Mar.</u>
  filius Dergani <u>11 Iun.</u>
  filius Nielli Naoigiallach <u>18 Aug.</u>

Fedhlemidius
  filius Eochodii <u>24 Mar.</u>
  filius Fergussii <u>9 Iun.</u>
  Legiferus <u>15 Ian.</u>
Feicius (Tiehius)
  filius Finchadii <u>24 Nov.</u>
Fergussius
  Dubdedius <u>24 Mar.</u>

filius Alildi <u>12 Dec.</u>
filius Conalli <u>9 Iun.</u>
filius Eochadii Moimedonii <u>24 Mar.</u>
filius Sednai <u>4 Apr.</u>
Feradach
  *23 Mar.*
Fiachrius
  filius Eochodii <u>10 Ian.</u>
Fiachus
  <u>15 Feb.</u>
  Suigde, filius Fedhlemidii <u>15 Ian.</u>
Finchuo (Finnchaemhius)
  filius Tiehii (Feicii) <u>24 Nov.</u>
Fingenus
  filius Demani <u>3 Ian.</u>
Finnach
  *22 Mai.*
Finnbarrius
  filius Fraici <u>10 Ian.</u>
Finnchadius
  filius Conlae <u>24 Nov.</u>
Finnchaemius
  filius Coemscragii <u>13 Mar.</u>
  filius Feicii <u>24 Nov.</u>
Finnloga
  filius Dergrogae <u>16 Ian.</u>
Fintanus
  filius Conchradii <u>12 Dec.</u>
  filius Malii <u>15 Feb.</u>
Finus
  see Restitutus
Forga
  filius Dallani <u>24 Mar.</u>
Fraicus
  filius Cathchuonis <u>10 Ian.</u>

Gabhrenus
  filius Corcrani <u>17 Feb.</u>
Gallianus
  imperator 13 Ian., 14 Sep.
Garuanus
  filius Senani <u>30 Mar.</u>
Gressene
  <u>18 Aug.</u>

Helena
  mater Constantini *10 Mar.*
Herod
  rex 28 Dec.

Iulianus
  impius 26 Iun.

(MDr, *MTur*, <u>MC</u>, (IMY))

(MDr, *MTur*, <u>MC</u>, (IMY))

Sedna
   filius Labani <u>4 Apr.</u>
   filius Trenii <u>24 Nov.</u>
Senachus
   filius Fergussii <u>12 Dec.</u>
Senanus
   <u>3 Mar.</u>
   filius Muredacii <u>30 Mar.</u>

Tadgaeus
   <u>24 Nov.</u>
   filius Kieni <u>16 Mar., 30 Mar.</u>
Tailgluin
   filius Brogani <u>30 Mar.</u>
Taurinus
   praefectus 17 Iul.
Tiberius
   Caesar 25 Mar.
Tiguernachus
   filius Finchuonis <u>24 Nov.</u>

Tranquillinus
   pater Marci et Marcelliani 18 Iun.
Trenius
   filius Buani <u>8 Mar.</u>
   filius Tigernachi <u>24 Nov.</u>
Tulchán
   *21 Oct.*
Tuscus
   consul 29 Iun.

Uthecharius
   <u>12 Dec.</u>

Zacharias
   pater Iohannis Baptistae 24 Iun.
Zebedeus
   pater Iacobi 25 Iul.

# GENERAL INDEX

(References are to pages. Cross-references are normally to the Index of Saints)

Laurence
of Rome, devotion to at Armagh 4, 5,
feast of 154
O'Toole see Ua Tuathail, Lorcán
Lawlor
H. J. 13
Lazarus
135
Legg, J. W.
11n
Leighlin/Lethglenn
priory CW 56. See also Laisrén
Leinster
182, Augustinian priories in 8
Leitrim
b., GY 49
Lent
see *Inid*
Leogathus
St 18n
Leontius
St 19
*Letavia*
see Brittany.
Letha/*Latium*
50
Liemania
mother of saint 167n
Liathros
church 144
*Liber Angeli*
4
*Liber de romanis pontificibus/ Liber
pontificalis*
137, 141
Limerick
Co. 126
Lismalin
tl./p., TY 129
Lismore
Ireland 63, 102, 192, diocese of 163,
provenance of MC 164–6, 170, 192
SCO 74
Lismullin/*Lis Moling*
convent at and provenance of MTur
129–30
*Lobar*
see Colmán Lobar, Finán Lobar
Lombardy
111
Lon/Lonanus
20n

Longford
Co. 28
Lothra/Lorrha
TY, priory/st of 3, 55
Loughcrew
p., Fore b., MH 151
Lough Derg
on r. Shannon 49
Louth
church 17, 49, 172
Louvain
MG at 184
Lowe
E. A. 11n
Luachair
Moling of 129
Lucas/Luke
evangelist 14n, 103, 136
Lucy
of Syracuse 37, 136
Lynn
see Lann Meic Luacháin
Lupus
St 92

Maccarthenus
pedigree of 167n
Mac Cuilinn
of Lusk 20n, 21
Mac Nisse
of Clonmacnoise 20n, 139
Máedóc (Áed)
Ua Dúnlaing, of Leinster 166
Máel Brigte
Irish form of Marianus 184
Máel Doid
14n
Máel Máedóc
see Malachy
Máel Ruain
of Tallaght 4n, 20n, 21
Máel Rubae
of Apurcrossan, Bangor 20n, 21
Mag Abna
159
Maghera
see Ráth Murbuilg.
Maigniu/Maignenn
of Kilmainham 20n, 21
Malachy/Máel Máedóc
of Armagh 8, 10n, 42, 105, 163
Manchán/Manchanus
Liath Mancháin 4n, 9, 14n

Martyrology of Tallaght (MT)
10n, 29–31, 33, 35, 47, 49, 58–9, 61,
78, 84, 89, 94, 100–1, 103, 112,
118–19, 124, 132, 133–61 *passim*,
166, 190, 192, 194
Martyrology of Turin (MTur)
27, 30–3, 49, 50, 68, 78, 84, 121–61,
165, 174n, 185, 188, 190–1n
Martyrology of Usuard (MU)
copy of in Ireland 16, *auctaria* of 18,
145, *Altempsianus* version 45, 59,
64; *Antverpiensis Major* version 27,
34, 90; *Aquicinctinus* version 42;
*Bruxellensis* version 18–19, 23, 27,
30–1, 34, 36, 39, 41, 52, 63, 71–2,
77, 79–80, 82, 87, 99, 102, 108–18,
120, 152; *Centulensis* version 26–7,
29, 34, 36, 44; *Grevenus* version
19n, 28, 35, 38–50, 52, 55–7, 62–4,
66–71, 74, 76–7, 79–80, 82, 86–7,
93–4, 97–8, 101, 103, 108, 110,
113–20, 160; *Hagenoyensis* version
58, 104; *Lubecana et Coloniensis*
versions 35, 44, 45, 48, 50, 56–7, 66,
74, 79, 86; *Matricula Carthusiae
Ultrajectinae* version 27; *Molanus*
version 52, 69, 116; *Rosweydinus*
version 90
Martyrology of York
Irish version (IMY) 121, 125, 185–94
Mary
cult/feasts of 8, 36, 136
Mary
mother of Philip and James 8
Maryborough West
b., OY 39
Masán
feast of 128
Matthaeus/Matthew
apostle 103, 193
Maurus
*discipulus sancti Benedicti* 4n, 14n, 19n
Mc Carthy
D., 10n, 195n
Meath/*Media*/Mide
Co./kingdom 16, 93, 128–9, 148, 151,
166n
Medranus and Tomanus
of *Britannica Arcluidensis* 166
Meehan
B. 122
Meic/*Filii* Nessáin
of Ireland's Eye 21

Mercia
187
Metz
103
Mide
see Meath
Midlands
provenance of Commentary on MO
127–8, churches in 165
Milan
18n, 82
Misael
4n
Missal
see Drummond
Mobí
St 4n, 14n, 98, 101
Mochellóc
St 14n
Mochoemocus
pedigree of 166n
Mocholmóc
St 14n, 15n
Mochta
of Louth 20–1, 49
Mochuaróc
St 4n
Mochuta/Carthach
4n, 188, 192, mother of 164
Mogruddon
ep. 43
Moinenn
entry on 126
Moling
of Luachair 4n, 129
Molotha
ghost saint 13
Monaghan
Co. 49
Monaincha
20, 27
Monanus
*levita in Scotia* 43
Monasterboice
114
Moray
SCO 40
Mo-Sacru
abbot of Clonenagh 166
Mothairén (Mothoria)
St 14n
Mothers of the saints
tract on 165

255

Mothuu
St 14n, 84
Movilla
tl., Newtownards p., Ards L. b., DN 63,
95
Moybolgue
see Bailieborough
Muckno
p., Cremorne b., MN 49
Mugain
St 14n, 15n
Muidocus
pedigree of 167n
Muirchertach
king of Tara 128
Muirchú
Life of Patrick by 142
Muirgein
of Glenn Uisen 34
Mundrehid
Offerlane p., Upperwoods b., LS 97
Munnu
St 4n, 14n, 15n
Munster
166, 177

Nabor
St 78
Nathí
St 84
*nativitas/gein*
see Colmán Ela, Iohannes Baptista,
Laurentius, Lucas, Marcus, Maria,
Mathae, Philippus, Thomas
Nem
alias Benedictus 178
Nevers
Patricius of 90
Newgrange
MH 128
Newry
abbey of 7n
Newtownards
p., Ards L. b., DN 63
Niall Glúndub
time of 166
Nicomedes
St 67
Ninian
St 97
Normans
arrival of 44. See also Anglo-Normans

Northumbria
58, 186n
Novatus
St 72

Ó Cléirigh
Mícheál 1, 164
Octaves
see Andreas, Apostoli, Iesus Christus,
Laurentius.
Offaly
Co. 39, 44
Offaly W.
b., KE 112
Offerlane
p., Upperwoods b., LS 97
Oghanus
ep. 42
Oisíne
St 7n
*Omnes sancti Europae*
14n
Onchú
St 14n, 15n
Ordnance Survey
129
Ormond Upper
b. 27
Oskamp
H. 1, 3, 10–11
O'Sullivan
W. 11n, 122, 130n

Palestine
60
Parvum Romanum
26
Patricius
of Nevers 14n, 90
Patrick/*Patricius*
St. 2, 4, 7n, 10, 12n, 20n, 21, 93, 142,
166, 183, 186–7
Paul
see Peter
the Hermit 125, 139
Paulinus
of York 194
Perthshire
SCO 1
Peter and Paul
cult/feasts of 4, 5, 8
Philip and James
8

# INDEX OF COMPUTISTICAL/ASTRONOMICAL ENTRIES

260